SPANIARDS IN MAUTHAUSEN

Representations of a Nazi Concentration Camp, 1940–2015

Spaniards in Mauthausen is the first study of the cultural legacy of Spaniards imprisoned and killed during the Second World War in the Nazi concentration camp Mauthausen. By examining narratives by and about Spanish Mauthausen victims over the past seventy years, author Sara J. Brenneis provides a historical, critical, and chronological analysis of a virtually unknown body of work.

Diverse accounts from survivors of Mauthausen, chronicled in letters, artwork, photographs, memoirs, fiction, film, theater, and new media, illustrate how Spaniards became cognizant of the Franco government's relationship to the Nazis and its role in the victimization of Spanish nationals in Mauthausen. As political prisoners, their experiences differ from the millions of Jews exterminated by Hitler, yet they were nevertheless objects of Nazi violence and murder and witnesses to the Holocaust. Of the more than seven thousand Spaniards incarcerated in Mauthausen, just over two thousand survived.

(Toronto Iberic)

SARAH J. BRENNEIS is an associate professor of Spanish at Amherst College.

Spaniards in Mauthausen

Representations of a Nazi Concentration Camp, 1940–2015

SARA J. BRENNEIS

University of Toronto Press
Toronto Buffalo London

ISBN 978-1-4875-0133-4 (cloth)   ISBN 978-1-4875-2131-8 (paper)

♾ Printed on acid-free, 100% post-consumer recycled paper with vegetable-based inks.

[Toronto Iberic]

Library and Archives Canada Cataloguing in Publication

Brenneis, Sara J., author
Spaniards in Mauthausen : representations of a Nazi concentration camp, 1940–2015 / Sara J. Brenneis.

(Toronto Iberic ; 34)
Includes bibliographical references and index.
ISBN 978-1-4875-0133-4 (cloth)   ISBN 978-1-4875-2131-8 (paper)

1. Mauthausen (Concentration camp).   2. Concentration camps – Social aspects – Austria – Upper Austria.   3. World War, 1939–1945 – Social aspects – Spain.   4. World War, 1939–1945 – Prisoners and prisons, German.   5. Prisoners of war – Spain.   6. Spaniards – Austria – Mauthausen – History – 20th century.   I. Title.   II. Series: Toronto Iberic ; 34

D805.5.M38B74 2018   940.54′7243094362   C2017-906329-4

This book has been published with the assistance of Amherst College.

University of Toronto Press acknowledges the financial assistance to its publishing program of the Canada Council for the Arts and the Ontario Arts Council, an agency of the Government of Ontario.

To Eric and Charlie

Contents

Illustrations

Acknowledgments

This book is the fruit of a decade of research in Spain, Austria, and the United States, aided every step of the way by scholars, colleagues, friends, and family, who offered timely advice and assistance.

As the project began to take shape, a number of individuals and institutions were of particular help: Margarita Lobo and Trinidad del Río Sánchez at the Filmoteca Española; Rosa Toran and Isidoro Teruel Manchón at the Amical de Barcelona; Mar Palomo Delgado at the Fundació Mercè Rodoreda; Francesc Rosés at the Museu d'Història de Catalunya; Doris Warlitsch and Ute Bauer at the Archiv der KZ-Gedenkstätte Mauthausen; Jordi Riera and Triangle Blau; and the librarians and staff at the Biblioteca de Catalunya in Barcelona and the Biblioteca Nacional in Madrid. Georg Iggers, Llorenç Soler, and Montse Armengou generously shared their expertise and work. Benito Bermejo provided early encouragement that facilitated my entry into a scholarly community studying the deportation in Spain.

During the book's later stages, the following aided the project: I wish to thank Robin E. Cookson at the US National Archives; Laila Ripoll and Mariano Llorente with Teatro Micomicón; Paul Jaskot and the Holocaust Educational Foundation; Alfons Aragoneses and the Institut Universitari d'Història Jaume Vicens i Vives at the Universitat Pompeu Fabra; and Laura Fontcuberta and David Doménech with the Amical de Mauthausen. Tomaz Jardim, Pepe Sedano Moreno, Paul Cahill, Victoria Maillo, Ilan Stavans, Ron Rosbottom, and Tara Daly provided welcome feedback at various stages of the project. Gina Herrmann deserves special mention as my sounding board and cross-country collaborator for the past five years. This book would not have been possible without the support of my parents, C. Brooks and Virginia Brenneis.

Two grants decisively moved the research for this book forward, for which I am profoundly grateful: the Amherst College Faculty Research Award Program, as funded by The H. Axel Schupf '57 Fund for Intellectual Life, and a National Endowment for the Humanities Fellowship. However, any views, findings, conclusions, or recommendations expressed in this publication are solely my own, and do not necessarily reflect those of the National Endowment for the Humanities nor Amherst College.

Portions of Chapter Two previously appeared as articles in the journals *Letras Femeninas* and *History & Memory*. I thank the editors for their permission to reprint.

While working on this project, I had the good fortune to meet two Mauthausen survivors, Ramiro Santisteban and Alejandro Bermejo. Their strength of spirit was evident, and they, along with all of the Spaniards of Mauthausen, have been my inspiration.

Eric has been there for me throughout the life of this project; Charlie arrived in time to join us at the seventieth anniversary commemorations at Mauthausen as a six-month-old. This book is dedicated to them.

SPANIARDS IN MAUTHAUSEN

Representations of a Nazi Concentration
Camp, 1940–2015

Introduction: Memory and Legacy of the Holocaust in Spain

Spaniards in Mauthausen: A Shared Trajectory

José de Dios Amill was the first Spanish Mauthausen survivor to publish his memoirs in Spain after the death of Francisco Franco, the country's dictator from 1939 to 1975. Dios Amill walked a fine semantic line between identifying himself as a Holocaust survivor and as a non-Jewish victim of the Nazi concentration camps. In his 1995 memoir, *La verdad sobre Mauthausen*, he distinguished between the brutal treatment of Jews in Mauthausen and the relatively less inhumane treatment of Spaniards. Nevertheless, he took umbrage with the exclusion of Spaniards in accounts of victims of the Holocaust at a moment in the 1990s when, in Spain and worldwide, the Shoah had become a prime topic of discussion:

> Sobre el holocausto nazi hay un sinfín de libros que describen la persecución del mundo hebreo pero se ha escrito muy poco, y gran parte del mundo lo ignora, sobre los milliones de personas no judías que también perecieron en los campos de concentración. Por parte de todos los estados, a excepción de Israel, ha habido un deseo por silenciar o minimizar la realidad de estos seis milliones de seres que también fueron exterminados, tanto como los judíos. (Dios Amill 58–9)[1]

Spanish Republicans figured among the millions of victims of the Nazis' racial and political genocide. As non-Jews, they were not formally Holocaust victims. Nevertheless, they suffered and were killed at the hands of the Nazis in concentration camps. Their ordeal, as Dios Amill attested, continues to be largely overlooked.

The Holocaust, for most of the world, is a widely discussed crime against humanity. Scholars, novelists, filmmakers, and artists have produced an enormous body of work on Nazi policies of persecution and genocide. These ongoing cultural dialogues encompassed the first published accounts in the 1940s, which predate our current conception of the word "Holocaust," through the passing of the last Nazi concentration camp survivors in recent years.[2] Yet in Spain, discussions of the Holocaust arrived late, and not just for survivors like Dios Amill.

The decisive victory of Franco's Nationalist forces in the Spanish Civil War (1936–9) created a culture of repression and fear, particularly for vanquished Republicans in the early post-Civil War years. Franco courted the Axis powers during the first half of the Second World War, but by the end of the conflict he had distanced himself from Hitler. Although Franco appealed to the Allied powers for recognition and aid, his repressive regime prevented open communication about Spain's past, leaving the country at loose ends to define its pertinence to the Second World War. As Europe and the United States were beginning to come to terms with the realities of the Holocaust in the 1960s and 1970s, Spain remained silent on the subject. Once Franco's death in 1975 brought the dictatorship to a close, a number of publications began to expose Spain's links to the war, revealing Franco's diplomatic relationship with Hitler and the fact that Spaniards were among the millions killed in Nazi concentration camps, including Mauthausen. Nevertheless, both Spain's transition-era and democratic governments operated under an implicit pact of silence that continued to prevent a free exchange about the Spanish Civil War and Spain's relevance to the Second World War.

Only during the past fifteen years have the Spanish government and Spanish citizens alike begun to turn their attention in earnest to Spain's legacy, in what many scholars consider a surge in re-evaluations of historical memory that arrived with the turn of the century. However, Spain's conversation about the Holocaust lags behind its re-examination of the Spanish Civil War. Doubts about whether the country can legitimately claim to have been affected by the Holocaust when it was officially neutral in the Second World War, and counted among its citizens very few Jews persecuted by Hitler, have left Spain at a loss as to how the country fits into the narrative of the Nazi genocide. In a nation where the word "holocausto" has been appropriated to describe Franco's purge of leftist sympathizers and anti-Semitism remains ingrained, how is Nazi aggression relevant to Spaniards and their collective history? And why has this relevance been eclipsed by national political questions that hold Spain at arm's length from the Holocaust writ large?

This study of the accounts and stories that emerged from the Spanish experience of Mauthausen and its subcamps, the Nazi *Konzentrationslager* where the majority of Spain's victims were imprisoned and killed, provides a definitive response. Between ten and fifteen thousand Spaniards were sent to Nazi concentration camps throughout Germany and Austria; more than five thousand of them were killed by the Nazis.[3] This number is strikingly low in comparison to the estimated six million Jews exterminated by the Nazis. By and large, the Spaniards deported to Nazi camps were not Jewish.[4] Most were Republicans or Republican sympathizers who resisted Franco during the Spanish Civil War; some were civilians in exile. To this end, they do not figure into the premeditated program to exterminate the Jews planned and propagated by the Nazis: they are not victims of the Holocaust. Rather, they are victims of the policies and practices of the Nazis and witnesses to the Holocaust. Yet their relative insignificance in the grand narrative of the Holocaust and Spain's late-arriving cognition about its role in the Second World War do not constitute reasons to exclude the Spaniards in Mauthausen from the collective memory of the nations and peoples who were victimized by the Nazis.

In *Perpetrators, Victims, Bystanders: The Jewish Catastrophe, 1933–1945*, Raul Hilberg defined the three main groups comprising the Holocaust: the primary perpetrator, Adolf Hitler, along with his Nazi followers; the "perpetually exposed" Jewish victims (x), which included Jewish survivors (186–91); and the bystanders who "were not 'involved,' not willing to hurt the victims and not willing to be hurt by the perpetrators" (xi).[5] The Spaniards in Mauthausen fall under none of these distinctions. Although European Jews were the primary victims of Nazi genocide, other national, political, and ethnic groups, including Spanish Republicans, were among those "targeted by the Nazis for mistreatment, subjugation, enslavement, and, in some cases, death" (Rosenfeld 4). The Spaniards deported to Mauthausen were not Jewish, yet they were also victims of these Nazi atrocities.

But all of the Spaniards in Mauthausen cannot be so neatly classified. Many Spaniards worked with the Nazis as functionaries in the Mauthausen offices or as *Kapos* in the camp's external work *Kommandos*. One Spanish *Kapo* was found guilty of murder at the Mauthausen trials at Dachau in 1947 and hanged in 1949.[6] These individuals unquestionably benefited from their positions of privilege; many survived because of their interactions and relative security under the protection of the

SS. Are they to be considered willing collaborators with the Nazis or victims of a perverse system in which they were forced to comply or risk deadly consequences? The Spaniards in Mauthausen can be located along a "continuum of victimization" described by Ervin Staub: "[a]s the continuum of destruction progresses, there is a parallel progression of psychological changes in victims" (31). Regardless of whether they were walking dead *Muselmänner*, office functionaries tasked with assuring that the daily lethal operations of the camp ran smoothly but who performed subtle acts of resistance, or the prisoner-*Kapos* who were directly or indirectly responsible for the death of their fellow prisoners, the Spaniards in Mauthausen are nevertheless all victims of Nazi aggression, both physical and psychological. The "psychological changes" each individual traced on a path of victimization depended on his relative security and on his hope or lack thereof for survival. That is, within the term "victim" lies more nuance, more of the grey zone identified by Primo Levi, which demands continued examination on an individual level.

Holocaust scholars have also shown that limiting our understanding of survivors to Jews who survived the concentration or death camps excludes others, such as children sent into hiding, or Jews who narrowly avoided deportation to the death camps but were nevertheless displaced by the threat of Nazi genocide. As with "victim," we must expand our definition of "survivor" to encompass non-Jews who avoided death at the hands of the Nazis in a variety of ways. In the case of the Spaniards deported to Mauthausen, survivors include those who remained alive until the camp's liberation (though many died of starvation and disease in the days immediately after liberation), those few individuals who managed to escape the camp by means of bureaucratic intervention from Spain, and the women and children who arrived at the camp's main gate, only to be rerouted back to Spain without their husbands and sons.[7] These individuals are not survivors of the Holocaust per se; rather, they are witnesses to the Holocaust and victims of the same violent practices that comprised the Nazi genocide of Jews. Nevertheless, Spaniards in Mauthausen were not victimized in the same manner as the Jews – they were not subject to policies of extermination, for one – a distinction that I note throughout this book.

Using archival documents and photographs, memoirs, artwork, films, historical accounts, and novels as evidence, I argue for the Spanish deportees' rightful place among peoples affected by the policies of Nazi genocide, including the Holocaust. Although it seems that the

Spanish nation as a whole has only recently begun to examine the injustices perpetrated against its citizens between 1939 and 1945, victims of Nazi oppression and their families confronted the persecution of Spanish Republicans as early as 1940. Throughout the long years of Franco's dictatorship and the official silence during the Spanish transition to democracy, Spanish Mauthausen survivors have been telling their stories, both privately and publicly. As the number of survivors dwindles, their children, grandchildren, and communities of committed writers and filmmakers have continued to recount the experiences of the Spaniards in Mauthausen in innovative ways. Thus the story of the Spanish victims of Mauthausen has reached a new generation and feeds the deliberations over Spain's connection to the Holocaust. The nature of the Spanish experience of Mauthausen – given that the Spaniards imprisoned and killed there were not Jewish – inherently differentiates a Spanish representation of Nazi persecution from representations of the Holocaust by other groups. This, by extension, has prevented the example of Spain from being included in much of the theoretical work on representations of the Holocaust.[8] Nevertheless, understanding Spain's relevance to the Second World War and Nazi oppression is central to attaining a more complete conception of the consequences of Nazi racial and political policies.

This book is not a comprehensive historical study of Mauthausen and the place of Spaniards in the Nazi genocide. Rather, it investigates the Spanish narratives that depicted the Mauthausen concentration camp while exploring the historical background to these stories as necessary context. These narratives translated the experience of Mauthausen into words or images, creating a collective memory out of experience and legend. As we will see, the authors of works as diverse as historiographies, letters, drawings, photographs, memoirs, historical novels, documentary films, and new-media narratives have laboured to capture Spain's collective memory of Mauthausen over the past seventy-five years. These creations remain relatively unknown inside Spain and entirely unknown outside the country.

Whereas Spanish Republicans killed during and after the Spanish Civil War are now publicly mourned in Spain, the Spanish Republicans victimized in Mauthausen have largely remained unacknowledged ghosts in contemporary Spanish society. Obituaries, monuments, excavations of mass graves, and governmental recognition of the plight of the Spanish Republicans persecuted during the Civil War and Franco dictatorship began to appear in Spain at the turn of the twenty-first century.[9] Yet despite suffering similar atrocities, the Spaniards deported to Nazi concentration camps during the Second World War have become what Judith Butler calls "unthinkable and ungrievable" losses (xiv) in Spain's historical memory. There has been no public outpouring of grief for the Spanish victims of Mauthausen. They are "interminably spectral" (Butler 33–4) figures haunting the periphery of Spain's recognition of its past traumas.

Giorgio Agamben writes that concentration camp prisoners were "stripped of every political status and wholly reduced to bare life" (171); that is, a life devoid of citizenship and political identity. To this end, Agamben argues that the Nazi concentration camp is a perversely "absolute biopolitical space" in which the "human beings [were] so completely deprived of their rights and prerogatives that no act committed against them could appear … as a crime" (171). Franco denied the Spaniards in Mauthausen their Spanish identity; the Nazis denied them their biopolitical identity. The Spanish Republican bodies that perished in Spain under Francoism were identifiable national enemies within the state. The Spanish lives lost to Mauthausen, on the other hand, remained unnamable because they were diminished to their bare life outside of Spain's borders. The Spaniards in Mauthausen are, therefore, harder to "remember" or memorialize since they have been denied their natural right to be mourned at the national level.

Dehumanized first by the Franco regime, which forced them into exile and negated their Spanish citizenship, the Spaniards deported to Mauthausen and other concentration camps were then violently attacked physically and emotionally by the Nazis during their long imprisonment. The process of dehumanization begun in Spain and continued under the Nazis thus affirmed the Spanish state's "derealization" of the deportees (Butler 34). In 2006, the sociologist Alejandro Baer asked, "¿Puede haber una cultura de la memoria del Holocausto cuando no hay una cultura de la memoria de la tragedia española?" (*Holocausto* 238).[10] Today, the answer to Baer's question is a resounding no: even with a growing historical memory of the Spanish Civil War, the country's collective memory of the fate of its citizens in Nazi concentration camps and its role in the Holocaust is weak and imprecise. Until Mauthausen's Spanish victims gain the recognition afforded the Republican victims of the Spanish Civil War, they will continue to be spectres in Spain's collective memory. By analysing the stories and accounts inspired and created by the Spaniards of Mauthausen, this book seeks to make these individuals and their experiences corporeal.

To understand the trajectory of thousands of non-Jewish Spaniards to Mauthausen and other Nazi camps, one needs a clear sense of Spain's relationship to Hitler's Germany and the country's documented role in the Second World War. The Spanish Civil War pitted a military insurgency against the democratically elected Republican government in a conflict that lasted three years, from 1936 to 1939. Although rebelling against the legally elected Spanish government, the Nationalists gained momentum as they drew tangible support from other European nations. The Nationalists and their military leader Francisco Franco aligned themselves in spirit with the project of National Socialism established by Adolf Hitler in Germany in 1933, and maintained an alliance with Benito Mussolini's fascist aims in Italy. The Republican militia drew from a loose coalition of anarchists, communists, unionists, and international fighters, pulled together to push back against a growing tide of fascism in Spain.

The Nationalists under Franco were able to count on German and Italian military planes and munitions, giving them a marked strategic advantage on the battlefront. Although he abhorred Spanish Catholicism and its political and social power, Hitler was nevertheless complicit with Franco in the Spanish Civil War. The Führer sent his infamous Condor Legion to bomb the nation's cities, including, most notoriously, the town of Guernica, and provided the Nationalists with modern armaments. By involving himself in the Spanish conflict, Hitler aimed in part to draw attention away from his accelerated movements to control Western Europe, but also, like the Italian army, to combat the spread of communism. Nations that would only a few years later band together as Allies remained neutral in the Spanish Civil War, and so the small squadrons of American, British, Soviet, and Canadian soldiers fighting for the Republic, composed entirely of volunteers, were unable to match the military strength Franco amassed with the help of his Axis alliances.

As the Spanish Civil War staggered to an end, thousands of Spaniards streamed across the border into France, seeking both a respite from intense bombings and protection from the Nationalist reprisals against those who had fought for or been sympathetic to the Republic. Movements in Western Europe were constricted, however. Most Spaniards remained in France, housed in crowded, dirty, and inhospitable refugee camps along the country's southern shoreline. Only a lucky contingent of Spanish refugees was able to obtain the necessary permissions and contacts abroad to press on to the relative safe havens of the United

Kingdom and the Americas. By April 1939, Franco, meanwhile, had won the Spanish war. Although some refugees managed to be repatriated without reprisals, it became apparent to those who had been active on the Republican side of the conflict that returning to Spain would result in a fate far worse than the lice, sand, and barbed wire they had to contend with in France: to stay alive, they had to remain in exile.[11]

To escape their miserable conditions in the barbed-wire enclosures of Agde, Argelès-sur-Mer, and Banyuls-sur-Mer, among other French internment camps, some vanquished Spanish Republicans volunteered for *Compagnies de travailleurs étrangers* (CTE or Companies of Foreign Workers),[12] the French Foreign Legion, or other outposts of the Resistance movements. Although often coerced to join, there was a common desire among these men who had fought with or supported the Spanish Republic to continue the fight against fascism by any means possible. Many were ordered to the Maginot Line to work on fortifications and thus were easily captured when Germany occupied France in 1940. They were swiftly sent to German prisoner-of-war camps or *Stalags*. Although some held out hope that they would be repatriated to Spain, it would become clear that they were personae non gratae to Franco and their fate would be left in the hands of the Nazis.

There were also Spaniards deported to Mauthausen directly from refugee centres in France. As the historians Benito Bermejo and Sandra Checa have detailed, these individuals – the young and the old – were neither involved in the Spanish Civil War nor were resistance fighters in France (*Libro memorial* 16–19). The most infamous of these innocent victims were the Spaniards on the convoy from Angoulême, France. Some 900 men, women, and children were deported to Mauthausen from the French refugee camp Les Alliers in Angoulême on 20 August 1940. Four hundred and thirty men and adolescent boys were detained in the concentration camp, while the women and children were sent back to Spain to meet a hostile welcome under Franco's rule (18–19). This event would soon form a cornerstone of Spanish narratives of Mauthausen, illustrating Franco's callous disregard for civilian countrymen, women, and children embroiled in Germany's ever-widening European campaign.

On 15 March 1939, two weeks before the official end of the Spanish Civil War, Hitler invaded Czechoslovakia. Franco was indebted to Germany for its intervention in the Spanish conflict, and as the Second World War appeared on the horizon, Spain quickly adopted a policy of "non-belligerence" towards Germany. This was, strictly speaking, a policy of neutrality, but a neutrality that placed Spain firmly on Hitler's side of the growing aggression in Europe. A tug of war between Franco and Hitler continued through the early months of the war, as Hitler pressed Franco to support Germany. Spain was a country in ruins after the Civil War, unable to lend manpower to Hitler's already tightly organized army. Yet Spain provided Germany with a strategic geographic military outpost, supplied wolfram for Hitler's war machine, and pressured France to acquiesce to Hitler's control. For his part, Franco wanted to expand Spanish control to the south in Morocco and Gibraltar with the help of German muscle. These negotiations culminated in a face-to-face meeting between Franco and Hitler in Hendaye, France on 23 October 1940. Although Franco wanted concrete concessions from Hitler, the Führer made pains not to agree to anything specifically. The two leaders signed a secret protocol, the Treaty of Friendship and Alliance, making Spain's support of Germany and Italy official. Franco's policy of compliance towards Hitler's Germany and his disowning of the exiled Republicans thus left the Spaniards languishing in German *Stalags*, stripped of citizenship and at the mercy of the Nazis. They were then deported to concentration camps across the Third Reich.

Franco's foreign minister and brother-in-law Ramón Serrano Suñer would attest that the Spanish government had no knowledge of the imprisonment and deaths of Spaniards in Nazi concentration camps. The emergence of correspondence and documents exchanged between officials in Spain and the Spanish Embassy in Berlin has proved this claim to be entirely false. Letters and records exist between the Consulate and the Commander of Mauthausen regarding the ashes and personal effects of Spaniards who died in the camp. Serrano Suñer was complicit in their deportation, having discussed the policy with Hitler himself during a meeting in Berlin in September 1940, a month before Franco's own encounter with Hitler in Hendaye. As Antonio Vilanova wrote in 1969, "Es preciso insistir que fue Ramón Serrano Suñer, cuñado de Franco y su ministro de gobernación, el que incitó, en su viaje a Berlín, en septiembre de 1940, a las autoridades alemanes a extremar su crueldad con los españoles republicanos atrapados" (*Los olvidados* 227).[13] While Serrano Suñer was still in Berlin, the Gestapo released an edict that mandated the forced imprisonment of the *Rotspanienkämpfer*, the Spanish "reds" who fought for the Republic and had been captured by the Germans (Bermejo and Checa, *Libro memorial* 19). The timing of this official deportation order on the heels of Serrano Suñer's meeting with Hitler was no coincidence (Bermejo, *El fotògraf de l'horror* 55–6).

In an open letter in the Spanish newspaper *El País* in 1979, the Catalan journalist Montserrat Roig accused Serrano Suñer of being complicit in the murder of Spaniards in Nazi concentration camps. Although Roig challenged the aging bureaucrat that "[u]sted tiene en sus manos parte de las claves de nuestra historia, y a estas alturas no se puede eludir ninguna responsabilidad" ("Carta abierta a Serrano Suñer"), Serrano Suñer would go to his grave denying that the Spanish government was aware of the existence of Spaniards in the Nazi camps.[14] One Spanish survivor, who was a teenager at the time of his internment in Mauthausen, through a well-documented diplomatic intervention initiated by a letter from his mother to Spain's office of the Minister of Foreign Affairs, was sent back to Spain as a minor in 1940. Consequently, this young man could attest to the presence of his countrymen in the concentration camp (Armengou and Belis, *El convoy de los 927* 273–5). The women and children on the convoy from Angoulême, France who were returned to Spain could also testify that their husbands and fathers had been sent to Mauthausen in 1940. The truth is that Franco, Serrano Suñer, and other high-ranking Francoist officials were quite aware that there were Spaniards among the millions murdered by the Nazis in concentration camps across Austria, Germany, and Poland. But these Spanish men and women were more than simply unwelcome in postwar Spain: having fought against Franco in the Spanish Civil War, they were no longer considered Spanish nationals. Moreover, they would have been persecuted and in many cases killed had they returned to Spain. To Franco, their fate in the camps was nothing more than the outsourcing of their persecution to the Nazis. In Mauthausen and in concentration camps across the Nazi empire, their bare lives could disappear just as effectively as they could in Spain. They had entered into a "space of exception" (Agamben 169), vanishing before they were even dead.

By the end of 1943, the Allies were applying more pressure on Spain to remove itself from its "special" relationship with Germany. Spain had officially backed away from its non-belligerence policy but was still far from fully neutral in the conflict, breaking off diplomatic relations with Germany only after the war had officially ended on 8 May 1945 (Preston, *Franco* 530). By mid-1944, Franco and his ministers began to doubt an Axis victory, and started backpedalling from their friendly relationship with Germany, recalling Spanish "Blue Division" forces fighting for the Nazis in Russia.[15] Spain's relationship with the US and the Allies was still cool. International opinion towards Spain was generally negative by the end of the war, resulting in various embargoes and refusals to recognize the dictatorship as a legitimate government, despite Franco's last-ditch efforts to land on the side of the Allies. Indeed, one of the most debated of these efforts was Spanish propaganda that emphasized the country's heroic efforts to save the Jews. The truth about Franco's involvement with displaced Jews is in fact much more complex.

Spain banished Jews from the Iberian Peninsula in the fifteenth century, and there were, consequently, very few Sephardic Jews in the country by the middle of the twentieth century. The few Jewish communities left in Spain in the 1930s were generally met with a public hostility encouraged, in part, by political conservatives and the Catholic Church (Avni 51–2).[16] Although Jews were given legal equality under the Second Republic's constitution, Franco's efforts at repealing laws that permitted religious tolerance left Jews in Spain in limbo at the end of the Spanish Civil War (68). This lack of resolution was also reflected in the whiplash between the Franco regime's contradictory policies and practices towards Jews during the Second World War. Franco was a party to the pervasive paranoia regarding a Jewish-Masonic-Bolshevik conspiracy in Spain, yet never ordered the expulsion of Jews from the Iberian Peninsula, despite rumours that this demand was imminent (69–70). As Serrano Suñer wrote to the Spanish ambassador to Romania in 1941, "en la legislación española no existe discriminación alguna en relación con los judíos que residen en España" (qtd in Avni 315).[17] Indeed, Franco had argued for a philosephardic view of the superiority of Sephardic Jews over other Jewish ethnic groups, and initially kept in place a policy of accepting Jews of Spanish ancestry back into Spain without much bureaucratic red tape (Payne 214).[18] In reality, this meant that "[t]he leadership of the Franco regime adopted a policy that would ignore the existence of Jews in Spain but still was disposed favorably toward the cultural tradition of Spanish Jews" (Avni 72). When faced with an onslaught of Jewish refugees as well as Sephardic Jews displaced by the war, however, the Spanish government imposed byzantine regulations and restrictions that severely limited the number of Jews who were able to escape Nazi persecution by fleeing to or through Spain. Initially, as France fell to the Nazis, Spain was open to refugees in transit, accepting a strict quota of Jews inside its borders at any one time. By October of 1940, however, these initial regulations had become even more restrictive. In March 1943, Franco closed the Spanish border with France to anyone, Jewish or otherwise, without a transit visa, which was supremely difficult to obtain (Payne 219). By 1944, the demands for proving Sephardic ancestry and Spanish citizenship had become increasingly arcane (Avni 128–63). Aside from a handful of high-ranking officials and diplomats at select Spanish embassies, few individuals merited the laudatory statements Franco would later use to sell Spain's heroic involvement in saving Jews to the Allies.[19] Franco's ultimate refusal to provide safe passage to Jews through Spain was commensurate with his disdain towards the Spanish nationals discarded in Nazi concentration camps. The myth the dictator created of himself as a saviour of Jews is similar in spirit to the false notion that Spain was a distant observer of the Second World War, unaware of the slaughter of her own people in Mauthausen and other Nazi concentration camps.

The camp at Mauthausen rose out of the wealth of its granite quarry, by exploiting the natural resources of the Austrian landscape and the human resources of its prisoners. Mauthausen was one of the two major *Deutsche Erd- und Steinwerke* (DEST or German Earth and Stone Works) quarry camps,[20] and was the sixth concentration camp established in Nazi Germany (Jaskot 37). The site, on a hillside above the Danube River Valley about twenty-two kilometres outside of Hitler's childhood town of Linz, was chosen strategically. It boasted a ready supply of granite from three previously established quarries – Wienergraben, the Mauthausen quarry, leased from the city of Vienna; Kastenhof, also leased and set a short distance from Mauthausen; and Gusen, purchased from the Poschacher quarry firm and located a few kilometres from the main camp (35) – and a rail line. These were necessities for strengthening the camp's structure and growing its population. German and Austrian prisoners began constructing the camp in late May or early June 1938. By 1939, the quarries were in full operation (39). The intention was that this rugged granite fortress would outlast Hitler himself.

The first convoy of Spanish deportees arrived at the Mauthausen town train station on 6 August 1940 (Pike, *Spaniards in the Holocaust* 63; Toran, *Vida i mort* 159). The Spaniards were among the first to haul cut rock up and down the Wienergraben's notorious 186 steps.[21] The quarry work was brutal, as were the abuses exacted by the *Schutzstaffel* (SS) and the prisoner-*Kapos* working in the quarry details. In Mauthausen, "a prisoner feared being assigned to the stone-quarry work details of DEST, for it implied almost certain death" (Jaskot 46). Production was high at Mauthausen. The quarries served the dual purpose of disciplining the prisoner population as well as providing stone to build the Nazi empire. The Nazis were unconcerned that these punishments diminished its labour force; there was a constant influx of new slave labour. As Spanish Republicans continued to arrive throughout 1940 and 1941, they were singled out for the construction of the camp and work in the quarries because many had previous experience in the construction trades. As such, "[t]heir numbers were greatly depleted through abuse in the stone quarries and, particularly, in building the walls of Mauthausen" (137). The Nazis essentially worked their Spanish construction crew to death by feeding them minimal rations, forcing them to work in extreme weather conditions, and shooting them for perceived (or invented) negligence.[22] But forced labour was not the only way the Spanish prisoners of Mauthausen suffered and died.

Mauthausen was feared as a singularly brutal concentration camp. The main camp of Mauthausen and its system of satellite camps across Austria – including Gusen, Steyr-Münichholz, Ebensee, and Melk[23] – were, by Nazi standards, a Category Three *Konzentrationslager* or concentration camp. The only category three concentration camp, Mauthausen housed criminals, Roma, and prisoners who were considered by the RSHA (*Reichssicherheitshauptamt* or Reich Main Office for Security) beyond hope of redemption (Le Chêne 36; AMM (Archiv der KZ-Gedenkstätte Mauthausen) 24). In practice, this designation meant that the prisoners had no hope of surviving the camp. For the first few years of its operation, Mauthausen's prisoner population was exclusively male. It was a concentration camp focused on forced labour, not an extermination or death camp, although it did have a gas chamber.[24] Fewer Jews arrived in Mauthausen than other Nazi camps, though most of those who did were exterminated upon arrival.[25] Further designated as a "Nacht und Nebel" (Night and Fog) camp, Mauthausen incarcerated political prisoners who were considered a threat to the German state and were thus marked for disappearance within the Nazi camp complex.[26] There was an international assortment of *Nacht und Nebel* prisoners at Mauthausen – Spaniards, Poles, Russians, Germans, French – all of whom wore an inverted triangle to designate their particular crime, ancestry, or sexual orientation. The Spaniards wore the blue triangle of immigrants for their refugee status with the letter "S" for *Spanier*. This demarcation placed Franco's refusal to recognize them as Spanish citizens in conflict with their agreed-upon nationality. According to the Nazis, the Spaniards were also guilty of political conspiracy against the German state, having fought against Franco, Hitler's ally, in the Spanish Civil War. Between the backbreaking work, the medical experiments in the *Revier* or infirmary, the paltry nourishment, inhumane living conditions, and the ubiquitous SS violence, a Spanish prisoner's chance of survival in Mauthausen was slim. Mauthausen's designation as a "work camp" was merely a euphamism for "slave labour camp:" prisoners were sent to the camp to work until they died.

Mauthausen was organized into an orderly array of buildings, divided into living quarters for the SS officers, barracks for the prisoners, and one for the prostitutes (available only to the SS and select *Kapo* prisoners), the administrative offices, the *Revier*, the crematorium, the showers, the gas chamber, and the kennels, with a path leading from the main camp to the quarry (AMM 23; Lechner; Holzinger and Kranebitter 66). Prisoners of various nationalities were housed together, with the Russians quarantined in tents outside the main complex of barracks and the Jewish prisoners who were allowed to live more than a few hours after arriving at the camp housed in their own block. The Spaniards had little direct contact with these imprisoned Jews, however, and as political prisoners they experienced what amounted to an entirely different camp. Nevertheless, throughout 1940 and 1941, the Spaniards died at an alarming rate, particularly in Gusen. Yet as more Russians arrived from the war's Eastern front, the Nazis refocused their killing efforts. After 1942, the chances of survival improved immensely for those Spaniards who managed to live past their first two years in Mauthausen. The parsing of the international prisoners into discrete spaces and fates in Mauthausen mirrors the way Spanish political prisoners have been separated from studies of the Nazis' other non-Jewish victims. Despite numerous postwar movements to memorialize these victims, memories of the Spaniards have largely been abandoned.

Mauthausen prisoners with particular talents were often selected as *Kapos* or *Prominenten*, both roles that Spaniards would assume. The *Kapos* were chosen as especially brutal or violent specimens, charged with aiding the SS in disciplining the other prisoners. Although the *Kapos* and the *Prominenten* held special roles inside the camps, only the *Prominenten* were involved in the camp's administration (Le Chêne 38–9). These prisoners were selected on the basis of their professional strengths or linguistic abilities, such that a prisoner who spoke both German and Spanish could find himself working alongside Gestapo officers in the bookkeeping office, or a prisoner with a medical background might be forced to aid German doctors in the *Revier* to administer deadly injections. Many of the *Kapos*, and those among the *Prominenten* who were responsible for the deaths of fellow prisoners, were considered Nazi collaborators and paid for their crimes when surviving prisoners sought retribution after Mauthausen's liberation.

The Spanish role in the inner offices of Mauthausen is one of the primary reasons so much documentation from the camp survived the Nazis' general purge of records and photographs in the days before liberation. A number of Spaniards in particular were selected to work in the records office and Mauthausen's photography laboratory. Others were able to gain roles in the administration of the camp through connections to the camp-wide Communist Party organization, well populated by Spaniards. They surreptitiously kept duplicate copies of records and photographs that documented the prisoner population of the camps, the names and images of SS officers, public killings, and visits by high-ranking Nazi officers, many of which they were able to hide and reclaim after the Americans liberated the camp in May 1945. These documents and photographs became key evidence against the Nazi machine and particular officers during the Nuremburg trials, where one Spanish ex-prisoner would testify, and later at the Mauthausen trial at Dachau. They also continued to ground historical texts on Mauthausen and Nazi Germany with irrefutable details for decades to come.

More than seven thousand Spaniards were deported to Mauthausen, mostly men who had fought for the Republic in the Spanish Civil War.[27] But older men and young boys innocent of any involvement in the Spanish conflict were also deported to Mauthausen from refugee camps in France after Franco's government failed to respond to German requests for their repatriation to Spain. Between five and seven Spanish women were also transferred from Ravensbrück to Mauthausen in the waning days of the war.[28] The exact number of Spaniards in Mauthausen has been debated. Accurate records do not include those who were killed upon arrival, before being entered in the camp registry; or in the days leading up to liberation, when record-keeping in the camp had been suspended. The information most frequently cited, however, comes from Casimir Climent i Sarrión, a Spaniard who worked as a clerk in the *Politische Abteilung*, the Gestapo's branch office in Mauthausen. Climent kept duplicate records of all prisoners, paying special attention to his countrymen. He counted 7,187 Spaniards who entered the Mauthausen complex between 1940 and 1945; 238 who were transferred to other camps or sent back to Spain; 2,183 who were liberated; and 4,765 who were killed (Climent Sarrión).[29] The Spanish survivors of Mauthausen agreed that they held an often-privileged position in the camp, one that was radically different from the treatment of the Jewish prisoners there. Many were, in Primo Levi's characterization, the "saved" and not the "drowned" (*If This Is a Man* 93). Nevertheless, Climent's numbers provided the counterstory to this privilege: more than 65 per cent of Spaniards imprisoned in Mauthausen or one of its subcamps died.

The Holocaust, *el Holocausto*: Coming to Terms

In part because of its complex ambivalence towards the terms "Holocaust" and "holocaust," Spain has been unable to claim a stake in larger discussions about the Holocaust and the policies and practices of the Nazis. Understanding how these designations are used and defined in Spain and among Holocaust scholars today is central to grasping the space that Spaniards in Mauthausen occupy in the Spanish consciousness. As James Young explains, the "names we assign this period automatically figure and contextualize events, locating them within the continua of particular historical, literary and interpretive traditions" (*Writing and Rewriting* 85). To this end, "[t]he differences among names also explain the great gulfs in understanding between different nations and people, reflecting disparate experiences of the periods as well as the different shapes respective national mythologies and ideologies necessarily confer on events" (87). Spain tends to consider the events of the Holocaust in relation to its own volatile past, reflecting the country's unique experience and perception of this historical moment.

In Spain, the term "holocausto" is now often used to refer to Franco's single-minded persecution of Spanish Republicans and Republican sympathizers during and after the Spanish Civil War. Paul Preston's volume *The Spanish Holocaust* (translated as *El holocausto español*) and Montse Armengou and Ricard Belis's documentary and book *Las fosas del silencio. ¿Hay un holocausto español?* (*The Graves of Silence. Is There a Spanish Holocaust?*) are both examples of this wider usage of "holocaust."[30] Preston explains that he finds "holocaust" appropriate to the scale of the violence perpetrated by the Franco regime and its fixation on the enemy as "instruments of a 'Jewish-Bolshevik-Masonic' conspiracy" (*The Spanish Holocaust* xi). However, he acknowledges that he uses the word "holocaust" in a comparative context in the hope that his rendition of a "Spanish holocaust" will "suggest parallels and resonances that will lead to a better understanding of what happened in Spain during the Civil War and after" (xi–xii). Armengou and Belis similarly see their usage of "holocausto" as drawing attention not only to the Franco regime's bloody vengeance but also to the fact that the Shoah has gone through a process of recognition and commemoration, while the results of Franco's repression have been forcibly forgotten in contemporary

Spain (*Las fosas del silencio* 23–4). In both cases, the authors do not argue that the concept of the uppercase-H "Holocaust" as the systematic extermination of Jews by the Nazis during the Second World War should expand to include the violence that consumed Spain during the Spanish Civil War, but rather that the definition of lowercase-h "holocaust" as a large-scale slaughter or massacre appropriately describes the killings enacted in Spain under Franco from 1936 to the mid-1960s. Some Holocaust scholars and scholars of contemporary Spain agree that the word "holocaust" is useful as an analogy to other forms of genocide. However, using the term as a dual signifier has also contributed to a lack of precision and understanding in Spain as to what constitutes the Holocaust.

Equating the Holocaust with Franco's persecution of Spanish Republicans during the Spanish Civil War is problematic, not least because of the difference in order of magnitude of the number of victims. By Preston's estimates, Franco's forces killed some 420,000 people in the theatre of war, through extra-judicial killings during it, and in executions immediately afterwards (*The Spanish Holocaust* xviii).[31] This number contrasts sharply with the estimates of six million Jews and five million non-Jews murdered during the Holocaust. Another significant difference between Franco's and Hitler's programs of persecution resides in each dictator's burden of proof for extermination: while Franco targeted only political opponents, Hitler targeted those who were biologically or racially different from the Aryan race, in addition to political opponents.

Preston's and Armengou's uses of "holocausto" to describe Franco's reign of terror – lack of capitalization notwithstanding – breeds confusion and misinformation. It conflates Franco's purge of Spanish Republicans during the Spanish Civil War with the Nazis' purge of Jews during the Second World War. Isabel Estrada has written that other terms such as "campo de concentración" and "exterminio" have also been misused in Spanish discourse about the Franco dictatorship. She argues, "Spain never had extermination camps like Auschwitz, constructed for the purpose of annihilating the Jewish population" ("To Mauthausen and Back" 41). Using the terms "concentration camp" and "holocaust" to refer both to purely Spanish phenomena – such as camps in Spain where Franco imprisoned detractors who may have been killed but were not exterminated en masse, and Franco's persecution of Spanish Republicans which did not reach the level of a "final solution" or mass extermination – as well as elements primarily associated with Hitler and the Nazis is ultimately imprecise, even reckless. However, these discussions have also had the positive effect of fueling the conversation about the Holocaust in Spain.

Naturally, this debate includes the impressions of the Spanish survivors of Nazi concentration camps themselves. Mauthausen survivors like José de Dios Amill view themselves as victims of Nazi persecution tantamount to the Jews. Similarly, the titles of other Spanish Mauthausen survivor memoirs – including *Nacianceno Mata, un canario en Mauthausen: memorias de un superviviente del holocausto nazi* (*Nacianceno Mata, a Man from the Canary Islands in Mauthausen: Memories of a Nazi Holocaust Survivor*) and Ignacio Mata Maeso's *Mauthausen: memorias de un republicano español en el holocausto* (*Mauthausen: Memories of Spanish Republican in the Holocaust*) – also implicitly argue for the inclusion of the Spanish experience of this Nazi concentration camp in the wider narrative of other, non-Jewish victims of the Holocaust.

However, other Spanish concentration camp survivors, most notably Jorge Semprún, argue vehemently against including themselves among Holocaust victims (Munté 131–3; Ferrán and Herrmann 26–8). Semprún's defence of the singularity of the Holocaust by definition excludes him, a non-Jew imprisoned in Buchenwald for his activities with the French Resistance, in its categorization. Semprún and Dios Amill – two among thousands of Spaniards who were imprisoned in Nazi concentration camps – demonstrate the spectrum of opinions of Spaniards who were victimized in the Nazi *Lager* or camp system. There is no one emblematic victim of the Nazis: there are millions of individuals, each of whom suffered a unique trajectory through the Second World War, the concentration camps, and the Holocaust. Certainly there are points of convergence for the Spaniards in Mauthausen; other prisoners in other Nazi camps had similar experiences. Nevertheless, as the variety of Mauthausen representations considered in this book will demonstrate, each Spanish deportee lived his own Mauthausen, similar but not identical to the Mauthausen experienced by his compatriots. Whether these men were victims of the Holocaust or non-Jewish victims of Nazi genocide is a distinction that, as we will see, continues to be debated in Spain and elsewhere.

Alejandro Baer has argued that the conflation of the Shoah with what has come to be known as a "Spanish holocaust" allows Spain to conceptualize the Holocaust in the country's own terms ("The Voids of Sepharad" 108–9). He also presents as "una interpretación del Holocausto muy española" the idea that if Spanish Republicans are considered victims of the Holocaust like the Jews, this allows for a redefinition of the

Holocaust as describing more than a singular Jewish victimization and aligns Spanish anti-fascist rhetoric with anti-Nazi rhetoric ("Memoria de Auschwitz" 113).[32] This interpretation, while controversial outside of Spain, nevertheless forces Spaniards to face the country's politics of memory surrounding both conflicts (the Spanish Civil War and the Second World War), providing an opening for public discussions about the Spanish Republicans deported to Nazi camps. The counterargument more common to scholars outside Spain, on the other hand, considers comparing the Shoah to other traumatic events in human history a dilution or banalization of the Holocaust.

Spain has had an ambivalent relationship to the Holocaust, a topic that was severely constricted in public discourse during Franco's long dictatorship. As Baer has explored, present-day Spanish anti-Semitism and a persistent conception that Spain was neutral in the Second World War have impeded a fuller understanding of the country's involvement in the conflict ("Memoria de Auschwitz"; *Holocausto*). Even as Spain entered a democratic period of more open discourse in the 1980s and '90s, Baer recounted that "en España el Holocausto siguió siendo un tema 'de judíos y de alemanes'" (*Holocausto* 238) despite the knowledge that Spaniards were also killed by the Nazis.[33] In a country where "the voids, the silences and the abiding prejudices regarding Judaism" define ideas about the Holocaust (Baer, "The Voids of Sepharad" 114), a comparative perspective is needed to spur an inclusive dialogue. The process of examination that the Holocaust has undergone beyond the Iberian Peninsula serves as a guide.

Michael Rothberg sees advantages to using the term "holocaust" as a comparative signifier: "the use of the Holocaust as a metaphor or analogy for other events and histories has emerged precisely because the Holocaust is widely thought of as a unique and uniquely terrible form of political violence" (*Multidirectional Memory* 11).[34] In Spain, the ability to understand the Holocaust both as a metaphor and as a historical moment allows conversations about the Holocaust to apply more directly to events that occurred inside the country's borders. This, according to Rothberg, is a way that countries such as Spain can deal with their national "form[s] of political violence," facing issues of their past through contemporary modes of recognition (such as commemorations, exhumations, and reparations).

A primary disagreement among Holocaust scholars outside of Spain is whether non-Jewish victims of the Nazis should be considered victims of the Holocaust alongside the Jews. Henry Friedlander summarizes the commonly held position in favour of the singularity of the Holocaust to refer exclusively to Jewish victims:

> [H]istorians have categorized the Nazis' murder of the European Jews as totally different from their murder of other groups. [Gerald] Reitlinger's work showed that while the Nazis persecuted, incarcerated, and often killed men and women for their politics, nationality, religion, and behavior, they applied against the Jews a consistent and inclusive policy of extermination. In their drive against the Jews, they even killed infants and the very old, a policy they did not follow in their treatment of such enemies, for example, as communists, Poles, Jehovah's Witnesses, and homosexuals. (xii)

Friedlander argues, however, that the Nazis employed a policy of extermination to Roma and the handicapped, two other groups who were also "biologically selected target[s]" (xii).

Michael Berenbaum captures this central disagreement among Holocaust scholars through the perspectives of two of the most well-known Holocaust survivors in the United States: Simon Wiesenthal and Elie Wiesel. Wiesenthal argued for the inclusion of non-Jewish victims in categorizations of the Holocaust, a stance that, Berenbaum argues, "mirrors his experience in Mauthausen where Jews constituted only a minority of those incarcerated" (21). Wiesel, on the other hand, feared that the inclusion of non-Jews as victims of the Holocaust would diminish the overwhelming suffering and persecution of Jews by the Nazis. Berenbaum concludes that "[t]here is no conflict between describing the uniqueness of the Jewish experience during the Holocaust and the *inclusion* of other victims of nazism" (32; emphasis in the original). In fact, he argues that including Jews and non-Jews alike as victims of the Holocaust is "an intellectual, historical and pedagogical prerequisite to conveying the truth of what occurred in the Holocaust" (33). Berenbaum sees an imperative in this inclusion. "Historical accuracy," he writes, "should unite ethnic communities who wish their dead to be remembered with Jewish survivors who appropriately want the Judeocentric nature of the experience to be told" (33). This pluralizing of the Holocaust makes room for the experiences of Spaniards in Mauthausen and other Nazi concentration camps to inform our overall understanding of the Nazi program of genocide.

The historian Doris Bergen has also defended the use of the "Holocaust" to refer to Jews and non-Jews victimized by the Nazis. Although she recognizes that "Jews were the main target of Nazi genocide" (ix–x), she points out that the Nazis also targeted the disabled, Roma, Slavic people, communists, homosexuals, Jehovah's Witnesses, Afro-Germans, "and other people considered unwanted in the 'new European order'" (x). Spanish Republicans were among those groups labelled undesirable by Franco, Mussolini, and Hitler. Bergen posits that "[w]hether or not one considers members of any or all of these groups to belong under the label 'victims of the Holocaust,' their fates were entwined in significant ways with that of the Jews targeted and murdered in the Nazi quest for race and space" (x). This "intertwining" of victims is particularly noticeable at Mauthausen, a concentration camp populated by an array of international prisoners, both Jewish and Gentile. Bergen argues that all of the victims of Nazi persecution "shared with the genocide of the Jews personnel, methods of killing and goals of so-called racial purification" (x). The Nazis had the same impulse to destroy all of these groups; had they not lost the war, it is conceivable that they could have even expanded their genocidal targets. If one argues that the goal of political persecution was tantamount to the Nazis' program of racial-religious persecution, the Spanish Republicans in Mauthausen can be seen as Holocaust victims alongside the Jews.

Jews were, however, the targets of Hitler's "Final Solution," and, unlike the Spanish prisoners in Mauthausen, were gassed and exterminated en masse. In particular towards the end of the war, in 1944 and 1945, Jews were targeted almost exclusively by the Nazis as Hitler sought to speed up the process of extermination. But even before this period, Jews were singled out in Mauthausen and other camps for particularly inhumane treatment. As Daniel Jonah Goldhagen has written: "In every respect, the Jews fared the worst; within a given camp or institution, Germans treated Jews far more harshly, fed them more miserably and assigned them the most exhausting and demeaning jobs" (312–13). As such, Jews in concentration camps were much less likely to survive the war – whether or not they were gassed – than political prisoners like the Spaniards. There are other fundamental differences between the Jewish experience of the Holocaust and the Spanish experience of Mauthausen. The Nazis spent a decade systematically working towards the extermination of the Jews of Europe: imposing restrictive laws, segregating Jews into ghettos, deporting Jews to concentration camps, and murdering them in a macabre variety of methods such as gassing, shooting, medical experiments, starvation, lethal injection, and forced labour. Although the Spanish Republicans in Mauthausen were not subjected to this systematic treatment, and were not persecuted for their race, religion, or culture, they were killed in many of the same ways as the Jews, with one important exception. Many fewer Spaniards were gassed at Mauthausen. By some accounts, individual Spaniards found themselves among a convoy of Jews sent to the camp gas chamber purely by accident; others were gassed at nearby Hartheim Castle.[35] It is clear that the Jewish experience of the Holocaust must be differentiated from the Spanish Republican experience of Nazi persecution as less systematic, based purely on political opposition, not racial superiority, and ultimately less lethal.

Thinking of the Holocaust writ large as both a "Jewish Holocaust" and a denominator that includes other populations targeted in the Nazi genocide follows the theses of Berenbaum, Rothberg, and Bergen that a more inclusive understanding of the Holocaust begets a more thorough conception of what actually happened during Hitler's reign. For some time, scholars have been investigating the persecution and murder of "other" groups, such as Roma, the disabled, homosexuals, and Jehovah's Witnesses victimized under Nazi Germany; a systematic historical investigation of all Spaniards killed by the Nazis is still lacking.[36] Notwithstanding the distinct experiences of the persecution of these other groups, the Nazis targeted them all. In this sense, the wider concept of the Holocaust as it is understood to be the program of Nazi genocide targeting certain undesirables – no matter the reason for their undesirability – would apply to the Spaniards in Mauthausen. Moreover, a narrow geographic view of the Holocaust as localized primarily in Northern Europe does a disservice to the wider geographic reach the conflict actually had.[37]

Separating the slaughter of Jews during the Holocaust from the victimization of Spanish political refugees in Nazi camps during the Second World War prevents a dangerous game of historical revisionism. Nevertheless, it is clear that Spain's role in the Holocaust and Spaniards' subjugation in Nazi camps is a much more complex situation than was originally understood or than was portrayed for years by Francoist historiography. The stories told by the Spanish prisoner population of Mauthausen are a central facet of this historical and cultural trajectory. In this book I will respect the singularity of the Holocaust while honouring the understanding that the Spanish Mauthausen victims have of their experiences.

Recent scholarship into previously marginalized non-Jewish victims of the Nazis has given a voice to people whose lives were deemed unworthy under the moral codes of National Socialism. The memories and histories of Roma, the handicapped, and homosexuals targeted by the Nazis provides a counternarrative to the stories of Spanish Republicans, which have been roundly set aside from Holocaust memories.[38] The disabled were targeted as "defective" humans in Social Darwinist terms; homosexuals were deemed sexual deviants; Roma were seen as racially impure. Handicapped children and adults were the Nazis' first victims, slaughtered en masse at killing centres such as Hartheim Castle, where Spaniards transferred from Mauthausen would be gassed only a few years later. Homosexuals died in concentration camps in similar numbers as Spaniards: approximately 7,000 total (Jensen 344, note 122). Roma share a long history on the Iberian Peninsula, predating the late-fifteenth-century Catholic kings, and are integral to the culture of Spain. All of these groups posed obstacles to the Nazi quest for racial purity and world domination; all were killed in the barracks and gas chambers of Mauthausen and its subcamps; all have representatives who return yearly to Upper Austria to keep their memories alive. Although these non-Jewish victim groups cannot be blindly equated, Spanish deportees, the disabled, homosexuals, and Roma targeted by the Nazis share a common thread that links not only their memories but also the impetus to defend their relevance to Holocaust scholarship. Thus, how Spaniards in Mauthausen have been remembered dovetails with the evolving memory of these fellow "others" set upon by the Nazis.

Where some may see a stagnation or saturation – the "end of the Holocaust," in Alvin Rosenfeld's parlance (7) – there is, in fact, a pattern of continuous development of our understanding of the Holocaust. The absence of a thorough investigation into the history and representation of Spanish Republicans deported to Mauthausen – juxtaposed with the growing body of scholarship on other "others" – reminds us that there are, indeed, stories left to be told. There are elements of the Holocaust and the Second World War that still remain in the shadows; these details offer different voices and new perspectives on what is roundly considered the defining historical catastrophe of the twentieth century. Far from participating in a competitive victimhood, the stories of the Spaniards deported to Mauthausen complement a European memory of the Holocaust. In other words, the memory of the Spaniards in Mauthausen matters not only to Spain's historical memory but also to the collective history and memory of the Second World War and the Holocaust.

Inviting Spain's collective and individual memories of the Second World War, Nazism, and the Holocaust to participate is consequential to the project of building a transnational European culture of memory.[39] Semprún, speaking on the sixtieth anniversary of the liberation of the Nazi camps in 2005, argued that a collective European project would only succeed "'when our memories have been shared and brought together as one'" (qtd in Leggewie).[40] Spain is and has been frequently sidelined on the geographic and conceptual margins of Europe. As the rest of Europe began to awaken to the tragedy of the Holocaust in the 1960s, Spain was still ruled by a dictator who censored and controlled the free flow of information. While the late 1970s and early 1980s saw the beginning of a trend towards Holocaust commemoration in the rest of Europe, Spain was just emerging from its dictatorship, and committed to moving forward with the formation of a democratic government unencumbered by discussions of the past. It was not until the 1990s, as the rest of Europe had arrived at a period of "normative formation and institutionalization of cosmopolitanized memories" of the Holocaust (Levy and Sznaider 17), that Spain finally began its tentative process of examining the past. Yet there have been no truth commissions, no indictments of Franco-era criminals, no *Vergangenheitsbewältigung* in contemporary Spain.[41] An understanding of the Spaniards in Mauthausen opens the possibility that Semprún imagined: a shared memory of Nazism, the Second World War, and the Holocaust that unites instead of divides. This truly transnational memory of the Holocaust has "the potential to become the cultural foundation for global human-rights politics" (4), thus affecting future change in ways yet unimaginable.

Our continued investigation into the Holocaust unlocks the seeds of good and evil that allow us continually to reassess our own humanity, that is, how we treat others and how we would like to be treated. One only need look towards the rise of the political far right, the resurgence in extremist hate speech, and the global immigration crisis to see the imperative to seek out our common history so as not to fall into the traps of legally codified intolerance. As Bergen writes, "the Holocaust was an event in *human* history" that continues to have repercussions throughout the world even today (1; emphasis in the original). We, as scholars and humans, are duty bound to understand it to the best of our abilities. The Spaniards in Mauthausen, by this token, are not just a collection of 10,000 men and women displaced by politics and war to a concentration camp in Austria; they are humanity in relief. They are our collective past, reminding us of the urgency of our present and future. Their memory is as relevant today as it was yesterday and will be tomorrow.

The Politics of Memory: Mauthausen in Spain's Collective Memory

The meaning of "Mauthausen" in Spain has transformed over time. For those Spaniards who experienced the concentration camp firsthand, Mauthausen was a built environment that became their prison, their home and, for the majority, their grave. It was a space defined by violence and oppression, resistance and camaraderie; at first foreign and then startlingly familiar as the days, months, and years of abuse and imprisonment wore on.

For the Spanish survivors, Mauthausen was a memory both immediate and remote. It inspired some to record their journeys to the concentration camp and their drive to survive there. For many other survivors, Mauthausen was a memory they willed to the furthest reaches of their consciousness. Painful and harrowing, Mauthausen was better left forgotten and untold than relived in the years after their liberation.

For Spaniards who lived through the Second World War but had no firsthand experience of Mauthausen, the camp was either a legend or a ghost. For the minority who knew of its existence, Mauthausen began to assume a symbolic significance: it was fascism incarnate, it was Spain's continued isolation from Europe, it was a force of evil barely imaginable. Encompassing this symbolism, exiled Spanish Mauthausen survivors in 1962 funded the construction of a monument to their fallen compatriots in the camp-turned-memorial site, without any aid or recognition from the Spanish government. Indeed, absence was the dominant theme for these Mauthausen survivors, who were invisible during the Franco regime. For those Spaniards who were unaware of the camp during these years – the majority – Mauthausen was nothing more than a spectre. While the genocide of Jews in the Holocaust became more and more apparent after the war, the Spanish experience became more distant, more ephemeral, a phantom neither seen nor heard. For most Spaniards during the latter half of the twentieth century, Mauthausen and its Spanish victims disappeared entirely.

In the years after Franco's death, however, Mauthausen returned from the brink of oblivion. It became a space of memory for those who did not witness the camp or live through the war, but who sought answers and truth from the camp's lived history. Mauthausen's resurrection represented a desire to understand the camp as part of a collective memory of the Spanish experience of the twentieth century. Those Spaniards who saw Mauthausen cast in this light of remembrance drew on the significance of the camp in the lives of their countrymen who lived and died there. Availing themselves of the memories of survivors, many sought to rebuild Mauthausen in the Spanish imagination, to bring it back from its state of abandonment and understand both its literal and symbolic significance for the Spanish nation and people. In this post-Franco period, survivors and their families participated in a number of significant early efforts to memorialize the Spaniards in Mauthausen. They communicated with Montserrat Roig about her volume on the history of Catalans in Nazi camps. They installed, piecemeal, a series of small monuments and plaques in regional cemeteries and plazas in communities throughout Spain to honour the deportees (Toran, *Amical de Mauthausen* 129–32). And they began to organize annual journeys to Austria to visit Mauthausen as it developed from an abandoned concentration camp to a comprehensive memorial site, to remember those who would never return.

In the most recent iteration of Mauthausen's presence in the Spanish collective memory over the past fifteen years, the camp has been reimagined as a space of commemoration and recognition. Plaques, memorial sites, and mounds of stones dedicated to the Spanish deportees dot the camp and the Spanish landscape, attesting to the almost entirely symbolic place Mauthausen now assumes in the Spanish consciousness. As the number of remaining Spanish survivors dwindles, the camp is no longer conceptualized as a lived space, but as an imagined one. Mauthausen and the stories of the Spaniards who lived and died there are the inspirations for new creative endeavours that seek to reinvigorate the legacy of the camp in myriad ways. However, as the symbolism invested in Mauthausen reaches towards unique representations and genres, the tangible experience of the camp as a prison and a grave felt by its survivors and victims is diluted and distorted. Compared to the now numerous memory sites dedicated to the victims of the Spanish Civil War in Spain – in the sense of Pierre Nora's *lieux de mémoire*, "material, symbolic, and functional" modes of remembrance created by a "play of memory and history" and underwritten by a "will to remember" (19) – the country is only beginning to create tangible and intangible national referents to the victimization of Spanish nationals by the Nazis.[42] Without these conspicuous sites of memory of the Holocaust in Spain, it remains difficult to visualize and mourn the Spanish Republicans deported to and killed in Mauthausen.

What once was a lived environment is today a monument; stories that were at one time grounded in the memories of survivors have become the provenance of interested observers, personally unconnected to the camp itself. Nevertheless, Mauthausen has gained a place in the Spanish consciousness as more of the population becomes aware of its significance in a long-form view of Spanish history. Whereas only some 7,200 Spaniards experienced Mauthausen as a concrete, built environment, arguably tens or hundreds of thousands of Spaniards have encountered Mauthausen as a symbolic space of reconciliation with Spain's past. At the same time, a historically accurate understanding of the Spanish experience of the camp has given way to heroic myths and legends told in broad strokes. The lived essence of Mauthausen as a concentration camp has all but disappeared. By analysing the gamut of Spanish representations of Mauthausen as thoroughly as possible, through its every iteration in the Spanish collective memory – from built environment to ghost to symbol – this book makes an invisible space visible.

The notion of collective memory has become a flashpoint in contemporary Spanish cultural studies. Historical and collective memory have drawn the interest of a variety of scholars throughout a spectrum of fields, though the majority take the Spanish Civil War as their cultural touchstone.[43] Maurice Halbwachs' original theorizations about collective memory are particularly informative when looking at Spanish Mauthausen narratives. Although Halbwachs differentiated between historical and collective memory – a difference that has all but broken down in contemporary scholarship – his emphasis on the "social frameworks for memory" (Halbwachs and Coser 38) is relevant. This concept illustrates how the memory of Mauthausen has moved from the realm of experience to the realm of imagination. Halbwachs understood that collective memories are rooted in individual memories that differ in content and intensity. However, the individual "is able to act merely as a group member, helping to evoke and maintain impersonal remembrances of interest to the group" (Halbwachs 50) in the construction of a collective memory. Although these group memories necessarily begin with the recollections of the individual – in the case of Mauthausen, with the survivors themselves, who are uniquely able to recount their experiences in the concentration camp – they soon become the provenance of the collective. As time passes, Halbwachs wrote, collective memory "erodes at the edges as individual members ... become isolated or die, [and] it is constantly transformed along with the group itself" (82). In this way, the individual memories, although lost as the individuals themselves disappear, live on and evolve through the collective.

Halbwachs' understanding of collective memory has informed both Holocaust studies and cultural studies of the Spanish Civil War, but similar theorizations on Spanish memory of the Holocaust and Nazi persecution are still lacking. Jo Labanyi posits that studies of the trauma of the Holocaust have not been applied to Spain because the Latin American model of repressive dictatorships appears to be more comparable. Holocaust discourse offers a vocabulary for framing the issue of historical memory in terms of a legal discourse on human rights violations "in the rest of Europe," Labanyi writes, but "never had significant impact in Spain" (27). Spain, as Labanyi, Baer, and Estrada have all argued, saw itself as divorced from the Holocaust because of its historical legacy: namely, the expulsion of the Jews in 1492, the continued relative absence of Jews in Spain through the modern era, and ongoing anti-Semitism in the country, which has prevented Spaniards from associating their experience of the Nazi policies and practices of genocide with the Holocaust.[44]

Even at a moment of growing consciousness in Spain about Spaniards in Nazi concentration camps, there is, as Baer has called it, a "weak" or "nonexistent" memory of the Holocaust ("Memoria de Auschwitz" 110). A recent protest by family members of Spanish Mauthausen survivors illustrated this disconnect. As reported in the Spanish newspaper *El País*, a small number of relatives of Spanish Mauthausen victims were denied entry to a Holocaust commemoration at the Senate building in Madrid in 2014. The confusion between the collective memory of the Holocaust and that of the Spanish Civil War arose in this instance not because the protestors were relatives of Spanish victims of Nazi aggression, but because they were denied entry into the Senate building for protesting Franco-era disappearances in Spain. In fact, the spokesperson for the Amical de Mauthausen, a survivor organization based in Barcelona, affirmed that since Spain began observing the Holocaust Day of Remembrance in 2005, "'Los republicanos españoles deportados a los campos de concentración nazis han estado representados y se ha encendido una de las seis velas en su memoria y recuerdo'" (Junquera).[45] This episode demonstrates the overwhelming attention devoted to victims of Franco's violence during and after the Spanish Civil War, which tends to overshadow a similar movement to understand Spain's involvement, no matter how small, in the Holocaust.

Two contemporary theorists, Michael Rothberg and Andreas Huyssen, have given us a way to move forward through this minefield of competing memories. Rothberg's development of "multidirectional memory" as counteracting the "ugly contest of comparative victimization" (*Multidirectional Memory* 7) sets a course to consider the memories of the Spaniards in Mauthausen as complementary to more well-established Spanish Civil War and Holocaust memories, not at odds with them. Considering memory as unbound by national and group identities, "an open-ended field of articulation and struggle" (21), permits us to look at the Spaniards in Mauthausen in a new light, to use "faculties that allow us to grasp traumatic pasts as relational without sacrificing specificity" (Rothberg, "Trauma, Memory, Holocaust" 289). When not defined solely as "Spanish," "Catalan," or "Republican" – identities they, themselves, at times resisted – the deportees become individuals whose memories are in productive dialogue with others. As Rothberg notes, this "'revisiting' and rewriting of hegemonic sites of memory" (*Multidirectional Memory* 310), namely the Spanish Civil War/ Holocaust historical continuum, "has the potential to create new forms of solidarity and new visions of justice" (5).

Huyssen also sees transnational memory, a "memory without borders" or a "productive remembering" (*Present Pasts* 4, 27), as a more generative approach to the past. He argues, moreover, that a "transnational discourse of human rights …[or] the creation of objects, artworks, [and] memorials" (9) are more fruitful ways to unpack historical trauma. In Spain, where no truth commissions have ever addressed the scars of the Spanish Civil War and Franco dictatorship and judicial efforts to adjudicate the past have been stymied, a transnational multidirectional memory that takes into account both the individual histories and their artistic representations seems to offer the most productive means of reconciling the country's past with its present and future.

Since the turn of the twenty-first century, Spain has begun to address information and memories about the Spanish Civil War that were suppressed for decades. Just as there has been a popular movement to understand the historical details of the Spanish Civil War and postwar era – spawning non-governmental organizations like the Asociación para la Recuperación de la Memoria Histórica as well as a tide of historical texts, novels, films, art, and journalism – this same impetus is beginning to extend to Spain's role in the Second World War, and in particular, the Spanish role in the Holocaust. There are similar motivations behind both of these interconnected movements: the passage of the Ley de la Memoria Histórica in 2007, which lent a governmental stamp of approval to efforts to unearth Spain's past atrocities; the ceremonies marking the sixty-fifth anniversary of the start of the Spanish Civil War in 2001 and the sixtieth anniversary of the liberation of Mauthausen in 2005; and the realization that the memories of a first generation of survivors of both conflicts will be lost forever if they are not recorded now.[46]

Thus, a movement that began in earnest in the first decade of the twenty-first century to return to the battlegrounds of the Spanish Civil War and the prisons of the Franco dictatorship, soliciting the testimony of those on the margins of Spain's official history, has influenced the early stages of a similar movement to revisit Spain's role in the Second World War. Accounts of Mauthausen have expanded over the past decade: there have been multiple efforts to record the testimony of survivors, a surge in historical research facilitated by the opening of Civil War and Second World War–era archives in Spain (with, for instance, the availability of correspondence between the Spanish embassy in Berlin and Franco's government), and an uptick in commemorations that recognize the Spanish presence in the camp (with Prime Minister José Luis Rodríguez Zapatero's official visit to Mauthausen in 2005, for instance). These movements aid in forming a more complete and public picture of Spain's role in the Second World War, a multidirectional memory of a particularly charged period in the country's history. In these ways, the historical continuum that connects the Spanish Civil War to the Second World War also connects the collective memory of the Civil War and Franco era with the collective memory of the Spanish role in the Holocaust. The resulting "transversal" memory archive, as Rothberg describes it, "cuts across genres, national contexts, periods, and cultural traditions" (*Multidirectional Memory* 18). The generically diverse archive of Spanish Mauthausen representations may take as its thematic core a common experience of Nazi victimization within a specific concentration camp, but nevertheless it traverses a wide and endlessly overlapping field of cognition.

When historians speak of a "cultural turn,"[47] they identify a shift in the way the story of history is constructed. Instead of limiting themselves to primary sources, historians who make this turn incorporate diverse cultural materials into their construction of history, admitting that government documents and the firsthand testimony of survivors tell only a partial story of the past. Indeed, photographs, films, memoirs, and fictional narratives are cultural relics that, when combined with other primary sources of the past, produce an integrated history.

A more inclusive history also incorporates areas often omitted from Holocaust studies – the role of non-Jews, the dilemma of Jewish collaborators, and issues of gender and sexuality, for instance – into the field. This integrated history is not discipline-specific, that is, it encourages elements of art history, film, media, and literary studies to become part of the historical conversation. Yet, just as historians judge primary sources on their provenance and relative accuracy, so, too, must those committed to an integrative history judge their sources. A memoir cannot be read and interpreted in the same manner as a short story; a documentary film and a graphic novel are two distinct types of narratives.

For a cultural study of Mauthausen that traces a variety of sources through seven decades, understanding the differences among the material, when it was produced, and its intended audience is crucial. Although David Wingeate Pike and Montserrat Roig have written authoritative historical volumes on the Spaniards in Mauthausen, they are not integrative histories. Neither Roig's *Els catalans als camps nazis* nor Pike's *Spaniards in the Holocaust: Mauthausen, the Horror on the Danube* consider memoirs or fictional accounts by Spanish survivors as primary sources. Both texts leave the historical narrative of Spaniards in Mauthausen in the past, not looking beyond the memories of survivors for their chronicles. For an inclusive cultural rendering of the Spanish experience of Mauthausen, I examine material from across a broad spectrum of genres as well as a lengthy time period. Thus, in Rothberg's words, I "constitute the archive by forging links between dispersed documents" (*Multidirectional Memory* 18), charting how individual and social reactions to the Spanish experience of Mauthausen have changed over time and depend on the status of the author: survivor, second- or third-generation relative of a survivor, or interested non-survivor.

What is now known about the existence of Spaniards in Mauthausen, their daily life and death, emerged from the camp records and photographs Spaniards were able to clandestinely copy; artwork and letters produced during the war from inside the main camp, its subcamps, and *Kommandos*; and the testimonies of survivors, written years or decades after their liberation. As the legacy of Mauthausen has grown in Spain, non-survivors have appropriated the story of Spaniards in the camp and created historiographies, films, novels, and artwork based on the survivors' experiences. These two forms of representation – one grounded in firsthand memory, testimony, and documentation, and the other based on secondhand (or thirdhand) postmemory of the experience of others – raises a number of questions that overlap with the polemical debates over representations of the Holocaust.[48]

Even firsthand testimony and documentation provided by survivors can blur the lines between reality and fiction. Survivors may emphasize certain details and omit others, portraying Mauthausen as they experienced it or wished it to be portrayed, but not necessarily precisely as it was. To that end, only a survivor can "know" Mauthausen as it existed during its years of operation as a concentration camp: even if documentary films had recorded Mauthausen during the war, they too would constitute a subjective portrayal. The Nazi depictions of the Warsaw Ghetto for propaganda purposes demonstrate this dilemma: constructed as so-called accurate portrayals of the ghetto and its Jewish inhabitants, these films have been proven to be highly subjective representations of the Jewish residents of the ghetto that were assembled to evoke certain emotions and reactions in their viewers.[49]

Evidence of the Spaniards in Mauthausen is similarly subjective. The composition of the text, photograph, document, or film substantiating the presence of Spaniards in Mauthausen depends on the proximity of the author to the firsthand experience of the camp and on his or her intentions, political or otherwise. Thus even a document as seemingly objective as Casimir Climent's registry of Spaniards who entered and died in Mauthausen is subjective: Climent recorded only Spaniards. He was unable to include those who perished before they entered the camp or after records were suspended during the days leading to liberation, and omitted some of the details of the cause of death (perhaps because he did not have access to that information). Moreover, he implicitly imbued his records with an intentionality of keeping the memory of those who died in Mauthausen alive beyond the liberation of the camp and its transformation from an active space of history to a past space of memory.

Similarly, the images taken and preserved by the Spaniards working in the Mauthausen photography lab tell another subjective story about the camp. As Gina Herrmann has observed, the photographs Francesc Boix saved and took were often artfully composed to demonstrate the presence and even the subtle dissent of other Spaniards in Mauthausen as they witnessed daily atrocities ("Camera Caedens"). Even the seemingly mundane identification photographs of SS officers were designed to elicit a reaction in their viewers. They were kept to identify perpetrators of crimes against humanity calmly posing for a snapshot at a moment when they were operating under a perverse legal system.

Recent Spanish films that aim to portray Mauthausen's place in Spain's history are also subjective representations of a space that no longer exists. Documentaries such as *El comboi dels 927* and *Cerca del Danubio* reflect the filmmakers' own political biases. The directors purposefully composed them to elicit an emotional reaction from the viewer. The archival footage of liberation and the memories of the survivors in these documentaries may reflect a historical reality, but they are filtered through a modern lens that repositions the deportees as heroic agents and aligns Mauthausen's significance within a larger historical trajectory that includes the Spanish Civil War and Spain's postwar dictatorship.

As these representations stray from firsthand accounts, they also approach the contentious realm of fictional texts attempting to capture what their author never saw in person. In Holocaust studies, fiction has long been criticized for turning a historical atrocity into whitewashed entertainment. Theodor Adorno's oft-quoted comment that at "the final stage of the dilectic of culture and barbarism ... [t]o write poetry after Auschwitz is barbaric" (*Prisms* 34) captured the sentiment that Holocaust fiction and other creative endeavours risked minimizing the atrocities suffered by millions of Holocaust victims.[50] Adorno's subsequent indictment that "[a]ll post-Auschwitz culture, including its urgent critique, is garbage" even more succinctly pinpoints an anxiety over the "barbarism" that marks post-Holocaust cultural expression (*Negative Dialectics* 367). Spanish representations of Mauthausen have also strayed into the "barbaric" territory of popular entertainment, though they have not elicited the same critical vitriol as Spanish texts on the Holocaust, such as Antonio Muñoz Molina's *Sefarad*. This novel, which by turns portrayed and fictionalized the experiences of a number of well-known Jewish survivors of the Holocaust, was criticized for dehistoricizing the Shoah. These criticisms raise a number of crucial questions about who has the right to represent the Spaniards of Mauthausen, whether non-survivors who did not witness the camp as deportees may create accurate accounts or fiction, and whether it is more acceptable for a Spaniard to represent his countrymen imprisoned in Mauthausen than to represent European Jews from foreign countries, who speak languages he does not know, and write about places he has never seen.

More recently, these issues have collapsed onto Javier Cercas's *El impostor*, a rendering of the false concentration camp survivor Enric Marco, which questions the effect of what Cercas calls "la llamada memoria histórica" (293 and throughout) in Spain and across Europe.[51]

Marco's elaborate farce, dissected in Cercas's characteristically self-indulgent style, revealed another sort of fiction created out of the experiences of the Spanish deportees: one that deliberately impersonated the real suffering of the thousands of actual Spanish victims of the Nazis. Cercas's popular book has thrown questions of the history and memory of the Spanish deportees into a collective memory melee in Spain that encompasses everything from the Spanish Civil War to the 2009 economic collapse. However, the author's assertion that "[l]a industria de la memoria resultó letal para la memoria" (307) as concerns the Spaniards in Nazi camps is false: indeed, *Spaniards in Mauthausen* itself is proof that the "historical memory industry" has not killed off Spain's collective memory of the country's victims of Nazi atrocities.[52]

Fictional representations of experiences in Mauthausen by non-survivors – from Mercè Rodoreda's 1947 short story "Nit i boira" to recent endeavours like *El impostor* – though they challenge the parameters of who is allowed to represent the Holocaust, nevertheless permit us to examine both author and text on a spectrum between two opposing motivations: from a popular banalization of the Holocaust for monetary gain at one extreme to a transnational aperture inviting new generations to discover a fundamental historical truth at the other. As I will show, in many of these diverse texts, elements at both ends of the spectrum are at work. Though they stray from firsthand accounts that bear witness to Mauthausen, these representations, regardless, figure into a moral imperative to remember Spain's experience of the Nazi concentration camps and the Holocaust.

This book is a comprehensive chronological study of the Spanish representations of Mauthausen created, published, exhibited, or screened from 1940 to 2015. Filling the void left by Spain's chronic undervaluation of accounts of the Nazi persecution of Spanish Republicans, it examines narrative fiction, film, images, memoir, historiography, and media inspired by the experiences of Spaniards detained or killed in Mauthausen during the Second World War. Through this evidence, I address how Spaniards became aware of the Spanish government's connections to Nazi concentration camps, when the Spanish populace began to be cognizant of the victimization of Spanish nationals in Mauthausen, and how the cultural material demonstrating Spain's connection to the Holocaust and Nazi genocide has evolved over time, changing the landscape of Holocaust studies and collective memory. Thus, this book reveals how Spaniards have interacted with knowledge and memories of the Holocaust and Nazi genocide from the moment Spanish nationals began to be deported to Mauthausen in 1940 to the present day. By tracing how Mauthausen continues to be represented in art even as its living memory recedes to the past, I explore how direct or indirect witnesses to a moment of historical importance translate what they have experienced into a form of artistic expression. These works of art have influenced Spanish culture over the decades, despite the country's immersion in the oppressive silence about the past imposed by the Franco dictatorship. They continue to influence Spanish culture today.

There is no single authoritative account of the Spaniards in Mauthausen: each representation is a subjective approximation that reflects a particular time period, authorial perspective, political persuasion, and genre. To this end, fact-checking each and every detail in the array of works produced by the survivors, historians, novelists, filmmakers, and visual artists of the Spanish experience of Mauthausen is not the goal of this study. Each representation of the camp is an interpretation that depends on who the author is and what his or her intentions are, where and when the work was produced, what genre it is, how it has been constructed, and who the presumed audience or reader is. Just as the Spanish prisoners who entered Mauthausen were a heterogeneous population, so too are these narratives. Examining the diverse survivor accounts and non-survivor representations born of this subject, one must find shared experiences and common denominators to get the clearest picture of what Mauthausen meant for the Spaniards. Each text and film evaluated in this book tells a different aspect of a collective story that, as a whole, argues for the inclusion of the Spaniards in Mauthausen in a European culture of memory of the Holocaust.

As a cultural study, no source lies beyond examination in this book. It is only by placing these cultural artefacts under a microscope that we may gain a more profound understanding of the interactions among the individuals, the historical events, and the creative enterprises they inspired. Wherever possible, I incorporate primary source material in this volume. This includes first editions, original manuscripts, documents from public and private archives, interviews, and photographs. I also rely on historians who have studied primary source texts. It is worth noting that, although this book is about the "Spaniards in Mauthausen," the majority of the individual representations authored, documented, drawn, photographed, or filmed is the work of Catalans. Although not all were written in the Catalan language, I have laboured to include and translate texts in their original Catalan when available.

Any text – whether creative, historical, or testimonial – will reflect the interests and opinions of its author and the zeitgeist of its time. Primary source material in the form of documents, photographs, letters, and lists harbour the implicit concerns of their authors, artists, or safeguarding entity. Nevertheless, these biases are informative: they allow me to study historical, autobiographical, and creative texts as the product of unique individuals and the reflection of particular moments in time. To that end, the Catalan identity of many of the individuals examined in this volume, although not necessarily directly addressed in the text, is relevant: a disproportionate number of Catalans figured among the Mauthausen deportees. Their language and culture was repressed by Franco and thus they were marginalized twice over, denied their Catalan identity as well as their Spanish identity by the dictatorship authorities who deported them to Nazi camps. By largely grouping the deportees as "Spanish," however, I recognize the Catalan deportees' overwhelming self-identification and acknowledge that they lived during a historical moment when a movement towards Catalan cultural autonomy and self-determination was manifestly impossible. Nevertheless, where applicable, I will address how the Catalan identity of certain individuals influenced their depiction of Mauthausen and thus how a particularly Catalan culture of memory has become available over the course of time via these materials.

Chapter 1 examines documentation and graphic representations of Mauthausen from 1940 to 1945, the period when it operated as a concentration camp imprisoning Spaniards, among other foreign nationals. Spaniards and Catalans formed a core network within the bureaucracy of the camp and performed clandestine acts of resistance by keeping records of the entry and deaths of their countrymen and women, creating artwork representing the Nazis and the prisoners, saving photographic evidence of the camp, and communicating to the best of their abilities with family members in Spain. These snippets of the inner workings of the camp reveal the depth to which the Nazis targeted Spaniards. In addition, they lay the groundwork for the continued resistance of Mauthausen survivors labouring to bear witness to their experiences under the repressive atmosphere of the Franco dictatorship. Spaniards were also witnesses in the Allied war crimes trials at Nuremberg and the US trials at Dachau between 1945 and 1947, where their oral testimonies provided our first public impressions of Mauthausen. To this end, their legal testimony became another avenue by which they represented the inner workings of Mauthausen to the public in the months after their liberation.

Chapter 2 traces the first four Spanish representations of Mauthausen, published between 1945 and 1963 in France, Mexico, and Spain by Catalan authors. This period was characterized by survivors' efforts to represent their experiences accurately, primarily through oral and written testimonial accounts, but also through fictional texts. The first published representations of Mauthausen written by Spaniards begin to appear in 1945, contemporaneous with early Holocaust narratives published in the rest of Europe. Nevertheless, these Spanish stories and accounts, released both inside and outside of Spain, have been all but ignored in favour of much more well-known European narratives. They are the unknown pioneers in the nascent genre of the Spanish Holocaust narrative.

Chapter 3 explores the first wave of Spanish Mauthausen survivor accounts, which began to appear in the 1970s, while Franco was still in power. Courting controversy by positioning himself as a central and heroic figure in his memoirs, Mariano Constante nevertheless brought early visibility to Spanish concentration camp survivors over the course of the decade. The first attempt to visually record the Spanish experience of Mauthausen on film came about in 1975, the year of Franco's death. Llorenç Soler's documentary, *Sobrevivir en Mauthausen*, signalled the beginning of a new visual genre of storytelling about the Spanish experience of the concentration camp. Finally, in 1977, Montserrat Roig published her groundbreaking historical account of Catalans in Nazi camps based on interviews she conducted with survivors. This text exposed basic information, horrifying details, and the voices of dozens of Catalan survivors of Nazi camps to a wide audience inside Spain. Roig's text became the cornerstone of all successive historical and testimonial treatments of the Spaniards in Mauthausen.

Chapter 4 moves into the fully democratic period in Spain, which nonetheless began with a profound public silence about the Spanish experience of Mauthausen. Not until 1995, when the second wave of survivor accounts began to emerge, would Spain see a fleeting open public acknowledgment of the country's role in the Second World War. These survivor accounts continued to be published well into the twenty-first century and ushered in a new era of Mauthausen representations. As the number of living survivors diminishes, the next generation of family members and committed artists have begun to experiment with new and innovative ways of representing the Spanish Mauthausen experience. A host of documentary films emerged in the early 2000s, followed by a number of fictional texts that addressed questions of historical memory as it related to Spanish victims of Nazi policies and practices. Among these texts are historical novels, a graphic novel, a play, and a narrative published on the social network Twitter that have taken the story of the Spanish Mauthausen survivors in new and at times contentious directions, using contemporary media.

Today, Mauthausen stands firmly as a memorial to the victims of Nazi genocide in the rolling hills of Austria. Chapter 5 concludes by examining the contemporary presence of the camp as a physical and conceptual space in the consciousness of Spaniards more than seventy years after it was liberated. Yearly commemorations of the camp's liberation bring renewed attention to underlying political disputes between survivor organizations and the Spanish government. Meanwhile, the limited archival video and oral testimony of Spanish survivors has allowed the country to stake a small claim in research on the Holocaust. Mauthausen will continue to shape Spain's discussions about historical memory long after the last Spanish survivors of Nazi concentration camps are gone. As a physical camp, the Spanish prisoners built Mauthausen's walls and installations – carving the rock, hauling the stone, and moving the earth – and died in its quarry and barracks. As a space of remembrance, this same Mauthausen will outlive its witnesses and remain a symbolic site for successive generations who seek to understand the Nazis' crimes and Spain's past trauma.

The representations of the Spaniards in Mauthausen are the stories of a collective victimized and intentionally forgotten by not one but two totalitarian regimes. They are examples not unlike the modern-day accounts of victims – refugees, political dissidents, and civilian casualties – born of war and migration worldwide. Putting voices and names to their collective suffering combats the ambivalence these Spanish targets have encountered at home and abroad since the end of the Second World War. Opening a discussion of Spain's relevance to the Holocaust is a way for the country to further consider how individual lives matter, how victims deserve to be mourned, and how memories demand to be remembered in the collective consciousness. In turn, the resulting dialogue stimulates a conversation about our ethical obligation to remember all victims of genocide and political persecution.

1 The View from Inside: Clandestine Representations and Testimony of Mauthausen, 1940–1946

Documentation: Casimir Climent and Joan de Diego inside the Mauthausen Gestapo Offices

On 6 August 1940, the first convoy of Spaniards arrived in Mauthausen. These approximately four hundred men were deported from *Stalag* XIII-A in Moosburg, Germany. In retrospect, what they experienced in Moosburg was a relatively comfortable incarceration as prisoners of war. Mauthausen, however, came as a shock. As they entered the main camp, an interpreter or seasoned prisoner warned the Spaniards that their existence in Mauthausen could only end one way: death.

Convoys of Spaniards deported from German *Stalags* and French refugee camps to Mauthausen arrived almost continuously throughout 1940 and 1941.[1] The old and the sick were exterminated immediately upon entry into the camp, never to be recorded in Mauthausen's official rolls. The Nazis put the rest of these inaugural convoys of Spaniards to work constructing the camp itself, carving Mauthausen's imposing walls out of the camp's granite, installing the quarry's infamous 186 steps, and building the stone foundations for the SS offices and barracks. The labour was inhumane, and the Spaniards who did not collapse from hauling hulking stone blocks on their backs in wooden clogs up the slippery quarry ramp were often shot or pushed off the so-called Parachute Jump to their death by the SS. Others were quickly transferred to the killing site of Gusen, the Mauthausen subcamp about four kilometres away where a significant population of Spaniards was killed. Those who died were quickly replaced by more incoming prisoners: the last convoy of more than a hundred Spaniards arrived on 19 December 1941, though more Spanish Republicans would continue to arrive in Mauthausen in smaller groups until April 1945 (Marsálek 141–50). In these Spaniards, the Nazis found a continually refreshed stable of slave labour to exploit.

Given their isolation in the German prisoner of war or French refugee camps and the lack of any real information about the Nazi concentration camp system, the Spaniards on the first transports to Mauthausen were blind as to its function and operation. As Joan de Diego, a Catalan man on the first convoy to the camp recalled, "no teníamos ni idea absoluta de aquello" (de Diego Interview).[2] They would learn quickly that Mauthausen had earned its reputation as one of the most violent and exploitative of the Nazi concentration camps.[3] The Spaniards occupied the lowest rung of the camp hierarchy when they arrived in 1940 and 1941, beneath even the Austrian and German criminals who had comprised the majority of the camp's population up until then. The historian Rosa Toran explains, "els espanyols, sense cap protecció, ocupaven el graó més baix en l'escala concentracionària i van anar a raure als comandos més durs, sota l'hostilitat dels deportats amb més poder" (*Vida i mort* 215).[4] The greatest number of Spaniards died in 1941 in Mauthausen and Gusen, worked or starved to death.[5]

By the end of 1941, however, those who had survived those first cruel months had become camp veterans of sorts, and began to infiltrate positions of relative safety within Mauthausen. Some Spaniards became *Kapos*, the notorious prisoner-guards who controlled their fellow prisoners, often through violence. Others held positions among the *Prominenten*, selected according to their former profession and intelligence to work in the records offices of the camp. By 1943, moreover, Spaniards had assumed a variety of lesser tasks in Mauthausen that nevertheless spared them the worst of the working conditions: as barbers, tailors, kitchen labourers, mechanics, woodworkers, and interpreters. Toran estimates that about two hundred Spaniards attained some sort of privileged position in Mauthausen, "sense perdre de vista la raó de l'internament i sense oblidar que l'obtenció i la conservació del lloc no era fruit de la condescendència dels caps nazis, sinó de la lluita diària" (*Vida i mort* 218).[6] Many of these singled-out Spaniards were members of the camp's communist organization, a fact that would influence not only their imprisonment in Mauthausen and their increased chance of survival, but also their portrayal of the camp in the years after their liberation.

This "daily struggle" provided an impetus for many of these Spaniards to record clandestinely the details of their existence in Mauthausen. The Spaniards quickly unified themselves inside Mauthausen, despite the political differences that had divided them during the Spanish Civil War. According to one French prisoner, "'the Spanish "collective" ... alone, up until 1943, had the character of a solid organization in which communists joined with anarchists, socialists and republicans'" (qtd in Pike, *Spaniards in the Holocaust* 123). Aided by this secret organization, a significant number of Spaniards took advantage of their limited means and tools to create and preserve a living documentation of the camp, guarding materials ranging from secretly recorded lists of prisoners to cartoons making light of their interminable imprisonment.

Produced at great personal risk, these documents, photos, drawings, and letters have become our earliest record of the Spanish experience of Mauthausen. They were created contemporaneously with the Spaniards' years of imprisonment and Mauthausen's full operation as a concentration camp, thus providing a rare glimpse inside the camp during the Second World War. They are images and information filtered through the eyes of men who were wholly cut off from the outside world, struggling to survive in an entirely inhospitable environment. Moreover, these cultural artefacts – many of which survive to the present day in national and personal archives – have informed and illustrated decades of testimony, memoir, and research about the Nazi concentrationary system, as well as the Spanish experience of Mauthausen. From the Nuremberg trials to the most recent popular journalism on Spaniards in the Holocaust, these foundational materials continue to form the cornerstone of what we see and imagine when we think of the Spanish Mauthausen population. They are a living record of an otherwise unimaginable past.

Joan de Diego was among the first Spaniards to arrive in Mauthausen on 6 August 1940 and one of the few to survive the five years until the camp's liberation. He worked in the quarry for approximately eight months before being selected in March 1941 to join the *Lagerschreibstube*, the camp administrative office. De Diego had taught himself German and could make sense of the Spanish names that confounded SS officials. The arrival of the Spaniards in Mauthausen brought administrative difficulties that the Germans had not encountered with Polish and Czech prisoners: "la ortografía de los apellidos de aquellas personas, el sistema del doble apellido español, los nombres de los lugares de procedencia" (Bermejo and Checa, *Libro memorial* 25), among other linguistic and cultural idiosyncrasies, posed a particular obstacle for Nazi record-keeping in Mauthausen.[7] De Diego was promoted to third secretary of Mauthausen on 1 March 1941 (Pike, *Spaniards in the Holocaust* 128), becoming, as he described it, the "embajador de los españoles" in the camp who could bridge these language barriers (de Diego Interview).[8] As a consequence, he also became a witness to the inner workings of the camp: he knew the identities of the SS officers, met Heinrich Himmler on one of the Nazi leader's inspection visits of Mauthausen, and came into frequent contact with his countryman Casimir Climent i Sarrión, who also worked in one of the camp administrative offices (*Spaniards in the Holocaust* 128–30).[9] These encounters would be essential for identifying the thousands of Spaniards who died in the camp.

Climent arrived in Mauthausen on 25 November 1940, and also worked in the quarries for his first months of imprisonment. He was promoted to clerk in the *Politische Abteilung*, the Gestapo's branch office in Mauthausen, under Karl Schulz on 16 March 1941. Climent also knew German and had been an officer for the Spanish Republic during the Civil War. Like de Diego, he could capably organize the growing list of Spaniards in the camp by their multiple surnames. In the Gestapo office, Climent was tasked with "todo lo que hacia referencia a los asuntos de Espanoles [*sic*]" (Cohen 224),[10] such as organizing the index card file of the incoming prisoner information, mailing victims' ashes to their families, and keeping track of Gestapo and prisoner correspondence (Pike, *Spaniards in the Holocaust* 33).

Both de Diego and Climent unwittingly found themselves in possession of a wealth of information related to the lives and deaths of the Mauthausen prisoner population in the camp's administrative offices. Moreover, as native Catalan and Spanish speakers, they were often solely responsible for the records documenting their fellow countrymen's presence in Mauthausen. They, like all of the Spanish prisoners of Mauthausen, witnessed unspeakable atrocities. Some of this cruelty they saw up close, inside the buildings where they worked. De Diego watched as SS officers hanged prisoners for sport from the rafters of the office, leaving them there in agony as de Diego was expected to carry out his duties (Pike, *Spaniards in the Holocaust* 129). Climent saw the Gestapo officer Schulz fatally burn a Jewish prisoner on the wood stove in plain view of the office workers (55). No doubt motivated by the tortures they witnessed, yet threatened by the very same violence should they disobey their SS overseers in even the slightest way, both de Diego and Climent took an active role in preserving documentation that would become integral to identifying the Spaniards in Mauthausen for decades to come. In the years after the Second World War, they also became key witnesses to the Nazi reign of terror in courtroom testimony and oral histories they provided until their respective deaths.

De Diego described his entry into the camp's offices as a life-changing event. As Mauthausen's third secretary in the *Lagerschreibstube*, he attained "cierta personalidad por razón de que [estaba] en la oficina ... te daba una autoridad que no tenía ningún preso en el campo" (de Diego Interview).[11] This authority was a privilege afforded few other Mauthausen prisoners but also a cross to bear, as de Diego became a witness to some of the most lethal atrocities committed in the camp. As his German improved while working in the offices, he was given more complicated tasks, until he was in charge of the "actos de defunción" ("death registry," de Diego Interview). This record was the multi-volume *Todesmeldung*, the running registry of deaths in Mauthausen: the list contained some 3,000 entries when de Diego began adding to it and some 200,000 entries by the time the camp was liberated (Roig, *Els catalans* 307). De Diego had to learn the meanings behind the different "administraciones" or the ways prisoners were killed (de Diego Interview). These could include alleged suicides, disease, exhaustion, hangings, and electrocutions, among the many other ways that the SS killed the Mauthausen prisoners. For the death list, de Diego translated these causes of death into the Nazis' own particular parlance, which ultimately obfuscated the actual cause of death (Toran, *Joan de Diego* 119). Prisoners transferred to Hartheim Castle, a Mauthausen outpost where convoys of prisoners were killed in its gas chamber, for instance, were recorded in the official registry as having been transported to the "sanatorium" of Dachau (*Joan de Diego* 119; Roig, *Els catalans* 288). Through his work in the offices, de Diego became fluent in these coded ways of masking the actual causes of death of the prisoner population.

De Diego's growing knowledge about the inner workings of the camp, the Nazis' obsession with record-keeping, and the subterfuge through which the SS documented their mass killings of prisoners would become invaluable after the camp's liberation. In one instance, de Diego was ordered to retrieve identity cards from corpses in the Mauthausen gas chamber (Toran, *Joan de Diego* 120); in many others, he accompanied the corpses from the gas chamber to the crematorium, with his record book under his arm (Roig, *Els catalans* 307). These experiences transformed him into an eyewitness to the Holocaust: "me permitió saber que habían cámaras de gas" in Mauthausen (de Diego Interview), a fact that was still in doubt in the years after the end of the Second World War.[12]

In the days leading up to liberation, de Diego was confronted with a singular dilemma: the SS demanded the incineration of all of the camp's documentation, including the death registry that de Diego had been keeping so carefully. Meanwhile, de Diego had been collaborating with Climent and another Spaniard in the *Politische Abteilung*, Josep Bailina, to keep complete clandestine records of the Spanish prisoners in the camp. In these chaotic final days of the war, de Diego saved a crucial piece of evidence by secretly rescuing Mauthausen's *Unnatürliche Todesfälle* or Unnatural Deaths register from the SS pyres and delivering it to the American forces (Pike, *Spaniards in the Holocaust* 34–5; Roig, *Els catalans* 499).[13]

In a parallel experience, Climent's work in the Gestapo's Mauthausen office would also prove definitive for the documentation of the Spaniards in the camp. Just four days after the liberation of Mauthausen, Climent gave a sworn statement to Eugene S. Cohen, an investigating officer of the US Army. He attested that his work in Mauthausen was focused on matters related to the Spaniards in the camp, in particular: "al mantenimiento del orden dentro de la cartoteca general y ultimamente se me encargó de lo que hacia referencia a las mujeres presas en el campo" (Cohen 224).[14] This "cartoteca" was the main index file of the camp, ultimately containing some 180,000 entries (Vilanova, *Los olvidados* 216). Although the SS kept a copy of each index card, at one point in 1944, Climent recalled that he was ordered to create a new, more detailed registry (Roig, *Els catalans* 502). Climent clandestinely kept the old copies of the index cards for each Spanish Republican in the camp. These extra cards, which he hid under stacks of blank index cards in the office, contained detailed information on the prisoner's birthplace and birth date, his number and transfer date from a German *Stalag* to Mauthausen, and the date of any further transfer to one of the Mauthausen subcamps or *Kommandos*. With the help of de Diego, Climent was even able to add the Spanish prisoners' home address to his secret card file and compile an additional handwritten list of all the Spaniards to pass through Mauthausen, the only exception being those who were killed immediately upon arrival in the camp (Pike, *Spaniards in the Holocaust* 34; *Els catalans* 571–776).[15] These actions proved that Climent was not only just as meticulous a record-keeper as his Nazi captors, but also, as the Mauthausen survivor Antonio Vilanova wrote, that he was nothing short of an "hombre tan valeroso, tan paciente y tan cuidadoso que ... fue el héroe que hizo posible que se puedan conocer los nombres y fechas de todos los españoles muertos en Mauthausen y sus kommandos" (*Los olvidados* 200).[16]

In saving the lists and index card files of the Spanish Republicans, Climent had amassed some 14 kilograms of documents that needed to be safely hidden in order to survive Schulz's order to burn all the *Politische Abteilung* paperwork as Allied forces approached (Pike, *Spaniards in the Holocaust* 33–4; Roig, *Els catalans* 502–3; Le Chêne 109; Vilanova, *Los olvidados* 216). Climent recounted that an SS official attempted to persuade him to flee the camp with the Gestapo officers as the Allies neared, but he refused, collaborating instead with the Americans (Cohen 224). When the US Army liberated Mauthausen on 5 May 1945, Climent approached Sergeant Benjamin B. Ferencz with a box – which he had apparently buried for safekeeping – containing identification cards and photographs of all of the SS who had been in Mauthausen (Pike, *Spaniards in the Holocaust* 34). Ferencz was struck by Climent's foresight, though he could not identify Climent by name, writing that he was "'moved by the blind faith which inspired the unknown prisoner to risk his life in the conviction that there would one day come a day of reckoning'" (qtd in Jardim 68; qtd in *Spaniards in the Holocaust* 34). Climent, de Diego, and others also smuggled eight copies of these lists out of Mauthausen. After liberation, they distributed them widely to the International Red Cross as well as survivors' and Spanish political organizations in France (Vilanova, *Los olvidados* 216–17). These hundreds of pages of lists are a carefully constructed record of the Spanish trajectory to Mauthausen. They divide the collective into the survivors, those who were gassed, those who were transferred to other concentration camps in Nazi Germany, and those who died in Mauthausen and Gusen. With detailed entries that track each individual through his origins in Spain to his deportation and the date of his death in Mauthausen, Hartheim, or Gusen – or to his liberation, for the fortunate few – the yellowing folios of de Diego's and Climent's legacy survive as one of the earliest compendiums documenting the Spanish presence in Nazi camps, preserved at the Museu d'Història de Catalunya in Barcelona among Joan de Diego's personal archives.[17]

Climent, like de Diego, was an eyewitness to scores of Nazi atrocities. Both men were afforded some modicum of liberty to move about the camp and were therefore privy to more of what went on inside Mauthausen than the average prisoner. In the days immediately following the American liberation of the camp, US Army officials interviewed Mauthausen survivors and perpetrators in preparation for the upcoming Mauthausen trials. The resulting Cohen Report, declassified by the

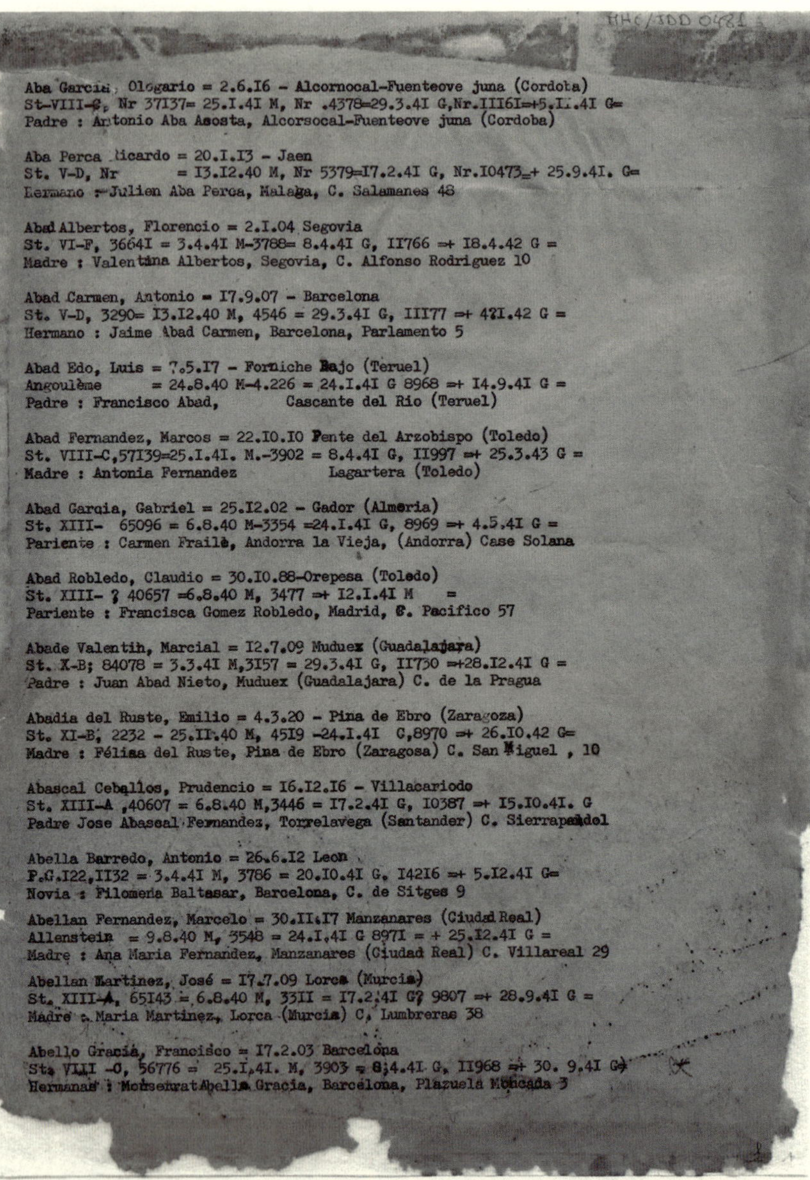

```
Aba Garcia, Olegario = 2.6.I6 - Alcornocal-Fuenteove juna (Cordota)
St-VIII-C, Nr 37I37= 25.I.4I M, Nr .4378=29.3.4I G,Nr.III6I=+5.I.4I G=
Padre : Antonio Aba Asosta, Alcorsocal-Fuenteove juna (Cordoba)

Aba Perca Ricardo = 20.I.I3 - Jaen
St. V-D, Nr        = I3.I2.40 M, Nr 5379=I7.2.4I G, Nr.I0473=+ 25.9.4I. G=
Hermano : Julien Aba Perca, Malaga, C. Salamanes 48

Abad Albertos, Florencio = 2.I.04 Segovia
St. VI-F, 3664I = 3.4.4I M-3788= 8.4.4I G, II766 =+ I8.4.42 G =
Madre : Valentina Albertos, Segovia, C. Alfonso Rodriguez 10

Abad Carmen, Antonio = I7.9.07 - Barcelona
St. V-D, 3290= I3.I2.40 M, 4546 = 29.3.4I G, III77 =+ 4?I.42 G =
Hermano : Jaime Abad Carmen, Barcelona, Parlamento 5

Abad Edo, Luis = 7.5.I7 - Forniche Bajo (Teruel)
Angoulême      = 24.8.40 M-4.226 = 24.I.4I G 8968 =+ I4.9.4I G =
Padre : Francisco Abad,         Cascante del Rio (Teruel)

Abad Fernandez, Marcos = 22.I0.I0 Pente del Arzobispo (Toledo)
St. VIII-C,57I39=25.I.4I. M.-3902 = 8.4.4I G, II997 =+ 25.3.43 G =
Madre : Antonia Fernandez         Lagartera (Toledo)

Abad Garcia, Gabriel = 25.I2.02 - Gador (Almeria)
St. XIII-  65096 = 6.8.40 M-3354 =24.I.4I G, 8969 =+ 4.5.4I G =
Pariente : Carmen Fraile, Andorra la Vieja, (Andorra) Case Solana

Abad Robledo, Claudio = 30.I0.88-Orepesa (Toledo)
St. XIII- ? 40657 =6.8.40 M, 3477 =+ I2.I.4I M     =
Pariente : Francisca Gomez Robledo, Madrid, C. Pacifico 57

Abade Valentih, Marcial = I2.7.09 Muduex (Guadalajara)
St. X-B; 84078 = 3.3.4I M,3I57 = 29.3.4I G, II730 =+28.I2.4I G =
Padre : Juan Abad Nieto, Muduex (Guadalajara) C. de la Pragua

Abadia del Ruste, Emilio = 4.3.20 - Pina de Ebro (Zaragoza)
St. XI-B; 2232 - 25.II.40 M, 45I9 -24.I.4I  C,8970 =+ 26.I0.42 G=
Madre : Félisa del Ruste, Pina de Ebro (Zaragosa) C. San Miguel , 10

Abascal Ceballos, Prudencio = I6.I2.I6 - Villacariodo
St. XIII-A ,40607 = 6.8.40 M,3446 = I7.2.4I G, I0387 =+ I5.I0.4I. G
Padre Jose Abascal Fernandez, Torrelavega (Santander) C. Sierrapandol

Abella Barredo, Antonio = 26.6.I2 Leon
P.G.I22,II32 = 3.4.4I M, 3786 = 20.I0.4I G. I42I6 =+ 5.I2.4I G=
Novia : Filomena Baltasar, Barcelona, C. de Sitges 9

Abellan Fernandez, Marcelo = 30.II.I7 Manzanares (Ciudad Real)
Allenstein = 9.8.40 M, 3548 = 24.I.4I G 897I = + 25.I2.4I G =
Madre : Ana Maria Fernandez, Manzanares (Ciudad Real) C. Villareal 29

Abellan Martinez, José = I7.7.09 Lorca (Murcia)
St. XIII-A, 65I43 = 6.8.40 M, 33II = I7.2.4I G? 9807 =+ 28.9.4I G =
Madre : Maria Martinez, Lorca (Murcia) C. Lumbreras 38

Abello Gracia, Francisco = I7.2.03 Barcelona
St. VIII -C, 56776 =  25.I.4I. M, 3903 = 8.4.4I G, II968 =+ 30. 9.4I G=
Hermanas : Monserrat Abella Gracia, Barcelona, Plazuela Moncada 3
```

1.1 First page of the "List of the Dead" [Joan de Diego Archive, MHC (Fons Amical de Mauthausen)]

US government in 2006, contained a one-page statement by Climent
that constituted the first governmental documentation of a Spanish survivor of a Nazi concentration camp. In his 9 May 1945 deposition Climent testified to having been a firsthand witness to murder:

> Como todos los que han vivido en este campo, he podido comprobar las
> ejecuciones, – algunas veces numerosas, – tanto de hombres como mujeres,
> algunos no mayores de edad. Fusilamientos, muertes mediantes camaras
> de gases toxicos, abandono de gente hambrienta, en recintos en donde
> morian privados de todo alimiento, es decir un sinfin de actos de sadismo.
> (Cohen 224; lack of accentuation in the original)[18]

In his corroborating testimony to Montserrat Roig, Climent, like de
Diego, asserted that he witnessed the killing of men of every nationality in Mauthausen (*Els catalans* 302–3).

Climent's deposition to the US Army, a legal testimony in the tru-
est sense of the word, is a concise document with a precise function.
Swearing that he had "declarado la verdad" ("nothing but the truth,"
Cohen 224; 222), Climent began a process of describing, detailing, and
elaborating the truth as he witnessed it in order to bring justice to both
the victims of Nazi oppression and the perpetrators of the crimes. His
voice – lent a particular tone of authority given the responsibility the
Nazis invested in him as a functionary in the camp Gestapo office –
inaugurated the written testimony of Spanish victims of the Nazis, and
continued to resonate throughout the historical documentation recording the experiences of Spaniards in Mauthausen.

Nevertheless, Climent's testimony, along with de Diego's saved lists,
were subjective accounts. Regardless of the authority granted them by
the US government or the Museu d'Història de Catalunya, these documents highlighted details of great importance to these two Spanish
Mauthausen prisoner-functionaries: namely, the presence and violent
deaths of their countrymen and women in the camp. They exhibited
Climent and de Diego's desire to make public the plight of Spaniards in
Mauthausen as quickly and in as official a manner as possible.

The Cohen Report figured into the Mauthausen trial, part of the larger
judiciary proceedings that took place at Dachau in 1946. Although this
active participation on the part of Climent and other Mauthausen survivors "enabled Holocaust victims to play a meaningful role in both
bringing their former captors to justice and establishing what had
occurred at Mauthausen in the preceding seven years" (Jardim 215),

the Mauthausen trial received very little international press and has been all but forgotten in the shadow of the Nuremberg trials. Nevertheless, the trials at Dachau inaugurated a period during which both Climent and de Diego were deeply involved in calling for justice for the victims of the Nazis. Twenty years later, in 1967, both men were witnesses at the trial of Karl Schulz, chief of the *Politische Abteilung* in Mauthausen, in Cologne, Germany (Pike, *Spaniards in the Holocaust* 291; Toran, *Vida i mort* 262). Climent and de Diego also testified at the 1970 trial of Georg Renno, the doctor responsible for the fatal transports to Hartheim Castle (Toran, *Joan de Diego* 275). Finally, de Diego testified before the US Consulate General in Bordeaux in 1986, in a legal process to halt the naturalization of former Nazis attempting to become American citizens (276).

Beyond their contributions to the international efforts to adjudicate Holocaust perpetrators, however, the information Climent and de Diego gathered and saved has had an impact on virtually every historical study of Spaniards in Mauthausen since the camp's liberation. Antonio Vilanova worked with Climent and de Diego's lists in his 1969 historiographic account, *Los olvidados: Los exilados españoles en la segunda guerra mundial* (*The Forgotten: The Spanish Exiles in the Second World War*). Evelyn Le Chêne credited Climent's archives as the "basis for any history of Mauthausen" (11) in her 1971 book, *Mauthausen: The History of a Death Camp*. Roig interviewed both men and included reproduced pages from their lists as well as an appendix of more than 200 pages culled from Climent's index card file of the Catalan prisoners in Mauthausen in her 1977 historiography *Els catalans als camps nazis* (*Catalans in Nazi Camps*). David Wingeate Pike depended on the lists and testimony of both survivors in his authoritative *Spaniards in the Holocaust* (2000). De Diego was one of the Spaniards who contributed his detailed oral history to the Mauthausen Survivor Documentation Project through the *Archiv der KZ-Gedenkstätte Mauthausen* (AMM, Mauthausen Camp Archive) in Vienna in 2002. Benito Bermejo and Sandra Checa considered de Diego, Climent, and Bailina "tres nombres claves" whose intervention in saving documents made the information that emerged from Mauthausen "particularmente completa" compared to data from other Nazi concentration camps (*Libro memorial* 25).[19] Their *Libro memorial: Españoles deportados a los campos nazis (1940–1945)* (*Memorial Book: Spaniards Deported to the Nazi Camps [1940–1945]*) from 2006 is the fruit of such detailed historical information. Even the 2010 online census of Spanish deportees to Nazi camps coordinated by Alfons Aragoneses was based in part on the lists from de Diego's personal archive.

As we consider how Spanish representations of Mauthausen were produced during the camp's period of operation and immediately after liberation, Climent and de Diego's documentation and testimony are of crucial importance. As tangible materials that attest to the lives and deaths of Spanish Republicans in Mauthausen, these lists and index cards are inanimate witnesses to a moment in history that the Nazis tried to erase. The archivists of this documentation, prisoners themselves who suffered alongside the men and women recorded on the registries they were forced to keep, risked death in guarding these cards and papers. They, too, are witnesses not only to the nefarious activities of the Nazis in Mauthausen, but also to the extremes to which their captors went to first record and then destroy the evidence of their crimes.

Climent and de Diego are the first of many Spanish prisoners of Mauthausen who looked beyond the stone walls of their prison towards a future that would need proof of the Holocaust to convince those who had never set foot inside a concentration camp of what occurred there. These two men knew before their own survival was assured that the representations of Mauthausen they were secreting away would be invaluable as records of the past. They understood the importance of this documentation for posterity just as well as the Nazis did. It is in history's best interest that Climent and de Diego outsmarted their captors to claim a piece of that history for the Spaniards in Mauthausen.

Artwork by the Spanish Prisoners

Like those assigned to the camp administrative offices, Spaniards were selected to work in the *Technische Abteilung* (technical division) and more specifically the *Baubüro* (construction or technical design office) in Mauthausen because of their professional skills as artists or draftsmen. Capitalizing on their access to paper, pencils, and ink, some of these men created artwork that went above and beyond the maps and blueprints they were forced to draw for the Nazis. The fact that thousands of Holocaust victims and witnesses were moved to create artwork of one form or another during their imprisonment across the Third Reich has prompted scholars like Irving Howe to ask: "Should not art have a sufficient sense of its own limitations to keep a certain distance from the unspeakable?" (Blatter and Milton 10). Yet as Janet Blatter has argued, victims of the Holocaust created artwork during their imprisonment in ghettos and concentration camps for a variety of reasons, from a desire to preserve their sense of identity to a need to chronicle any aspect of their experience (31–4). For scholars of the Holocaust, this artwork "reflects its time both in its subject matter and in what it reveals about the artists themselves and the conditions under which they worked" (22). A closer look at the artwork created by Spanish Republicans during their imprisonment in Mauthausen is a snapshot of the time, place, emotion, and identity of the individual artist and the moment. Works created from 1940 to 1945 that have survived until today are some of the earliest Spanish visual representations of Mauthausen and the Holocaust. As Howe writes, these works of art "testify to the will of the doomed to live out their few remaining days as human beings who speak, create and fantasize, human beings who stretch out their hands to those of us they could not know as anything but an unseen future" (11). They turn an anonymous mass struggle to survive into the vision of one individual pushed to his limit who nevertheless retains a sense of self in the concentration camp.

Artwork created by Spaniards while they were still imprisoned in Mauthausen has survived piecemeal, oftentimes only discovered in the personal archives of survivors. The loss of this clandestinely produced artwork was commonplace: only a fraction of the hundreds of thousands of works of art created by Holocaust victims in the camps escaped confiscation or destruction by the SS, damage by the elements or Allied bombings, being given or traded away, or being destroyed by the artist himself (Blatter and Milton 37). Like all art of the Holocaust, there is no one coherent narrative for the works of Spanish Republicans in Mauthausen: from delicate pencil drawings to colour cartoon greeting cards, Spanish prisoners captured many facets of the concentration camp experience. In their official capacities in the technical offices of Mauthausen, they drafted maps of the camp, secretly making copies for the Spanish resistance organization. At the behest of SS officers, they also drew pornographic images. All of these examples provide a representational window into Mauthausen during its years of operation, when Spanish prisoners sought a means of expression and documentation in any form they could manage.

Manuel Alfonso Ortells arrived in Mauthausen on 13 December 1940, and was promoted to the camp *Baubüro* office on 5 May 1941 (Bermejo and Checa, *Libro memorial* 361; Strozier 26). Alongside a number of other Spaniards, including Eduardo Muñoz Orts and Manuel García Barrado, Alfonso worked on maps for the camp's construction operations

(Strozier 22). But his position inside one of the camp's administrative offices also afforded him the opportunity to travel to other sites outside the main camp as part of the "equipo de geómetras (vermesung)" ("geometrician team" Alfonso Ortells 60). In this way, he supplied the Spanish resistance organization with copies of maps and drawings, including those of the region surrounding the main Mauthausen camp. At least one of these clandestine sketches, depicting the position of the armoires, table, and door inside the technical design office and titled "Baubüros," survived (Alakus et al. 112). With access to drafting materials, Alfonso also created drawings and propaganda, which he described as small works of art for his friends in the camp. He recounted: "a veces hacia dibujos a escondidas para celebrar el aniversario de los amigos; hacia postales que después firmábamos y asi se hacia un buen recuerdo" (Alfonso Ortells 66; lack of accentuation in the original).[20] He signed these works of art with a small bird, which to him symbolized a desire for liberty and inspired the nickname "El Pajarito" ("The little bird," "Artistas y científicos" 6).

Alfonso's greeting cards and caricatures depicted life inside Mauthausen, sometimes in darkly humorous ways. In one example, a man with an oversized head smiles as he rides a bicycle down a curving road, leaving behind the burning remnants of what are clearly the walls of Mauthausen. A directional road sign surrounded by blooming flowers says "Final Muchos Años" ("Destination Many Years") and a small bird draws a lazy spiral in the sky. This is a greeting card – indicated by the text that reads "Muchas felicidades" ("Many congratulations") in the foreground – produced circa 1944 in pencil on the back of a work order (Blatter and Milton 174).[21] Alfonso's improvised medium of the blank side of a functionary document was a common use of pilfered materials by concentration camp artists, who would avail themselves, at some risk, of any available material (25). The card portrays a desired freedom from the confines of the concentration camp, after the wished-for destruction of the camp. The road sign promises that once outside the camp's walls, the man on the bicycle may hope to enjoy a long life; indeed, Alfonso's signature bird of liberty flies in the same direction. Moreover, as the most dominant aspect of the drawing, the ex-prisoner's head – perhaps a caricature of one of Alfonso's compatriots in the camp[22] – suggests a newfound individual identity that was lost amid the dehumanizing routine of Mauthausen. Although neither Alfonso's specific intentions nor the recipient of this card is known, the work is characteristic of the artist's melding of humour and seriousness

1.2   Greeting card by Manuel Alfonso, circa 1944 [Mauthausen Memorial Archives/Archiv der KZ-Gedenkstätte Mauthausen]

of purpose that reveals a longing to survive to see the end of the Second World War.

Alfonso did survive Mauthausen, and would live to write his memoirs. While the drawing of the man on the bicycle is archived at the Mauthausen Memorial Archives in Vienna, Alfonso retained many other examples of his concentration camp artistry, some of which he reproduced in his autobiography. There is a caricature, presumably of Mauthausen Commandant Franz Zeireis feeding piglets with a baby bottle, dated 21 December 1944. This drawing depicts the pigs that Zeireis kept in the concentration camp, which were afforded better treatment and meals than the Spanish prisoners in his charge (Alfonso Ortells 108).[23] Another greeting card shows a man with striped prisoner pants walking by the prostitutes' barracks (109). Without any identifying details, this card clearly demonstrates one of the daily routines of Mauthausen: the ability of male prisoners with additional privileges – including some Spaniards – to visit the prostitutes who were housed in separate barracks in Mauthausen.[24] Two drawings portray the brutal work of the prisoners in the quarry and the constant threat of death. In one, two figures lie inert and bleeding at the barbed wire fence near a watchtower as prisoners cut and haul stone nearby under the vigilance of a prisoner-*Kapo* (104). Undated, this coloured pencil work is a rough sketch of the Mauthausen working conditions; the men are faceless representations of any or every prisoner. The other, a more carefully crafted watercolour, shows a group of prisoners about to carry one of their own on a pallet up the long quarry stairs towards the main camp (105). Red bloodstains dot the stairway and the man, who is, presumably, dead. These seem to be early drawings from Alfonso's ordeal; greeting cards from 1944 "celebrate" the Spaniards' improved conditions and longevity in the camp (109–10). By 1945, Alfonso had spent five years in Mauthausen, with no apparent end in sight. All of the works of art the artist included with his memoirs are simple drawings that nevertheless manage to communicate complex emotions about one man's life in the camp and his aspirations beyond the walls of Mauthausen.

Alfonso, like many other Holocaust artists, was also compelled to draw for SS officers and *Kapos* in order to obtain food or better treatment. In exchange for a mildly pornographic drawing created for one of the barrack captains, for instance, Alfonso was able to secure a plate of food (Llor 58). In fact, Alfonso credited his survival to this type of work: "'El dibujo me salvó la vida en Mauthausen. Gracias a eso me salvé'" (56).[25] Although pornographic and other commissioned works created by the Spanish artist-prisoners of Mauthausen for the SS and *Kapos* have not survived, they are mentioned in other sources. The character Emili in Joaquim Amat-Piniella's fictionalized memoir *K.L. Reich* – a foil for the author – is a talented artist who is compelled to draw pornography for the SS officers. Similarly, one of the other men who worked alongside Alfonso in the *Baubüro*, Muñoz, nicknamed "Lalo," drew works specifically for the entertainment of his captors (Strozier 22).

Muñoz and other Spaniards also created artwork and clandestine maps inside Mauthausen. Before the Spanish Civil War, Muñoz was trained as an artist at the Escuela de Bellas Artes in Valencia; he counted Pablo Picasso as his mentor upon his liberation from Mauthausen (Strozier 22). His colour caricature from 1944 of Alfonso drawn as a bird, perched on a fig tree branch with a ball and chain around one of his talons, survived thanks to its inclusion in Alfonso's private collection (Strozier 25; Llor, unnumbered colour page after 128). The drawing was signed on the reverse side by dozens of Spanish Republican compatriots in the camp, under the heading "Te homenajeamos efusivamente, esperanzados en la pronta desaparición de la bolita," a reference to the end of the Spaniards' long incarceration (Llor, unnumbered colour page after 128).[26] Beyond sending their well wishes to Alfonso, the signatories' handwriting indicated that they, too, were suffering the same interminable imprisonment.

Other examples of works of art created by the Spaniards in Mauthausen can be found in various sources. Joan de Diego's greeting card with a message in Czech over embossed flowers dated 17 July 1943, and Antonio Fradera's small colour drawing of a bullfighter with a Spanish flag, dated 1944 from Gusen, are collected in a catalogue for an exhibit at the Visitor's Center of the Mauthausen Memorial site (Alakus et al. 102, 09). Pablo Escribano's original colour greeting card celebrating one of his countryman's soccer skills, dated a few days before the camp's liberation, is also on display at the Mauthausen Memorial museum in Austria (Holzinger and Kranebitter 213). Roig reproduced a hand-drawn map of Mauthausen created by a Spanish member of the clandestine resistance organization in her historiography (*Els catalans* Figure 71, after 512). The exhibition "Supervivencia, testimonio y arte: Españoles en los campos nazis" ("Survival, Testimony and Art: Spaniards in the Nazi Camps"), which originated at the Centro Documental de la Memoria Histórica in Salamanca in 2010, included a number of drawings and prints created inside Mauthausen before 1945 as well as others made after the camp's liberation.

Perhaps the best-known creation by a Spanish Mauthausen inmate is more accurately described as graphic art. By most accounts, the artist Francesc Teix was responsible for the famous banner hung across Mauthausen's main gate to greet the troops who would liberate the camp. Provided with bed sheets stolen from the SS by the Spanish clandestine organization and sewn together, Teix laboured for two days on the enormous sign hidden in the washroom of barrack 11 (Pons Prades and Constante 273). Just as he was finishing his layout of the banner on 5 May 1945, however, inmates spotted the first squadron of American troops approaching the camp. Teix hurriedly completed his sign; in photos of the banner, the final word is compressed, nearly running off the last sheet. Teix's work reads, in all capital letters, "Los españoles antifascistas saludan a las fuerzas libertadoras" ("The Antifascist Spaniards Salute the Liberating Forces"). Drawings of the flags of the United States, Great Britain, and Russia adorn the centre of the banner, with English and Russian translations of the message on either side below the Spanish text. Created out of a sense of euphoria at the prospect of the Spaniards' freedom as well as the pragmatism of identifying themselves as a welcoming and organized contingent of the camp's prisoner population, Teix's situational artwork was lost in the days after the camp's liberation. However, the banner as it was installed on the inner façade of the gate into the main camp, surrounded by prisoners, was photographed first by Francesc Boix on 5 May, and subsequently by the US Signal Corps (Holzinger and Kranebitter 252–4). This final work of Spanish Mauthausen prisoner art has become an iconic symbol of the Spanish resilience and organization in the camp.

After American forces liberated Mauthausen, many of the surviving Spanish ex-prisoners remained in the camp as displaced persons for a number of weeks. Artwork created during this time and in the following year had a greater chance of surviving to the present day. Indeed, the "Supervivencia, testimonio y arte" exhibit was able to gather a number of these post-liberation works of art by the Spanish Republicans. Unlike the caricatures and greeting cards forged in captivity – subtle works of protest cloaked in frivolous genres less likely to draw the ire of the Nazis should they be discovered (though still explicitly forbidden) – those works made immediately after the end of the war betrayed a darker impression of the Spaniards' years of imprisonment. Ramón Milá Ferrerons arrived in Mauthausen as a child with his family in the convoy from Angoulême, France, on 20 August 1940. In his five years of imprisonment, he experienced more desperate conditions in the

subcamp of Gusen as well as some relief when he joined the Poschacher *Kommando* in Mauthausen. During the camp's years of operation,
Milá drew at the behest of SS or *Kapos* in exchange for his continued
survival (Strozier 23–4). He worked in the carpenter's labour detail in
Gusen but also drew decorations for a theatrical production the Spaniards mounted inside Mauthausen in 1944 (Roig, *Els catalans* 391). His
artwork from 1946, however, shifted focus to the brutalities he either
experienced or was privy to while in Mauthausen. In a pen and ink
sketch, a shadowy figure of a guard whips naked skeletal prisoners
agonizing under the showers. The sketch included a caption in French
that explained the scene as the cold shower "extermination massive et
rapide" in Gusen ("massive and rapid extermination," Strozier 23). This
is a scene that Milá would not have witnessed, but that was a notorious
form of extermination in Gusen. His drawing removed any identifying features from the SS, instead calling attention to the anguished and
pained faces of the victims.

In two other drawings from 1946, Milá represented moments in Mauthausen that visually attested to the daily cruelties experienced in the
camp. In a pencil sketch, the sinister figure of an SS officer holds a Jewish prisoner by the arm as a *Kapo* viciously whips him (Strozier 13). The
Kapo wears an inverted triangle, denoting his status as a prisoner, while
the Jewish victim wears a striped uniform and the Star of David on his
arm. In a colour pastel on black paper from 1946, Milá depicted a shirt-
less, emaciated, and barefoot prisoner carving stone inside the camp's
barbed wire fence (18). The artist's medium of colour pastels is another
indication that this work was created after Mauthausen's liberation,
when the Spaniards had greater access to materials. This freedom to
create starkly honest representations of their imprisonment – including
scenes that suggest that some Spanish artists were direct witnesses to
the persecution of Jews in the Holocaust – is in evidence in artwork created long after 1945.[27]

Although most of the artwork created by the Spanish Republicans
remained largely unknown, a few drawings were included in international postwar publications or bulletins for survivors' organizations in
France. Muñoz's pen and ink illustration of two prisoners loaded down
with large quarry stones, one collapsing, just in front of Mauthausen's
imposing gate, accompanied an article in the French periodical *Regards*
on 1 July 1945 (Strozier 22). Two pen and ink drawings – one of two
prisoners dragging a naked corpse; another of a naked man tied by the
wrists to a tree, dead or on the verge of death – were included with Mercè

Rodoreda's short story "Nit i boira" when it was first published in the Mexican magazine *La Nostra Revista* (*Our Magazine*) in 1947. The illustrations, attributed only to "Clavé" and without any definitive source information, indicate the wider distribution of some artwork created by Spaniards in concentration camps.[28]

The Spaniards who created artwork inside Mauthausen began a mode of visual representation of their experience of the camp that would grow to encompass photographs and documentary film in the decades to follow. These early images, like the documentation that Joan de Diego and Casimir Climent copied and saved, were made at great personal risk to the artists. Even an image as seemingly innocuous as a greeting card contained the unambiguous wish for freedom, which would have been interpreted as insubordination by the Nazis, was punishable by death. These simple drawings and cards had to be kept entirely secret; yet among the Spanish prisoners, they were expressions of solidarity. Some, like the hand-drawn maps and interior plans of the camp, were tools of survival. Not only would they aid the Spanish Republicans in navigating the camp and organizing their resistance efforts, they would also serve as evidence of the inner workings of Mauthausen to the outside world should liberation day ever arrive. The fact that the Spaniards were able to save these drawings and maps demonstrated a foresight beyond the barbed wire of their prison to a postwar existence that counted on images to help tell the story of the Spaniards in Mauthausen between 1940 and 1945. They translated the emotions and moments that only the Spanish prisoners who were inside Mauthausen's stone walls witnessed into visual imagery that captured a particular moment in time otherwise inaccessible and unimaginable to the rest of the world.

Francesc Boix and the Mauthausen Photographs

By 1941, Spaniards had assumed privileged positions inside Mauthausen's administrative and technical offices. This same year, two Spaniards were also chosen to work in the camp's *Erkennungsdienst*, the identification service or photographic laboratory. Antoni García Alonso was a trained photographer and became an assistant first to Fritz Kornatz and then his successor Paul Ricken, the official Mauthausen SS photographers, developing film and supervising prints and enlargements (Pike, *Spaniards in the Holocaust* 134–5; Bermejo, *El fotògraf de l'horror* 106). Shortly after his arrival in the photo lab, García requested an assistant. The camp's Spanish clandestine organization was able to select Francesc Boix Campo, a young prisoner who had been working as a camp interpreter until his promotion to the photo lab (*Spaniards in the Holocaust* 138). Boix entered the lab in August of 1941 (*El fotògraf de l'horror* 103; *Boix Testimony* 3438).[29] Another Spaniard, José Cereceda, entered the lab in 1943 (*El fotògraf de l'horror* 104). Stocking the *Erkennungsdienst* with Spaniards was a turning point in the exposure of the inner workings of the Mauthausen concentration camp to the rest of the world after the end of the Second World War. The photographs and negatives that Boix saved came to embody Nazi brutality and the excesses that occurred in concentration camps across the Third Reich where photos could not be salvaged. Moreover, Boix had a particular influence on the representation of the Spanish population and experience of Mauthausen. His post-liberation photographs remain the source from which subsequent visual representations of the Spanish Republicans in the camp have sprung. Simply put, Boix has become a tragic icon of the Spanish Mauthausen imprisonment.

Most of the principal Nazi concentration camps had an *Erkennungsdienst*. In Mauthausen, the photography office was responsible for taking identity photos of the SS as well as every prisoner upon arrival.[30] The service also documented the camp's construction, prisoner deaths, – by firearm, suicides, and accidents, according to Ricken[31] – and the medical or physical abnormalities of the prisoners. Finally, the SS photographers were tasked with recording important or unusual events in the camp, such as visits by members of the Nazi chain of command, the arrival of large convoys of prisoners, and public executions (Bermejo, *El fotògraf de l'horror* 107; Pike, *Spaniards in the Holocaust* 135; AMM 30). This type of official Nazi photography only infrequently survived the war: prints and negatives were roundly destroyed in the days before the Allied forces liberated each successive camp.[32] If they did survive, these photographs were often recovered without any context: questions persisted about how they were produced and presented, by whom, and under what circumstances (Zelizer 1).

Sybil Milton spent many years working with Holocaust photography at the United States Holocaust Memorial Museum in Washington. She lamented the lack of identifying information for prints and negatives saved from Nazi camps because "[h]owever eloquent the image, photographs are not self-sufficient and unambiguous without supplementary information" (Milton). Holocaust prints and negatives were often missing basic information, such as the identity of the photographer and the date the photo was taken. Moreover, when Holocaust photographs were organized to preserve and catalogue them, coherent sets of images were frequently split up among different entities (Milton). Not only did Boix save thousands of negatives, but he also answered many of the lingering contextual questions about the official SS photographs in his initial cataloguing of the photos as well as his testimony at the Mauthausen trial in Dachau and the Nuremberg trials. Due to the efforts of Mauthausen survivors, museums, and archives to retain and curate these photos in the decades after the liberation of the camp, they exist today as a virtually intact body of images.

However, the official SS photographs saved from Mauthausen present a one-sided perspective of the camp: they "[offer] a narrow, incomplete and often haphazard view of a much more complex reality" (AMM 16). Photographs that capture only the perspective of the SS undermine the task of understanding a more complete history of the Holocaust. As Jean-Marie Winkler, the general coordinator of the Mauthausen Memorial photography exhibit, elaborates, "[t]here is a danger here that the living memory of the inmates, who alone can testify to the horrors experienced in the camps, will be replaced by the apparent reality caught on the glossy prints" (18). At Mauthausen, however, photos that explicitly present the prisoners' point of view counter this Nazi narrative. This second type of photograph proved invaluable to later representations of the Spanish experience of the camp. In the chaos immediately following the camp's liberation, Boix availed himself of one of the Leica cameras assigned to the Identification Service. He became, in his own estimation, a "war photographer," and began to document his surroundings.[33] Boix's post-liberation photographs focused on various installations in Mauthausen – the quarry, the gas chamber, the prisoner barracks – as well as on the individual survivors themselves. Given his allegiance to his Spanish compatriots and the camp's robust resistance organization – who openly gathered in the days after Mauthausen's liberation – Boix's focus was mainly on his fellow Spaniards. Nevertheless, Boix's perspective and opinion of what merited capturing stood in stark contrast to the official SS photos of Mauthausen: life, not death, was at the centre of Boix's viewfinder. As Winkler writes, "[w]hen the survivors take hold of the camera, it is to create an image of themselves that is in deliberate contrast to that of their executioners" (20).

Our ability to contrast Mauthausen's official photography with Boix's post-liberation photographs would not have been possible without the extraordinary intervention of the Spanish prisoners to preserve

1.3 Francesc Boix in the days after Mauthausen's liberation with his "War photographer" armband visible, 1945. Photographer unknown. [MHC (Fons Amical de Mauthausen)]

prints and negatives slated for destruction by the Nazis. Although there are a number of versions recounting the story of how Boix and members of the Poschacher *Kommando* were able to save SS negatives and smuggle them outside of the camp before the Allied forces arrived, the basic narrative remains clear.[34] According to García, before Boix entered the *Erkennungsdienst* in 1941, he and the other prisoner-workers were making five prints of each photo negative for the SS and one secret sixth print, which they hid among other "inferior" prints in a drawer (Pike, *Spaniards in the Holocaust* 138). According to Cereceda, however, secreting away photos and negatives was "asunto de Boix. García y yo no hacíamos otra cosa que ver, oír y callar" (qtd in Gómez).[35] In either interpretation, it is clear that the practice of clandestinely hiding prints and negatives increased when Boix entered the photography lab. By 1944, Boix had assumed greater responsibility in the *Erkennungsdienst*: he was promoted to secretary and oversaw the other prisoners in the lab (Bermejo, *El fotògraf de l'horror* 117). Although García felt that Boix's actions – namely, fraternizing with SS officers, openly fighting with other Spanish members of the clandestine resistance organization, and revealing the organization's plans to Ricken (Pike, *Spaniards in the Holocaust* 175) – put the three Spaniards in the photography lab at risk, other survivors attested that Boix was fully committed to the resistance cause and that his relationship with SS officials inside the camp ultimately saved Spanish lives (*El fotògraf de l'horror* 120).[36] A number of Mauthausen survivors, including former members of the Poschacher *Kommando*, remembered Boix with great fondness, throwing García's characterizations of Boix as a loose cannon into doubt.[37]

By 1944, Boix was actively copying and hiding a second set of negatives of the official SS photographs. In March 1942, members of the Spanish clandestine resistance movement inside the camp began to smuggle photographs out of the laboratory and hide them in various locations around the camp (AMM 32–4). This secret enterprise became even more urgent in 1944, as the conditions in Mauthausen worsened in conjunction with the beginning of the Nazis' retreat. Boix and the resistance organization enlisted the young men of the Poschacher *Kommando* in moving the prints and negatives outside of Mauthausen entirely. These boys – most of whom had arrived as barely teenagers with the convoy of Spanish families from Angoulême in 1940 – were afforded a privileged work detail with Poschacher industries, located in the town of Mauthausen.[38] Anton Poschacher was a Nazi Party member from Mauthausen with various industrial interests who employed these young

Spanish prisoners at his town quarry beginning in 1943. As time went by, the Poschacher *Kommando* boys were given better working and living conditions, until they had the freedom to enter and leave the main camp at will, pass through the town of Mauthausen without drawing any suspicion, and spend the night in barracks outside the camp.

Many former members of the Poschacher *Kommando* claim partial responsibility for the process of hiding the thousands of negatives, hundreds of duplicate prints, and SS identification photos saved by Climent.[39] Sewing the photos and packets of negatives into the lining of their coats or concealing them in the soles of their shoes, various Poschacher boys passed through the gates of the camp and delivered the contraband to the resistance organization's contact in town, Anna Pointner. An Austrian woman sympathetic to the cause of the Spanish Republicans and the concentration camp prisoners, Pointner concealed the negatives and prints behind a rock in her garden wall until members of the resistance organization could return to claim them after the camp's liberation.

As Jesús Tello Gómez recalled, although certain boys were directly involved in the process of saving the negatives, "'todo el mundo [en el *Kommando* Poschacher] se calló y gracias a este silencio se pudo llevar a cabo'" the operation (Llor 179).[40] Boix credited a collective effort in captions he recorded on the backs of some of the prints that were saved: "Fotos SS salvades per l'organització clandestina del PCE i JSU a Mauthausen," referring to the Partido Comunista de España and Juventudes Socialistas Unificadas, two clandestine Spanish political parties active inside Mauthausen (Bermejo, *El fotògraf de l'horror* 124).[41] The preservation of negatives and prints of official SS photographs of Mauthausen was a dangerous and ambitious project carried out by a collective effort of Spaniards.

The content of the SS photos is just as incredible as the story of their survival after the Nazi purges. The images demonstrate the carefully crafted Nazi narrative of economic progress and domination over the prisoner population from various time periods. Photos from 1940 to 1943 were taken by one of the two SS subofficials in charge of the photography lab – Ricken or Kornatz – and show the construction of Mauthausen and Gusen. They document the building of the major installations in the two camps, such as exterior walls, central offices, SS barracks, and guard towers. They also capture the state of Mauthausen's quarry, which was the source of the camp's stone buildings and foundations and a sign of its economic prowess within the concentration camp system.

These images often lack any human presence. When we are afforded a glimpse of the prisoners responsible for the labour in the quarry and the construction of buildings and walls, it is from afar. In these instances, it is nearly impossible to determine their identities with any certainty. One photo of prisoners actively working on one of Mauthausen's exterior walls is an exception, however. It pictures two men carrying a pallet of stones between them as well as perhaps a hundred men in the background in the process of cutting, hauling, and placing rock. The two men in the foreground are dressed in the prisoner's striped uniform and cap. Although their identification numbers are not visible, one can discern an inverted triangle with an S in the middle on a patch on their chests, marking them as Spaniards. They look towards the camera, giving both the photographer and the future spectator the possibility of identifying them.[42] The Spaniards were among the first prisoners to be deported to Mauthausen, and were integral in the construction of the camp. This photo is not only a testament to that fact, it also gives a rare glimpse of individual prisoners in active labour in the camp. The background of the photo, on the other hand, contains the more typical scene of a mass of anonymous prisoners in addition to a long view of Mauthausen's entrance towers and iconic eagle emblem, with the rolling Austrian countryside tantalizingly out of reach. Unlike the majority of those thematically dedicated to the camp's construction, this photo betrays a fleeting glimpse of the human toll of that backbreaking labour. Like other SS photos, however, the men's expressions are blank and they are treated as objects demonstrating a greater purpose: the strength of Mauthausen and its economic – that is, human – potential.

Another popular theme among the salvaged official photographs is the identities and lives inside Mauthausen of the SS themselves. Unlike the SS photos of prisoners, most of the officials, subofficials, and soldiers in these images look straight at the camera from a few feet away. Many have subsequently been identified. These official portraits include images of Franz Ziereis, the commander of Mauthausen; Eduard Krebsbach, among the primary SS doctors in the camp; Werner Fassel, the subofficial responsible for the *Politische Abteilung* under Karl Schulz; and Ricken. In other photographs, the SS recline in the sun, play cards in the barracks, or stroll the camp grounds (AMM 115–21; Toran and Sala 126–38). Juxtaposed with the surviving prisoner identification portraits, the SS portraits clearly communicate power and organization: they are the embodiment of the Nazi

1.4 Construction work at Mauthausen, with two unidentified Spanish prisoners in the foreground. Photographer: Paul Ricken or Fritz Kornatz [MHC (Fons Amical de Mauthausen)]

ideal. In prisoner identification photos, in contrast, the men in striped uniforms with shaved heads stare expressionless at the camera, communicating an utter powerlessness, their identities traded for the numbers clearly marked on a placard in the bottom right-hand corner of the photograph (AMM 90–1). The images of incoming convoys of Russian prisoners of war include full-body portraits of prisoners dressed in tattered clothing before the camp's so-called Wailing Wall. Although some men looked into the camera's lens with what can be interpreted as defiance, the majority communicated defeat and fear in the hunched positions of their bodies and their pained expressions (AMM 83–89; Toran and Sala 178–89).

The dehumanization of the Mauthausen prisoner population is also evident in the SS photos of masses of inmates in the camp's *Appellplatz* during inspections. Forced to give the Nazi salute, perform ridiculous gymnastic exercises, or suffer disinfections naked, these images show that any sense of dignity or autonomy among the prisoners had been erased (AMM 93–7; Toran and Sala 190–3). In a similar vein, the SS photographs of the dead documented the ultimate goal of this process of dehumanization: annihilation. Illustrating the "unnatural deaths" that Joan de Diego recorded inside the camp's administrative office, photos of men sprawled on the ground or grasping the electrified barbed wire fence recorded the Mauthausen prisoners' last moments of suffering. While in many of these images the bodies are face down – one amid an incongruous field of wildflowers – in others, gaping mouths and hollowed-out eyes present the photographer and viewer with an inescapable and personal image of death (AMM 101–7; Toran and Sala 210–19). Ricken admitted in his declaration before the War Crimes Branch at the Mauthausen trial in 1947 that he would at times manipulate the photos to achieve a more technically correct image (Bermejo, *El fotògraf de l'horror* 108). In 1943, the Nazis ordered the cessation of photos documenting the dead; Boix was ordered to destroy all photographs this same year in Mauthausen (Schmidt and Loehrer 14–15; *Boix Testimony* 3444). The fact that Boix and other Spaniards in Mauthausen preserved these illicit images remains one of the most enduring acts of resistance to emerge from inside the concentration camp.

In addition to photos of the SS formations, Boix saved a series of images that document two of Heinrich Himmler's inspections of Mauthausen. Himmler, as *Reichführer* or supreme leader of the SS, oversaw the Nazis' concentration camp empire and visited Mauthausen in April 1941 and again at a later, unknown date. Boix pinpointed the date of Himmler's first visit and identified the author of the photos as Ricken during his testimony at Nuremberg (*Trial of the Major War Criminals* 264). In photos of a smiling Himmler greeting SS officers, touring officer barracks, and inspecting the quarry, other Nazi officers are also clearly identifiable: Ziereis; Georg Bachmayer, Ziereis's second-in-command at Mauthausen; Ernst Kaltenbrunner, a high-ranking SS officer; and August Eigruber, the governor of the province of Linz, were all members of Himmler's welcoming committee in the camp (AMM 123–7; Toran and Sala 144–67). These photos became integral to Boix's testimony at Nuremberg and Dachau and to the ultimate death sentence for Himmler: they documented that Mauthausen was known to and operated by the Nazi high command.

Moreover, they would turn the tables on the power play between the SS officers and the Mauthausen inmates. Boix, a prisoner meant only to be exploited by the Nazis, brought these photos to the International War Crimes Tribunals at Nuremberg and to the Mauthausen Concentration Camp Trial at Dachau as a means of asserting his power to settle accounts with his victimizers. Although Boix survived Mauthausen, his untimely death six years after liberation was due to his treatment at the hands of the Nazis. These photos are not only his legacy but have come to represent the collective memory of all the Spaniards in Mauthausen.

Boix's agency in saving photos from the official SS archives of Mauthausen is reason enough to credit him with some of the earliest representations of the inner workings of a Nazi concentration camp. Yet Boix's work documenting Mauthausen and Gusen after they had been liberated by American forces was another key facet of his efforts to record the Spanish concentration camp experience for posterity. Between the 2 and the 4 May 1945, the SS had departed the main camp of Mauthausen; they fled Gusen on the morning of 5 May. Members of the Vienna fire brigade were left in charge of the prisoners, who at the same time had taken matters into their own hands. By the time a squadron of the 11th Armored Division of the US Army arrived at the gates of Gusen and Mauthausen at midday on 5 May, the prisoners had disarmed the Viennese firemen, and the International Committee – Spaniards as well as men of other nationalities who operated the underground resistance organization in Mauthausen – had taken over security in the camp. By all accounts, the Americans left the now-liberated Mauthausen ex-prisoners on their own overnight, returning with the full command of the 11th Armored Division on 6 May (Pike, *Spaniards in the Holocaust* 242; Toran, *Vida i mort* 235–6; AMM 130, 140). What went on while the camp was under the sole control of the International Committee remains under debate, but it is clear that some of the ex-prisoners took this opportunity to exact vengeance on a number of the prisoner-*Kapos* who remained in their midst and to hunt down fleeing SS guards (*Spaniards in the Holocaust* 243–5; Gallart Vivé 302–3).

With a recovered Leica at the ready, Boix canvassed Mauthausen and Gusen during and after the 5 May liberation, photographing scenes of the arriving American troops;[43] the Mauthausen quarry, gas chamber, and the Gusen tunnels; moments of relaxation among his fellow ex-deportees; female survivors of Mauthausen; and the resumption of political meetings among the Spaniards in the camp during the weeks after liberation. Never one to shy away from the camera, Boix also included himself among a number of portraits of his compatriots and in his series of photos documenting Ziereis's deathbed confession. Boix was, after all, both reporter and victim of the Nazi atrocities committed at Mauthausen. He was as involved in capturing images from the camp and of its former prisoners as the Army photographers from the US Signal Corps, to the extent that some photos taken by the Americans have been credited to Boix and vice versa.[44] At least one of Boix's post-liberation photographs documented a mass of naked corpses piled outside the Russian camp, an image strikingly similar to the visual documentation the US Army photographers collected in Mauthausen and other Nazi concentration camps (Bermejo, *El fotògraf de l'horror* 163; Schmidt and Loehrer 18).

Boix's main focus, however, was on the individuals and the sense of humanity that survived the Nazis' attempts at total annihilation and dehumanization in Mauthausen, as illustrated by the SS photographs he saved. Ex-deportees with rifles slung across their shoulders and men in their striped prisoner uniforms in front of the barbed wire fence posed for portraits that highlighted their newfound power to control how and where they were photographed (AMM 171–7; Toran and Sala 228–32; 236–9). Since the SS did not photograph incoming Spaniards for identity portraits, these post-liberation portraits served as commemorative reminders of their imprisonment. They "reverse the dehumanised gaze of the *Erkennungsdienst* mug shots when they honorifically restore the individual's subjectivity through their very articulation as portraits" (Loew 34). Although they have subsequently been mistaken for SS portraits of the Spanish prisoners at the outset of their imprisonment, Boix's photos in fact documented the survivors in their earliest moments of freedom. These photos also functioned to "establish their [the ex-inmates'] identity as concentration camp survivors and confirm their credibility as witnesses" (AMM 128). In this sense, these photos constituted a testimonial twice over: they bore witness to the survival of men who would bear witness to the Nazis' program of pathological violence in Mauthausen.

The Spanish deportees anticipated the arrival of their American liberators by stringing Francisco Teix's banner across one of the Mauthausen gates. Boix captured a number of images of the Spanish Republicans and other Mauthausen survivors greeting the American troops and posing en masse in front of the banner between the 5 and the 7 May

(AMM 136; Toran and Sala 240, 244). The solidarity of the Spanish ex-deportees is clearly on display in these images, even though not all of the Spanish survivors are pictured. Although there were ideological and political differences among the Spanish prisoners before liberation, and these differences would continue to divide the Spanish survivors after liberation, on the occasion of their salvation from Nazi evil, they gathered as a collective entity. These photos showed the relief and joy visible on the faces of the individuals who were now ex-deportees, finally freed from their Nazi captors. Boix documented the Spaniards' refusal, moreover, as stateless, displaced persons, to acknowledge defeat by photographing the first open meeting of the Spanish Communist Party on 13 May in the former Mauthausen showers (AMM 184–5).[45] He captured images that suggested the success of the Spaniards' lengthy efforts to document the inner workings of the camp. Photos of members of the Poschacher *Kommando* posing with Pointner outside her home illustrated the necessary link between Spaniards and an outside member of the resistance movement in creating a visual record of Mauthausen for posterity (Toran and Sala 233; Bermejo, *El fotògraf de l'horror* 176–7).

While Bachmayer, Mauthausen's second in command, poisoned himself, his wife, and his two children as American forces closed in, Ziereis, the commander of Mauthausen and its subcamps, fled (Pike, *Spaniards in the Holocaust* 249; Toran, *Vida i mort* 235). On 23 May 1945, a contingent consisting of an American corporal and ex-prisoners discovered Ziereis in a town more than 100 kilometres from Mauthausen, wounded him, and took him to the military hospital that had been set up at Gusen (AMM 204; *Spaniards in the Holocaust* 262–3; Bermejo, *El fotògraf de l'horror* 165). As Ziereis agonized, Boix photographed his interrogation and the final hours before his death on 24 May. Boix was the only photographer to capture Ziereis, surrounded by American military personnel and former Mauthausen inmates, in this state of powerlessness. By publishing the full contact sheet of negatives of Boix's Ziereis series, Benito Bermejo uncovered a telling juxtaposition: Boix had included a photo of eight frail, shaved men in another part of the Gusen Military Hospital on the same roll of film (*El fotògraf de l'horror* 166–9). Taken just before the images of Ziereis began, this photograph underscored the human consequences of Ziereis's command over Mauthausen and its subcamp empire. The suffering these men experienced was the direct result of the Nazis' policies as carried out by SS officers like Ziereis. But one Nazi commander's death is little consolation for the hundreds

1.5 Spaniards gathered in front of the main Mauthausen gates strung with Francisco Teix's banner, after their liberation, May 1945. Photographer: Francesc Boix [MHC (Fons Amical de Mauthausen)]

of thousands of men and women who perished in Mauthausen and its subcamps, as illustrated in this photo of infirm men at Gusen. In some images in the Ziereis series, Boix looks on – his homemade "war photographer" armband visible – acting again as a dual witness to the scene: witness to the interrogation and death of Ziereis as well as a witness who consciously chronicled the beginning of a post-liberation era of accountability for high-ranking Nazis (AMM 204–5; Toran and Sala 256–9; *El fotògraf de l'horror* 164–9).

Boix was, as Camila Loew writes, "the photographed and photographing photographer" (32), self-consciously capturing Mauthausen in its immediate post-liberation state from a variety of angles and vantage points. Maureen Tobin Stanley argues that "Boix's stills of Mauthausen,

1.6 Gusen survivors, May 1945. Photographer: Francesc Boix [MHC (Fons Amical de Mauthausen)]

although they are visual, not verbal, and capture the polyvalent, multiple stories of others, not only of himself, must be deemed a memoir, a memorialistic account of lived subjectivity" ("Stills of Mauthausen" 40). Following this line of thinking, Boix's photographs constitute one of the earliest – if not the earliest – representations of Mauthausen by a camp survivor.

The trajectory of the official SS photos as well as Boix's post-liberation photos after Mauthausen's liberation in May 1945 follows their transformation from materials documenting the camp to images that form part of the collective memory of the camp. They comprise, moreover, Boix's testimony of his experience inside Mauthausen, and – along with the documents saved by Climent and de Diego and the artwork by Spanish Mauthausen prisoners – form a corpus of the earliest representations of Mauthausen. In the days immediately after Mauthausen's liberation, members of the Spanish resistance organization recovered the photos and negatives from Pointner, the Austrian woman who had been hiding them in her garden wall. Boix shepherded the photos into the hands of the Communist press in France where they became front-page images in the summer of 1945. The French magazine *Regards* and newspaper *Ce Soir* published spreads of the Mauthausen SS photographs in July and August 1945 (AMM 39–41).[46] Boix commented later that he singled out *Regards* as one of the destinations for his photo collection because Robert Capa's photojournalism had been published in the magazine during the Spanish Civil War (Bermejo, *El fotògraf de l'horror* 181). Additional photos from Boix's collection appeared in a 1945 French book on Mauthausen. The author of this volume, despite using official SS images saved by Boix and others as well as a number of Boix-authored photos of the interrogation of Ziereis, did not directly credit Boix (Tillard; *El fotògraf de l'horror* 181). Another Czech photo book published in 1946 or 1947 used an ample number of the photos Boix both took and saved without crediting their photographer (*Mauthausen*; *El fotògraf de l'horror* 181). These publications demonstrate the reach Boix's photos had in postwar Europe. They continued to shape European visual imaginings of the concentration camps throughout the twentieth century.

Boix was called before the International Military Tribunal proceedings in Nuremberg, Germany on 28–9 January 1946. On the stand, he explained that he was a Spanish refugee who had arrived in Mauthausen on 27 January 1941 (*Trial of the Major War Criminals* 263), that he was first employed as an interpreter in the camp, and then "[a]fterwards my work was with photography, developing the films which were taken all over the camp showing the full story of what happened in the camp" (272). To that end, he brought twenty-four photographs from his collection that were entered into evidence (Schmidt and Loehrer 16–17). A number of these photos were projected in the courtroom as Boix provided their locations, subjects, approximate dates, and authors. Although Boix was not present when the majority of the photographs were taken, he developed the negatives and confirmed the details of the prints given his knowledge of Mauthausen and the attentive record-keeping procedures that were followed in the photography lab. In this way, Boix identified photos of Himmler, Kaltenbrunner, and Albert Speer in Mauthausen, thus proving the men's firsthand knowledge of the camp and the Nazi concentration camp system.

Yet Boix's Nuremberg testimony was not limited to what he could identify in the SS photographs. He constantly tried to provide additional details about life and death inside Mauthausen for the prisoners. In a notorious exchange, he began to explain how it was that Spanish Republicans were sent to concentration camps. The lead attorney, Charles Dubost, interrupted him before Boix could testify to Franco's involvement:

> BOIX: … We heard that the Germans had asked what was to be done with Spanish prisoners of war who had served in the French Army, those of them who were Republicans and ex-members of the Republican Army. The answer …
> M. DUBOST: Never mind that … (*Trial of the Major War Criminals* 267)

Had Dubost allowed Boix to finish his thought, at least a hint of Franco's involvement in the deportation of Spanish nationals to Nazi camps would have entered into the public record decades before it became common knowledge in Spain.

In his second day of testimony at Nuremberg, Boix described the Russian prisoners as "human scarecrows" (*Trial of the Major War Criminals* 270) who were subject to the harshest conditions, which led to their deaths; he recounted the treatment of Polish and Yugoslav prisoners, whose position in the camp, he said, was "comparable only to that of the Russians. Until the very end they were massacred by every means imaginable" (271); he characterized the prisoner-*Kapos* as men who "preferred to live like beasts, like savages, like criminals," elaborating that many of his comrades could have become *Kapos*, but "preferred to be beated [*sic*] and massacred, if necessary, rather than become a Kapo" (*Trial of the Major War Criminals* 273); and recounted the charade of the Russian officers who arrived in 1943 and were photographed in humane conditions, only to be tortured and killed later on.

One of the most extraordinary aspects of Boix's testimony at Nuremberg was his insistence on providing even more information and detail than what the lawyers solicited. At one point, when asked about the Soviet prisoners in Mauthausen, he said, "I cannot possibly tell you all I know about it; I know so much that one month would not suffice to tell you all about it" (*Trial of the Major War Criminals* 270). Although the Tribunal was primarily interested in what Boix witnessed firsthand – Lord Justice Sir Geoffrey Lawrence, acting as the lead judge or president of the proceedings, told Boix: "I don't think the Tribunal wants to hear more details which you did not see yourself" (278) – Boix was driven to bear witness to as much as he possibly could. The Nuremberg trial was Boix's international soapbox and he was determined to use this opportunity much the same way he was driven to distribute his photographs to the press. Since Boix was the sole Spaniard to testify at Nuremberg, his voice ultimately represented the thousands of Spaniards who fell victim to the Nazis in Mauthausen and other camps and could not bear witness in such a public forum. In the months immediately after the camp's liberation, Boix's photos and testimony began to piece together the story of Mauthausen from the vantage point of a survivor who had risked his life to be able to bring news of what would eventually become known as the Holocaust to the wider world.

Boix died in 1951 from medical issues stemming from his imprisonment in Mauthausen. The photos he distributed to the international press and took to Nuremberg and Dachau began to be dispersed to various survivor organizations and Spanish ex-deportees in France. They came to illustrate dozens of books and documentaries on Mauthausen and the Holocaust, becoming iconic images of the Spanish experience of the Second World War and the concentration camps. The Mauthausen Memorial in Vienna made an effort in the early 2000s to gather the full collection of Mauthausen photographs and negatives. They found the collection spread out across a number of state-run and personal archives: in the Mauthausen Memorial's own photo archives, at the Museu d'Història de Catalunya,[47] and in the Mauthausen survivor Mariano Constante's private collection (AMM 38).[48] The editions published by the Mauthausen Memorial as *The Visible Past: Photographs of Mauthausen Concentration Camp* and by the Museu d'Història de Catalunya as *Mauthausen: crònica gràfica d'un camp de concentració* (*Mauthausen: Graphic Chronicle of a Concentration Camp*) are the most complete collections of these photographs to date.

At one point during Boix's testimony at the Mauthausen trial at Dachau in 1946, he admitted: "If I had known that I would have to appear before such a tribunal, I would probably have remembered" more precise dates about his photographs (*Boix Testimony* 3445). Yet Boix's contributions to Spain's collective memory of Mauthausen endured despite the difficulties he encountered remembering details while imprisoned in the camp and after his liberation. The visual record he preserved combats the memory imprecisions that afflicted all concentration camp survivors. It "connects the unimaginable with the imaged" (Zelizer 13), illustrating what may otherwise be impossible to visualize. There are, as Barbie Zelizer has written, "limitations of words in shaping the atrocity story" (49) of the Holocaust. The textual survivor narratives that emerged in the years following Mauthausen's liberation captured the horrors of the camp in a less immediate way than the photos of the dead, the gas chamber, and the amazement of the newly freed inmates. These photos are a visceral connection to the concentration camp during its years of operation. They put the spectator in the place of the SS and the prisoners to experience Mauthausen from inside its stone walls and barbed wire. Boix's efforts in preserving, taking, shepherding, and promoting his collection of photographs, interpreted as one act of sacrifice and bravery, was his survivor memoir. These images tell the story of Mauthausen in a way that no other cultural artefact could. They are our first glimpse of the inside of this Nazi concentration camp: a window into a world that would remain unfathomable to non-survivors and an unbroken connection to history and memory that inspired many others to continue to tell the story of the Spaniards in Mauthausen.

The News at Home: Prisoner Correspondence and Reporting in Spain

The Spanish prisoners in Mauthausen were cut off from the rest of the world. From 1940 to the end of 1942 they were allowed no contact with anyone from the outside; the only news that reached them was from incoming prisoners.[49] In this way, they were treated as *Nacht und Nebel* (NN) prisoners although the majority of the Spaniards were not officially designated as such (Roig, *Els catalans* 250–1).[50] However, around the same time that a number of Spaniards were afforded new privileges inside the Mauthausen administrative offices, the Nazis began to allow the Spaniards to correspond with their families back home. Beginning in 1943 and ending in 1944, the Nazis permitted the Spanish prisoners to send postcards of no more than twenty-five words every six weeks to Spain in Spanish – an exception to the normal rule that prisoners write only in German – and to receive limited correspondence from home (Pike, *Spaniards in the Holocaust* 131; Batiste Baila, *Mariner del "Maria Rosa"* 184–7). Both outgoing and incoming missives were highly censored, but the prisoners still managed to communicate the essential information to loved ones in Spain: that a husband, son, or father was imprisoned in Mauthausen. Although most of this personal correspondence remains in family archives, the story of one Spanish Mauthausen prisoner's letters to his friends and family inaugurated a new phase of research into the presence of Spaniards – and Catalans, in particular – in Nazi concentration camps decades after the war's end.

Although some information about the Spaniards in Mauthausen trickled into Spain via these letters home, in general the country was ignorant of its role in the Holocaust for years. The few who saw Spaniards enter Mauthausen with their own eyes – the exiled women and children on the convoy from Angoulême, France who were turned back to Spain, and the Spanish teenager who was sent back to Spain after diplomatic intervention, in 1940 – did not speak publicly about what they witnessed during the early months of the camp's operation. Franco's dictatorship was particularly oppressive during these post-Spanish Civil War "years of hunger" in Spain. The press and public discourse were tightly controlled during the Second World War such that most of the news emerging from Europe was propaganda from Nazi Germany and Vichy France used to fortify Franco's standing among the Axis powers. There would be no personal accounts of Mauthausen in Spain in any public forum until 1946, with many more emerging after Franco's death in 1975.

When the Allied powers began to liberate the concentration camps, beginning in late 1944, Spanish newspapers, alongside the international press, published short bulletins, photographs, and news reports chronicling these discoveries. Spanish newsreels showed viewers Bergen-Belsen and Buchenwald as British and American forces discovered the Nazi massacres committed inside these camps. Yet explicit reports of the Spaniards in Mauthausen were not among these first news stories. The Spanish newspaper *ABC* reported on Francesc Boix's testimony against Albert Speer at Nuremberg on 30 January 1946, but Boix was identified as a Mauthausen survivor with the French name "François Boix," and nowhere in the article was his nationality revealed ("El proceso de Nüremberg"). Information about the Spaniards in Mauthausen would take decades to come out in the press. In 1945 and 1946, only those Spaniards who knew a Mauthausen survivor personally had any real chance of understanding what had happened to their loved one during the war. In most cases, however, Spanish family members of a Mauthausen victim would have to wait until Franco's death to confirm that their loved one had been among the millions killed by the Nazis.

Pere Vives i Clavé was a bright and visionary young Barcelona native who crossed the border into exile in 1939 and entered a series of French internment camps. He was deported to Mauthausen on 22 July 1941, and died there of an injection to the heart three months later, at the age of thirty-one (Aragoneses, "Censo de deportados"). In the French camp of Agde, Vives met the poet Agustí Bartra, with whom he struck up a quick friendship. The two circled the internment camp at night, discussing literature as they walked the sandy confines. When Bartra was released from Agde in 1941 he travelled from Paris to a castle full of Spanish exiles at Roissy-en-Brie, France, and finally to Latin America. Along the way, he and Vives began a copious exchange of letters, as Vives made his way towards his death in Mauthausen and Bartra towards his life in exile.[51] Vives' family in Barcelona also received a steady stream of letters and postcards written in Catalan, Spanish, or French, whichever language the censors allowed at the time, as Vives was pulled ever closer to Mauthausen. The French internment camps permitted more lengthy and frequent exchanges of correspondence – though still subject to censorship and the vagaries of international mail during wartime – than would be allowed in Mauthausen.

Vives' last communiqués from *Stalag* VI-C, the prisoner of war camp from which he was sent to Mauthausen, were short and full of longing. He expressed love for his family and his wish to maintain contact with them, a desire that was irretrievably constrained by the war.[52] Vives' letters to Bartra ended with his transfer to Mauthausen. Bartra only learned of his friend's death when Vives' sister Carmen contacted him in 1946. Together, Bartra and Vives' family pooled their cache of letters and postcards written by Vives between 1939 and 1941 into *Cartes des dels camps de concentració* (*Letters from the Concentration Camps*), only published decades after Vives' death. The letters, as Bartra expressed in his prologue to the volume, possessed "una riquesa espiritual, un interès humà i de document del nostre temps" (Vives i Clavé 10).[53] Vives' perspective in the letters and postcards was that of a man with limited access to the growing strife outside his confines: although he knew only that "el führer ho ha espatllat tot" ("the Führer has ruined everything," 28), the contemporary reader can trace his march towards certain death as he followed the familiar trajectory from exile in France to deportation to Mauthausen.

Vives' letters lend a face and a humanity to the thousands of Spaniards who wound up as anonymous numbers in the *Lager* system. Unlike the survivors who lived to tell their stories, he had no historical perspective, no knowledge of the political trap into which he had fallen. In this sense, Vives was akin to a Holocaust diarist in his letters, writing as the events unfolded with no foresight into the outcome of those events, unlike "the survivor-memoirist [who] begins his testimony with full knowledge of the end, which inevitably contextualizes early experiences in terms of later ones" (Young, *Writing and Rewriting* 30). What Vives knew was that he was not allowed to write about the French internment camp, much less mention the name of his ultimate destination: Mauthausen.

He praised the French among whom he worked on his labour detail for their particular sympathy to the Spanish refugees. He did not know whether what he had heard about boats taking refugees to Mexico was really true, but he knew that the farther he got from Agde and Argelés, the second internment camp in which he lived, the worse the conditions got. Even though he felt "ple i responsable de meu destí" ("fully responsible for my destiny," Vives i Clavé 54) and said he didn't want to insinuate anything, in his last letter to Bartra he sent his friend the address of his family in Barcelona. This gesture revealed that Vives was prescient that his struggle to survive would only get more difficult as conditions worsened in the Nazi concentration camp system.

In his letters to his family, Vives mentioned his chronic bronchitis and the old friend from Barcelona whom he had encountered in the Agde camp: "Y también Amat!!! el que venia a estudiar a casa con Colominas y los otros, más inteligente y sensible que antes" (63).[54] "Amat" continued to be a presence in Vives' letters, just as Vives would become a presence in Joaquim Amat-Piniella's novel *K.L. Reich*. In the novel, Vives inhabits the character of Francesc, who, after suffering from a chronic lung ailment that he has had since he entered the fictionalized Mauthausen, dies from an injection to the heart in the camp infirmary. Amat-Piniella dedicated *K.L. Reich* to Vives, demonstrating his friend's enduring presence among Spanish Mauthausen survivors.

Vives' postcards to his family from a German prisoner of war camp were shorter than the letters from the French internment camp. In them, he pled for news of his friend Amat, who was sent to another *Stalag*, and also for news from home. He was seemingly ignorant of the tight controls preventing his family from responding to his letters: "Pourquoi ne m'écrivez-vous pas?" (88).[55] Looking for a positive spin on his dire conditions, he wrote that "[l]a souffrance pendant cette longue epreuve, m'a appris beaucoup de connaissances que j'aurais toujours ignoré" (87).[56] He continued to assert that he was "en bonne santé" ("in good health," 86). His family held out hope that he was alive, despite having gotten his last note from Germany in June of 1941. They did not learn of Vives' death until 1946, when a recently released survivor from the camp contacted the family to relate Pere's last moments. The friend, almost certainly Amat-Piniella, wrote to Vives' sister Carmen that her brother had not suffered in the camp. She passed the news of Vives' death on to Bartra:

'Va sortir malalt d'Agde. Arribar a Mauthausen era fatal. Compreneu? En un camp d'extermini no és possible de seguir cap tractamente. Una injecció va acabar-ho tot. L'amic ens jura que ell no sospitava res. Una nova cura, es pensava. Aparentment, això és tot, sembla. Però quin món de pensaments, de sofriments mentals, que no sabrem mai, va precipitarlo i el va vèncer?' (10)[57]

Vives died – presumably of a benzene injection (Pike, *Spaniards in the Holocaust* 84) – in the Mauthausen infirmary on 31 October 1941 (Aragoneses, "Censo de deportados"). This same friend delivered Vives' index card with his faint signature – almost certainly among the registry cards that Casimir Climent saved until liberation – to Vives' family in 1946, proof to them that "'Pere moria a Mauthausen tot sol'" (9).[58]

Vives' letters are a window into the soul of an individual Spanish refugee. They are an incomplete and fragmented account of the trajectory of one man pushed farther and farther away from his family and his homeland, who nevertheless accepted his fate bravely, writing letters that in the moment undoubtedly allowed him to continue to live another day. These communications give the contemporary reader a sense of what it was like to face a wholly unknown and threatening future, and demonstrate how those fears and hopes could be expressed to people who have not lived through them. In 1939, Vives wrote his family from the French internment camp of Saint Cyprien: "Mi estado moral es excelente. ... No sería un hombre si me asustara ante los estados inconfortables" (61).[59] Indeed, Vives showed extreme fortitude and strength in his letters, channeling the voices of thousands of other Spaniards whose letters and accounts never reached their destinations, were never written, or were never published. When *Cartes des dels camps de concentració* was finally published in Spain in 1972 as a disquieting volume of letters composed in three different languages, it began a movement of rediscovery that would radiate through the decades. Montserrat Roig cited reading Vives' letters as a main impetus to start the research that would culminate in *Els catalans als camps nazi*.[60] Amat-Piniella dedicated his novel "A en Pere Vives i Clavé, assassinat pels nazis el dia 31 d'octubre de 1941, en memòria d'una amistat fraterna" (*K.L. Reich* n.p. [1963b]).[61] And, in a curious twist of history, Bartra spoke of Vives to his fellow Spanish exiles in the castle in Roissy-en-Brie, one of whom was the author Mercè Rodoreda. Rodoreda composed her short story "Nit i boira," based on the experience of a Catalan refugee in a Nazi concentration camp in 1946, and published it a year later in Mexico (chapter 2). Vives' letters revealed the inner joys and miseries of one man who travelled the long road from Spain to Mauthausen. Although he did not live to bear witness to the cruelties he saw and felt in the Nazi camp, his letters remain tangible evidence of his experience as a Catalan man caught up in the horrors of the Third Reich. They reached Spain at a crucial moment when the country as a whole was only vaguely aware of the Nazi concentration camps and completely ignorant of the presence of Spaniards in them.

Other Spaniards in Mauthausen experienced the severe restrictions on outgoing communication that was the camp's policy until 1943. Alfonso López Yañez recalled that although his family was actively trying to identify his whereabouts through letters to the International Red Cross, "[e]stuvimos nosotros después de tres años practicamente sin tener correspondencia con la familia" (Soler, *Sobrevivir en Mauthausen*).[62] When the Spaniards were finally able to write their families beginning in 1943, they were severely limited in what information they could relay. López Yañez recounted that in their initial correspondence, the Spaniards were not allowed to stray from an approved text: "Estoy bien. Mandad paquete. Besos y abrazos."[63] Although these packages from home did arrive, López Yañez remembered, they were pillaged by the SS. In later letters many prisoners would tell their families that they had everything they needed so the SS would be unable to steal from subsequent packages (*Sobrevivir en Mauthausen*).

The initial rules that prisoner postcards could only contain twenty-five words seems to have been relaxed, so that eventually the Spaniards were permitted forty and then two hundred words (Roig, *Els catalans* 252–3). In Mauthausen, they were given a postcard printed with instructions in Spanish and German informing them of the regulations concerning their communication, including that the content of their postcards remain "solamente de caracter personal y familiar" ("only of a personal and familiar nature") and prohibiting the inclusion of photographs in packages from home. The other side of these postcard forms contained address information for the recipient as well as the prisoner's number and identifying information about the camp: *Lager Mauthausen (Oberdonau) Deutschland*. Thus a prisoner's family could ascertain that their loved one was in a camp named Mauthausen in the Upper Danube area; whether they understood that this was a Nazi concentration camp as opposed to a prisoner of war camp is unclear.[64]

In a postcard Joan de Diego sent his family in December 1943, he wrote: "No dudo que son muchas las familias que dejaran escapar de sus ojos unas lagrimas de recuerdo a seres queridos, que bajo un cielo extranjero esperan que las pasiones humanas reintegradas al cauce de la paz devuelva a ellas la felicidad pasada" (de Diego "Postcard").[65] The reference de Diego made to "the cause of peace" was as close as he could get to alluding to his circumstances of being trapped in a conflict that was larger than any one individual. Despite de Diego's privileged status inside the camp's administrative offices, this postcard was one of only two he was permitted to send in 1943 and 1944 (Pike, *Spaniards in the Holocaust* 131).[66]

Josep Miret Musté sent a postcard to his mother in February 1944 despite his designation as an NN prisoner not permitted any outside contact. He circumvented these requirements with the aid of the Spaniards inside the Mauthausen administrative offices and by signing his postcard with a pseudonym, Josep Castells (Roig, *Els catalans* 253). His card demonstrates even less political engagement than de Diego's, and is thus more representative of the majority of the postcards the Spaniards sent home. Miret Musté wrote his mother that "[m]i salud y situacion no pueden ser mejores pero lo seran más todavia cuando pueda estrecharla en mis brazos y decirle como el alejamiento aumenta mi cariño" (*Els catalans* n.p. after 512; lack of accentuation in the original).[67] Without more detail as to his situation and condition, Miret Musté's mother – like the thousands of other family members of Mauthausen prisoners in Spain – would have had no real idea that her son was facing a daily struggle to survive in the camp. Indeed, she likely did not learn of his death in the subcamp of Floridsdorf on 17 November 1944 until long after the end of the Second World War (Aragoneses, "Censo de deportados"; *Els catalans* 618; Bermejo and Checa, *Libro memorial* 276).

Although Spaniards had become aware of the atrocities the Nazis committed in concentration camps across the Third Reich by the end of the war, it would take decades before they would unravel the extent to which their own loved ones were among the victims. The letters Vives i Clavè sent from various French internment camps and German POW camps as well as the postcards other Spaniards sent from Mauthausen constituted rare proof to a subset of the prisoners' families of their whereabouts after leaving Spain. In this sense, these missives, alongside the documentation, artwork, and photographs created and saved by the Spaniards in Mauthausen, are time capsules that capture the lived experience of being imprisoned in a Nazi concentration camp. Nonetheless, because the prisoner postcards from Mauthausen contained very little information that might have allowed a small portion of Spain's population to grasp the gravity of their loved ones' plight, they are more notable for what they do not reveal. The full story of the experience of the Spaniards in Mauthausen was yet to be told.

Confirmation of the existence of Nazi concentration camps reached Spain at the same time it reached America and Western Europe. Soviet forces were the first to liberate Nazi concentration camps along the Eastern Front, arriving in the Polish camp of Majdanek in July 1944 and continuing on to liberate camps such as Treblinka and Auschwitz in the summer of 1944 and the beginning of 1945 (USHMM "Liberation"; Zelizer 49). The Russians did not publicize these first rescues as much as the Americans did with the liberation of the camps on the Western Front. The Spanish press only alluded to them (Zelizer 50–1). One news brief in the widely circulated Spanish monarchist daily *ABC* from 1 January 1945, contained the newspaper's sole reference to Auschwitz before the end of the war: "los bolcheviques han logrado alcanzar la línea Suchau-Andrichau-Auschwitz, donde fueron detenidos" (qtd in Aynat 18).[68] In his systematic analysis of every page of *ABC* between 1 July 1944 and 31 December 1945, Enrique Aynat found only one allusion to the persecution of the Jews. An article by the foreign correspondent Eugenio Suárez published on 1 February 1945 downplayed the magnitude of the Nazis' policy of extermination while bolstering Spain's role in saving Jews: "'En cuanto a la persecución de los judíos, [...] el nuncio de Su Santidad, monseñor Angelo Rotta, y la Legación de España hicieron grandes esfuerzos para atenuar la violencia emprendida contra ellos,'" (qtd in Aynat 19).[69] As scholars have demonstrated, members of the Spanish diplomatic corps did more to save Jews than Franco did, despite the myth the dictator perpetuated to this end (Introduction).[70] Nevertheless, it is a great exaggeration to claim that the Spanish government intervened on behalf of the Jews in any significant way.

Members of Franco's government – in particular, Spanish diplomats and returning Blue Division soldiers – knew, to a certain extent, about the fate of Jews during the Second World War. The historian Bernd Rother has uncovered documents attesting that Blue Division soldiers returning from the Eastern Front informed the Franco government of the cruel mistreatment of Poles and Russians as early as April 1942; that British and American sources provided Franco with information on the German mission of exterminating the Jews and "rumours" of a Jewish genocide as early as March 1943; and that the definitive "objetivo de la política alemana con respeto a los judíos deportados" directly from Spain was known to the Spanish government by June 1943 ("German policy objective with respect to deported Jews," Rother, *Franco y el*

Holocausto 125–6). In July 1944, the Spanish ambassador to Hungary, Ángel Sanz Briz, confirmed that there were extensive rumours of Jews being deported by the trainload to "un campo cerca de Katowice (por lo tanto, a Auschwitz)" ("a camp close to Katowice (and therefore, to Auschwitz)," (128) where they were gassed and their bodies used for fat production. And in August 1944, information reached the Spanish government from witnesses who confirmed the killing of Jews in Auschwitz and Majdanek, news that was corroborated by Sanz Briz's diplomatic contacts (128). Notwithstanding the accumulating confirmation of the genocide of Jews, the Franco government refused to mediate with the Germans for the French Jews imprisoned in concentration camps. Nor, as we have seen, did Franco intervene on behalf of the Spaniards in Mauthausen, about whom he was fully aware.

Despite the rumours running through the regime and among certain circles in Madrid about Nazi concentration camps and the slaughter of Jews, this information was not made public until the end of the war because the press was entirely controlled by Franco (Rother, *Franco y el Holocausto* 129). It was not until American and British forces began to liberate camps closer to the Western Front in the spring of 1945 and the scope of the genocide became obvious to the public that the Spanish press published news briefs relating the dire conditions in the Nazi camps. However, both Rother and the historian Paul Preston have found that during this time the Spanish press deemphasized Nazi atrocities by cloaking them as the logical consequences of the chaos of war as opposed to the earliest indicators of Hitler's widespread campaign of extermination (*Franco y el Holocausto* 129; Preston, "Franco and Hitler" 1). Moreover, reports in the Spanish press about Nazi violence and the extermination of Jews were undercut by a complete lack of images, comparisons with the Russians or Spanish Republicans, or juxtapositions of Spanish historical triumphs with the Allied victory (Álvarez Chillida 414–16). Nowhere in these early news reports was the presence of Spaniards among the victims of the Nazis made explicit.

Attention in the Spanish press to the Nazi concentration camps began to appear with more frequency after the discovery and liberation of Buchenwald by American troops on 11 April 1945, and of Bergen-Belsen by British forces four days later. The Spanish documentary series *Noticiarios y Documentales* (*News Broadcast and Documentaries* or *No-Do*) released a number of newsreels portraying the liberation of Nazi camps in 1945 that were screened in Spanish cinemas. One focused on Buchenwald, showing the crematory ovens, gaunt and bald prisoners, and stacks of human remains as a British delegation toured the camp shortly after its liberation. The voice-over narration clarified that in Buchenwald "sufrieron martirio y muerte miles de presos políticos de diversas nacionalidades, incluso alemanes" ("Libres").[71] In a similar vein, the *ABC* special reporter Carlos Sentis accompanied a British delegation to Dachau after its liberation by American forces on 29 April 1945. Sentis described the visceral horrors he witnessed inside the camp as he spoke with survivors of different nationalities. "Todo es tan trágico," Sentis wrote, "que roza siempre lo grotesco."[72] Although they focused on the international community of survivors in each camp, no mention was made in either of these reports of the Spanish prisoners in Buchenwald, Dachau, or any of the other Nazi camps where they were imprisoned.

Combing the Spanish press from April and May 1945, the historian David Wingeate Pike found only one reference to Mauthausen in *Ya*, the Catholic daily newspaper published in Madrid. The news brief carried a dateline of Paris, 14 May 1945:

El tercer ejército de EE UU ha descubierto un campo de concentración al este de Salzburgo, en Austria, que hace de los de Buchenwald y Dachau <<un juego de niños>>, según ha declarado un coronel del Ejército estadounidense a un corresponsal de la prensa combinada americana. Añade que este campo estaba destinado a los presos políticos forzados a trabajar en minas de cal durante horas y horas, sin más comida que un cazo de sopa de patata al día. (qtd in Pike, *Franco y el eje* 290)[73]

Without mentioning the name of the concentration camp, this report emphasized the brutality of Mauthausen and alluded to its sizable political-prisoner population. Among those political prisoners, of course, were thousands of Spaniards who nevertheless remained anonymous in the Spanish press for another year.

While Joan de Diego, Casimir Climent, Manuel Alfonso, Francisco Boix, Pere Vives, and others frantically sought to document the depth of what was happening to them and their fellow countrymen in Mauthausen, their families back home remained almost entirely ignorant of their plight. The omissions littering the Spanish press during and just after the end of the war silenced the desperate voices of the Mauthausen captives. The Spanish public was sentenced to wait – in some cases for decades – for the knowledge that their own countrymen and women were victims of Nazi persecution.

2 Postwar Impressions: The First Published Representations of the Camp, 1945–1963

Although it is a common perception that the Spanish experience of Mauthausen was entirely unknown in Spain until after Francisco Franco's death, the reality is that four Spanish authors published stories and accounts of the camp in Spain, France, and Mexico between 1945 and 1947. Three of these four authors were Mauthausen survivors with firsthand knowledge of the camp's operations and legacy; the fourth was an exiled author with a personal connection to the camp. All four were Catalan. Their narratives constitute the earliest published representations of Mauthausen by Catalan – and thus Spanish – authors with a reach beyond the Iberian Peninsula. The works of Mercè Rodoreda, Carlos Rodríguez del Risco, Joaquim Amat-Piniella, and Amadeo Sinca Vendrell, contemporaries of better-known early Holocaust writers such as Robert Antelme, Olga Lengyel, Primo Levi, David Rousset, and Władysław Szpilman, who published their survivor narratives in France, Italy, and Poland in 1946 and 1947,[1] have never entered the canon of Holocaust literature written by non-Jews.[2]

The texts by these three Catalan Mauthausen survivors and their contemporary in exile do not stray far from canonical works published by Holocaust survivors in the years immediately after the war. Early works of Holocaust literature from Western Europe revealed stories that had never been told before, as "there was no known precedent for Auschwitz and Buchenwald, except perhaps by analogy to Dante" (Roskies and Diamant 115). Publishers downplayed the Jewish origins of some early Holocaust authors, in part to appeal to French and Italian readers weary of the topic (113). Much like the authors of the earliest Spanish Holocaust literature, who were not Jewish, Western European "first-generation testimonials ... did not constitute one literature ... [E]ach author had returned with a different experience, literally speaking a different language" (115). This diversity is evident not only in the earliest works of concentration camp fiction by Rodoreda and Amat-Piniella, both written originally in Catalan, but also in the early deportation memoirs of Rodríguez del Risco and Sinca Vendrell, composed in Spanish. These two memoirs particularly reflect the thematic threads of heroism, the pursuit of a "higher cause" and "self-empowerment and self-determination" that the scholar Margaret Taft has identified in Jewish narratives of the Holocaust from 1944 to 1946 (107–8). The three Mauthausen survivors in this cohort – Rodríguez del Risco, Sinca Vendrell, and Amat-Piniella – had unique experiences of the same camp, depending in part on their political outlook, whether they held a privileged position in the camp, and how they perceived the communist clandestine organization of the Spaniards.

All four of these pioneering Catalan authors brought their first impressions of the Holocaust to a small but significant audience inside Spain, to their countrymen in exile, and to committed observers abroad at a moment when discussions of the Nazi genocide were strictly controlled in Franco's Spain. With the exception of Rodríguez del Risco's anomalous wide-release newspaper series, the Catalans' respective publications were, like the narratives of their Jewish counterparts, "driven and directed by the victims and survivors, with little involvement from communities outside their own" (Taft 5). To that end, these authors' perceptions of the Nazi genocide are influenced by personal experience and a cultural environment rife with anti-Semitism, misinformation, and misconceptions common in the years immediately after the Second World War. Yet they also reflect accurate information that would be corroborated by the historical record in the decades to come. They present a fraught view of the Holocaust through Catalan eyes, exploring issues of morality, nationality, religion, and responsibility in their quest to comprehend the events surrounding the Nazi genocide and its effect on a specific community of Spanish deportees. However, each of these texts in its own way also recognizes the defining distinction between Jewish and Spanish populations in Nazi camps: the Jews were slated for extermination; the Spaniards were not. In that they all address the presence of Jews in Mauthausen and have shaped conceptions of the Holocaust in Spain, they must be considered Holocaust literature.[3]

The Holocaust narratives by Catalan authors that emerged from 1945 to 1947 pushed the limits of public discourse and raised questions of accountability at a time when no official acknowledgment of Spain's complicity in the Nazi purges was forthcoming. Many of these early Spanish representations of Mauthausen could not be published under the dictatorship's strict censorship regulations, in part because they were written in Catalan. They would have to wait until after Franco's death to find a publisher and an audience inside Spain. Even those that were released in Spain were hidden in plain sight for decades, unavailable to and unknown by the Spanish public. Nevertheless, the dozens of Spanish representations of Mauthausen that came out in subsequent years can trace their origins to these four groundbreaking texts. Taft's observation that "[v]ictims and survivors who confronted their experiences throughout the 1940s did so in a way that ultimately helped other survivors shape an identity that was meaningful, purposeful and empowering in the post-war world" (5) holds true both for early Jewish and Catalan authors of the Holocaust. These four texts are the foundational works of Spanish Holocaust literature.

Carlos Rodríguez del Risco's Serialized Memoir "Yo he estado en Mauthausen" (Spain 1946)

By the last Nazi count on 4 May 1945, some 2,184 Spaniards in Mauthausen were still alive, though an unknown number died in the days after liberation, from dysentery and starvation-related causes (Toran, *Vida i mort* 162). Out of a continued animosity towards the Franco regime and fearful of reprisals in a Spain now fully under the dictator's control, the majority of the Spanish survivors of Mauthausen settled in France after the war. Although Mauthausen was the last of the Nazi concentration camps to be liberated, only a year later it was among the first to inspire a Spanish survivor's tale: the testimonial narrative of a deportee who lived through a Nazi concentration camp and managed, against all odds, to return to Spain.

Carlos Rodríguez del Risco's firsthand account of his five years of imprisonment in Mauthausen appeared in Spanish in 29 serialized instalments between 26 April and 1 June 1946, in the Falange newspaper *Arriba*. A defender of the Spanish Republic when he fled his homeland at the end of the Spanish Civil War, Rodríguez del Risco did a political about-face during his deportation and imprisonment, renouncing his "renegade" defence of the Republic in favour of a newfound devotion to Franco and the Nationalist cause. Rodríguez del Risco's final thoughts in the last instalment of his series underscored his complete political conversion:

Católico por convicción, soy soldado de la Iglesia; español fervoroso, seré siempre un leal servidor de mi Patria. Y mi Patria está hoy, quieran o no comunistas y renegados, representada unánimemente por Franco, hombre providencialmente elegido para librarla de la más formidable hectombe de todos los tiempos. (1 June 1946, 3)[4]

As the first Spanish and Catalan author to publish an account of his experiences in a Nazi concentration camp, Rodríguez del Risco was the unwitting founder of a genre that lay dormant for decades in Spain before resurging after the death of Franco. That the author released his serialized account in the Franco regime's officially sanctioned fascist newspaper one year after his liberation makes his story both foundational and propagandistic. "Yo he estado en Mauthausen" ("I Have Been in Mauthausen") is a disquieting text that clashes with common knowledge of the Holocaust, supplying counter-versions of history that offend accepted moral sensibilities pertaining to Jews and Spanish Republicans. This dialectic has made Rodríguez del Risco's story untouchable in critical circles, demonstrating what Irving Howe calls "the sheer difficulty – the literary risk, the moral peril – of dealing with the Holocaust in literature" (179–80). Rodríguez del Risco's firsthand testimony of Mauthausen has never been re-edited, republished, or cited in a scholarly study.[5] Yet despite its limited dissemination, contradictions, and offensive nature, the text is a groundbreaking Holocaust survivor account. As the first Holocaust narrative published in Spain – and indeed among the first to be published in Europe – Rodríguez del Risco's account set the stage for decades' worth of Spanish representations of the Holocaust and Nazi concentration camps while drawing attention to the paucity of those representations published under Franco.

By 1946, Spaniards had been allowed little information about Nazi concentration camps under Franco's strict control of the press and were completely unaware that their countrymen had also suffered directly under Hitler's reign. "Yo he estado en Mauthausen," published in a major Francoist newspaper, was the exception. Like historical revisionists or Holocaust deniers, however, Rodríguez del Risco complicated his survivor's account by grounding it in a politically motivated manipulation of facts. Visible amid the author's relativist, anti-Semitic, and pro-Francoist diatribes, nevertheless, is accurate historical information about Mauthausen and the Second World War: material that would be corroborated by historians and fellow survivors in the decades to come.

Reading for these accuracies positions the text as historically relevant despite and because of its political contextualization. It reveals information previously unknown in Spain while demonstrating the Franco regime's control and manipulation of this information.

Given the obscurity of Rodríguez del Risco's series, the contentious nature of the political and historical underpinnings of the text, and its offensive portrayal of Jews, the author's contribution stands apart from the Spanish concentration camp narratives that followed it. It is politically anathema to other works of the genre from Spain, produced by a country that, according to the popular perception, was not involved in the Holocaust and did not produce Holocaust literature.[6] But although "Yo he estado en Mauthausen" is the account of a Gentile unsympathetic to the extermination of the Jews happening around him, it is one of many, in James Young's words, "versions of the Holocaust" to emerge from "various literary forms, cultural and religious traditions, and precedent experiences [that] have indeed shaped the Holocaust" (*Writing and Rewriting* 5). In his version, Rodríguez del Risco illuminated the unique experiences and perspectives of a Spanish witness to history caught in the Nazi *Lager* system. By critically approaching Rodríguez del Risco's anti-Semitic pro-Franco chronicle we are asking that the genre of Holocaust literature expand to incorporate even the most odious of non-Jewish survivor accounts steeped in historical revisionism. Deborah Lipstadt has argued that instead of dismissing Holocaust deniers as purely serving their own self interests, there is historical importance in "illuminat[ing] and demonstrat[ing] how the deniers use [their] methodology to shroud their true objectives" (2). Although Rodríguez del Risco straddled the line between Holocaust survivor and trivializer, his memoir is an example of the kind of historically contextualized manipulation that will become even more common in the decades after the end of the war.

Rodríguez del Risco's text must be assessed, as Hayden White argues, on "the basis of [its] fidelity to the factual record," but as a narrative account, it "consist[s] as well of poetic and rhetorical elements by which what would otherwise be a list of facts is transformed into a story" (28). Rodríguez del Risco's story comprises not only factual material about Mauthausen, but also the author's rhetorical reliance on the Spanish literary traditions of the serialized novel and conversion narrative, and his propagandistic foray into Holocaust-denier territory. Thus, Rodríguez del Risco's text demonstrates what White calls the "inexpungeable relativity in every representation of historical phenomena," and in particular the difficultly of discerning historical truth in a written representation of the Holocaust (27). "The relationship between historiography and survivors' accounts has been uneasy," observes Henry Greenspan (Hayes and Roth 423), but that unease does not allow us to ignore a particularly fraught entry in the genre of written Holocaust testimony. In short, although "Yo he estado en Mauthausen" exists in a category by itself, it nonetheless remains firmly rooted in the Spanish literary canon as well as in the genre of early Holocaust memoir, and deserves a critical gaze.

"Yo he estado en Mauthausen" purports to be serialized nonfiction, billed by its recurring, italicized subtitle as an adventure tale: "*Carlos R. del Risco relata en exclusiva para 'Arriba' sus siete años de aventura en el exilio*" ("*Carlos R. del Risco relates exclusively for 'Arriba' his seven years of adventure in exile*"). Like the nineteenth-century Spanish *folletín* or serialized novel, Rodríguez del Risco's tale is a hero's journey from loss to liberty published in brief, regular instalments that would have been easily found, purchased, and read by a working- or middle-class Spanish public.[7] This identification with a popular literary genre from the nineteenth-century positions "Yo he estado en Mauthausen" as an accessible, classic adventure story, complicating the fact that the author's chronicle is the product not of his imagination, but rather of the true-life ordeal he survived while the largest genocide of the twentieth century was happening around him.

Rodríguez del Risco followed the path of thousands of other Spaniards who fled their country after the end of the Spanish Civil War, although documentation about his movements is scarce. His published account never goes into detail about his life in Spain during the Civil War. However, the essentials of his progression through France, Germany, and Austria during the Second World War, about which he wrote in the *Arriba* articles, have been confirmed in the database of deportees edited by Alfons Aragoneses and by the historian Benito Bermejo.[8] Born on 5 May 1901 in the Catalonian town of Vilanova i la Geltrú (Bermejo and Checa, *Libro memorial* 299), Rodríguez del Risco's trail runs cold until, by his own account, on 5 January 1940, he was part of a French battalion fighting the Germans on the banks of the Moselle River, alongside other Spaniards who fought in the Spanish Civil War. His written saga began here, *en medias res*, like most serialized novels, as he recounted the reception he and his fellow soldiers received a month later from the French townspeople when they exhibited a captured Nazi flag: "Cuando el día primero de febrero llegábamos de descanso al pueblo Base-Ham, sus habitantes, al ver la bandera nazi que temolábamos como 'gran trofeo de guerra', nos hizo objeto de grandes ovaciones. Estaba comprobado *nuestro heroismo*" (Rodríguez del Risco, 26 April 1946, 4; emphasis in the original).[9] Whereas this type of anti-fascist rhetoric was gaining momentum in postwar narratives beyond Spain's borders, Rodríguez del Risco's assertion in a Falangist newspaper that exiled Spanish Republicans fighting against Hitler were considered heroes defied Franco's commonly held and mandated assumption that these men were traitors. Dan Diner notes that the memory of the Spanish Civil War tended to overshadow the Holocaust in postwar Spain: "the history of extermination proper was only given legitimate space when it adopted the political semantics of anti-fascism's master-narrative," iconically captured by the Spanish conflict ("Icons of European Memory Juxtaposed" 33). Yet Rodríguez del Risco used precisely the opposite narrative. The author's opinions about his Republican compatriots grew more and more negative as the series wore on, revealing a conversion narrative that pulled him towards increasingly fascist rhetoric. Given Rodríguez del Risco's silence in any other published form, however, it is impossible to discern how much of this pro-Franco stance reflected the author's own beliefs and how much was imposed by his editors.

The information available about Rodríguez del Risco's trajectory obtained by Bermejo and Sandra Checa as well as Aragoneses is for the most part corroborated in the pages of Rodríguez del Risco's text. Rodríguez del Risco was, at some point during his service in the French military, captured by the Germans and sent as a prisoner of war to *Stalag* XI-B near Fallingbostel, Germany.[10] On 8 September 1940, he was deported to Mauthausen, entering with the official prisoner number 4,286, among the first groups of Spaniards to arrive in the camp.[11] He spent his five years of imprisonment in Mauthausen in the main camp as well as the subsidiary camps of Gusen and Steyr, the latter a subcamp associated with a notorious work detail that the author describes extensively in his articles.[12]

Despite his relatively protected status as a political prisoner, Rodríguez del Risco singled out the deprivations and cruelties he and his fellow Spanish nationals suffered at the hands of the SS and prisoner-*Kapos*. Soon after arriving in Mauthausen, Rodríguez del Risco revealed that "el martirio había comenzado" ("the torment had begun"): he and his barracks companions were forced to haul 50-kilogram stones up the quarry steps fourteen times, and, at the end of a twelve-hour work day with only a small ration of food in their stomachs, were left "rendidos, extenuados y apaleados" by the SS ("collapsed, exhausted and beaten," 3 May 1946, 3). Although Rodríguez del Risco criticized a standard punishment throughout his imprisonment of twenty-five lashes from the SS and the *Kapos* for infractions such as smoking a cigarette in the barracks or protesting the lethal injection of fellow Spaniards, he saved his severest condemnation for the conditions in the camps that were beyond human control. Rodríguez del Risco called the harsh Austrian climate, magnified by the wet rags the prisoners wore, "un martirio mucho peor que los castigos, el trabajo y el hambre" in the camps, resulting in the deaths of the first Spanish prisoners ("a suffering much worse than the punishments, the work and the hunger," 6 May 1946, 3). Although Rodríguez del Risco witnessed and experienced the cruelties of Mauthausen firsthand, it is clear that he was spared the very worst of the abuses.

As a result, and unlike most of his Spanish compatriots, Rodríguez del Risco survived Mauthausen and was liberated on 5 May 1945, from the Gusen II subcamp (26 May 1946, 3).[13] Although Bermejo has confirmed that Rodríguez del Risco returned to Spain after his liberation and died there years later, with no direct descendants, details about Rodríguez del Risco's life and death in Spain after the war are otherwise limited (Bermejo, "Re: Información viaje.doc"). Only by piecing together the press laws governing Spanish newspapers in the 1940s as well as the rampant anti-Semitism of the Franco regime does one begin to glean a picture of how the articles that comprise "Yo he estado en Mauthausen" came to be published in Spain at a time when information about the atrocities of the Holocaust was severely constricted.

By 1946, Spanish newspapers were constrained by the Franco regime's 1938 *Ley de prensa* (Press Law), which strictly controlled the editorial staff and content of the country's periodicals. Newspapers were required to uphold the regime's tenets; a publication that diminished the "'prestigio de la Nación, o del Régimen, entorpez[ó] la labor del Gobierno en el nuevo Estado o [sembró] ideas perniciosas entre los intelectualmente débiles'" faced severe punitive measures (qtd in Fernández Areal 187).[14] After 1944, the Franco regime and the Falange were eager to distance themselves from their fascist origins, yet the Spanish press continued to follow the fascist example of anti-Semitic rhetoric through the end of the war and after, as Rodríguez del Risco's articles demonstrated (Lazo Díaz 180–1).[15]

Despite the stranglehold that Franco's *Ley de prensa* had on free expression in Spain, Rodríguez del Risco was able to publish his true-life account of Mauthausen months after his liberation, seemingly without impediments. In reality, *Arriba* was the only imaginable place a former defender of the Republic could tell his (mediated) side of the story, in a medium that was guaranteed to adhere to the dictator's standards. As the voice of the Franco regime and the Falange, the Spanish wing of the Fascist Party and the only legal political party after 1939, *Arriba* was a newspaper that by its definition upheld the values of the dictatorship. In 1946, a survivor's account of Mauthausen could only have been published inside Spain under the auspices of the Franco regime and the Falange, who could control its content and message. Without this stamp of approval from Franco's censors, a literal account of Mauthausen from the vantage point of a Spanish Republican would have incurred severe repercussions from the regime and never have reached the public. It remains a mystery, nevertheless, why the Franco censors were not more concerned about the level of historiographic detail about the Holocaust in Rodríguez del Risco's articles, which contradicted the regime's standard whitewashing of this type of information. Its publication in a nationally circulating newspaper distinguishes "Yo he estado en Mauthausen" as perhaps the most widely read twentieth-century Spanish account of the Holocaust.[16]

While Rodríguez del Risco provided irrefutable historical details about Mauthausen, it is unthinkable that *Arriba* would have printed "Yo he estado en Mauthausen" without subjecting it to the regime's rigorous standards, and only with an ulterior motive in mind. It thus stands to reason that the author's account was manipulated or edited, either by Rodríguez del Risco himself or by the editors of *Arriba*, to conform to the prevailing political rhetoric of the Franco dictatorship, serving the crucial function of couching a localized history of the Holocaust as political propaganda in support of the regime. However this editorial manipulation was achieved, it incorporated Rodríguez del Risco's conversion from Republican to Francoist into the serialized account of his adventure. A rhetorical trope since Saint Augustine's *Confessions* in the fourth century, the conversion narrative became a seminal element of the Spanish literary canon in the sixteenth century with such religious conversion texts as Santa Teresa de Ávila's *Vida* and San Juan de la Cruz's mystical poetry. Thus, Rodríguez del Risco's conversion narrative upheld not only the political standards of the Franco regime but also its ideological positioning as the second coming of Spain's Golden Age.[17] In his structural distillation, James Fernández identifies the four elements that coalesce in the conversion narrative as the union of "a new, converted and writing self" with "an ultimate, ideal reader," taking a backward glance at "an old, unredeemed self" for the benefit of "a community of human readers" (29–30). Rodríguez del Risco's conversion narrative manifested these four tropes as the union of Carlos, the Franco-supporting memoirist, with the Falangist, pro-Franco ideal *Arriba* reader who, over the course of the articles, looks back at Carlos, the unredeemed Republican soldier, for the enlightenment of the Spanish postwar population. This conversion – captured particularly in the series' closing citation, cited previously, in which Rodríguez del Risco pledged loyalty to the Catholic Church, Spain, and Franco – relegated the historical truths buried within "Yo he estado en Mauthausen" to window dressing on Francoist propaganda. Yet, as a closer look at the articles reveals, Rodríguez del Risco's attention to historical detail in his account of Mauthausen was not so easily tempered.

After defending his battalion's heroism and establishing a first-person authorial voice in the first instalment of "Yo he estado en Mauthausen" – two key traits shared with the Spanish serialized novel and the conversion narrative – Rodríguez del Risco's Francoist political concessions became more apparent in the second instalment. The author's patriotic leanings stirred as he gazed over the border at Hendaye, Spain. While pining for his homeland, the author wrote: "contemplaba, a veces con amargura, otras con alegría, las tierras de mi España, en las que, si antes de la guerra había producido enormes cicatrices, ahora vivía en paz y tranquilidad mientras el mundo se desangraba en el caos de la guerra" (27 April 1946, 1).[18] The "before the war" to which the author referred was during the representative government of Spain's Second Republic, which he defended in the Civil War. Following the author's revisionist interpretation, however, the Republic was solely responsible for the divisions in Spain that tore the country apart. And then, instead of enjoying the "peace and tranquility" that Franco brought as dictator to Spain, the author was enmeshed in a "chaotic" war far from home. Indeed, upon his return to his battalion, Germany declared war on a France Rodríguez del Risco called "[a]l camino de la derrota, no era sino un pueblo desmoralizado, sin cohesión, semibolchevizado," and he was sent to the Maginot Line (27 April 1946, 4).[19] The author's condemnation of France as a "semi-bolshevik" nation began a thread of anti-communist sentiment in the articles, in which he referred to himself and his compatriots with the pejorative term "rojos." During the Spanish Civil War, the communist or "red" faction of the Republican militia was Franco's primary target and would remain firmly in the dictator's crosshairs after the war. Thus, by using the term "reds" and denigrating the Republic, Rodríguez del Risco echoed the dictator's rabid anti-communist stance and the Nazis' pejorative *Rotspanier* (Spanish Red) denomination, thus indicating a sympathy for the victors of the Civil War who had defeated his own band of Republicans. These attitudes would have been interpreted as acts of treason to many of his countrymen in Mauthausen, but were clear gestures towards the author's gradual conversion to Francoism.

Similarly, after his capture on the front line and transfer to a *Stalag*, Rodríguez del Risco praised his German captors as humane and sympathetic to the Spanish plight: "Desmostraban especial interés y simpatía por España y nos aseguraban con la mayor seriedad que después del soldado alemán, el español era el mejor del planeta" (30 April 1946, 7).[20] This praise planted the notion that conditions under the Germans were not "tan terrible" as other reports from survivors indicated ("so terrible," Rodríguez del Risco, 30 April 1946, 7).[21] Moreover, it underlined a political affinity between Germany and Spain that worked to Franco's advantage during Spain's Civil War as well as during the Second World War, when Nazi concentration camps eliminated scores of his political adversaries (1 May 1946, 4).[22] Yet by 1946, as Spain was attempting to curry favour with the victorious Allied forces, this comparison of Nazi and Spanish soldiers in Rodríguez del Risco's narrative built a tension between Franco's authoritarian regime seeking international legitimacy and the vanquished Republican counter-insurgents, muddling the author's imprecise political bias with his propagandistic voice.

Once he was deported and imprisoned in Mauthausen, however, Rodríguez del Risco lauded the Germans less, describing the cruelty, torture, and inhumane conditions he suffered under the Nazis in stark terms. This assessment was in line with how fellow survivors in memoirs published decades later would contrast their treatment in the *Stalags* versus in Mauthausen. Rodríguez del Risco's account of the layout and hierarchy of the camp, when corroborated with the comprehensive historical and testimonial texts published in Spain after Franco's death, was also detailed and accurate. He mapped the organization of the camp barracks, described with precision the grueling labour in the quarry and in the Steyr *Kommando* to which he was assigned, and mentioned the trainloads of Jews who were exterminated within hours of arriving in Mauthausen. He related with exactitude an event that became the touchstone of later historical investigations of the Spaniards in Mauthausen: the arrival of a convoy of entire Spanish families from

Angoulême, France, in August, 1940.[23] Although he arrived in Mauthausen some three weeks later and did not claim to have witnessed the events himself, Rodríguez del Risco nonetheless described the visible emotions on the faces of these newly arrived prisoners, presumably gathered from the accounts of others: "La estupefacción, la rabia y el terror se apoderó de todos, pero todas las protestas que formularon resultaron inútiles. Hicieron descender del tren a los hombres y niños mayores de diez años, y pese a la desesperación de las mujeres, madres, hermanas y esposas que quedaban en los vagones fueron internados en Mauthausen" (6 May 1946, 3).[24] Rodríguez del Risco later learned that the women and children from the convoy were sent back to Spain to face an uncertain future as enemies of the Franco regime.[25]

The ebb and flow of Rodríguez del Risco's political alliances – exemplified by his shifting attitudes towards his fellow Spaniards, as well as towards the Germans and the Jews – contradicts the author's pro-Francoist message, but also arouses continued suspicion about his editors' and the regime's role in shaping in the articles. Although his was most likely not the only hand composing "Yo he estado en Mauthausen," the series cannot be dismissed entirely as a work of political propaganda because of the glimpses of historical revelations that had never before been seen in Spain. The contemporary reader steeped in knowledge of the Holocaust will find the task of identifying false representations fairly straightforward despite the fact that Rodríguez del Risco and his editors enlisted what Lipstadt calls a "basic strategy of distortion" in these articles in which "truth is mixed with absolute lies, confusing readers who are unfamiliar with the tactics of the deniers," much less with the underlying historical facts of the Holocaust (2). The Spanish reader in 1946, on the other hand, would have been aware neither of the existence of these tactics nor of the underlying truth.

Rodríguez del Risco's attention to history fractured in the 7 May instalment, when he relieved Hitler of any guilt associated with the concentration camps, calling the Führer:

un verdadero patriota [que] siente la necesidad imperiosa de trabajar por el resurgimiento de su país ... elevando a la nación muy por encima de aquellos que la humillaron con la victoria militar ... [E]se hombre, sin duda alguna extraordinario, no pudo ni debió nunca – a mi juicio – conocer la verdadera y triste realidad de los horrores dantescos en los campos de concentración. (7 May 1946, 4)[26]

According to Rodríguez del Risco's relativism, the real masterminds behind the cruelties he suffered and witnessed in the concentration camps were Hitler's advisors and the SS. Furthermore, the author argued that the National Socialist Party and the SS manipulated the prisoners into becoming the real authors of the violence perpetrated in the concentration camps: "el mayor número [de muertes] haya que cargarlos a los jefes de barraca, cabos y enchufados; presos todos ellos como sus víctimas, pero inducidos por las S.S. con métodos más o menos violentos" (29 May 1946, 3).[27] Although in subsequent publications his fellow survivors would also indict many of the prisoner-*Kapos* for their cruelty, Rodríguez de Risco's exculpation of the Nazis is outlandish. These are opinions shared by those who deny or trivialize the Holocaust and pro-Nazi propagandists after the war; they are that much more jarring coming from a prisoner who watched the horrors of a concentration camp unfold around him. Yet as the example of Paul Rassinier, a Buchenwald and Dora survivor, demonstrates, Rodríguez del Risco was not the only concentration camp survivor to negate aspects of the Holocaust. Lipstadt points out that since Rassinier was himself a concentration camp prisoner, he could not very well deny the brutal conditions of the camps; rather, he elected to shift blame from the top of the Nazi hierarchy to the lower orders of the SS and the *Kapos* in his early writings, much as Rodríguez del Risco did (Lipstadt 54–5).

Rassinier's first memoir, *Le Passage de la Ligne*, also relied heavily on anti-Semitic statements to craft a denial narrative from the vantage point of an individual who had witnessed Holocaust atrocities first-hand (Lipstadt 51–2). Similarly, Rodríguez del Risco's account was infused with anti-Semitic rhetoric, customary in the Francoist press of the era and in narratives from the returning Blue Division soldiers (Núñez Seixas "Sharing or Witnessing Destruction?"). Whereas the author empathized with the Spaniards arriving in Mauthausen, he betrayed little depth of feeling for the Jews who were killed before his eyes. The arrival of a transport of Jewish prisoners from Holland who were brutally murdered by SS dogs prompted Rodríguez del Risco to proclaim a rash of hateful diatribes against the Jewish race, based solely on his observations of the Jewish population of Mauthausen. The author singled out the Jews in Mauthausen for what he considered their lack of humanity. According to Rodríguez del Risco, they were "hipócritas, falsos y egoistas, y por un poco más o menos de comida daban lugar a escenas como la de un hijo pegándole a su propio padre" (8 May 1946, 3).[28] He only backpedalled on his own hypocritical indictment – pardoning Hitler while finding the Jews guilty for their own slaughter – when considering the SS's inhumane treatment of the Dutch Jews: "Sin embargo, su martirio rebasó los límites de lo humanamente concebible" (8 May 1946, 3).[29]

According to later historical and testimonial accounts, the Spaniards in Mauthausen had limited contact with Jewish prisoners, the majority of whom were exterminated almost immediately upon arrival in the camp. Yet Rodríguez del Risco's anti-Semitic condemnation is reminiscent of the calculated treatment of Jews by the Franco regime during the Second World War. As we have seen, Franco may have bragged to the Allies about his personal intervention on behalf of the Jews of Europe once Hitler's downfall was certain, but in reality his regime did very little to help European Jews escape capture by the Nazis. The regime, moreover, crafted a mythical reverence for the Spanish Catholic kings who expelled the Jews from Spain in 1492 and thus "unified" the Iberian Peninsula. Rodríguez del Risco's opinion of the Jews in "Yo he estado en Mauthausen" is indicative of a continued public anti-Semitism in Spain after the war, certainly encouraged by the newspaper's editorial mandate. It also displays one prisoner's moral conflict regarding the value of human life in the camp, as Rodríguez del Risco recognized the Nazis' dehumanization of the Jews while at the same time dehumanizing them himself. The articles threaten anyone who attempts their dissection with the complications of both Franco's posturing towards the Jews, decades of debate over ethical representations of the Holocaust, and the author's own prejudicial and minimizing stance.[30]

Rodríguez del Risco's account might have resulted in nothing more than a forgettable and grotesque parody if not for the author's accurate representation of other historical facts and the timing of his publication. The author bore witness to the aid Casimir Climent and Joan de Diego provided to their fellow countrymen in the camp Gestapo offices; to Heinrich Himmler's inspection of Mauthausen, in full view of the prisoners; to the formation of a Spanish clandestine organization, headed by members of the Spanish Communist Party (which Rodríguez del Risco dismissingly called "el Comité Rojo de Mauthausen" ["the Red Committee of Mauthausen," 17 May 1946, 3]); to the Nazi medical experiments performed on the international prisoners; and to the chaos that accompanied the arrival of American forces on 5 May 1945. He named individuals from high-ranking Nazis to camp prisoner-*Kapos*, accusing them of torture and murder, while also identifying those prisoners who were, in his opinion, to be commended for their bravery and self-sacrifice.[31] Although he never saw it himself, Rodríguez del Risco also explained that "[e]n Mauthausen – según nos decían – se había instalado la 'cámara de gas'" (22 May 1946, 3).[32] He nevertheless described how incoming prisoners, particularly Jews, Russians, Poles, and Czechs, were stripped of their clothing, handed a piece of soap, and led to their death in the gas chamber. In characteristic fashion, he focused his condemnation on the news of an errant Spaniard who arrived in a convoy of other prisoners and was mistakenly gassed despite the efforts of the camp's second-in-command to save him (22 May 1946, 3).

It would take scholars decades to compile historiographies containing the same detailed information about the Spanish experience of Mauthausen that Rodríguez del Risco delivered to a wide audience in 1946. The historical details that the author included would never be aired publicly in tribunals or governmental commissions inside Spain, positioning the testimony of survivors as the fundamental source of information available about Spaniards in Mauthausen.[33] Rodríguez del Risco's account firmly negates the long-standing notion that Spaniards living under Franco's dictatorship were denied any information about the presence of their countrymen in Nazi concentration camps. It also contradicted the prevalent conception of the era that Spaniards were not involved in the Second World War at all. This information may have been hidden in the pages of a regime newspaper under layers of deceit and delusion, but it was still available.

Rodríguez del Risco's uncorroborated observations thus form complex counterparts to the author's accurate historical details. From his assurance that the Spaniards in Mauthausen celebrated the news of Largo Caballero's transfer from one concentration camp to another, enthused that the former leader of the Spanish Socialist Party would suffer as his followers had (16 May 1946, 3),[34] to his glowing description of the camp coffee as "malta bastante bien preparada" ("fairly well prepared malt," 4 May 1946, 4), an opinion antithetical to all other Spanish testimony about the miserable coffee in Mauthausen, Rodríguez del Risco's contradictory reports watered down the believability of the author's tale.[35] His series is an editorializing testimony, making the task of judging the work on its historical merit an intuitive process and aligning it more than the author or his editors perhaps intended with a work of fiction. Rodríguez del Risco's articles are an apt example of Lawrence Langer's notion of represented or mediated reality in survivor testimony, imbuing a survivor's account with "some kind of teleology, a view of experience invested with meaning and purpose" (26). In "Yo he estado en Mauthausen," this teleology is captured in Rodríguez del Risco's or his editor's intent to transform his experience in a Nazi concentration camp into a work of political propaganda supporting the Franco regime. The series also demonstrates what Robert Eaglestone has called the "doubleness" of the genre of testimony, in which "the texts lead to identification and away from it simultaneously" (43). Rodríguez del Risco draws the critical reader in with historiography while pushing him away with propaganda and falsifications.

Only one original copy of Rodríguez del Risco's serialized account is readily available. A stapled packet of "Yo he estado en Mauthausen," each article clipped from the yellowing pages of the 1946 newsprint edition of *Arriba*, resides in the National Library in Madrid. Rodríguez del Risco's articles lie in the archive, as Aleida Assmann has theorized it, "situated halfway between the canon and forgetting," in a "state of latency, in a space of intermediary storage" (335–6). A closer look at the archived microfilm images of the newspaper reveals, however, that some of Rodríguez del Risco's more fallacious entries are not included among the National Library's originals. In particular, Rodríguez del Risco's entry excusing Hitler from any culpability for the existence of the concentration camps – a treatise that interrupts the chronological flow of the narrative – is found only in the microfilm.[36] Another missing original includes Rodríguez del Risco's condemnation of the Republican fighters who "se mancharon las manos de sangre," and his declaration that after the "espantosa tragedia de Mauthausen," the majority of Spaniards wished to return to Spain, because "por dura e inflexible que fuese la justicia que la madre Patria nos impusiera, teníamos un rayo de esperanza en la caridad cristiana del Generalísimo [Franco]," an assertion that would be proven false by the migratory patterns and anti-Franco sentiments of the vast majority of Spanish survivors after their liberation (13 May 1946, 3).[37]

The National Library's originals end abruptly after Rodríguez del Risco's liberation from Mauthausen, leaving the author stranded in France, one among thousands of Spanish exiles. In actuality, there were two additional articles in the series, available only on microfilm. They account for the author's break with the Spanish Communists in France and his safe passage back to Spain in 1945, a homecoming at odds with the long-term exile of his fellow Spanish survivors. Rodríguez del Risco's return to Spain was explained away in the articles by the author's non-sanguinary participation in the Spanish Civil War and a series of bureaucratic connections that allowed him the good fortune of crossing back into Spain without threat of imprisonment or death for his defence of the Spanish Republic. The omissions made evident through a comparison of the originals of "Yo he estado en Mauthausen" with the microfilm, though perhaps the result of the political preferences of a library donor, effectively censor some of the most egregiously propagandistic entries in the series. These missing pages from Rodríguez del Risco's story in the National Library's original are a fitting symbol for the erasure of the text from the canon of Spanish concentration camp narratives, Franco's desire to veil his allegiance to Hitler after the Allied victory, and the absence of Spain in Holocaust studies as a whole.

The Spanish survivors who wrote about their experiences in Nazi concentration camps after Rodríguez del Risco – Jorge Semprún and Mariano Constante the best known among them, but also Sinca Vendrell and Amat-Piniella, as we will see – invariably took the defence of the Republic's political ideals and their continued dissension with Franco's dictatorship as their guiding principles. Although Spanish concentration camp survivors were anything but a homogenous group – especially politically, as they encompassed the communists, anarchists, trade unionists, and even those apolitical individuals who defended the Spanish Republic – they are categorically neither apologists for Hitler nor Franco. Rodríguez del Risco, embodying traits that most Spanish concentration camp survivors found deplorable, remained a figure so marginalized that in a body of highly self-referential narratives authored by Spanish Mauthausen survivors, he was never mentioned again by anyone, in any form. Including Rodríguez del Risco's voice in this body of Holocaust-related literature adds a contentious, complicated, and marginalized interpretation of Spain's Civil War and the country's role in the Second World War to the discussion, demonstrating that not all Spanish Mauthausen prisoners continued the fight against Franco, fundamentally disagreed with fascist ideology, or remained in exile once liberated. Rodríguez del Risco, the first Spanish Mauthausen spokesman, ruptured some of the commonly held "universal truths" about the survivors of concentration camps offered in the Spanish memoirs, films, and novels that would follow over the next seventy years. It is in part because of this counter narrative that Rodríguez del Risco's perspective must be considered among the Holocaust accounts of Spanish survivors.

Rodríguez del Risco never surfaced again publicly; he, like his series of articles, lived out the rest of his life in obscurity. Yet "Yo he estado en Mauthausen" was the first text to tell a story of life and death from the little-seen perspective of a Spanish prisoner inside a Nazi concentration camp. This is a frame of reference that is still rarely considered in overarching studies of the literature born of the Holocaust; Rodríguez del Risco's testimony implicitly questioned what kinds of texts could be included in this genre. Spain's role in the war in Europe, the concentration camps, and the postwar period has traditionally been considered tangential to a precise understanding of this historical period from a continental European vantage point. Yet Rodríguez del Risco's writing in and of itself made the argument that Spaniards were not only present and involved in the conflicts with Nazi Germany, but that they were cognizant of the importance of recording this involvement. Moreover, the text demonstrated that the regime considered this record political baggage for Franco despite his disavowal of the Republican exiles. Even though "Yo he estado en Mauthausen," in all its moral and political contradictions and condemnations, is not representative of the body of Spanish concentration camp narratives, it fits into wider Spanish literary traditions and touches on historical facts that would be paramount to subsequent studies of the Spanish role in the Holocaust.

There is no denying the polemical place of Rodríguez del Risco's account within Holocaust narrative; indeed, some would argue that it holds no place. But Rodríguez del Risco did not go so far as to deny the evidence of the Holocaust he himself witnessed. Instead, he demonstrated in no uncertain terms that history and testimony are not always complementary. This mismatch is even greater when Rodríguez del Risco's account is contextualized and considered as a publication inextricably linked to Franco's totalitarian regime. Yet as Young notes, "the critical reader accepts that every Holocaust writer has a 'different story' to tell ... because *how* victims and survivors have grasped and related their experiences comprises the actual core of 'their story,'" that is, the context tells a story along with the text (*Writing and Rewriting* 38–9). Positioning Rodríguez del Risco's words in the cultural and political climate of 1946 Spain and understanding the text's brazen flouting of its responsibility as the country's first Nazi concentration camp narrative paints an overall portrait of "Yo he estado en Mauthausen" as only the beginning of a much larger discussion of the place of Holocaust representations in Spain throughout the twentieth and twenty-first centuries.

Amadeo Sinca Vendrell's Personalized Historiography
Lo que Dante no pudo imaginar (France 1946)

Amadeo Sinca Vendrell was among the few to arrive in Mauthausen on the first convoy of Spaniards on 6 August 1940 who survived until liberation. Given his knowledge of English, he was employed as a translator and thus attained a relatively privileged position in the camp. Only a few months after his liberation, he distilled his five years of imprisonment into a personalized historiography of Mauthausen: *Lo que Dante no pudo imaginar. Mauthausen-Gusen 1940–1945* (*What Dante Could Not Imagine. Mauthausen-Gusen 1940–1945*).[38] In her prologue to the 1980 edition of the book, Federica Montseny, the noted anarchist and Minister of Health under Spain's Popular Front in 1936, described it as the first Spanish account of a concentration camp, and the first of Mauthausen in particular: "Otros libros se han escrito sobre lo que fueron los campos de exterminio en Alemania. Otros supervivientes han descrito su martirio y las mil muertes vividas. Pero éste tiene el mérito de haber sido el primero que se escribiera" (Sinca Vendrell, *Lo que Dante no pudo imaginar* 31).[39] Sinca Vendrell's treatment is, in fact, the first published book by a Catalan survivor on the Spanish experience of deportation and imprisonment in Mauthausen. By extension, it is among the earliest Spanish-authored treatments of the Holocaust.

Although both men were liberated from the subcamp of Gusen II, Sinca Vendrell, unlike Rodríguez del Risco, settled in France and would remain there for the rest of his life.[40] Sinca Vendrell also published his personalized historiography in Spanish, but his book could not be released in his home country until 1980. A portrayal of the Spanish experience of the Nazi camp that, unlike Rodríguez del Risco's account, did not defend the actions of Franco and Hitler and, moreover, praised the solidarity of the deported Spanish Republicans in Mauthausen, was prohibited in dictatorship Spain. *Lo que Dante no pudo imaginar* was published in France in 1946 by Imprimerie Descoins, a French press with an editorial interest in Spanish politics, in a limited printing run of 1,500 copies (*Lo que Dante no pudo imaginar* 15). Sinca Vendrell's book, part-memoir and part-historiography, mainly reached his local community of Spanish exiles living in France; it would have to wait until well after Franco's death for an audience inside Spain. Nevertheless, *Lo que Dante no pudo imaginar* joined Rodríguez del Risco's "Yo he estado en Mauthausen" as among the pioneering accounts of the Nazi camps by a survivor of any nationality.

By virtue of being unencumbered by Franco's censors, Sinca Vendrell's 1946 first edition might be considered more reflective of the Spanish experience of Mauthausen than Rodríguez del Risco's series of articles from the same year. Whereas Rodríguez del Risco ended his newspaper articles by extolling Franco's actions in "liberating" Spain, Sinca Vendrell began his account by calling the dictator to account for "selling" the exiles' freedoms and Spain's liberties to the Germans and Italians:

> Millares de españoles procedentes de otros campos de Francia, nos encontramos concentrados en una gran planicie rodeados de alambradas y vigilados como prisioneros de guerra, a pesar de que nuestro único crimen (si ello puede calificarse como tal) fue el de defender noblemente con las armas en la mano y el pensamiento firme, las libertades de nuestro pueblo que el traidor Franco, vendido a los tiranos de Alemania y de Italia, nos arrebataron después de 32 meses de lucha. (*Lo que Dante no pudo imaginar* 63)[41]

Writing within months of each other, Sinca Vendrell's Mauthausen memoir reflected the survivors' continued preoccupation with justice whereas Rodríguez del Risco's memoir distanced itself from the original cause of the Spanish Republicans. The moments where these two narratives converge and diverge demonstrate two ways of reconciling with the past that will find corollaries in Mauthausen survivor memoirs stretching into the twenty-first century.

Sinca Vendrell's account went beyond the genre of personal memoir to include an overarching history of the Spaniards in Mauthausen. But the author necessarily relied on his own perspectives and opinions, which, along with his use of metaphor and exaggerated prose, tempered his original goal of a providing an entirely objective historical representation of the Spanish experience of Mauthausen. This blending of the personal and the historical, one could argue, is entirely understandable given the date of the text's composition. In 1946, the year after Mauthausen was liberated, Sinca Vendrell had access to a limited body of historical work on the Nazi camps; his source material emanated from his own memory and the private archives of fellow Spanish Mauthausen survivors. The reader, therefore, experiences Mauthausen solely through the author's subjective perspective as a Spanish survivor.[42] This subjectivity does not preclude the presence of factual information: in *Lo que Dante no pudo imaginar*, subjectivity and objectivity are not mutually exclusive. In his role as a non-professional historian and Mauthausen memoirist,

Sinca Vendrell provided a personalized account of his lived experience of the camp while also sketching an overarching history of Mauthausen. For all intents and purposes, Sinca Vendrell and Rodríguez del Risco were innovators of a new genre in the realm of the entirely novel field of Spanish Holocaust studies: the personalized historiography.

In his preface to *The Drowned and the Saved*, Primo Levi considered the role of "privileged" survivors like Sinca Vendrell in the creation of a Holocaust consciousness:

> [T]he best historians of the Lagers emerged from among the very few who had the ability and luck to attain a privileged observatory without bowing to compromises, and the skill to tell what they saw, suffered, and did with the humility of a good chronicler, that is, taking into account the complexity of the Lager phenomenon and the variety of human destinies being played out in it. It was in the logic of things that these historians should almost all be political prisoners ... [who] disposed of a cultural background which allowed them to interpret the events they saw. (*The Drowned and the Saved* 18)

Levi stressed that these men, unlike the Jews and the criminals, had access to data, enjoyed "tolerable" living conditions, and because of their experiences as "antifascist combatants ... they realized that testimony was an act of war against fascism" (18). Sinca Vendrell brought his experience as a Republican officer in the Spanish Civil War to bear on his representation of Mauthausen, exploring the complex panorama of individuals he encountered in the camp with a critical eye. Levi wrote that the passage of time and distance from events meant that later representations of the camps would become "blurred and stylized," in part influenced by what the survivors read and internalized after leaving the camps (19). It stands to reason that Sinca Vendrell, as both a political prisoner who enjoyed a certain level of privilege in Mauthausen and as a self-appointed historian who recorded his memories of the camp just after he was liberated but before this process of "blurring" set in, captured a version of the camp that was both immediate and personal.

In a 1981 personal letter to a Spanish historian, Sinca Vendrell defended the authenticity of his narrative explicitly because he was among the first Spaniards to arrive in Mauthausen: "Solamente somos nosotros (como yo) uno de los supervivientes que fuimos los primeros llegados al campo de MAUTHAUSEN y Gusen lo que sufrimos y sabemos verdaderamente la catastrofe que alli ocurrio durante los

5 años vividos en estos campos jamas olvidados por nosotros" (Sinca Vendrell, "Letters" 4 Dec. 1981; emphasis and accentuation in the original).[43] Sinca Vendrell's Mauthausen narrative lacked the retrospection and authority that became common in later Spanish accounts of the Holocaust. Instead, it reflected the author's unmediated reaction to the Nazi atrocities he witnessed over the course of five years.

The author's account began in the French interment camps – called "campos de concentración" in the text.[44] He integrated data on the Spanish prisoner population in the French camps with exclamations about the Spaniards' continued high spirits and upstanding morals: "¡Qué de ilusiones ... amigo lector!" ("What hopes ... my friend, the reader!" Sinca Vendrell, *Lo que Dante no pudo imaginar* 66). This second-person narration invited the reader to accompany the author on his journey of discovery, again underlining the scarcity of comparable accounts of the Nazi camps at this point in time. As his narrative continued, Sinca Vendrell recounted his capture by the Germans while assigned to a French labour detail near Amiens on 20 May 1940. From there, the author recorded his passage through three separate German POW camps – *Stalag* Trier, *Stalag* XIII A in Nuremberg, and *Stalag* VII A in Moosburg (77–86) – describing the general lack of food, the exhaustion of the marches between POW camps, and the humiliations perpetrated on prisoners of different nationalities by the Germans.[45] Although he provided details that grounded the narration in historical fact, Sinca Vendrell also infused his prose with literary flourishes:

> El hambre empezaba a hacer sus estragos en nuestros fláccidos estómagos, cubiertos con el manto de la noche en la bruma espesa; los focos de los coches que pasaban por la carretera nadaban como una nube, dando un resplandor azulado, fugaces y temerosos de alumbrar nuestros miserables cuerpos. (75)[46]

This florid description translated unimaginable conditions into tangible images that the reader – who may, after all, have encountered Sinca Vendrell's account as his first textual exposure to the experience of the French camps, the German *Stalags*, and the Nazi *Lagers* – could better envision. This literary technique extended to Sinca Vendrell's overarching metaphor, clearly presented in the book's title, comparing Mauthausen to Dante's Inferno.[47]

Indeed, in the book's second chapter, Sinca Vendrell and his compatriots were deported to Mauthausen and entered a visceral hellscape. The author described the men's arrival as a literal descent as they perceived "en las tinieblas ... un precipicio sin fin" (Sinca Vendrell, *Lo que Dante no pudo imaginar* 88), the initial signs of the horrors they subsequently witnessed on a daily basis.[48] They first discerned the camp's exterior walls, guarded by "[l]as famosas águilas imperiales, creación del espíritu monstruoso hitleriano, [que] presedían el tétrico recinto" (87).[49] Hitler was a monstrous ghost, absent in the flesh yet present through his total control over the camp.[50] The atmosphere outside the gates of Mauthausen produced a physical reaction in the deportees: "Hedor denso se esparcía al exterior del campo, enrareciendo la atmósfera y privando la respiración, produciendo en nuestros estómagos efectos de nauseas."[51] From the outside, the Mauthausen fortress was like "un siniestro fantasma"; the men heard "gritos de dolor... quejidos y rugidos guterales" (88) emanating from the lost souls trapped inside.[52] It was no coincidence that the terrifying sounds of suffering that reached the men before they entered the camp appeared to emanate from the stomachs of those inside, just as they produced an immediate nausea in the men outside. The Nazis' starvation tactics were a centrepiece of the Spaniards' collective agony in Mauthausen.

Sinca Vendrell made his literary comparison explicit when he stated: "Mi impresión era tan intensa que el interior del campo me lo imaginaba como si fuese el infierno de Dante."[53] Yet the author availed himself not only of Dantesque imagery, but also implicitly patterned his entry into Mauthausen on Francisco de Quevedo's canonical seventeenth-century narrative "El sueño de la muerte" ("The Dream of Death"). Sinca Vendrell, like Quevedo, was the narrator and subject of this nightmarish journey. Trying to capture the terror of the unknown interior of Mauthausen, the author imagined the even more grotesque scenes that awaited him on the other side of the gates: stairs covered with blood, chairs of fire, disfigured skeletons, and instruments of torture. His movement through this imaginary purgatory was soon confirmed by what he experienced once he passed through the Mauthausen gates: "la realidad corroboró rápidamente dicha visión, contemplando cómo nuestros cuerpos famelicos, eran instrumento del sadismo criminal, entronizado por el sistema nazi-fascista alemán" (*Lo que Dante no pudo imaginar* 88).[54] This "German Nazi-Fascist system" enthroned at the centre of the camp was its sinister overlord: Satan himself. Just as Dante encountered an inscription reading, in part, "Abandon all hope, ye who enter here" as he passed through the gates of Hell, so, too, did Sinca Vendrell face a similar admonition upon entering Mauthausen. A Spanish *Kapo* named

Enrique warned the men: "'¡Españoles, seguramente no habréis oído hablar hasta el presente del Mauthausen...! Mauthausen es el Campo de la Muerte. Aquí desacatar las órdenes, se paga con la vida'" (88–9).[55] Once inside the camp, the author remembered seeing only "seres esqueléticos, figuras descompuestas con aires de locura, cuerpos mal vestidos y andrajosos, con aspecto repugnante que producían el doble contraste de dolor y temor" (89).[56] Sinca Vendrell's descent into hell was now complete.

Anticipating a reader's scepticism as to the necessity of this extended metaphor comparing himself to Dante and Mauthausen to the Inferno, Sinca Vendrell wrote that "hacer la descripción de tanta misera es difícil" (89).[57] This understated admission acknowledged that what the author and his fellow deportees experienced defied comparison to elements present in the world of the living. It was an early indication of the seeming impossibility of capturing the horrors of the Holocaust in mere words: the atrocities committed by the Nazis constituted a singularly unimaginable violence for the author and his readers. To this end, Sinca Vendrell challenged his audience to put themselves in the shoes of the deportees, to imagine Mauthausen from the inside. As he wrote about the brutal conditions and treatment in Gusen, the author paused to entreat the reader to think carefully about what he described: "En estas condiciones, querido lector, haz un parentesis en tu pensamiento, para detenerte en el cuadro doloroso que miles de rostros reflejaban después de tan grandiosos sufrimientos" (109).[58] This tactic is what Eaglestone calls an "over-identification," common in Holocaust testimony. The narrative "allow[s] the Holocaust to become assimilated into everyday experience and ... readers [to] identify ('role-play') with the victim narrators" (Eaglestone 63). Unlike Rodríguez del Risco, who alienated some readers with his counterfactual details, Sinca Vendrell invited his audience to share in his narrative account. Although he was committed to eliciting this identification with his fellow deportees, Sinca Vendrell also admitted that capturing such violent surroundings was an impossible task: "Gusen, no hay pluma que lo describa. No hay expression gráfica que pueda emplearse para señalar la realidad del campo de Gusen" (*Lo que Dante no pudo imaginar* 109).[59] In Sinca Vendrell's narrative, the Nazi camps were at once describable and indescribable, a tension that reflected the paradox of living a day-to-day existence in the extraordinarily inhospitable surroundings of a Nazi concentration camp.

Although he relied on certain literary techniques to communicate the essence of the deportee experience, Sinca Vendrell, like Rodríguez del Risco, also grounded his account in historical fact. He included the names of individual Spaniards housed in his barracks in Gusen II and identified particularly cruel SS officers by name. He described the Gusen tunnels, where prisoners fabricated planes and other armaments, and the failed attempt by the SS to lure the prisoners into the tunnels to exterminate them all before the American forces arrived. He detailed the main Mauthausen work *Kommandos* and explained the insignia that each national group was assigned. He related the arrival of Jewish women from Germany and Poland who were forced to serve as prostitutes in Mauthausen. His factual information was primarily based on events he witnessed in the camp, as he stated explicitly: "Hago esta narración y afirmo haberlo presenciado" (*Lo que Dante no pudo imaginar* 114).[60]

Thus, Sinca Vendrell's book primarily focused on the experiences of Spaniards like himself in Mauthausen, in particular detailing the beatings, tortures, and killings committed by the Nazis. His judgment of the SS – whom he labelled "super-verdugos" ("super-executioners") – placed them among the most ignominious torturers in history, and framed their actions in a way that Spaniards familiar with their own history would grasp: "Sus procedimientos cimentados en el crimen, en la ignominia y en el trabajo forzado, superaban los tiempos de la inquisición y todos cuantos la humanidad había sufrido a través de sus luchas" (*Lo que Dante no pudo imaginar* 90).[61] This recollection of the Spanish Inquisition grounded the narrative in an infamous historical precedent that also targeted Jews. It compared what would come to be known as the Holocaust to one of the most brutal periods in Spain's history, positioning – as Rodríguez del Risco did – the experience of the Spaniards in Mauthausen in relation to the Iberian Peninsula's long tradition of conquest and conversion.

Sinca Vendrell vowed to remember the names of the SS who caused him and his compatriots such suffering, despite understanding that they were assigned a space of relative obscurity in the Nazi concentration camp system: "yo bien sé que los fatídicos nombres de Mauthausen y Gusen, pasarán desapercibidos en el conjunto de los campos de exterminio" (*Lo que Dante no pudo imaginar* 147).[62] The author also made a point of recording the treatment he observed of Jews in Mauthausen. In one instance, he watched as a group of SS forced a number of Jewish prisoners to choose to either jump over the edge of Mauthausen's quarry precipice or be shot: "Ni un gemido, ni un grito de dolor, salieron jamás de los pechos de estos hombres tan vilmente asesinados" (100).[63]

One can interpret the author's description as admiring the Jews' bravery in the face of such wanton annihilation. But Ulrich Winter argues that Sinca Vendrell "openly shows his resentment at the Jews" by identifying their lack of solidarity as they march passively towards their demise (111). However, Sinca Vendrell skirted the open anti-Semitism obvious in Rodríguez del Risco's account by focusing on the injustices of the Nazis instead of a perceived complacency of the Jews. By contrasting the privileged positions of the Spaniards in Mauthausen and their active resistance to the episodes in which he witnessed the Jews isolated and brutally targeted for extermination, Sinca Vendrell's book presented an early depiction of the Final Solution and a subtle acknowledgment of the singularity of the Jewish Holocaust. Neither of these concepts would have been commonly understood in the author's circles in 1946.[64]

Sinca Vendrell was also present for the convoy from Angoulême, France that arrived on 24 August 1940, bringing entire Spanish families to the gates of Mauthausen. The author wrote: "De la expedición de Angoulême, hay que hacer resaltar un hecho expresivo lleno de crueldad. Los españoles ... llegaron hasta la estación de Mauthausen con mujeres y niños de corta edad" (*Lo que Dante no pudo imaginar* 93).[65] He described the cruelty of separating these Spanish families, as the women called out to the SS from the train cars: "'¿Dónde llevan a nuestros maridos e hijos?'" (94).[66] The rumour that ran through the camp was that the women and younger children were returned to Spain, but the prisoners in Mauthausen were unable to confirm this. Extolling the patriotic virtues of these women, who accompanied their husbands in the fight against fascism, Sinca Vendrell underscored his political alliances to the Spanish Republic and the fight against Hitler. This perspective again distinguished Sinca Vendrell's account from Rodríguez del Risco's: the two survivors ended up on opposing sides of history.

Indeed, Sinca Vendrell was committed to the cause of solidarity in Mauthausen. He consistently emphasized the high moral standing and heightened capabilities of the Spaniards working together in the camp, oftentimes considering the thousands of Spaniards in Mauthausen as a single entity. When the first Spaniard died in the camp, Sinca Vendrell reported that he and his compatriots held a moment of silence in his honour: "Nuestro dolor se reflejó unánimemente" (*Lo que Dante no pudo imaginar* 95).[67] But at times his defence of the character of his fellow deportees obfuscated the realities of living in Mauthausen. Sinca Vendrell claimed that only in exceptional cases did Spaniards patronize the prostitutes, and that the "vicios anti-naturales ... de perturbación amoral" that tempted other men in the camp – that is, homosexual behaviour – "fueron rarísimos entre los españoles que convivíamos en el campo" (110).[68] Subsequent revelations from Spanish Mauthausen survivors contradict Sinca Vendrell's assertions: some Spaniards engaged in homosexual behaviour, the prostitution trade, or both, in Mauthausen.

According to the author, the privileges the Spaniards enjoyed in almost every aspect of Mauthausen's operation benefited others as well: "nuestras intervenciones en la enfermería, en la higene del campo, en los trabajos de cantera, en la intendencia, en la cocina y en el régimen y trato general del campo, fue intensa y beneficiosa [*sic*] para todos" (*Lo que Dante no pudo imaginar* 129).[69] Sinca Vendrell's pride in what he called the "Acción Solidaria" ("Solidarity Action") in the camp contributed to his determination to seek justice for those who suffered under Nazi rule. He pledged that the fight "por liberar a España y vengar a nuestros hermanos de no importa qué nacionalidad, asesinados vilmente en Alemania" would continue (146).[70] Although exaggerating the extent to which the Spaniards' clandestine organization brought about improved conditions for prisoners of other nationalities, and arguably for other doomed Spaniards, Sinca Vendrell's single-minded insistence on justice for all Mauthausen victims was prescient of the postwar trials that attempted to adjudicate Nazi crimes on behalf of the victims of the Holocaust.

During a particularly lethal exercise in Gusen in which prisoners were forced to stand naked outside in formation for hours in below freezing temperatures, leaving 500 people dead, Sinca Vendrell promised himself that "si escapábamos con vida, luchar[ía] por hacer justicia. Promesa que yo, como uno de los supervivientes, trato de cumplir recordando a mis hermanos de cautiverio, honrando su memoria y manteniendo con firmeza mi palabra" (*Lo que Dante no pudo imaginar* 113–14).[71] The author kept his promise by writing his book, which he imagined assuming its rightful place in the annals of history: "Todo este proceso doliente dedicado a los muertos, esta palabra que cumplo, va idealmente a engrosar el terrible *dossier* de Nuremberg" (147).[72] Though Sinca Vendrell composed *Lo que Dante no pudo imaginar* during the Nuremberg trials, his account would not contribute in any public way to the postwar trials in Europe, nor would Spanish victims of Nazi camps as a collective see their day in court. The author remained in exile in France, committed to publicizing the ordeal of the Spaniards in Mauthausen and working for decades just so his book would see the light of day in Spain. He remained in contact with other exiled Spanish Republicans in France and scholars working on resurrecting the story of the Spanish deportees until his death in Toulouse in 1989.[73]

By the time Sinca Vendrell published his definitive volume in Spain, his was no longer the first book to address the experiences of Spaniards in Mauthausen. Montserrat Roig, Eduardo Pons Prades, Mariano Constante, and Manuel Razola had all published books on the topic by 1980, leaving Sinca Vendrell's contribution one among many historical treatments of the Holocaust in Spain after Franco's death. Nevertheless, Sinca Vendrell's 1946 account – not doomed to obscurity like Rodríguez del Risco's series – informed many of these and other subsequent historical publications.[74] Although it has garnered minimal critical attention in subsequent decades, Sinca Vendrell's volume remains at the core of "the genealogy of Spanish Holocaust discourse" (Winter 113). *Lo que Dante no pudo imaginar* allowed other survivors and those who did not experience Mauthausen directly to imagine what Dante could not: the Spaniards' will to survive in the face of Nazi atrocities in the inferno called Mauthausen.

Mercè Rodoreda's Short Story "Nit i boira" (Mexico 1947)

The narrator in Mercè Rodoreda's 1947 short story "Nit i boira" ("Night and Fog") described how the little red fish in his fishbowl captivated him as a boy. By instinct, the fish turned away from the glass side of the tank before running into it. In a curious game, the boy would select the only red fish with a distinctive white spot on its side, take it out of the water until its eyes bulged, put it back in the bowl to recover, and repeat this process until the fish died. In concentration camps across the Third Reich, the Nazis tortured their human captives like the boy did with his goldfish, until they, too, died of exhaustion, starvation, or disease, or were killed outright by their captors. The Jews, marked with the yellow Star of David, tantamount to the red fish with the white spot, were slated for extermination. But the other fish, like the narrator and protagonist of "Nit i boira," a political prisoner imprisoned in a Nazi camp during the Second World War, suffered a similar fate at the hands of the SS: "Em treien i em tornaven a la cel·la. Me'n treien per apallissar-me i m'hi tornaven perquè em refés, per poder-me apallissar una altra vegada" (Rodoreda, "Nit i boira" 231).[75]

Although the protagonist defended his childhood game, saying "vaig fer-ho per joc, perquè volia veure què faria, no pas desitjant que morís," there is nevertheless an ironic similarity between the way he treated his fish and the way he was treated as a prisoner in a concentration camp.[76] He was grateful that he did not stand out like the Jewish prisoners marked for death: "ací, al camp, estava tan content de no tenir una taca blanca" ("Nit i boira" 231).[77] Rodoreda, a Catalan author who composed "Nit i boira" in France only a year after the end of the war, also remained in her own transparent fishbowl, removed from Spain without any knowledge of how long she would be trapped in exile. Rodoreda's life, as Carme Arnau pointed out in the prologue to the 1978 edition of the story published in Spain, like the protagonist's life, was also divided by the Spanish Civil War, which "ha tallat la seva vida en dues meitats irreconciliables" (Rodoreda, *Semblava de seda* 10).[78] The wavering ethics of Rodoreda's concentration camp prisoner echoed the author's ambiguity towards her own relatively safe haven in exile, while also reflecting the moral relativism of the Nazi *Lagers*. Faced with the Nazis' unflinching fascist ideology, Rodoreda explored the theme of moral transgression during the Holocaust long before this term was employed to refer to the extermination of Jews during the Second World War. With "Nit i boira," Rodoreda became the first Spanish or Catalan woman to publish a work of fiction based on a Nazi concentration camp.

Rodoreda's narrator was detained in Nazi-occupied Bordeaux on 14 March 1943, sent to a French prison, and then deported to a concentration camp. Based on his trajectory and the language of the story, the protagonist is also Catalan, one of thousands of Spaniards – the majority of them Catalans – deported to concentration camps from French internment camps, *Compagnies de travailleurs étrangers*, and the French Foreign Legion after the Spanish Civil War. Although the camp, like the narrator, remains unnamed, Rodoreda's careful attention to historical detail suggests that "Nit i boira" could be modelled on Mauthausen. The title of Rodoreda's story is one indication of the identity of the camp: "Nit i boira" refers to the Nazi's *Nacht und Nebel* policy of removing political adversaries – the majority of whom were not Jewish – from occupied zones, and interning them in camps such as Mauthausen where the goal was to make them simply disappear. Moreover, the story references the international prisoners in the camp – the Catalan narrator specifically mentions Poles, Frenchmen, and Belgians – the tunnels, and the incongruous beauty of the camp's landscape. In this way, Rodoreda hinted at knowledge about the interior structure of Nazi camps that, at the time of the story's publication in 1947, would have been known to some Spaniards exiled in France, but not to those who remained in Spain.[79]

In a 1972 interview, Rodoreda described her life in exile to Montserrat Roig: "'Durant l'exili no vaig escriure res perquè altra feina tenia per a sobreviure. Escriure en català, a l'estranger, es voler que floreixin flors al Pol Nord'" (Roig, "El somriure" 27).[80] Yet Rodoreda wrote "Nit i boira" while in exile in 1945 and 1946, and in writing about the natural beauty of a concentration camp in Catalan, the author did, indeed, manage to make flowers bloom in a place as uninhabitable as the North Pole. "Nit i boira" was one of a number of narratives representing the Second World War – era historical events that Rodoreda sent to contacts abroad while she remained exiled in France.[81] It first appeared in 1947 in *La Nostra Revista*, a politically engaged Catalan magazine published in Mexico between 1946 and 1954 with a distribution of 1,000 in the Americas and Europe (Manent 79). Given the magazine's limited reach and the heavy-handed censorship of the first decade of Franco's dictatorship, it is unlikely that more than a few clandestine copies of *La Nostra Revista* would have found their way to Spain. Thus, although "Nit i boira" had an immediate international reach, both Rodoreda and her story remained in exile. "Nit i boira" would not appear in print in Spain until 1978, three years after Franco's death and the year Spain's new constitution was ratified.

Rodoreda's narrative vision of Mauthausen lent a sublime poetry of the everyday to the experience of a concentration camp, intermingled with the brutality and moral ambiguity that would soon become commonplace in Holocaust narratives of the twentieth century. Writing about a concentration camp from the vantage point of a political prisoner trapped inside set "Nit i boira" squarely in the realm of politically engaged literature, yet Rodoreda's protagonist threw presumptions of ideology into doubt. He embodied the moral quandary of a deportee captured for his political leanings who nevertheless denied any political involvement, arguing that his detention was a misunderstanding. His seemingly sadistic tendencies, moreover, left him open to comparisons with his captors. Meanwhile, his initial vision of the camp as a "paradise" and the imagery that Rodoreda used to paint a space at once naturally beautiful and grotesque, laid the groundwork for a supremely ambiguous story, an ambiguity that was itself rooted in historical accuracy. Rodoreda's narrative raised a question that would become much more prevalent in the remaining years of the twentieth century, namely, whether a writer who did not witness the concentration camp experience herself had the right to fictionalize it. Two years before Theodor Adorno would famously challenge poetry after Auschwitz,[82] Rodoreda's confrontation of the moral complexities of this inescapable historical memory argued that this type of narration was, indeed, necessary. "Nit i boira" grasped the contradictions within the Nazi empire to which so few were able or willing to bear witness in the years immediately after the war.

Narrating in the first person, the prisoner's initial survival tactic in the camp was to pass unperceived: "fes el mort," "[ésser] una ombra," and "Ésser invisible. Invisible com una cosa" (Rodoreda, "Nit i boira" 231, 233).[83] When an officer asked him to implicate himself by identifying a woman in a photograph, he demurred and the Nazis beat him in punishment. But even his reaction to the violence of the camp reflected his wish to become an invisible shadow, dehumanized to the point of ignoring his own pain: "Els dos primers cops són els que fan mal. Al cap, de vegades, només el primer. Amagar la cara" (233).[84] Although he submitted to the camp order, the prisoner refused to place himself among the political adversaries labelled *Nacht und Nebel*. In fact, he had no desire to escape the camp to continue the fight, because he insisted he was never a part of the political resistance, and perhaps never even hated the enemy: "'Sortir d'ací, per què? N'hi ha que volen sortir per continuar. Si fos resistent o comunista ... Però no sóc comunista ni he fet mai res: no he ajudat a fer volar cap tren ni he fet passar mai cap consigna. Potser ni els he odiat ...'" (Rodoreda, "Nit i boira" 233).[85] In his own mind, he was a refugee caught in the middle of the conflict, much like Rodoreda herself. Although he claimed political disinterest, one must wonder if he was, in retrospect, negating the ideals that brought him to this camp, along with thousands of others who fought for the Republic against Franco and the Nationalists and who were dying at the hands of Hitler. In this sense, the narrator's inner torment reflected Carlos Rodríguez del Risco's outward contradictions.

Even as the bombing increased, Allied forces approached the camp, and his liberation neared, the narrator did not latch on to the notion of freedom. He did not want revenge, and he sank deeper into his "maresme il·limitat, serè."[86] This serene paralysis was his true desire: "tornar dintre un ventre, plegat, abaltit, voltat d'una tebior molla" (Rodoreda, "Nit i boira" 233).[87] Maria Campillo and Maureen Tobin Stanley have interpreted this "ventre" as a womb, in conjunction with a gendered reading of the story, which includes two brief flashbacks the narrator had to childhood interactions with his mother. However, the story does not indicate whether the author intended "ventre" to be read as a womb or a belly, a word that maintains a dual significance in Catalan. The main character of "Nit i boira" was also among the few male protagonists to populate Rodoreda's narratives, which in this story was a historically determined detail: the very few Spanish women prisoners imprisoned in Mauthausen arrived as evacuees from other camps in 1944 and 1945.[88] In either interpretation, however, this "ventre" is a both a sensual and a sensory-deprived corporeal space whose imagery opens and closes "Nit i boira," symbolizing the false sense of security provided by an enclosed space as confining as a womb, belly, or concentration camp. Reflecting on his surroundings in the first lines of the story, the protagonist juxtaposed a notion of protection with the violent desires of the mass of humanity in the camps to attain safety: "'Si tots els que som ací poguéssim tornar dintre un ventre, la meitat moriríem trepitjats pels qui voldrien ésser primers. Un ventre és calent i fosc i clos...'" (Rodoreda, "Nit i boira" 231).[89] As the story progressed, the narrator's will to live faded into a desire to disappear. He hid in a corner of the camp that evoked this humid belly or womb, waiting for the SS to find him and beat him into non-existence. The protagonist's retreat into a womb-like space was thus less a rebirth than a return to a state of oblivion that was political, as an unwanted Spanish refugee in Europe, and personal, as a submissive prisoner in a Nazi concentration camp, leading to the ultimate oblivion: his death.

Because this submission to the Nazi order coexisted with the controlling impulse he had exhibited as a child torturing his fish, the narrator, like this interior space, was ambiguous. He jabbed Meier, the prisoner who slept in the bunk next to him, with a spoon because the man's constant urination got on his nerves. When Meier later died, the protagonist kept his death a secret for two days so as to collect Meier's rations. When another prisoner discovered the ruse and stole Meier's bowl from the protagonist, Rodoreda's narrator beat this prisoner for being a thief. The actions of the protagonist confused right and wrong, a common transgression that Tzvetan Todorov has studied as a conflict between what he calls vital values and moral values in concentration camps, explaining that "for the vital values it is my life that is sacred; for moral values it is the life of someone else that is" (40). Jorge Semprún also described this conflict in *The Long Voyage*, his fictionalized account of his own imprisonment in Buchenwald: "In the camps, man becomes that animal capable of stealing a mate's bread, of propelling him toward death. But in the camps man also becomes that invincible being capable of sharing his last cigarette butt, his last piece of bread, his last breath, to sustain his fellow man" (60).

For the prisoner in "Nit i boira," his life depended on his invisibility, his ability to become a shadow in the camps. He resisted helping anyone but himself, saying that "com més en moren ací, més m'agrada."[90] His admission that the mounting death toll put him more at ease pitted an ethically deplorable outlook against the sheer will to survive. He imagined that the death rate in the camp would decline "si tots estiguessin quiets" if he told them, "'[f]eu reserves de força.'"[91] Yet this flash of magnanimity was counteracted by the protagonist's contradictory realization that if fewer prisoners died "aleshores hauria quedat jo sol. I m'haurien vist. Hauria estat visible" (Rodoreda, "Nit i boira" 231).[92] Although in other moments, his only desire was to fade into oblivion, here the protagonist did not want to stand out like the fish with the white spot. He wanted to blend into the masses – particularly the dead masses – to avoid the brutality of the SS. It seems, in fact, that the protagonist was on the brink of death as he recalled his years in the concentration camp, waiting for the SS to bring on the final release with their blows and render his invisibility complete. Rodoreda positioned this Spaniard in opposition to the Jews in the camp: his self-interest drove his desire not to be the primary focus of the Nazis' wrath.

The presence of the natural world in the camp and the story mirrored the protagonist's ambiguous emotions regarding his and his fellow prisoners' lives and deaths. The narrator wrote that "quan vaig arribar el camp em va semblar un paradís. La portalada ampla i les torres de guaita li donoven un aspecte de fortalesa: però a dins ... Hi havia, a l'entrada, unes barraques de fusta d'un verd tendre, amb parterres de flors, al voltant d'una placeta. No eren les nostres, és clar." (Rodoreda, "Nit i boira" 231).[93] The narrator's ability to see beyond the signs of death and control in the camp and the officer's quarters to the natural beauty of the flowers, mosses, and blades of grass that surrounded him reminds us of his humanity, his ability to see the living as well as the dead.[94]

This living metaphor resonates with the protagonist's desire to return to the interior space of a belly or a womb, but it also becomes entangled with the narrator's disconcerting musings on life and death. When a transport of sick prisoners arrived in mid-winter, they were alive but barely made a sound on the snow-laden landscape: "la flonjor de la neu ofegava la remor dels passos."[95] The new arrivals were "set out to dry" overnight, and "al matí encara n'hi havia set de vius. És bonic, un cadàver glaçat. Net" (Rodoreda, "Nit i boira" 231).[96] The passivity that the narrator assumed as his ethos in the camp was mirrored in the ostensible passivity of the Nazis: in their own perverse way, they let nature take its course by allowing the new prisoners to freeze to death. However, the Nazis' seeming inaction actually sped the prisoners' deaths. The beauty the narrator found in a frozen corpse and in the track drawn in the snow as he dragged one of the cadavers towards a pile of the dead juxtaposed natural and human cruelty, revealing the emotional contradictions inherent in a morally bankrupt existence.[97]

As his time in the camp progressed, the narrator's initial welcoming reaction to the beauty of the natural world around him degraded, becoming increasingly associated with the unnatural human cruelty of the camp. The tender leaves, the small blue insects, and the moss were useless excesses to him, and, moreover, nauseated him. Geraldine Cleary Nichols argues that the narrator in "Nit i boira" becomes progressively feminized over the course of the story as he fades into non-existence (408–9), but there is another way to read his transformation: he has internalized the moral ambiguities of the concentration camp itself. The prisoner-*Kapos* who beat their fellow prisoners, the SS who tortured by day and returned home to their families at night, the townspeople who smelled the crematory smoke yet did not speak out were all indicators of the moral relativism of the concentration camp. Rodoreda's protagonist ultimately embodied the ethical contradictions so prevalent in this historical moment, and they are what propelled him towards his longing for death.

Mercè Rodoreda was never held in a Nazi concentration camp. However, she knew a Frenchman who was imprisoned in Dachau and it is likely that her contacts with other exiled Spaniards in France would have made her familiar with the story of at least one Catalan, Pere Vives i Clavé, who perished in Mauthausen. Rodoreda suffered the consequences of political action even though she was not, strictly speaking, politically active, distilling the trauma of her exile experience into the concentration camp enclosure in "Nit i boira." Yet beyond the overarching exile metaphor, Rodoreda's attention to the nuances of the experience of a concentration camp for a male prisoner begs the question as to whether she was privy to a survivor's testimony. The author recorded acute details from the depths of the *Lager* experience, capturing the prisoners' arrival in the camp as they were stripped of their clothes and any remaining possessions, led to the showers, forced into the "dutxa gelada, dutxa bullent" (Rodoreda, "Nit i boira" 231), and then forced to wait naked for their striped prisoner's garb.[98] She identified the barracks where prostitutes were housed and captured the layout of Mauthausen. Beyond concrete details, she delved into the protagonist's mental state. When her narrator admitted that he never hated his bunkmate Meier, and that even he realized the absurdity of hating an anonymous Nazi – "Costa d'odiar un home si no li has vist mai la cara" (233)[99] – Rodoreda provided a trenchant criticism of Hitler's Final Solution, designed from the start to engender hatred for an entire race.

There seem to be two possible explanations as to how Rodoreda learned such intimate details about the inside of a concentration camp at a time when that sort of information was only beginning to emerge in the press.[100] In 1939, she was working for a Catalan government-run educational institution when she decided to flee Spain. She left in a transport of other Catalan intellectuals and government employees as the end of the Spanish Civil War approached. Rodoreda was sympathetic to the Republican cause and thus fearful of her fate in a Nationalist Spain, but never anticipated that she would live the next thirty-three years in exile. Rodoreda spent 1939 and 1940 in her first refuge at a house in Roissy-en-Brie, France, with other exiled Catalan writers, including, at different moments, Armand Obiols, Anna Murià, and Agustí Bartra. Murià's soon-to-be husband, Bartra, arrived at Roissy-en-Brie in 1939 after months in the French internment camp of Agde, speaking frequently of the close friendship he had developed there with Vives, with whom he continued to exchange letters until Vives was sent to Mauthausen. Murià wrote that everyone at Roissy-en-Brie knew about Bartra's friend: "Arribat a Roissy, avait tots sabérem els noms del seus amics del camp de concentració: Vives, Puig, sobretot Vives. Hi havia tingut llarguíssimes converses i es bescanviaven llargues cartes" (71).[101] Bartra eventually collected Vives' letters in a moving volume published in Spain that followed the path of a Spaniard unwittingly destined to die at the hands of the Nazis (chapter 1). Bartra finally learned from Vives' family in 1946 that his friend had been given a lethal injection to the heart in Mauthausen three years earlier. This news would most certainly have made its way to Rodoreda through her tightly knit Spanish exile community in France, which would have included other Spanish survivors of Mauthausen who knew Vives as well.[102]

Rodoreda and Murià struck up a friendship in Roissy-en-Brie that continued by letter in the 1940s while Murià and Bartra were in exile in Mexico and the Dominican Republic and Rodoreda stayed behind in France. Indeed, although she remained in contact with Bartra as well, it was Murià in Mexico to whom Rodoreda sent "Nit i boira" for inclusion in *La Nostra Revista*, where it appeared accompanied by two drawings of concentration camp prisoners in striped uniforms. In a final twist to the mystery of Rodoreda's connection to Vives and to Mauthausen itself, the drawings that accompany this initial magazine publication of "Nit i boira" were attributed to "Clavé." Although it is impossible to confirm that "Clavé" was Pere Vives i Clavé, there are no other Spaniards with that surname in the contemporary census of Spanish prisoners who entered Nazi camps during the Second World War (Aragoneses "Censo de deportados").

Rodoreda found herself in Paris when the Nazis invaded, and fled through bombarded cities in France with Obiols and their colleague at the *Revista de Catalunya*, Pierre-Louis Berthaud, to escape the mounting violence and persecution by the Nazis.[103] In a letter to Murià in December 1945, Rodoreda wrote that Berthaud had divorced and remarried after spending seven months in a concentration camp in Germany (Rodoreda and Murià 65). Campillo identified this camp as Dachau, and consequently argued that Rodoreda based "Nit i boira" on Berthaud's seven months imprisoned there ("Un viatge a l'infern" 85–6; "Memoria literaria" 337, note 51). However, details such as the prisoners who froze to death; the nearby tunnels; the accurate description of the wide front gates, guard towers, and SS barracks; and the clear presence of an international prisoner community are evidence that the setting for the story was Mauthausen.[104] In addition, the fact that the majority of the Spaniards imprisoned in Nazi camps were sent to Mauthausen and that the few who survived generally returned to France after liberation creates a strong argument for Mauthausen as the model for "Nit i boira." Rodoreda may have gleaned certain aspects common to Nazi camps from Berthaud's experience at Dachau, but the author's representation of a Spaniard's journey through the *Lager* system points to Mauthausen as her inspiration.

Thus, Rodoreda's story was the first work of fiction to emerge from the Spanish experience of Mauthausen and to reach an international audience, as modest in size as it was. It was also among the first representations of Nazi horrors by a woman, in a genre dominated in Spain and the rest of Europe by the voices of male survivors and historians. By the time the story was published in Spain in 1978, its immediacy had been eclipsed by Roig's much better-known historiographic volume, not to mention a number of survivor accounts of Mauthausen that were released in the mid-1970s.[105] Yet Rodoreda's courage in publishing this story cannot be dismissed: "Nit i boira" stands as an example of concentration-camp fiction before such a genre existed, and confronts the polemical territory of the moral relativism of prisoners facing the Nazis before Adorno, Todorov, or Semprún had begun to theorize about this topic. Moreover, Rodoreda's subtle representation of the persecution of the Jews through her metaphor about a red fish with a white mark on its side was uniquely compassionate among Spanish authors writing about Mauthausen. Nevertheless, the author made no attempt to narrativize the extermination of Jews in literal terms; it was a topic about which she would have had much less knowledge.[106] Her primary aim was to encapsulate the experience of one Catalan prisoner in Mauthausen.

Many Spanish Republican women were deported to the German concentration camp Ravensbrück from various points in France.[107] By virtue of little more than circumstance, Rodoreda herself could have suffered a similar fate. Instead, the author channelled her frustration with her exile existence in France through this historically engaged short story. In 1946, as she was composing "Nit i boira," she wrote to Murià, in exile in Mexico: "Tu dius que estàs cansada d'Amèrica, jo estic degouté de França. No saps mai si demà menjaràs. La vida és dura i desagradable" (Rodoreda and Murià 71).[108] The line between political engagement and neutrality was blurred when the violent overthrow of an elected government forced civilians into exile for fear of political reprisals. Yet the overarching ambiguity regarding an individual's survival in a hostile and foreign environment regardless of political disposition became eminently clear in "Nit i boira" as well as in Rodoreda's personal trajectory.

Comparing Rodoreda's "Nit i boira," written while the Nuremberg trials were still ongoing, with works that have the benefit of fifty years of hindsight and critical study illustrates the transformations of Spanish representations of the Nazi regime through the decades. Rodoreda's narrator imagined his future burden, if he were to leave the camp alive: "'Si surto d'ací viu, com seré? Sempre em semblarà que duc a passejar un riu de cadàvers'" (Rodoreda, "Nit i boira" 232).[109] That river of corpses would be what the survivors in subsequent historical texts, oral histories, and memoirs implored the public not to forget, but it was part of the daily existence and death in the camps that Rodoreda captured through her protagonist. "Nit i boira" is a fictional representation of a concentration camp steeped in the realities of the Nazi *Lager* system. But as carefully as any historically documented text, Rodoreda's narrative revealed the personal experience of one prisoner's arrival, existence, and death at the hands of the Nazis. "Nit i boira" is as engaged with history as any of the Spanish representations of Mauthausen that would follow it, but the text is all the more crucial for its attempt to capture the ambiguous morality of the daily concentration camp horrors that the author and the world could only begin to imagine so soon after the Nazis' defeat.

Joaquim Amat-Piniella's Semi-Fictional Novel
K.L. Reich (Spain 1963)

As Emili, the protagonist of Joaquim Amat-Piniella's novel *K.L. Reich*, contemplates his liberation from a Nazi concentration camp in Austria, he scans the former prisoners who surround him: "una massa d'homes i dones de totes les races i totes les classes, de totes les religions i de totes les ideologies, una massa que ho ha donat tot sense queixar-se, una massa desconeixedora del valor del seu sacrifici que és la més profunda palpitació del món" (Amat-Piniella, *K.L. Reich* 274 [1963b]).[110] This mass of men and women comprise the social microcosm of the camp: survivors of different backgrounds and beliefs who sacrificed years of their lives to the Nazi reign of terror. Those who did not survive the camp sacrificed everything. Although Emili sees this conglomeration of individuals as a united community of survivors, the novel's author positioned a microscope over one subset of these international prisoners: the Spaniards. In the prologue to the original 1946 manuscript of *K.L. Reich*, Amat-Piniella wrote: "Les xifres astronòmiques de jueus, russos, polonesos, francesos, txecs, etc., que han mort als camps nazis no rebaixen pas la importància de l'aportació catalana i espanyola a l'impressionant carnatge" (9–10).[111] The Catalans and Spaniards who were killed in Mauthausen "han de pesar en un balanç de l'esforç peninsular en la causa de l'alliberació d'Europa" (10).[112] *K.L. Reich* – and the decades-long battle the author waged to publish it – argued that the small but significant force of Spaniards caught up in the fight against Hitler had stories that demanded to be told.

K.L. Reich followed the Spaniards of Mauthausen who sacrificed their lives and livelihoods for a cause that went unrecognized in their homeland. As a survivor himself, the author sought to unveil the inner workings of a Nazi concentration camp while focusing on a cross section of the camp's Spanish prisoner population.[113] Amat-Piniella fleshed out a cast of Spanish characters who were imprisoned in the camp, as well as other individuals and groups to whom he would have had only limited access while he was a prisoner in Mauthausen. His fictionalized account nevertheless took the reader beyond the gates of the camp, into the innermost relationships and thoughts of the Spanish population as well as other international inhabitants of Mauthausen. Amat-Piniella presented a conflicting array of ideologies and actions that revealed the prisoners as individuals, anathema to the Nazis' conception of a uniform mass of anonymous deportees slated for extermination.

Published in a censored edition in Spain in 1963, Amat-Piniella's novel was one of the first books Franco's censors allowed that presented a Spanish perspective of a Nazi concentration camp. As we have seen, however, *K.L. Reich* was not the first narrative of the Nazi camps published in Spain: this distinction goes to Rodríguez del Risco's serialized newspaper account. Nevertheless, Amat-Piniella wrote *K.L. Reich* in 1945 and 1946 and published excerpts of the novel in France in 1945 and in Spain in 1947. Although the novel in its entirety would not find a publisher inside Spain until the 1960s, Amat-Piniella merits inclusion among the vanguard of Spanish Holocaust authors given his determination to draft and publish his fictionalized account of Mauthausen in the immediate postwar years. The fact that his early attempts to publish the manuscript found only limited success does not diminish the immediacy of *K.L. Reich*, a novel that represents the inner workings of Mauthausen, the plight of Jews in the camp, and the divisions among the Spanish prisoner population with an intimacy that had not been seen before, nor would be seen again.

Active in leftist politics and journalism in his native Catalonia, Amat-Piniella fought with the 80th Mixed Brigade on the Republican side of the Spanish Civil War. He crossed the border into France on 14 July 1939, a few months after the Republic's defeat. Following the familiar path of Spanish exiles through a series of French internment camps, Amat-Piniella landed in a Company of Foreign Workers fortifying the Maginot Line (Amat-Piniella, *K.L. Reich* 8 [2005]). As France fell to the Nazis in 1940, he was captured and sent to *Stalag* XI-B in Fallingbostel, coincidentally the same prisoner of war camp where Rodríguez del Risco was held. On 27 January 1941, he was deported to Mauthausen as prisoner number 6211. He would spend four and a half years in the main camp of Mauthausen and the external *Kommandos* of Ternberg, Vöcklabruck, Redl-Zipf, and Ebensee. On 6 May 1945, the day after Mauthausen was liberated by American forces, Amat-Piniella was freed from Ebensee (Aragoneses; Bermejo and Checa 288).

Like most of the first Spaniards who arrived in the camp in 1940, Amat-Piniella began his imprisonment in Mauthausen working under brutal conditions in the quarry, but he was soon able to procure better working and living conditions as a *Prominenten* in the camp's administrative offices. Thanks to the intervention of a fellow Catalan prisoner who drew pornographic images for the SS, Amat-Piniella was transferred to an assignment cataloguing the camp's civilian clothing, an event he credited with saving his life (Amat-Piniella, "Entrevista" 17).[114] Although his fortunes varied as he was transferred between different *Kommandos*, Amat-Piniella pinned his survival on, as he told Montserrat Roig in 1973, "la idea de sortir amb vida, i després poder-ho explicar" (23).[115] The notion of writing a book about his experiences came to him while he was still imprisoned in Mauthausen, as a way of maintaining his faith (23). He wasted little time after he was liberated bringing *K.L. Reich* to fruition.[116]

In the weeks after Mauthausen's liberation, Amat-Piniella made his way to Paris and then on to Andorra. He wrote the original manuscript of *K.L. Reich* during an eight-month period from September 1945 to April 1946 while living in exile in Sant Julià de Lória (Serrano i Blanquer, "Edició i recepció" 91). In 1948 he crossed the border into Spain, reuniting with his wife in Barcelona (Amat-Piniella, *K L. Reich* 9 [2005]). Despite the danger of returning to Franco's Spain, he continued to work on a novel that would conflict with the dictator's control of information about the Spanish involvement in the Second World War. In the preface to the 1946 manuscript, Amat-Piniella expressed doubt that his narrative would find an editor or a publisher, but emphasized why the story must be told: "el que aquí gairebé ningú no sap és que, entre els milions de persones de totes les nacionalitats que van trobar la mort als camps de Hitler, també hi havia catalans i espanyols" (Amat-Piniella, *K.L. Reich* 9 [1963b]).[117] Although Rodríguez del Risco's newspaper account was the first survivor publication to explicitly acknowledge the presence of Spaniards in Mauthausen, Amat-Piniella sought to provide a more nuanced story of the Spanish deportees. The author's novel contained its own biases and inaccuracies. However, Amat-Piniella's choice of fiction allowed him to circumvent certain demands of the censors and gave him the freedom to explore the pathos of the Spaniards in Mauthausen in a manner that a historical rendering would not allow. As Joan Ramón Resina has commented, this combination of history and fiction "raises questions about the generic status of witnessing and the relation of truth to a discourse that combines experience and imagination" (165). Nevertheless, Amat-Piniella was able to reach towards the essence of the concentration camp experience for the Spaniards with his visceral depiction of Mauthausen.

Amat-Piniella's novelistic recreation of the prisoner and guard population of Mauthausen is closely related to Rodoreda's short story "Nit i boira." Beyond sharing the Catalan language and an exploration of the moral relativism inherent in the fight to survive in a Nazi concentration camp, Amat-Piniella's novel also began as a short story published in exile. Although both Rodoreda's and Amat-Piniella's texts were written in 1946, Amat-Piniella's attempts to publish *K.L. Reich* in its entirety in the immediate postwar period were fruitless.[118] Nevertheless, he managed to publish two excerpts from the novel that hinted at the depth of the full text. In August 1945, only four months after Mauthausen was liberated, Amat-Piniella published a two-page vignette called "La fam" ("Hunger") in *Per Catalunya: bulletin d'information des catalans en exil* (*For Catalunya: Informative Bulletin of Catalans in Exile*). Dedicated to and edited by exiled Catalans in Nice, France, this periodical was only published four times between July and October 1945, with a small distribution among its target population. "La fam," written in Catalan, was told from the perspective of Vicenç, a concentration camp prisoner dying of starvation. Vicenç is a Valencia native who has been imprisoned in a camp where the *Kapos* speak German and he is forced to work in a quarry. He thinks only of his hunger, fatigue, and the cold, knowing that it is only a matter of time before he will be overcome by all three: "Vicenç estava condemnat i ell ho sabia, pero abans de morir es defensava com una bèstia assetjada" (Amat-Piniella, "La fam" 3).[119] He resists as best he can, gathering what nourishment he is able to find and protesting the lack of food to his fellow prisoners. As the short story ends, Vicenç thinks once again about a warm soup that would bring him back from the brink of death.

Amat-Piniella's first published postwar story never mentioned Mauthausen, the Nazis, or Austria, but it was clearly set inside the punishing confines of the Austrian concentration camp. This short piece was an introduction to a character so singleminded about his hunger that it led to his death in *K.L. Reich*. In the novel, Vicenç is a Spanish prisoner on the lowest rung of Mauthausen's hierarchy. "La fam" corresponded almost verbatim to a section of Chapter Three in both the original 1946 manuscript and the censored versions of *K.L. Reich* published in Spain in 1963. Amat-Piniella managed to publish one more excerpt of *K.L. Reich* in Spain before his long wait to release the entire novel ensued.

The November 1947 edition of the Catalan periodical *Antologia dels fets, les idees i els homes d'occident* (*Anthology of Western Facts, Ideas, and Men*) included the short story "Eutanàsia" ("Euthanasia") by Amat-Piniella. *Antologia* was a Barcelona-based magazine published monthly and in circulation for only a year, from May 1947 to May 1948. Although its print run was modest – 1,000 copies per issue (*Antologia dels Fets*) – it was dedicated to the larger cause of demonstrating Catalonia's relevance to the rest of Europe, as stated in the magazine's manifesto: "Antologia vol esser un esbarjós mirador, per on Catalunya pugui atalaiar Europa, amarant-se de veritable universalitat, a través de la qual afermarà i enrobustirà, pel contrast, la seva personalitat nacional" (Amat-Piniella "Eutanàsia" inside front cover).[120] Amat-Piniella's short story of the lethal injection of a Catalan concentration camp prisoner certainly conformed to these standards of connecting the small region in the northeast corner of Spain to the rest of Europe, in this case presenting Catalonia's relevance to the Holocaust. Published in Spain the year after Rodríguez del Risco's newspaper articles, Amat-Piniella's second excerpt from *K.L. Reich* was also the second text by a Catalan survivor of Mauthausen published inside Spain that addressed the Nazi genocide.

Although "Eutanàsia," like "La fam" and *K.L. Reich* itself, never mentioned the name of the concentration camp that provided its setting, *Antologia*'s editors left no room for doubt about the text's background in their short parenthetical introduction to the story:

Dels set mil espanyols que han passat pel camp de concentració alemany de Mauthausen, n'han sortit mil vuit-cents escassos. L'autor és un dels supervivents i, sobre els records del seu captiveri de quatre anys i mig, ha escrit un reportatage novel·lat amb el títol "K.L. Reich," inèdit encara, i del qual publiquem avui un capítol. (Amat-Piniella, "Eutanàsia" 52)[121]

The identification not only of Mauthausen but also of the author's status as a survivor of the camp in this prologue – written in Catalan no less, a language banned by the Franco dictatorship – challenged the official silence on Spain's role in the Holocaust. Much like Rodríguez del Risco's newspaper series, Amat-Piniella's story was a public acknowledgment of the presence of Catalans and Spaniards in Nazi concentration camps that languished in obscurity until the author was able to publish his full novel in Spain. Admittedly, *Antologia* had a much more limited impact than Rodríguez del Risco's outlet of *Arriba*, as it would have been seen by only a small and decidedly anti-Franco contingent of Catalans willing to risk reading a leftist publication. Nevertheless, "Eutanàsia" joined "Yo he estado en Mauthausen" as proof that evidence was available inside Spain in the immediate postwar years of the existence of Spaniards imprisoned and murdered in the Nazi camp.

Amat-Piniella's second published excerpt of *K.L. Reich* introduced the characters of Emili and Francesc, close friends who confront the latter's failing health in the camp. As Emili despairs, Francesc considers his own impending death a means of justifying the Spaniards' long fight against fascists: "la mort no m'espanta, perquè és, en certa manera, una compensació per als que hem lluitat sempre contra els nostres assassins. En matarnos ens donen la raó, justifiquen el nostre esforç" (Amat-Piniella, "Eutanàsia" 52).[122] Emili senses that his friend is not a single individual in the camp, but rather a man who belongs equally to those around him. His death represents the mortality of the collective, and "[s]ense ell, esdevenien incomprensibles la continuació de la vida al camp, la derrota dels alemanys i àdhuc la fi de la guerra" (54–5).[123] Eventually, however, Francesc enters the infirmary, despite the warnings of a Spanish doctor. He lies in bed next to a young Jewish boy who is desperate to know what will happen to them. Francesc's calm demeanour contrasts with the Jewish boy's cries as he is led into a separate room for his "treatment": "'No ... No ... Que em porteu a matar! Ja ho sé, que em voleu matar!'" (57).[124]

Amat-Piniella's inclusion of a Jewish voice in the story underlined the shared experience of the Spaniards and the Jews in Mauthausen, perhaps to an unrealistic extent. The protestations of this Jewish character are at odds with the passivity of the Jewish prisoners depicted in Sinca Vendrell's account. Soon after the Jewish boy is taken to his death, an infirmary *Kapo* takes Francesc to the SS doctor. Francesc realizes too late that the infirmary is an illusion: "'Sóc un idiota, va pensar; si no hi ha res de real en tot això! Ni metges, ni taules, ni pàmpol, ni jo!'" [125] Yet even as he is led into the injection room, Francesc continues to harbour the illusion that his death is not imminent. He asks the German doctor if the shot will hurt him, knowing the answer. The Spanish doctor responds that "[a]mb aquest tractament milloraràs. No tinguis por!" (Amat-Piniella, "Eutanàsia" 58).[126] The gasoline injection that kills Francesc is, in a perverse sense, what "improves" his deplorable conditions in the concentration camp: in death he will not suffer as in life. As Francesc slowly slides towards oblivion in the closing lines of the story, the SS doctor orders his dosage reduced, thus prolonging Francesc's agony in the interest of saving the gasoline to kill other prisoners. The cruelty of the Germans is self-evident in the story, particularly compared with the compassion that Emili and even the Spanish doctor demonstrate towards Francesc. Ultimately, "Eutanàsia" planted the theme of the value of compassion and solidarity in the face of extreme violence and cruelty that Amat-Piniella developed more fully in *K.L. Reich*.

The story Amat-Piniella published in 1947 was a significant episode from Chapter Eleven of the 1946 manuscript and the 1963 editions of the author's novel. Francesc is modelled on Pere Vives i Clavé, who was killed by a lethal injection of benzene in Mauthausen in 1941.[127] The relationship between Emili and Francesc reflected Amat-Piniella's enduring friendship with Vives. The author's rendering of Vives in "Eutanàsia" and again in *K.L. Reich* invited the reader to share the thoughts of a Spanish prisoner in Mauthausen in the moments before his death. Moreover, it presented the historical fact of the Nazis' reliance on lethal medical experiments such as benzene injections to exterminate prisoners throughout the concentration camp empire: not only Jews, but Spaniards as well. This horrifying treatment and the contingent suffering of its victim hinted at the multiple perspectives of victims and perpetrators that Amat-Piniella explored in the novel-length version of *K.L. Reich*.

Amat-Piniella was finally able to release *K.L. Reich* in its entirety in Spain in 1963, retaining the storylines and much of the original wording of "La fam" and "Eutanàsia." The novel was published by Seix Barral with the aid of the editor Carlos Barral, who brought many otherwise unpublishable postwar volumes to print in Spain. Released first in the Castilian translation, a Catalan edition was added later the same year.[128] However, by 1963, the landscape of Holocaust narratives had changed significantly: Amat-Piniella was no longer a pioneer in the genre. Most notably, 1963 saw the publication of Jorge Semprún's *Le grand voyage* (*The Long Voyage*). Published in French in Paris, Semprún's text – like Amat-Piniella's – fictionalized the author's experiences in a Nazi concentration camp. Semprún's narrative approach to the Holocaust took the reader into the mind of a Spanish exile deported to Buchenwald as he contemplates his current situation trapped in a boxcar with other deportees, the past that has brought him to this moment, and the future that prompts him to write about his experiences. While *Le grand voyage* has become a canonical Holocaust narrative, *K.L. Reich* is virtually unknown outside of Spain. Nevertheless, Amat-Piniella's work is as important as Semprún's in its early panoramic representation of a Holocaust consciousness. The fact that it was published under Franco's dictatorship in Spanish and Catalan editions – re-edited and translated many times since – has opened *K.L. Reich* up to a significant audience in Spain over the decades. Given its origins as a manuscript written in the months after Amat-Piniella was liberated from one of Mauthausen's satellite camps, *K.L. Reich* retains the immediacy of the earliest Spanish Holocaust texts discussed in this chapter.[129] It had a sizeable influence over the Spanish Mauthausen histories and memoirs published in the decades to come.

In his introduction to the re-edited version of *K.L. Reich* released in 2002, David Serrano i Blanquer enumerated the elements that were cut from the original manuscript to allow the 1963 Castilian and Catalan editions of the novel to evade Franco's censors: "las referencias despectivas del carácter germánico, de su antisemitismo, así como símbolos explícitos de carácter izquierdista o el compromiso de los españoles por las libertades republicanas" (Amat-Piniella, *K.L. Reich* 12 [2002]).[130] These references would have alerted Franco's censors and had to be suppressed in order to publish the book during the dictatorship, at a time when no other Spanish Holocaust narratives were permitted. Nevertheless, Amat-Piniella's censored novel still included other controversial storylines and elements frequently present in other early Spanish Holocaust narratives published outside the country. Examining Amat-Piniella's first attempts to reckon with his experience in Mauthausen allows us to better understand these tensions or "grey zones," as Primo Levi has called them, from the prisoners' perspective in the concentrationary environment.

Writing in 1969 in one of the first Spanish historiographical accounts of the Nazi camp, the Mauthausen survivor Antonio Vilanova recognized that *K.L. Reich* was "un único libro, que yo conozca, describiendo la vida y la muerte de los españoles en un campo de concentración alemán."[131] Yet Vilanova was disappointed that the author opted for a fictional encounter with Mauthausen over a historical study, lamenting that *K.L. Reich* "se trata el tema en forma novelada, con nombres figurados y donde muchos de los episodios que se relatan no corresponden, en todo o en parte, a la realidad. Y esto no es hacer historia, ni sirve para fines históricos" (*Los olvidados* 202).[132] Though Amat-Piniella did not pretend to write a historical account of Mauthausen, his novel served "historical ends" by providing a human portrait of a Nazi camp. Fiction, in its liberation from authentification, has the power to transmit the story running beneath the history of these events. Serrano i Blanquer argues that the novel is able to "ofrecer una determinada perspectiva moral ... un género que le permite llegar a la escencia a través del simbolismo y de la síntesis," (Amat-Piniella, *K.L. Reich* 13 [2002]).[133] This "essence" of the camp, the untold stories of individual and collective encounters with violence and generosity, is what distinguished Amat-Piniella's novel from much of the body of Spanish Holocaust narrative to precede and follow it.

Rodoreda's fictional approach to the camp confronted these moral imperatives as well, but Amat-Piniella also peppered his narrative with historically accurate episodes from the years of Mauthausen's operation. Rodoreda was never inside a Nazi concentration camp, thus her approach to the moral relativism inherent in the camp's operation and the prisoners' actions was based on a synthesis of what she learned from Spanish survivors and what she created out of her imagination. Amat-Piniella's approach to these same issues confronted the challenge of allowing the reader both to understand the camp as a real place and to feel the conflicts among the different strata of prisoners. Having lived these experiences himself, it is clear that Amat-Piniella's choice of the genre of fiction gave him the liberty to explore the inner thoughts and sensations of the Spanish prisoner population that would diminish the authority of a historical account. Yet the author did not eschew a historical approach entirely: beginning with the central protagonist, *K.L. Reich* presented clear allusions to people, places, and events that have been corroborated by the historical record.

The novel opens with the protagonist Emili, an embodiment of the author himself, arriving at the gates of an unknown concentration camp with Francesc, the character who was first introduced in "Eutanàsia." Although the name "Mauthausen" never appears, there are allusions to the geography and layout of the camp that pinpoint the novel's setting: the camp remained unfinished in 1940 and boasted a prominent quarry near the Linz-Salzburg rail line "construït després de la incorporació d'Àustria al Gran Reich alemany, dominant les aigües del 'bell Danubi blau,'" (Amat-Piniella, *K.L. Reich* 87 [1963b]).[134] Moreover, Amat-Piniella referenced other historical moments that have subsequently been confirmed as events that occurred in Mauthausen during its years of operation. At one point, the narrator describes that "un jove espanyol havia sortit del camp, repatriat per menor d'edat" (148), an unambiguous reference to the Spanish teenager sent home from Mauthausen after his mother wrote Spain's Minister of Foreign Affairs on his behalf.[135] The details of the liberation of the camp, in which American forces arrived and then left the ex-prisoners to fend for themselves for a night before taking control, also conform to the liberation of Mauthausen. The author's decision not to use the camp's real name nor to identify any of the characters based on real people with their real names in part reflected the fact that the prisoners had little idea of where they were: "Llevat del Danubi ... cap altra referència no era identificable" (216).[136] Moreover, from the prisoners' perspective, once they were trapped inside, this concentration camp could have been any of the dozens of Nazi camps dotting the Third Reich. The author captured the anonymity of the prisoners sent to die in oblivion with the generic identifier of the camp: "K.L. Reich."[137] Emili and Francesc's initial ignorance of camp life and death also betrayed a general ignorance among the novel's Catalan and Spanish readership of the Nazi *Lager* system and the day-to-day experience of being a Spanish prisoner in a concentration camp.

Amat-Piniella proceeded to examine a cross-section of the camp's social and power structure, from the weakest and most powerless prisoner to the German commander of the camp. Narrated in the third person, the novel assumes different points of view representing the voices and thoughts of these individuals positioned throughout the camp's hierarchy. The narrative descends from the prisoners who act as *Kapos*, in a position of power over their fellow prisoners; to the prisoners who, due to their relationship with the *Kapos*, or their favoured position within the International Committee or the organization of Spanish communists, are given slightly less arduous jobs within the camp that allow them to eat regularly; to the prisoners who hold no special position or favour whatsoever, and are doomed to work the more physically demanding jobs outside the camp and suffer an almost constant and overwhelming hunger. *K.L. Reich* examines each of these rungs on the concentration camp structural ladder through individual prisoners whose experiences and behaviour serve as archetypes within the community of Spanish prisoners. Nevertheless, the novel consistently returns to Emili's perspective. Thus, as the reader gradually descends into the concentration camp universe via *K.L. Reich*'s international cast of characters, our primary point of view is through a Catalan man who will come to know a certain amount of privilege in the camp as he attempts to remain aloof from the political battles among his countrymen.

At the very bottom of the camp hierarchy of Spaniards is the familiar character of Vicent, described as an easygoing man from Valencia who was accustomed to eating and living well before his imprisonment.[138] After only three months in the camp, Vicent is a shadow of his former self: he has lost the *joie de vivre* he enjoyed on the outside. Now he aspires to nothing more than to satiate himself, inventing imaginary banquets while he suffers the unending cold and is driven to exhaustion by the *Kapos*. He is governed almost exclusively by his stomach, dehumanized into his basest need: "En Vicent no sabia res, no comprenia res, no recordava res. Només tenia fam."[139] Vicent attains no special privilege within the camp and in that sense, his was the story of thousands of camp prisoners: "¡n'hi havia tants de casos com el seu, al camp!" (Amat-Piniella, *K.L. Reich* 69 [1963b]).[140] Amat-Piniella's descriptions of a man ruled by an unrelenting hunger were so central to the concentration camp environment that they were among the first elements of the novel he drafted.[141]

When Vicent steals another prisoner's bread, he is branded a thief and brutally tortured under the cold showers by the *Kapo* nicknamed Popeye. Vicent is barely breathing when the beating stops. The narrator describes a slow transition from life to death as the man's inert body lies on the wet pavement. Although Vicent does not die from starvation, his unending hunger is, ironically, what leads to his death. As the first detailed description of a death of a character whom the reader has come to know, Vicent's demise underscores his utter powerlessness.

Francesc also occupies a low rung in the camp's hierarchy. As was detailed in Amat-Piniella's 1947 excerpt from *K.L Reich*, "Eutanàsia," Francesc arrives in the camp suffering from a respiratory illness. Sick and unable to work at the rate of his fellow Spaniards, Francesc is targeted by the SS. In one episode, Francesc watches, with "l'estranya fascinació de la sang i de la tortura," as an SS officer beats a Jewish prisoner almost to death.[142] The SS officer, seeing him, indicates that Francesc should be the one to push the Jewish prisoner over the edge of a nearby precipice. Francesc refuses to participate in this macabre game, telling the SS officer: "'¡No puc fer això!'" (Amat-Piniella, *K.L. Reich* 115 [1963b]).[143] For his refusal, Francesc is beaten, but rather than give the officer the satisfaction of killing him, he jumps over the edge into the river below. He survives, but this act of self-sacrifice is punished with brutal labour. Francesc's mitigated act of heroism – substituting his own life so that he would not have to take the life of the Jewish prisoner – differentiates him from Vicent. Although Francesc is ultimately killed by the Nazis in a cruel act of torture not unlike Vicent's brutal beating, Francesc possesses a sense of human dignity that extends beyond his own wellbeing. Vicent, on the other hand, is primarily concerned with his own survival. While both men die senselessly at the hands of their captors, the differences in their world views demonstrate two extremes on a moral scale: from the selfish man who steals another starving man's bread in the interest of his own survival to the selfless man who risks his life rather than sacrifice another's.

One step up in the camp hierarchy of Spaniards from Vicent and Francesc are men like Emili and Rubio, who are given privileged positions in the camp. In part due to the organizational efforts of the other Spaniards, these men are guaranteed food and a protected place inside the camp's administrative offices to work. Rubio is a Spanish barber with ties to the camp's clandestine organization who collects detailed information about the inner workings of the crematories. Emili is able to better his situation in the camp when some of the SS officers realize he is a talented artist and demand that he draw them pornographic images; he also works in the kitchens and later in the photography lab.[144] The difference between being able to work inside in an office or kitchen versus outside in the quarry is essential to Emili and Rubio's survival, as the quarry's punishing conditions sped the deaths of most of the prisoners. In comparison, although Emili complains of the suffocating heat and odours of the kitchen where he works peeling potatoes, he is nevertheless afforded more food and protected working conditions.

Although Emili initially "s'aferrava a la idea d'una unió de tots els espanyols" (Amat-Piniella, *K.L. Reich* 80 [1963b]), he later becomes disillusioned with the effectiveness of the Spaniards' solidarity: "'La gent és apàtica i egoista. Ningú no creu que valgui la pena d'intentar res" (127).[145] Even though Emili demonstrates a general ambiguity towards the organizational structure of the Spaniards inside the camp, it is this structure that "organizes" the extra food and improved work details for fellow Spaniards.[146] Indeed, when Emili is transferred to a satellite camp, Rubio writes him that: "'Amb tant de privilegi estem a punt d'aconseguir el nostre somni inicial, que cap espanyol no passi fam ... [I] que cal la unió de tots per a les hores que s'acosten" (195).[147] Despite the gains he receives from these connected fellow prisoners, Emili is nevertheless true to his nonpartisan ideals. He considers the extra food that Rubio gives him as bribes from the clandestine organization, and eventually refuses to draw pornography for the SS officers. These acts force him to accept a slightly lower rung in the camp hierarchy than he would have attained by collaborating with the Spanish clandestine organization, as Rubio does. Emili is driven, instead, by the memory of his friends Francesc and Werner, a German prisoner, both of whom were killed by the Nazis in the camp. Unlike Francesc, Werner, Vicent, and thousands of others, Rubio and Emili survive their years in "K.L. Reich."

Ernest, a young Spaniard who assumes a position in the camp kitchen while becoming a German *Kapo*'s lover, embodies the moral ambiguity of the Spaniards who occupy the rung above Rubio and Emili in the camp hierarchy. Ernest's homosexual tendencies embarrass the Spaniards organizing in the camp. Through Rubio, they ask Ernest to change his behaviour, but he refuses. Ernest provides the Spanish organization with valuable information regarding the newly arrived camp prostitutes, whom his *Kapo* frequents. Yet the power of being a *Kapo*'s favourite goes to his head, and he preys particularly on older Spanish prisoners. In one case, he has a Spanish prisoner punished for stealing some potatoes (which were, in fact, stolen on the orders of the Spanish clandestine organization), even though Ernest is friendly with the man's son. The punishment is so severe that Ernest indirectly causes the man's death by handing him over to the SS. Ernest's behaviour clashes with the heterosexual norms and solidarity of the Spanish prisoners: "Els espanyols del camp, cada vegada més interessats en un redreçament moral que els fes quedar bé com a grup col·lectiu, repudiaven obertament la conducta de l'Ernest."[148] Nevertheless, Ernest wields more power than the majority of the Spaniards because of his relationship with the German *Kapo*; he undergoes a process of what the narrator called *"alemanyització"* ("Germanization," Amat-Piniella, *K.L. Reich* 196 [1963b]); emphasis in the original). Ernest ultimately pays for his treason to the Spanish cause, however. After the camp is liberated, the son of the man who died from the punishment inflicted as a result of Ernest's actions shoots him. Ernest's post-liberation death at the hands of a prisoner who had possessed no power in the camp is an ironic end to a man who enjoys lording his preferential treatment over his fellow Spanish prisoners.

At the top of the camp's Spanish hierarchy stands August, the Spaniard who holds the most power in the camp. A Valencian man who speaks German so well that Emili initially thinks he is German, August ingratiates himself with the German *Blockälteste* (block elder) nicknamed Popeye by means of his ability to communicate with the SS.[149] He is put in charge of his own *Kommando* of other prisoners, including Emili, who are transferred outside the main camp under August's authority. But August is by turns loyal and disloyal to the Spanish clandestine organization. He alternates between trying to protect the Spaniards, declaring that his position in the camp hierarchy allows him to save hundreds of Spanish lives; and not wanting his countrymen's clandestine operations to put the favours he receives from the Germans at risk. As August's thirst for power grows and the end of the war nears, the increasing divisions among the Spaniards involved in the clandestine organization become more pronounced: August's actions lead to the unravelling of the solidarity they so tirelessly seek.

August asks Emili to inform on the political activities of other Spaniards in the camp, suspecting that the communists are colluding with the Germans. When August declares himself the head of the clandestine operations, the men interpret this as a "'cop d'Estat militar'" introducing a "nou dictador" into their ranks (Amat-Piniella, *K.L. Reich* 203 [1963b]).[150] The Spaniards in the camp are a microcosm of Civil War–era Spain: political quarrels prompt a deep divison between political factions, resulting in a power vacuum that allows the ascent of a dictator. This breakdown in solidarity has a corrupting effect on the entire spectrum of Spanish prisoners:

> Quan hi hagué entre els espanyols una relativa abundància, la brega política entre comunistes i anticomunistes experimentà una intensitat inusitada ... Havien descobert que la generositat amb els desvalguts podia constituir algun dia un mèrit polític. I així deixava de ser generositat ... Capdavanters i seguidors s'apassionaven en la caça de prosèlits, com si de l'hegemonia en el grup espanyol del camp depengués l'esdevenidor de la pàtria i del món sencer. Els tebis, els neutres o els arribistes s'aprofitaven de la rivalitat i, si volen, podien vendre's a l'un o a l'altre. (204)[151]

August symbolizes the reigning ambiguity in the power structure of the Spaniards in the camp. He eventually renounces his position as the head of the Spanish contingent, leaving at the helm a Spaniard who does not speak German. As a result, the Spaniards' united front collapses. As liberation approaches, August has earned his fair share of enemies who want to bring him to account for his constant manipulation of his countrymen. But unlike Ernest, who is killed once the Spanish prisoners are left to their own devices by the Americans, August "[v]a sortir-ne més tard que els seus companys, sense deixar cap rastre. Els seus enemics no es pogueren donar el gust de 'demanar-li comptes'" (Amat-Piniella, *K.L. Reich* 243–4 [1963b]).[152] August's disappearance leaves unresolved the relationship between the Spanish clandestine organization and a man who toyed with the political upheaval and desperation of his fellow countrymen, much as *K.L. Reich* leaves the future of the Spaniards in limbo once the camp is liberated.[153]

The groundbreaking nature of *K.L. Reich* resided not only in this exploration of the spectrum of Spanish prisoners in the camp, but also in its portrayal of individuals outside the Spaniards' immediate camp community: namely, Jewish prisoners and Germans. Amat-Piniella's narration is at times sympathetic, and at times confrontational, towards the plight of Jewish prisoners, the ideals of Nazi officers, and the thoughts of German prisoners, allowing *K.L. Reich* to draw a three-dimensional portrait of the camp. On a camp hierarchy that extended beyond the Spanish population, the Jews were at the absolute bottom and the Nazi officers remained decisively at the top.

Hans Gupper, nicknamed "El Negre," was a fictional counterpart to Georg Bachmayer, the Nazi who was second-in-command at Mauthausen under Franz Ziereis from 1939 until the camp's liberation. Amat-Piniella devoted a significant portion of the novel to exploring Gupper's dreams for the development of "his" camp, wading into the perverted idealism of National Socialism. As Gupper surveys the camp, he is drawn to its organization and the way it is able to fortify the Reich with its quarry. He also surmises that prisoners are stealing food, a crime he wants to eradicate. Both this Nazi officer and the Spanish prisoner population are deeply concerned with food, though for different reasons. When Gupper asks one of his *Lagerälteste* (camp leaders), an obese SS functionary the prisoners nicknamed "King-kong," about who would be best suited to complete the construction of the camp, King-kong suggests the Spaniards. They are gathered for the work almost immediately. Thus the author makes the connection between the camp's commandant and the Spanish population explicit. It is nevertheless startling to imagine Amat-Piniella envisioning the concentration camp's function and utility from the point of view of a Nazi officer. It is this empathy that distinguishes *K.L. Reich* from the majority of the concentration camp narratives by Spaniards.

The description of Gupper leaves no doubt as to his position on the highest rung in the power structure of the camp, a violent instigator of the program of Nazi domination: "Cada grau i cada condecoració devien significar centenars de vides immolades a la 'gran Alemanya.' El flamant *Obersturmführer* de la SS havia adquirit l'aurèola dels herois a força de matar jueus i comunistes" (Amat-Piniella, *K.L. Reich* 51–2 [1963b]).[154] Yet despite his fame for killing Jews and communists, Gupper is particularly sympathetic to the Spaniards, aiding them with work assignments and exacting less severe punishments on them than on the camp's other prisoners. While some Spaniards defend Gupper's actions, Emili is not swayed, having witnessed how Gupper treated other prisoner groups: "'Les jueves que matava a destralades no l'emocionaven gaire'" (247).[155] Gupper offers the prisoners refuge with the Red Cross as the American forces approach the camp and does not attempt to escape along with other SS officers. The announcement arrives in the soon-to-be liberated camp that Gupper has instead poisoned himself, his wife, and his children. These details – particularly the commandant's sympathy for the Spaniards and the murder-suicide – aligns the character of Gupper precisely with Georg Bachmayer, who is mentioned in numerous Mauthausen survivor testimonies.[156] Gupper's idealistic vision of the camp and his ultimate martyrdom for the Nazi cause lends a counterbalance to the Spanish ordeal that is both fascinating and unsettling.

To be sure, Amat-Piniella included other Germans in *K.L. Reich* who provided a diverse perspective of the inner workings of the camp. Some, like a German crematory worker, remained nameless. Others, like Emili's friend Werner, were given an identity and fleshed out as multidimensional characters. Rubio encounters a German man in the crematory who puts his job into historical context, saying "'Entre els antics, la incineració era una cerimònia amb grandesa. Aquí cremen els morts per fer desaparèixer els rastres de l'assassinat" (Amat-Piniella, *K.L. Reich* 165 [1963b]).[157] Werner, on the other hand, looks towards the future: he encourages Emili to continue the organization of the Spaniards despite his frustrations. Werner also provides some insight into the German mindset, although he is not a Nazi. The narrator describes how German boys are taught that "considerant que la dona no era més que una màquina de fer fills per a la pàtria, estimant que l'exercici i la nuditat eren, no solament un camí, sinó una fita ... ¡Clima propici a totes les aberracions!" (146–7).[158] The Nazis stage Werner's death as a suicide, which infuriates Emili: "'És de ràbia que ploro, ¿m'entens?'" (164).[159] The friendly relationship between Werner and Emili presents a complex yet sympathetic image of a German prisoner who also became a victim of Nazi brutality. This cross-cultural relationship supplied another rarely seen perspective that distinguished Amat-Piniella's novel from other texts by Spanish Mauthausen survivors.

Popeye, the barracks boss, represented yet another German archetype in the novel. Imprisoned as an asocial criminal, Popeye lords himself over the Spanish prisoners, punishing them often and violently for the merest infraction. Although Vicent steals bread from Popeye and August manages to ingratiate himself with him, gaining slightly better treatment for himself and some of the other, weaker prisoners, the majority of the Spaniards view the German *Blockälteste* as a sadistic villain. Popeye is the first to beat Emili in the camp, he tortures Vicent to death, and he commits countless other atrocities witnessed by the prisoner population. As retribution, a group of prisoners hunts him down and kills him after the camp's liberation; Emili comes across Popeye's body, his head crushed by other victims of the *Blockälteste*'s tortures. Unlike many other pseudonymous characters, Amat-Piniella did not disguise Popeye: he was a German *Kapo* frequently mentioned in other accounts by the Spaniards in Mauthausen.[160] Though not as complete as the spectrum of Spanish prisoners that Amat-Piniella explored, this handful of German characters grounded the novel in a historically minded sense of the variation of German responses to the Nazi agenda.

Unlike the Spanish and German characters, there are very few individual characterizations of the Jewish prisoners: when they appear in the narration, they are nameless or anonymous figures amassed in large groups.[161] Nevertheless, the author laboured to include episodes of cruelty and humanity towards the Jews who entered the camp, relying primarily on Emili's eyewitness accounts to capture the stark difference between the treatment of Jewish and Spanish prisoners. For the Jews, there was no hierarchy: no individual Jewish prisoner had any more power or control over his or her ultimate fate than any other. In this sense, Amat-Piniella presented a clear picture of the Nazis' pogrom to annihilate the Jews through their brutal and singular treatment in a single camp.

Although the Spaniards saw only scant evidence of Jews entering the camp during its first years of operation, by 1941 enormous convoys of Jewish prisoners were arriving on a regular basis. The narrator described them as the Nazis' prime target: "Aquells centenars de jueus holandesos que acabaven d'arribar inauguraven la temporada dels grans carnatges. El camp de Hans Gupper ... començava aleshores a acollir els perseguits predilectes de la Gestapo" (Amat-Piniella, *K.L. Reich* 87 [1963b]).[162]

During this period, Emili witnesses waves of Jewish prisoners arriving and being brutally beaten, in part because of his position distributing clothing in the camp. He watches as a group of Hungarian Jews passes through the camp's gate and begins to understand the fundamental difference between himself and them: "'La seva mort és segura, més que la nostra. Almenys, més immediata" (Amat-Piniella, *K.L. Reich* 99 [1963b]).[163] At another point, Emili sees a further one hundred prisoners, including twenty Jews, beaten and killed almost immediately upon entry. What he watches is so violent that that he cannot sleep: "Un món d'espectres es movia sota els seus ulls closos, enmig d'un silenci més punyent que els udols de terror d'una estona abans" (144).[164] The fact that many Spaniards managed to survive in the camp while other prisoners – including those in the Russian camp – were slated for a rapid extermination bothers Emili on a moral level: "li semblava monstruosa la llei que obligava que tants morissin a fi que uns pocs poguessin sobreviure" (218).[165] Another Spaniard argues that the Spaniards tend to survive because they are long-term residents of the camp; their lives are not preserved at the cost of others' deaths. Nevertheless, Emili considers these scenes of torture and death as the demarcation between the population of Spaniards that has, on the whole, been allowed to live, and a population of Jews who are relentlessly murdered. This narrative thread asked Spanish readers of *K.L. Reich* to comprehend the deep-seated difference between being a Spaniard and being a Jew in a concentration camp: while one group had a chance of survival, the other had none. This was, in essence, Amat-Piniella's early argument for the singularity of the Holocaust.

When liberation finally arrives, the narrator describes how men of different nationalities reacted: the Yugoslavs sang patriotic hymns, the Spaniards acted as though they had seen this kind of celebration before, the Russians pursued their torturers, but "[e]ls pocs jueus que havien tingut la sort d'arribar a la fi arrossegaven els peus ... contemplaven les coses amb ulls de fura i no deien res" (Amat-Piniella, *K.L. Reich* 265 [1963b]).[166] Spectres until the very end, the surviving Jews mark liberation in silence. Because their voices were also seldom heard in the narration, *K.L. Reich* offered a glimpse of the suffering of Jews in the camp that also held this population at arm's length. Although the reader is never privy to the thoughts of Jews the way he is to the thoughts of the Spaniards, the novel's sympathy towards the persecuted Jews marked a departure from previous accounts. Neither Rodríguez del Risco's anti-Semitic tirades, nor Rodoreda's metaphorical approach, nor Sinca Vendrell's argument against the singularity of the Jewish experience provided the kind of sympathetic vision of the Jews that Amat-Piniella did. The fortunes of the Spaniards in this Austrian camp may have been distinct from those of the Jews, but the author's approach allowed the reader to begin to comprehend the complex and overlapping populations and hierarchies in one Nazi

Lager. This vision placed the Spaniards both contextually and experientially in the middle of the Holocaust.

During the camp's waning hours, as the SS flee and the International Organization is placed in charge, Emili finds a sense of serenity. As he wanders the camp, noticing the mark of "K.L. Reich" stamped on just about everything, he ponders the deaths he has witnessed. His friends Francesc and Werner died, victims of the Nazis' unjust cause, yet Emili senses the peace that both men found as "[u]na pau que no és passivitat i renúncia, sinó un estat moral actiu, com un estat de gràcia" (Amat-Piniella, *K.L. Reich* 275 [1963b]).[167] Despite the moral transgressions Emili witnesses and lives in the camp, he completes his four and a half years of imprisonment awash in this "active moral condition" that allows him to endure the camp: "Endarrera queda un passat d'horrors; endavant s'obre un esdevenidor d'esperances" (275–6).[168] Emili's transformation from passive prisoner unmoved by the solidarity of the Spaniards to active prisoner, recording the injustices occurring around him, if only to preserve them in his own memory, provides an ending to the story that is, as Serrano i Blanquer writes, "paradójicamente, existencialmente esperanzador" ("paradoxically, existentially hopeful," Amat-Piniella, *K.L. Reich* 11 [2002]). Amat-Piniella's novel pulled the reader into an intimate dialogue with a cross-section of the temporary residents of this camp, allowing a deeper understanding of the suffering caused by the Nazis and counteracted by the prisoners' humanity. As the last word from the first group of published Spanish representations of the Nazi concentration camps, Amat-Piniella's sensitivity towards his countrymen's place in a larger conflict foretold a body of Spanish Mauthausen accounts that would in the years to come create a public consciousness of the Holocaust heretofore unseen in Spain.

3 Transitions: Early Accounts
   of Mauthausen, 1970s

Spain in the 1950s and 1960s was still limping through a protracted recovery from its civil war. While Franco declared "25 Years of Peace" in 1964 – twenty-five years after the defeat of Republican forces in 1939 – a reconciliation was nowhere in sight. Divisions between the winners and losers of the war would continue to mark Spanish society for years to come. The majority of the Spanish Republicans who survived Mauthausen remained in France. Some affiliated themselves with French survivor organizations or political groups dedicated to the ex-deportees.[1] The negligible attention Spanish Mauthausen survivors and victims received inside Spain in the years immediately after the Second World War had long since dissipated. The Franco regime continued to enforce censorship laws and prohibit political gatherings. The Barcelona-based Amical de Mauthausen, founded in 1962 as an organization for survivors and family members of Spaniards killed at Mauthausen and other Nazi camps, was forced to operate underground, remaining illegal until after the death of Franco (Toran, *Amical de Mauthausen* 11). Even after the dictator's death in 1975, public awareness of the Spaniards of Mauthausen was minimal. The Amical was unable to publicize its activities, the Franco government remained averse to reexamining its past, and the majority of the ex-deportees were unwilling to return to a Spain unaware of – or even hostile towards – their suffering. The phantom figure of the Spanish Mauthausen survivor remained in the shadows.

Many of the earliest representations of the Spaniards in Mauthausen were initially published abroad or to no fanfare in Spain. As such, the victims were essentially invisible and any knowledge of the Spanish experience of Mauthausen in the twenty-five years that had passed since the liberation of the camp lay dormant in Spain. In Europe and the Americas, historical narratives, journalism, and survivor testimony of the Second World War, the concentration camps, and the Holocaust gained prominence in the late 1960s, spurred in part by coverage of the capture, trial, and execution of Adolf Eichmann between 1960 and 1962. In Spain, however, the first tentative attempts to come to terms with the realities of the Spaniards who had been caught by the Nazis for the benefit of a wider audience began only in the 1970s. This "historical gap" is similar to what the psychiatrist and Holocaust survivor Dori Laub identifies in testimony about the Shoah: a lapse in "collective witnessing" that "underscores the fact that these testimonies were not transmittable, and integratable, at the time" (Felman and Laub 84). In the case of Spanish survivor accounts of Mauthausen, Spain's political situation was one factor that created this blank memory space. Another factor relates to the trauma that the Mauthausen survivors had lived and seen. Mauthausen haunted them to such an extent that bearing witness to what they experienced would have been tantamount to reliving the original horror. As Cathy Caruth explains, relating traumatic events involves "a kind of double telling, the oscillation between a *crisis of death* and the correlative *crisis of life*: between the story of the unbearable nature of an event and the story of the unbearable nature of its survival" (7; emphasis in the original). The primary trauma of Mauthausen and its recurrence in the survivor's retelling reopens the scars of the original wound.

What Dominick LaCapra called "the aftereffects – the hauntingly possessive ghosts – of traumatic events" (xi) are sticky, not easily removed from the survivor's consciousness after the concentration camp. Yet the release of testimony may allow the survivor to finally shed those ghosts and heal his wounds. Speaking about the trauma, for Laub, is an act of "repossessing one's life story," which is necessary to be able to "complete the process of survival after liberation" (Felman and Laub 85). Bearing witness in a public forum not only benefits the survivor but also the listener. Beyond "purely documentary knowledge ... [t]estimonies are significant in the attempt to understand experience and its aftermath, including the role of memory and its lapses, in coming to terms with – or denying and repressing – the past" (LaCapra 86–7). The result for the witness, his or her interlocutor, and the listener, is, in Laub's words, a collective "reemerging truth" (Felman and Laub 85): not an empirical truth, but the essential truth of the survivor's experience.[2]

As censorship laws loosened and Franco neared death, Spanish survivors who bore witness in the 1970s began to exorcise the ghosts of their Mauthausen trauma. One survivor published a host of melodramatic tell-all autobiographies; five others risked Francoist limits on free speech to speak on camera about their concentration camp experiences; and more than forty exiled ex-deportees each provided their oral histories to a Catalan journalist. Collectively, these furtive attempts to break through the decades of silence on the subject of Spaniards in Mauthausen would lay the groundwork for future testimonial efforts and representations. Although significant in the chronology of Spain's developing consciousness of Mauthausen, they ultimately proved to be only flashes of recognition that would recede to the background as Spain's decade of transition came to a close.

The Mauthausen survivor Mariano Constante, who authored and co-authored four autobiographical books over the course of the decade about Spaniards in Nazi camps, looms large over the story of the Spanish ex-deportees. Indeed, Constante's quest to place himself not only at the centre of a quiet storm of survivor accounts but also at the centre of the resistance movement inside Mauthausen's walls from 1941 to 1945 eventually resulted in contention and controversy among his fellow deportees and some historians. Nevertheless, Constante commanded an audience and brought the experiences of the Spaniards of Mauthausen to light as Spain transitioned from dictatorship to democracy. The stories and data he included in his books began to form a core narrative of the Spanish experience of Mauthausen that toed a line between history and invention.

Llorenç Soler's 1975 documentary *Sobrevivir en Mauthausen* constituted the first attempt to reimagine Spain's relationship to the Holocaust in sounds and images. Although the film could only be viewed clandestinely in Spain until well after Franco's death, Soler's drive to record the first-person testimony of Spanish Mauthausen survivors stood at the vanguard of a rush of documentaries on the subject that would emerge at the start of the twenty-first century. These successive films mimicked Soler's cinematic techniques, biases, and narrative strategies. Thus, the same year as Franco's death, the Spaniards of Mauthausen began to come into focus onscreen.

The final turning point during the 1970s came when a young Catalan novelist and journalist suddenly became aware of the presence of Spaniards in Nazi camps. Montserrat Roig spent the decade investigating a story with no precedent. She interviewed Spanish concentration camp survivors, tracked Spain's newfound interest in the Holocaust, and even capitalized on an unexpected moment when she found herself seated next to Franco's brother-in-law to demand that the regime's government account for the deportation of thousands of its citizens to Nazi camps.[3] Roig's steadfast committment to understanding what, exactly, had happened to the contingent of Catalans and Spaniards who disappeared over the border in 1939 culminated in the 1977 publication of *Els catalans als camps nazis*. This lengthy historiography instantly became – and has remained – the authoritative account of the Catalan experience of the Nazi concentration camps. Roig spoke with dozens of survivors, corroborated their accounts, and left no room for doubt that the men and women who perished in or survived Mauthausen and other Nazi camps were an irreplaceable part of the country's collective memory. Although Roig's volume betrayed her own subjective sense of the topic, she brought a notoriety to the Spaniards of Mauthausen that would finally allow them and their stories to see the light of day.

The Proto-Survivor: Mariano Constante and the First Wave of Mauthausen Testimony

Eduardo Pons Prades' *Los que SÍ hicimos la guerra* (*Those of Us Who DID Fight the War*), published in 1973, was among the first historical narratives about the exile of 1939 and the destinies of the Spaniards who crossed the border. The author, a historian of and participant in the 1939 exile, defended the prerogative of those who had lived history to tell it: the book's title countered any attempts by those who were not there to recount the experiences of the war. In the prologue, the novelist Manuel Vázquez Montalbán wrote that "el libro adquiere en ocasiones niveles de epopeya no enjundiosa, casi de relato de aventuras, avaladas por la realidad" (Pons Prades 14).[4] Far from a criticism, Vázquez Montalbán commented that this style of writing resulted in "[u]n libro estimulante porque evidencia que, en las situaciones más comprometidas, más acosadas, la dignidad humana aporta una fuerza extraordinaria y es capaz de convertirse en un factor de cambio histórico" (Pons Prades 14).[5] Nevertheless, a historical text that borders on epic adventure story is a far cry from the apolitical chronicle of the past one might expect of a historian. Yet Vázquez Montalbán's assessment captured the ethos of a decade's worth of popular histories published on the subject of Spaniards deported to Nazi camps. Eschewing a rote accounting of the facts, these texts invited history's participants to weigh in on their experiences, crafting high drama out of the narrative. As a consequence, facts were at times cast aside in favour of the thrill of the firsthand perspective of a horrendous spectacle.

This style of writing was not confined to Spain in the 1970s, a decade that brought to prominence Hunter S. Thompson's "gonzo" brand of New Journalism in the United States and a seemingly endless parade of mass-market accounts of the Holocaust in Europe.[6] These splashy paperbacks coloured the early histories of the Spaniards in Mauthausen while bringing them more attention and a larger audience than they would have garnered otherwise. Nevertheless, they challenged the reader to tease out fact from embellishment, weaving together a historical timeline with the biased perceptions of their authors. Along with Pons Prades' entry, other books on Spaniards in Mauthausen published in Spain in the 1970s skirted the line between novel and testimony. Javier Alfaya's *Españoles bajo el III Reich* (*Spaniards under the Third Reich*, 1970) blended historiography and archival source material with the unedited testimony of Ricardo Rico, a survivor of Gusen. Antonio Aznar's *Mauthausen: exterminio de los españoles* (*Mauthausen: Extermination of the Spaniards*, 1976) was a novelistic approach to the memories of the Spanish deportees, as a survivor recounted a compatriot's last days in Mauthausen to the man's parents. Mariano Constante and his memoirs landed amid this atmosphere of adventure and drama, turning him into the controversial "original" Spanish Mauthausen survivor of the 1970s.

A native of Aragón, Mariano Constante Campo was a young Republican sergeant when he crossed the border into France in 1939. Like many other Spanish exiles, he joined a French work detail (*Compagnies de travailleurs étrangers* or CTE) to escape the miserable living conditions in the Septfonds internment camp, but was soon captured as a prisoner of war after the Germans breached the Maginot Line. He was deported to Mauthausen from *Stalag* XVII-A in Kaisersteinbruch on 7 April 1941 (Bermejo and Checa, *Libro memorial* 122), and was active in the communist clandestine resistance movement inside the camp. He was only 25 when he was liberated from Mauthausen on 5 May 1945. Living in exile in France, Constante published two accounts of Mauthausen in 1969 and 1971. The first, written with his fellow Spanish Mauthausen survivor Manuel Razola, was a collection of survivor testimonies interwoven with the personal accounts of the two authors. *Triangle bleu: Les républicains espagnols à Mauthausen, 1940–1945* was published in France in 1969 and in Spain as *Triángulo azul: los republicanos españoles en Mauthausen, 1940–1945* (*Blue Triangle: The Spanish Republicans in Mauthausen,*

1940–1945) a decade later. In Spain, the book was billed as a "reportaje histórico" ("historical report," Razola and Campo back cover) and included a strident political bias favouring the communists in Mauthausen. Although this text was Constante's first attempt to capture his version of the camp, it was not the first effort a Spanish reading public would have seen. That would have been Constante's second publication: *Les années rouges: de Guernica à Mauthausen* (*The Red Years: From Guernica to Mauthausen*), published in France in 1971 and in Spain as *Los años rojos: españoles en los campos nazis* (*The Red Years: Spaniards in the Nazi Camps*) in 1974.

Los años rojos was the first of three memoirs Constante published before his death in 2010. Like the first-person accounts of Mauthausen that preceded and followed it, Constante blended personal anecdotes with historical information. The author's own experiences – particularly those that were not corroborated by his fellow deportees or historians – are impossible to verify. His written testimony was subjective, prone to exaggeration and lapses in memory, while also providing details that the historical record has upheld. Constante emphasized above all the collective power and work of the Spanish Republicans inside Mauthausen in *Los años rojos*, providing examples that many of his fellow deportees supported in their own memoirs. Yet he placed himself and his efforts with the Spanish communist resistance at the centre of the narrative, depicting himself as a figure of utmost importance within the clandestine prisoner organization and inside the camp in general. The extent to which Constante aggrandized his role in the resistance would only be fully understood later, as other Mauthausen survivors started to add their testimony to the corpus and as historians unravelled the experiences that only a few would survive and desire to tell. Constante's star faded as the stories of other Mauthausen survivors began to eclipse his own. Yet at the moment that Constante's earliest memoir was published in Spain, the year before Franco died, it was the first of its kind: Antonio Sinca Vendrell's personalized historical text took another six years to reach a Spanish audience and Constante's collection of testimony authored with Razola another five. As such, Constante's first autobiographical account of Mauthausen stands out in the trajectory of the genre.

In a warning that opened the French edition of this memoir, Constante excused himself as a non-professional writer who was merely relying on his memories of a distant past: "Ce récit a été écrit d'après mes souvenirs, d'après de ma mère et d'après des notes prises en 1945.

J'ai tout classé par ordre chronologique. Je ne suis pas un écrivain" (*Les années rouges* n.p.).[7] This apology was removed from the 1974 Spanish edition, an indication that Constante's confidence in his authorial voice had grown. The author composed three memoirs, two co-written volumes, and a single-authored collection of memories of his Aragonian compatriots on the topic of the Spanish deportees to Mauthausen throughout his life.[8] Moreover, he appeared in the Spanish press and on television with increasing frequency throughout the 1970s, acting as something of a self-appointed spokesman for the Spanish ex-deportees. As Constante's self-confidence expanded through the decade, so too did his perceived stature among his fellow Spaniards in Mauthausen.

Constante later defended his presence at the centre of these texts and in the thick of history: he viewed himself as a man whom destiny had chosen to record and remember what he called the "Holocausto español" ("Spanish Holocaust") for those who were unable to do so (*Republicanos aragoneses* 7):[9]

> Nunca busqué el ser un 'mandamás' ni un 'tiralevitas' para obtener mandatos directivos que hicieron resaltar mis cargos y responsabilidades. En España, y fuera de ella, tuve la suerte, el honor sería más justo decir, que siempre fueron mis compañeros los que me designaron para dirigir organizaciones tanto militares como civiles, clandestinas o legales, para defender nuestros ideales, nuestras luchas, nuestros deberes y nuestros derechos morales y físicos. ¿Adquirí por eso notoriedad? No la busqué. (8)[10]

Although the persona of Mariano Constante was a constant presence in his body of work – even in texts that appeared to be impartial historical accounts – the author argued that he lent credibility to the testimony and accounts of others: "No es por vanidad el mezclar actividades personales con las de los compañeros oscenses; sólo así pueden llegar a ser comprendidas ciertas situaciones dificilísimas y casi increíbles. Mi participación en todos los momentos la considero necesario para darle mejor credibilidad a todo lo expuesto" (*Republicanos aragoneses* 16).[11] Constante's defence of his ubiquity in the many texts he authored and co-authored throughout the 1970s was patronizing to his fellow deportees, some two dozen of whom eventually wrote their own memoirs. In addition, the argument that he lent "credibility" to other accounts became problematic when Constante's own credibility was called into question. The historian David Wingeate Pike wrote, with some hyperbole, that "where exaggeration and fabrication are concerned, no writer on Mauthausen has matched Constante, whose distortion of the facts has left him despised by his compatriots" (*Spaniards in the Holocaust* xiv). Benito Bermejo also observed that, although Constante was one of the most prolific writers to survive Mauthausen, he caused some rancor among his fellow survivors because of the "excés de protagonisme per part seva, que sembla que ha estat a tot arreu (i a vegades, explícitament, gairebé ho pretén)" (*El fotògraf de l'horror* 121).[12] The tangled web of contemporary Mauthausen survivor testimony and memoir was, for better or for worse, inaugurated by Constante's first memoir.

Los años rojos began on 18 June 1936, with the first shots of the Spanish Civil War. A teenager at the time, Constante was nevertheless at the centre of the micro-conflict in the northern Spanish town of Huesca. His father was a socialist-leaning schoolteacher who fled to the mountains. His mother was detained shortly thereafter. Constante ended up following a different trajectory than the rest of his family, who remained in Spain after the conflict. The young Constante, as a Republican sergeant, trod a familiar route into exile as the Republican defeat became imminent: from French internment camps to a CTE to a German *Stalag*. When the Second World War broke out in September 1939, Constante professed that the Spaniards saw it coming: "Decir que esto nos sorprendió a los españoles sería mentir. Sin ser estrategas, ni políticos profesionales, hacía tiempo que habíamos previsto que la política de agresión de la Alemania hitleriana se desenvolvía de tal forma que, un día u otro, se lanzaría contra las naciones que se llamaban 'defensoras de la libertad'" (*Los años rojos* 57 [1974]).[13] Somehow, in the midst of his deportation odyssey, Constante claimed to have made observations that would only have been available with decades of hindsight.

Constante asserted that, although he changed his name and other identifying information upon entering the *Stalag*, the German Gestapo "me contaron mi vida con más detalles de los que yo era capaz de recordar" (*Los años rojos* 57 [1974]) when they interrogated him.[14] Indeed, the Germans would not have been able to obtain such detailed information about the activities of the Spanish prisoners during the Civil War without the collaboration of the Spanish government. An array of historians and investigative journalists agree that Franco was not only aware of the fate of Spanish Republicans in France and Germany, but that he was complicit in their deportation to concentration camps.[15] The Gestapo had access to files on the activities of the deportees during the Spanish Civil War, "que no podien haver obtingut sense la col·laboració de les autoritats espanyoles" (Toran, *Vida i mort* 95).[16]

Constante was deported to Mauthausen, arriving on 2 April 1941. In the *Stalags*, he observed that the Spaniards "[t]eníamos desacuerdos, desde luego, pero, frente al enemigo común, nuestra unidad era mucho más fuerte que en España" (*Los años rojos* 102 [1974]).[17] In Mauthausen, this sense of unity among countrymen only increased, giving Constante fortitude: "me sorprendía ver la dignidad con que nuestros compatriotas hacían frente a la adversidad ... Y la solidaridad era admirable. Éramos sostenidos hasta el final por los que aún se podían sostener" (128).[18] Constante was initially "protected" by a German *Kapo* and given the task of cleaning barracks, then rose to the rank of *ordenanza*, or porter, for the SS because of his German-language skills.[19] He focused, too, on describing the ways in which the Spanish clandestine organization grew and developed, fulfilling its goal of replacing the German *Kapos* who were liquidated and achieving what Constante called the Spaniard's "tela de araña [que] se hallaba bastante extendida" (149) into Mauthausen's administrative offices.[20]

Constante placed himself in the middle of this ever-widening underground Spanish resistance movement. The author recounted a series of extraordinary events in which he risked his life to advance the Spanish cause: secretly listening to the news on an SS radio, translating a Russian newspaper into German and Spanish, writing the Russian translation on the "Welcome Liberators" banner, fighting fleeing SS on the shores of the Danube River during the confusing period just after the camp's liberation, and travelling to meet with Russian and Swiss officials in the hopes of securing an exile route for the Spaniards into France. However, Constante only briefly mentioned what would in his later accounts become a source of division among his fellow survivors: the resistance movement's participation in the safeguarding of duplicate photos and negatives. In *Los años rojos*, Constante limited himself to crediting "Paco Boix" and Antoni García for "recuperating" SS photos, and wrote that the photos were "guardadas por los miembros de la organización española" (142 [1974]).[21] Later, during the days leading up to the camp's liberation, Constante wrote that the Poschacher boys, "los jóvenes españoles deportados – unos cuarenta" ("the young Spanish deportees – about forty," 174 [1974]), worked to smuggle photos and other evidence of Nazi crimes out of the camp. In successive memoirs, Constante would give himself more credit for saving the photos, much to the consternation of other Mauthausen survivors who remembered events differently.

Constante fleshed out his first Mauthausen memoir with a number of experiences that were unique among survivor narratives. For instance, the author lingered on the latent homophobia in Mauthausen and his own "aversión tremenda a los homosexuales" ("tremendous aversion to homosexuals," *Los años rojos* 118 [1974]). He described successfully defending himself from the sexual advances of a *Kapo* in his barracks. These details, much like the proud assertions by other Mauthausen survivors that they fought and won the right to pay for the services of the camp's prostitutes, appear dated and prejudicial to the contemporary reader.[22] Homosexuality in the camp, however, was an issue that arose over and over again in memoirs published by Spanish Mauthausen survivors in the early 2000s. The Spaniards' homophobia and the explicit persecution of homosexuals by the Nazis presented an uncomfortable alliance between victim and persecutor in the camp. Constante's offhand comments highlighted the extent to which sexuality among the Spanish Republicans in Mauthausen has been marginalized or ignored, an uncomfortable reality that survivors and historians of the Spanish experience alike have been reluctant to investigate thoroughly.

Constante also captured differences and similarities between the Spaniards and the Jews in Mauthausen. In a particularly memorable scene, a transport of Jews arrived speaking an antiquated Spanish, which Constante excitedly called "el castellano de Cervantes!" ("the Spanish of Cervantes!" *Los años rojos* 137 [1974]). Constante was delighted to discover that they were Sephardic Jews. When they were exterminated en masse the next day, however, Constante was so distraught he considered suicide. He recognized that the Jews, unlike the Spaniards, were subject to a rapid extermination: "La diferencia de los judíos con respecto a nosotros era que la exterminación nuestra se hacía de manera lenta, metódica, aprovechando nuestro trabajo, la de ellos era total y rápida" (132).[23] Like Joaquim Amat-Piniella before him, Constante acknowledged the profound difference between the slave labour of Spanish prisoners and the extermination of Jewish prisoners in Mauthausen: he was, consequently, a witness to the Holocaust.

Many of the details Constante narrated about Mauthausen in *Los años rojos* became part of the collective memory of the Spanish survivors, recounted in memoir after memoir. It was as unclear in Constante's account as it would be in later memoirs what the author witnessed himself and what he learned secondhand. Yet in the Spain of the early 1970s, the author's rendering of the harrowing experiences of Spaniards in Mauthausen was new. *Los años rojos* was the first Spanish Mauthausen memoir published in Spain since Rodríguez del Risco's series of articles in 1946. Unlike the earlier obscure account, Constante's was edited by a popular publishing house and reached a new generation of readers. As a reviewer in the *La Vanguardia* newspaper described it, "[e]l libro nos pone los pelos de punta y nos recuerda hasta que punto puede llegar la bestialidad humana" ("Los años rojos" 61 [1974]).[24] This comment could just as easily capture a horror film as a memoir recounting atrocities committed by the Nazis. The novelist Antonio Muñoz Molina described the author's role in this project as: "el joven Mariano Constante se ve arrastrado por la gran riada de los acontecimientos históricos, pero igual que ellos también actúa por un impulso de su voluntad, por un deseo entre cándido y temerario de unirse a una lucha que considera justa" (*Los años rojos* 11 [2005]).[25] *Los años rojos* is positioned halfway between a historical thriller and a publication that catapults its author into the fight to preserve what was then a scarcely acknowledged history. The novelist Javier Cercas characterizes the 1970s in Spain as a period when "ni siquiera la izquierda consideraba que la historia de la segunda guerra mundial, el Holocausto y los campos nazis formasen del todo parte de la historia española" (218).[26] Constante's first memoir began an uphill battle to include the experiences of the Spanish deportees in this larger historical context.

After his initial Spanish publication, Constante's voice became more authoritative. He authored or co-authored three more books in quick succession after *Los años rojos*, each adding to his creation myth as the Spanish Mauthausen proto-survivor. *Yo fui ordenanza de los SS (I Was a Porter for the SS)* was the second instalment in Constante's trilogy of memoirs, published in 1976. *Los cerdos del comandante: españoles de los campos de exterminio nazis (The Commander's Pigs: Spaniards in the Nazi Extermination Camps)*, a collection of narrated testimonies of Spanish Nazi concentration camp survivors written with Pons Prades, was published in 1978. Finally, the Spanish translation of Constante and Razola's curated collection of survivor testimonies originally published in France in 1969, *Triángulo azul: los republicanos españoles en Mauthausen, 1940–1945*, was released in Spain in 1979. Constante was a near-ubiquitous presence through the decade as the history of the Spaniards in Mauthausen started to gain an audience. As one *La Vanguardia* reporter wrote at the time, Constante was considered the "piedra filosofal para todo aquel que quiera saber algo acerca de la peripecia de nuestros hermanos republicanos que fueron objeto de la locura nazi" (Monegal, "Mariano Constante" 27).[27] As the decade wore on, the thousands of other Spanish Mauthausen survivors were overshadowed by Constante's desire to be at the forefront.

Yo fui ordenanza de los SS is a tale of solidarity, adventure, comradery, terror, and even humour, as experienced by the author during his four years in Mauthausen. Constante's second memoir is a page-turner, among the most engaging of Mauthausen survivor accounts. The cover illustration for the first paperback edition of *Yo fui ordenanza de los SS* clearly advertised the dramatic nature of the book:[28] it featured an imposing Nazi, teeth bared, in full SS uniform, including a prominent swastika armband, a whip, and a red feathered cape standing authoritatively on the skeletal heads of a flaming parade of hundreds of prisoners in striped uniforms. Constante was at once a reliable and an unreliable narrator in this volume, yet only the author knew when he was portraying his experiences accurately and when he was embellishing. By the mid-1970s, Constante had shed his modesty about his writing abilities, playing with a narrative timeline and recounting episodes that he did not witness in *Yo fui ordenanza de los SS* with the same amount of detail as the episodes he did witness. He tried to psychoanalyze his captors, exploring why, in his opinion, National Socialism became so powerful. The subjective nature of this account and Constante's hubris compromised both its standing as testimony – in that the author included information he gleaned secondhand but did not witness himself – and its historical authority. Nevertheless, it remained a foundational example of the genre of the Mauthausen memoir. Constante's sleight-of-hand in recounting "his" memories – while actually relaying the memories and experiences of others – became a trope in dozens of later texts. Perhaps more important, it made for an engaging read.

Constante expanded some of the same stories he recounted in *Los años rojos*, promoting his own involvement in the clandestine activities in the camp to a greater extent in his second memoir. The titles of these two books convey their subtle differences: *Los años rojos* was about the collective struggle of the Spanish "reds"; *Yo fui ordenanza de los SS* was about Mariano Constante's first-person experience and his individual role. A reviewer noted that, although *Yo fui ordenanza de los SS* did not include a substantially different account from Constante's first memoir, "sí abunda en los pormenores y letra pequeña de las inhumanas condiciones de vida en el campo y en los vericuetos y estrategias que habían de sortearse para poder conseguir algún cargo de ordenanza o fámulo de los SS, y así poder subsistir" (Monegal, "Noche y niebla" 39).[29] The reviewer called Constante "aquel republicano inmarchitable" ("that everlasting Republican," Monegal, "Noche y niebla" 39), whose fame as a deportee and Mauthausen survivor had, by 1976, become unmatched.

Pons Prades, in his introduction to *Yo fui ordenanza*, reminded the reader that the author sought to provide a panoramic overview of the Spanish experience of Mauthausen in his first memoir. In the second, Pons Prades described how Constante introduced the reader to "la misma entraña de la organización nazi creadora y explotadora del infierno concentracionario alemán" that operated as a foil to "el grupo nacional español" (*Yo fui ordenanza* 12).[30] Of his Spanish compatriots in the camp, Constante wrote that "[e]xcluidos los judíos – que fueron exterminados todos – nosotros éramos, junto a los soviéticos, el grupo nacional más castigado debido a que fuimos los primeros deportados políticos del Oeste europeo que entramos en aquel universo concentracionario y a haber sufrido los métodos de exterminación durante los primeros años de victorias nazis" (289).[31] Although there can be no doubt that the Spaniards suffered grave losses in Mauthausen, Constante's hyperbole challenged other national groups to defend their victimization, a tactless game. Particularly because Constante's survival was predicated on one of the many privileges afforded the Spaniards in the second half of their imprisonment, this statement reads as overwrought and unnecessarily competitive. But the battle between good and evil captured in this passage – the Spaniards versus the Nazis – sustained Constante's narrative. Although the forces of "good" triumphed in the end, the fact that so few Spanish deportees survived to witness their liberation, and then remained in the shadows of Spain's history during the 1970s, complicated their victory.

One of the distinguishing features of Constante's second memoir was his minute, armchair psychologist study of the daily activities, customs, and dispositions of members of the Mauthausen SS. Given his privileged position as a porter for the Mauthausen commander Franz Ziereis's secretary, Constante was able to observe the SS in what can only be called their "natural habitat," inside their barracks and among their fellow SS. Constante's "Impresiones sobre la mentalidad y actividades de los SS" (*Yo fui ordenanza* 85), as one of his chapters was titled, provided a portrait of the depravity and dehumanization he associated with the Nazis.[32] The lives of the SS, in Constante's estimation, "estaba totalmente alejada de cualquier realidad humana."[33] What was more, they lived "al margen de todos los principios fundados por y para los hombres" (86).[34] In one instance, Constante described how the SS treated "Carlos," a black man from Barcelona, as a freak of nature.

Constante considered the members of the SS the aberrations, not the Barcelonés, whom the Spaniards called, affectionately, "Nuestro Carlos" ("Our Carlos") and shepherded alive through to Mauthausen's liberation day (90–2). Constante came to realize that his attempts at understanding the underlying psyche of the Nazis were fruitless: "las [reacciones] de los SS jamás pude comprenderlas" (88); though it did not stop him from trying.[35]

Constante organized the narration of his second memoir as a reflection on his brutal first years in Mauthausen before becoming a protected prisoner at the service of the SS. In the spring of 1943, he recalled an SS ordering "'¡Los rojos españoles que saben hablar el alemán que salgan de las filas y se presenten ante mi!'" (*Yo fui ordenanza* 16).[36] Then an SS yelled for Constante by number: "'¡El rojo español número cuatro mil quinientos ochenta y cuatro del *block* trece, que se presente aquí inmediatamente ... !'" (17; emphasis in the original).[37] In his confusion at having been singled out, Constante wondered, betraying his self-esteem, "¿Habría descubierto que yo era uno de los dirigentes de la organización clandestina española?" (17).[38] He was called, in fact, to serve as an orderly or porter to the SS because he spoke German. Thus Constante began his dual role as one of the communist leaders of the Spanish resistance and one of the protected Spanish prisoners, afforded a job that allowed him access and privilege. The overall narration of *Yo fui ordenanza* benefited from the thirty-one years of hindsight Constante had accrued since his liberation from Mauthausen. Although the reader never encounters the present day in Constante's book, it is clear that this memoir took into account the intervening decades, during which time certain events that occurred in Mauthausen assumed additional significance.

One of these events was the clandestine copying and salvaging of hundreds of photographs and negatives from the Mauthausen photo lab. The story of Antoni García, Francesc Boix, and the Poschacher boys who printed, saved, and smuggled the illicit photos out of the camp has been perhaps the most enduring Mauthausen myth, recounted by an array of Spanish survivors (chapter 1). Constante leapt into the legend. In the version of the events included in *Los años rojos*, all credit was due to García, Boix, and the Poschacher boys; in the version he included in *Yo fui ordenanza*, Constante himself was a protagonist at the centre of the photo smuggling ring. In fact, Constante claimed that at the very moment he was called to serve the SS, he had dozens of photo negatives sewn into the shoulder pads of his jacket. The gravity of this juxtaposition was not lost on the author years later: "los clisés que un día servirían de testimonio histórico, y que precisamente habían sido extraídos a los SS por Boix y García, por iniciativa del primero" (22) were on Constante's person.[39] Boix and Joan de Diego were eventually able to save Constante's jacket and the photographic treasure it contained. The author proudly continued to wear the jacket, secretly pleased that the SS were unaware that "el ordenanza, que pasaba junto a ellos dieciséis horas al día, llevaba cosida en los forros de su chaqueta la prueba irrefutable de sus crímenes" (26).[40] Constante also described his role as one of the go-betweens in the delivery of the negatives from the clandestine group to the Poschacher boys, which occurred during soccer games when the boys were permitted inside the main camp and a hand-off was possible (267–9).

Constante's claims that he was a main actor in the saving of negatives from the Mauthausen photography lab has not been corroborated by other Mauthausen survivors involved in the actions or by historians. Moreover, it contradicted a more humble recounting of these same events in Constante's first memoir. Nevertheless, Constante continued to consider himself integral to this collective action. He recounted trying to join Boix at the Mauthausen trial in 1946 but being thwarted by the American authorities in his attempt to secure a passport (*Yo fui ordenanza* 292–3; *Republicanos aragoneses* 288). Boix did seem to have given Constante many of the prints and negatives still in his possession before his death, in that Constante has been cited by a number of Mauthausen historians as their photographic source.[41] But Constante's opinion of Boix had fluctuated yet again by the time he published his third memoir, *Tras Mauthausen* (*After Mauthausen*). In this 2007 volume, Constante once again contradicted his earlier accounts, relieving Boix of his hero status, praising García for his actions, and changing his own role from smuggler of photos to part of the team that recovered the photos after Mauthausen's liberation.[42] While he chided the authors of other accounts for their loose accountability to the truth – "¡Los mentirosos y falsificadores de la historia deberían tener mayor pudor y vergüenza y no inventar cuentos llenos de embustes!" (*Tras Mauthausen* 42) – Constante's own version of these events is ultimately difficult to pin down.[43]

Many of Constante's tales brim with bravado, and decoding the extent to which he was the protagonist, or merely part of the supporting cast, of clandestine actions in the camp is nearly impossible. Regardless, the solidarity of the Spaniards in the camp is a central mythical motif in the book. Friendships among Constante's countrymen had almost miraculous powers: "¡Eran capaces de levantar la moral a un muerto!" (51).[44] As Constante, Joan Pagès, Boix, de Diego, and other Spaniards began to infiltrate Mauthausen's inner offices, the author described himself and his fellow "'enchufados'" as like "un gran pulpo: un cuerpo, la organización clandestina, con tentáculos, cada uno de nosotros, que empezaba a llegar a todas partes" (51).[45] As the Spanish octopus stretched its tentacles into every facet of the camp's operation, its feats of resistance got more daring.

The Spaniards became experts at "organizing" food – a common camp euphemism for stealing – both to feed their sick or injured compatriots, but also to barter with the SS. Constante recounted his expertise in extracting extra food rations from the SS for whom he worked. In one tale, Constante recalled how one of the SS asked him to get him a good white shirt in exchange for tobacco, saying that "'los españoles sois los más 'bandidos' del campo. ¡Los españoles sois capaces de robarle a uno la camisa que lleva puesta!'" (*Yo fui ordenanza* 131).[46] This exchange is one of the moments of levity in a narration that includes dark descriptions of the cruelty and depravity of the Nazis. While this touch of humour makes Constante's book a particularly dynamic, readable tale, it also distances the Spanish experience from our common perceptions of "serious" Holocaust narratives. In his exaggerations and comical asides, Constante trades in a Holocaust trivialization similar in tone to Carlos Rodríguez del Risco's counterfactual account.

Yo fui ordenanza de los SS is full of examples of the ingenuity and solidarity of the Spanish resistance group. In fact, Constante gave what some Mauthausen survivors have countered was a false impression that all of the Spaniards in the camp formed a united front. Jacint Carrió i Vilaseca, for instance, argued in his survivor memoir that the Spanish clandestine group did not have as far a reach in Mauthausen as Constante has asserted: "S'ha parlat molt de l'activitat política clandestina deins dels camps d'extermini. És cert que existia però ben poca influència va tenir sobre el dia a dia de la majoria. Les discussions ideològiques eren cosa dels presoners situats en llocs clau, ben alimentats" (89).[47] Constante, as one of these well-fed and well-positioned prisoners, observed from a privileged vantage point. He claimed throughout *Yo fui ordenanza*, however, that the Spanish clandestine group's efforts to better the situations of its countrymen only began to bear fruit in 1943, and that he was as abused, starved, and mistreated as any other Spanish Mauthausen prisoner.

The hyperbole and imprecision saturating Constante's memoir had the effect of piquing the ire of fellow Mauthausen survivors. Constante's insistence on the primary role of the communists within the camp's resistance group aggravated political divisions present during the Spanish Civil War and subsequent exile (Toran, *Joan de Diego* 278). In response to Constante's request for clarification about particular events in the camp and figures pertaining to Spanish victims, de Diego responded with a terse: "no insisto sobre el numero de los que pasaron y fueron asesinados en el [campo], lo importante es haber demodtrado [*sic*] con pruebas los crimenes cometidos por los SS, sin olvidar la complicidad del regimen franquista" ("Letter to Mariano Constante" 1; lack of accentuation in the original).[48] In one article, Constante claimed that sixteen thousand Spaniards entered Mauthausen and that sixteen hundred survived, a wildly inaccurate estimate. He also wrote that he was among the only fifteen or sixteen Spaniards who were afforded privileged positions in Mauthausen, when the number was much greater (Monegal "Mariano Constante"). This particular assertion drew Casimir Climent out of his "silencio habitual" to chastise Constante for numbers that are "completamente imaginarias, por no decir falsas" (Climent Sarrión).[49] Climent perhaps captured his fellow deportees' disdain of Constante's endless overstatements best when he wrote that "Constante escrib[e] libros en los que él se pone como ejemplo, y en los que él dice que lo ha hecho todo en el campo y que ha servido tanto a un fregado como a un barrido. Por desgracia es verdad, él lo ha hecho todo, incluso algo que la mayoría de españoles no hemos hecho" (Climent Sarrión).[50] That is, the majority of the Spanish survivors of Mauthausen did not claim to be heroes, as Constante did time and time again.[51]

Constante's contradictions and heroic tales also raised doubts among historians of the Spanish deportation. Bermejo cited Constante's changing opinions of Boix as a source of distrust: "la seva relació personal amb Boix no havia estat tan bona com algun escrit seu havia fet suposar" (*El fotògraf de l'horror* 122).[52] Pike went even further to demonstrate his lack of confidence in Constante's accounts. In both *Los años rojos* and *Yo fui ordenanza*, Constante described an encounter with a particularly predatory SS nicknamed "La Niña" for his homosexual tendencies. According to Constante, "La Niña" tortured the author by repeatedly trying to drown him in a well. At one point, the SS officer:

se puso a aplastarme los dedos de las manos, haciendo girar sobre ellos sus botas herradas, como si estuviese aplastando un reptil. Al mismo tiempo que recordaba aquello me parecía volver a sentir el dolor pasado y mirándome los dedos pude comprobar que aquello no era una simple pesadilla: habían quedado deformados para siempre en aquella triste jornada del invierno de 1941... (*Yo fui ordenanza* 63)[53]

Pike, thoroughly sceptical of Constante's memories, took it upon himself to disprove this particular episode. In an encounter with the author in a hotel airport in France in 1997, Pike surreptitiously examined Constante's hands and proved to his own satisfaction that neither one was deformed (*Spaniards in the Holocaust* xiv).

But Pike's indictment of Constante extended beyond this scene. In the Spanish version of his history of the Spaniards in Mauthausen, Pike wrote:

Es triste que Mariano Constante, que podría haber hecho una útil contribución a la historia de Mauthausen, optara por la distorsión y la falsedad, invistiéndose con el papel de otros, con el resultado de que muchos de sus compatriotas, que sabían muy bien que la historia de Mauthausen exige un relato plano, sin adornos, miraran sus escritos con desprecio. (*Españoles en el holocausto* 18)[54]

Of course, this unadorned, "flat" story would presumably not have attracted readers in the same way as Constante's heroic and hyperbolic adventure tales have over the years. For Pike, these exaggerations were fodder for Holocaust revisionists, and thus posed a danger to the historical record and collective memory (*Spaniards in the Holocaust* xv). For Constante, at least according to Pike, they were his livelihood (xiv). In the 1970s, as the collective memory of the Spanish experience of Mauthausen was in its infancy, Constante was the most visible and productive of the survivors, publishing a book at least every two years between 1974 and 1979. What is at issue is whether his dissimulations were detrimental to the larger issue of recuperating the experiences of the Spaniards in Mauthausen for Spain's collective memory. Along with Montserrat Roig, Constante kept the Spanish deportees in the public's consciousness during the years immediately before and after Franco's death: he prevented them from disappearing entirely from Spain's historical landscape. Although his tendency to inflate facts and figures to suit his personal narrative are well established, he was still unquestionably a witness of Mauthausen who survived for four years inside the camp's walls.[55] This bona fide does not erase the problem of his egocentrism and lapses in judgment, but it does advocate for his inclusion in any serious consideration of the body of representation produced by and about the Spaniards of Mauthausen.[56]

Underground Images: Llorenç Soler's Documentary
Sobrevivir en Mauthausen (1975)

The earliest moving images of Mauthausen were contained in an eight-minute film recorded by the US Signal Corps soon after the liberation of the camp in 1945. This black and white film documented the aftermath of the Nazis' program of annihilation in Mauthausen and Gusen. The camera panned over the recognizable main gate of Mauthausen, cutting to scenes of Austrian townspeople tossing emaciated bodies onto horse-drawn carts as though they were sacks of potatoes. Close-up shots of the decomposing forms of prisoners were juxtaposed with footage of the walking dead: skeletal men being tended by fellow survivors. The only sound in this otherwise silent picture was the oral testimony of the American Jack Taylor, a US Navy lieutenant who appeared before the camera flanked by fellow survivors in front of the flapping welcome banner the Spaniards had hung across prisoners' gate. As Taylor described his capture by the Gestapo and being denied POW status, he called Mauthausen "an extermination camp, the worst in Germany" (Donovan, Kellogg, and Stevens). This cinematic document was immediate in all senses of the word: filmed mere days after the Nazis ceased their malicious killing operations, it offered frank and intimate moving images of the individual and collective toll the Nazis exacted at the Mauthausen complex. Taylor's on-camera placement of Mauthausen in Germany instead of Austria also showed the dislocation of the camp's survivors. Although the film was entered into evidence for the prosecution at the Nuremberg trials, it was not widely released. Thirty years later, however, it served as an epilogue to the first Spanish documentary to expose the horrors of Mauthausen.

The first widely known documentary film that captured images of Mauthausen was Alain Resnais' *Nuit et brouillard* (*Night and Fog*) from 1955.[57] This French film intermingled contemporary footage with "found" images. Many of the black and white photos threaded throughout the film were taken and saved by Francesc Boix and other Spaniards in Mauthausen, though they remained uncredited.[58] Resnais' film presented a decidedly subjective perspective of the Holocaust: the narrator never explicitly mentioned the Nazis' program of extermination of the

Jews. Instead, *Nuit et brouillard* framed the concentration camps against a background of the victimization of international prisoners and resistance fighters. At one point in the film, over images of the iconic Mauthausen quarry steps and photos of the prisoners hauling stone, the voice-over narration intoned: "Trois mille Espagnols sont morts en construisant ces étapes menant à la carriére de Mauthausen" (Resnais).[59] This brief mention constituted the widest international acknowledgment to date of the presence of Spanish deportees in Mauthausen.

Although *Nuit et brouillard* was not publicly screened inside dictatorial Spain in the 1950s and was banned at the 1956 Cannes Film Festival, it was shown and distributed across Europe in the mid-1950s (Dreyfus 40). In 1968, the French Amicale de Mauthausen offered a copy of the film to the Amical de Mauthausen in Barcelona, where it was shown in 1968 (Toran, *Amical de Mauthausen* 31). Joshua Francis Hirsch argues that the film is the first example of post-traumatic cinema, "draw[ing] attention not just to the past but to the traumatic effects of the past on us – its deformation of historical memory – and the necessity of working through those effects" (*Afterimage* 61). Examining the first Spanish documentary to delve into the subject of the deportation of Spanish Republicans to Nazi concentration camps through the lens of *Nuit et brouillard* demonstrates a similar process at work in the exchange between trauma and memory in a film that deals with a parallel topic. Twenty years later Llorenç Soler, like Resnais, adopted a "fragmentation of temporality, the restriction of point of view to the subjectivity of the witness, and formal and historical self-consciousness" (Hirsch, *Afterimage* 62) in his attempt to depict the Spanish experience of Mauthausen on film.[60] Although his film attained neither the reach nor the artistic merit of Resnais' celebrated feature, Soler inaugurated a visual approach to the topic that continues to reverberate in present-day Spain.

Sobrevivir en Mauthausen (*Survival in Mauthausen*) begins with a title card that immediately situates the film in a larger historical milieu:

> Muy cerca del final de la II Guerra Mundial, el Campo de concentración de Mauthausen, es el último liberado por las tropas aliadas. En este lugar, víctimas de la barbarie nazi, murieron – oficialmente – 127.000 deportados pertenecientes a diversas nacionalidades, entre ellos unos 7.000 ex-combatientes del Ejército Republicano Español. (Soler, *Sobrevivir en Mauthausen*)[61]

Conspicuously absent from this background information was any indication of the Franco regime's role in deporting Spaniards to Nazi camps. Soler began filming *Sobrevivir en Mauthausen* in late 1974, while Franco was still alive, the Amical de Mauthausen was illegal, and the filmmaker's passport had been confiscated due to his counter-government activities (Soler, *Los hilos secretos* 63). As such, the "historical self-consciousness" he manifested onscreen drew connections between the Spanish Civil War and the Second World War, but not between Franco and Hitler.

Soler was active in militant cinema circles in Barcelona during the dictatorship, focusing in particular on documenting transition-era Catalan society. The director has said that when he began this project, the topic of Spaniards in Nazi camps "era tabú y, en consecuencia, gozaba de la total ignorancia de la mayor parte de los españoles" (*Los hilos secretos* 61).[62] Although survivors broached their experiences in Mauthausen in a number of texts published in Spain beginning in 1945, we have seen that the topic nevertheless remained shrouded in secrecy. The first shot in *Sobrevivir en Mauthausen* visually captures this continued silencing: a man's silhouette, his face entirely obscured by shadow, against a washed-out white background. The first Spanish concentration camp survivor to appear on film is anonymous to such an extent that he seems to be part of a witness protection program. Soler filmed *Sobrevivir en Mauthausen* on a shoestring budget: the quality of the film was rough and the documentary at times evidenced amateur production techniques. Accordingly, the director has called *Sobrevivir en Mauthausen*, "un documental marginal, semiclandestino, rodado con escasos medios y desafiando los rigores de la censura franquista, condenado por ello a una existencia incierta y subterránea" (175).[63] As an example of Spanish militant cinema, however, Soler's film also found backchannels to evade Franco's censors and lend it revolutionary credibility (García-Merás 32).

These budget constraints, militant tendencies, and the undercurrent of fear of discovery that ran through the film were analogous to the decades-long ordeal the film's central figures had endured. The Spanish Mauthausen survivors were marginalized many times over: as exiled Spanish nationals rejected by the Franco regime, as concentration camp victims overshadowed by other national and racial groups, as survivors adrift in postwar Europe, and as emblems of Spain's collective memory overlooked in favour of the victims of the Spanish Civil War. "[A]quel grupo de supervivientes vivían en la marginación y en el olvido," the director wrote, like *Sobrevivir en Mauthausen* itself (Soler, *Los hilos secretos* 62).[64] Soler's documentary inhabited a similarly liminal space: created clandestinely and released under the radar of Franco's government, it lived an underground existence.

The man in shadow, who is never identified directly, is the Mauthausen survivor Joan Pagès.[65] The director threaded Pagès' testimony throughout the film, eventually bringing him out of the shadows, highlighting the deep grooves on his face and cutting to shots of his hands gesturing and holding a cigarette.[66] Pagès is the central figure in *Sobrevivir en Mauthausen*, joined by four other survivors who offer their testimony. After holding an equally central role in the clandestine resistance movement inside Mauthausen, Pagès returned to Spain, where he became the founding president of the Amical de Mauthausen.[67] He bore witness to the Spanish solidarity in the camp, demonstrating by his and his compatriots' mere presence before the cameras the effectiveness of the resistance movement in saving Spanish lives. They testified at length in the film about the formation, organization, and acts of resistance spearheaded by the Spaniards that allowed some prisoners to survive. Pagès described how members saved minuscule portions of their daily rations in an effort to aid the weaker prisoners among them. These and other actions, according to Pagès, resulted in a noticeable change in conditions in the camp and prestige for the Spaniards that also benefited prisoners of other nationalities. Pagès and the other witnesses thus restricted the film's thematic core mainly to their subjective memories of Spanish solidarity inside the camp. This subjectivity, identified by Hirsch as one of the tenets of post-traumatic cinema, excludes other equally pressing details from the Spanish experiences in Mauthausen. As we have seen in Constante's accounts and as we will see in Roig's historiography, however, at a charged moment of political transition in Spain, stories of conscientious objection and resistance like those in this militant film were particularly in demand.

Cutting among interview footage with these five Spanish and Catalan Mauthausen survivors – individually unidentified, but listed in the final credits – Soler weaved in tracking shots of present-day Mauthausen and scenes of Spanish urbanity.[68] This cinematic "fragmentation of temporality" (*Afterimage* 62) had a purpose that became clearer as the spectator began to comprehend the Spaniards' fight to survive in the camp juxtaposed with their invisibility in present-day Spain. As the camera panned across Mauthausen's walls, gates, and plazas, the physical space of the camp in the film became denuded, almost entirely devoid of human presence. This contrasted with the establishing shots of bustling Barcelona streets and costumed Nazis wrangling with staged prisoners in a theatrical production of Bertolt Brecht's *Terror y miseria del III Reich* (*Terror and Misery of the Third Reich*).[69] The difference between present-day Spain as lively and chaotic and present-day Mauthausen as dormant and inert introduced a metaphor that distinguished Soler's active recuperation of survivor testimony from the stagnant ignorance in Spain of the ex-deportees' plight. Despite Soler's efforts, the Spanish survivors' experiences seemed destined to remain buried in the quiet remove of the Austrian countryside.

The "formal self-consciousness" (Hirsch, *Afterimage* 62) in *Sobrevivir en Mauthausen*, in which the film's production constitutes an overt element of the narrative, veers away from the poetic questioning of *Nuit et brouillard*. Instead, Soler opted for a more coded message about performance: the director and the witnesses performed a version of the Spanish experience of Mauthausen onscreen. In a scene that combined the cinematic with the theatrical, Soler appeared riding in the passenger seat of a moving car as he clarified that the Brecht production that viewers glimpsed was only "una visión atenuada de aquella barbarie. Pero hoy todavía existen supervivientes que la sufieron en su propia carne. Su testimonio es imprescindible para conocer la verdad de los hechos" (*Sobrevivir en Mauthausen*).[70] That is, although by the 1970s the Holocaust and Nazism had become intermingled with diverse forms of entertainment, the survivors who described their ordeal were tangible proof of a reality that needed no dramatic enhancement. Moreover, the director's presence in the film – in a trench coat with a handheld microphone conducting interviews on a city street and in a moving vehicle, or appearing with film canisters and slide projectors conspicuously arranged in the background – underscored the performative quality of a filmmaker at risk, on the move, and conscious of his craft. Although one critique stated that Soler "ha desaparecido como autor" in the film ("has disappeared as author," Romaguera i Ramió and Soler de los Mártires 397), this was far from the truth. He laboured to be the Mauthausen survivors' collective memory incarnate in *Sobrevivir en Mauthausen*; his conspicuous efforts to make the Spanish survivors and himself visible in the documentary conversely accentuated the marginal existence of these men and their life stories in Franco's Spain.

Unable to provide a more direct accounting of the background and present-day situation of the ex-deportees in Spain for fear of censorship or reprisals from the Franco government, Soler used a set of now-familiar techniques to historically ground the film. He interspersed black and white photos of Nazi camps, Hitler, and the theatre of war – some of which were sourced, uncredited, from the collection saved by Boix – into the interviews. He acted as an on-camera narrator, highlighting his agency in the film's production while filling in context and details such as the location of Mauthausen relative to other Nazi concentration camps, the daily caloric value of the prisoners' diet in the camp, and the Nazis' program of "anulación de la personalidad, humilaciones, torturas físicas y morales, dejaciones y sadismo" against the prisoners.[71] And, in an effort to widen the scope of the film beyond descriptions of the Spanish solidarity in Mauthausen, Soler included more universal characterizations of Nazi abuses and cruelties. To this end, the director positioned the film as a localized account of Spaniards that nevertheless arrived at larger issues. In a voice-over narrating filmed courtroom scenes from the Nazi War Crimes Trials, Soler asked "¿Pero habrá algún tribunal de la historia capaz de juzgar en toda su magnitud el crimen colectivo de estas gentes? ¿Hay pruebas suficientes para ellos?" (Soler, *Sobrevivir en Mauthausen*).[72] Implicitly, the answer was no: the Nazis were never judged on par with the magnitude of their crimes; the evidence they left behind was never enough to indict all of them.

Sobrevivir en Mauthausen ends with a return to the first recorded images of Mauthausen from the US Signal Corps film. A projector rolls black and white footage of ex-prisoners grabbing potatoes from a supply truck, supporting gaunt and infirm fellow survivors, and walking past mounds of dead bodies. This is a film within a film: a construction of Mauthausen within another construction of Mauthausen, both designed with a particular purpose in mind. The Signal Corps film – "a specific moment in the vast process of destruction and breakdown" (Bathrick 290) – was created as evidence to indict the Nazis; Soler's documentary was created to demonstrate the heroism of, yet continued disregard for, the Spanish Republicans deported to Mauthausen. Both films were attempts to represent some kind of ultimate truth, one that so few were alive, willing, or able to describe.

Sobreviver en Mauthausen would never be widely released. Like other examples of Franco-era militant cinema, it would have been distributed primarily to university film clubs, neighbourhood associations, and the occasional liberal-minded parish church (García-Merás 32). Soon after the film was finalized in April 1975, it was screened for the 30th anniversary of the liberation of Mauthausen in the camp itself (Ríos Carratalá 45), and then, according to Soler, "se incorporó a los canales de difusión clandestina" (*Los hilos secretos* 64).[73] Relegated to back channels, this film has arguably had only a fraction of the number of viewers that

Nuit et brouillard had in the ensuing decades.[74] Nevertheless, *Sobrevivir en Mauthausen*, like its French predecessor, is a foundational Spanish film in the annals of representations of the deportation of non-Jews to Nazi concentration camps. It laboured to capture the original trauma of the deportation of Spaniards to Mauthausen and the contemporary trauma of living as a marginalized survivor of that experience. Twenty years later, a host of Spanish documentaries on the experience of the Nazi camps would reproduce a similar structure of survivor testimony intermingled with a subjective approach to the historical moment in the country's own version of post-traumatic cinema.

Soler took his cues from Resnais' documentary. In its juxtaposition of a clandestine past and present, *Sobrevivir en Mauthausen* carved out a niche for the unique story of the Spanish deportees, who may have been referenced in *Nuit et brouillard* but in reality claimed no space in the history of the Nazi deportation, the Holocaust, or the Second World War. The ex-deportees' memory of their trauma, thirty years after their liberation from Mauthausen, was necessarily coloured by their fragile political existence in Spain, the passage of time, and the difficulty remembering and describing events that took on an increased significance on the world stage with each passing decade. Although these fissures are invisible onscreen, they weigh on the narrative structure and visual content of the film. These same obstacles to resurrecting the memories of Mauthausen through survivor testimony were – at the same moment Soler was filming this documentary – presenting Montserrat Roig with similar challenges as she worked on her ambitious contribution to the collective memory of the Spaniards deported to Mauthausen.

Mauthausen "Discovered": Montserrat Roig's Historiography
Els catalans als camps nazis (1977)

Montserrat Roig was a young journalist only a few weeks away from publishing her first novel when she attended an event that would change her professional trajectory. Vicenzo Pappalettera, an Italian survivor of Mauthausen, and his co-author and son Luigi were in Barcelona on 6 October 1972 to present their book, *Los SS tienen la palabra: las leyes del campo de Mauthausen reveladas por las Schutz-Staffeln* (*The SS Have the Floor: The Laws of the Mauthausen Camp Revealed by the Schutz-Staffeln*; "Presentación del libro" 30). Translated into Spanish from the original Italian, the book did not include any discussion of the Spaniards imprisoned in the camp, but a handful of Spanish concentration camp survivors were drawn to the presentation. And so it was here, at the Institute of Italian Culture in the Eixample quarter of the city, that Roig met the Mauthausen survivors Joaquim Amat-Piniella and Joan Pagès for the first time. According to one historian, this was the "encontre que fou el punt de partida de l'obra monumental de Roig" (Toran, *Joan de Diego* 258).[75] Roig's "monumental work," *Els catalans als camps nazis* (*Catalans in Nazi Camps*), was the first publication of its kind in Spain: a thorough historiography and testimonial account of the Catalan survivors of Nazi concentration camps. It left a lasting mark on the story of the Spaniards in Mauthausen, establishing a narrative approach to the trauma of the camps and the victimization of Spanish Republicans that outlasted the author and her subjects.

Roig had read Pere Vives i Clavè's collected letters, Jorge Semprún's *Le grand voyage*, and Amat-Piniella's *K.L. Reich* before she met these Catalan survivors. Nevertheless, it was this personal encounter with men who had lived and suffered in Mauthausen that allowed Roig to understand that what she was reading was not ancient, but rather local history: "Aleshores vaig adonar-me que el nazisme no era per a nosaltres només cosa de les pel·lícules o dels llibres d'història, no altres només la 'qüestió jueva' o la resistència als països ocupats durant la guerra, el nazisme havia perseguit gent de casa nostra, gent que parlava la meva llengua" (Roig, *Els catalans* 13).[76] The stories of her own people – Catalans who were virtually unknown victims of Nazi atrocities – drove Roig to spend the better part of the 1970s immersed in their experiences. When her book was finally published in Spain in 1977, it was a revelation. Two generations of Spaniards were wholly unaware of the suffering their countrymen had endured in Nazi camps. Roig's book finally exposed a history that had been suppressed for more than three decades.

Born in 1946, Roig had no direct experience of the Second World War or the concentration camps. She was the first of a new generation of writers who revived coverage of Mauthausen with an entirely different perspective. For years, Roig delved into personal stories behind the Nazi camp, publishing articles in leftist newspapers and magazines positioned to challenge Franco's censorship laws and poised to usher in Spain's transition from dictatorship to democracy. Roig's articles about Mauthausen survivors and their families fomented the early cultural impact that Spaniards' firsthand experience of Nazi oppression would have on Spanish society at a time when Spaniards were only just starting to realize that the Holocaust held any relevance to their country. Her initial journalistic forays into the Spanish experience of Mauthausen and other Nazi concentration camps tracked the author's own process of discovery as she built her magnum opus. As Roig uncovered pieces of the larger puzzle of the Spaniards of Mauthausen, her readers gained access to information that had been previously stifled. Published years after Rodríguez del Risco's serialized articles, these reports also allowed Spanish victims of the Nazis and their families a renewed voice in the Spanish press. Roig's magazine and newspaper articles from the years just before and just after Franco's death began to unravel the experiences of the Spanish deportees and led to *Els catalans als camps nazis*, solidifying Roig's authority as a chronicler of the deportation.

By 1972, Roig had published a lauded collection of short stories as well as her first novel, *Ramona, adeu* (*Goodbye, Ramona*). She was 26, working as a journalist and active in anti-Francoist and feminist causes.[77] Franco was still in power, and Roig's pro-democracy activities placed her squarely among the ranks of intellectual resistors. After reading Vives' letters in 1972, she wrote an article for the progressive Catalan afternoon newspaper *Tele/eXprés* titled "Una historia provisional" ("A Provisional History"). It introduced readers to Vives, and also connected the dots between one man's untimely death and Nazi policies towards Spanish Republicans during the Second World War. Roig presented basic information about Mauthausen in the article: "un típico pueblo austríaco, de postal pintoresca, está situado en el valle del Danubio, entre bosques de abetos y prados."[78] She also provided approximate data about the number of Spaniards killed in the concentration camps: "[m]urieron unos 130.000 hombres, de entre ellos unos 5.500 españoles" (Roig, "Una historia provisional" 13).[79] Like the virtually unknown history of Spaniards in Nazi camps, this story was "provisional" in that more details would continue to emerge.

Indeed, six months later, in December 1972, Roig sat down with Vives' two sisters and the men she had met a few weeks earlier at the Institute of Italian Culture: Ferran Planes, who had known Vives in the French internment camp of Agde; and Amat-Piniella and Pagès, who had been with Vives in Mauthausen. The resulting interview, published in *Triunfo*, a leftist national magazine for the intellectual set, offered the reader an introduction to the Spanish experience of the Holocaust. Roig asked foundational questions, transporting her readers to a place and time that was wholly foreign to them: Who suffered the worst mistreatment in Mauthausen? How did some prisoners manage to survive? Were the townspeople aware of what was happening in the camp? How did the prisoners relate to the SS? Did anyone try to help the Jews? In 1972, the Spanish public had a limited understanding of the Holocaust. There was an almost complete absence of discussion of the topic in the media and in schools. Most Spaniards did not know that their country-men and women had been imprisoned and killed in Nazi camps. In this sense, Roig's interview began dispelling the myths upheld by Franco and his censors: that Spain was strictly neutral during the Second World War, that the Spanish government was unaware of Spaniards impris-oned in Nazi camps, and that the Nazis had only persecuted the Jews. The article also attacked some of the preconceived notions that an unin-formed Spanish reading public might have had about the experience of being a Spaniard in a Nazi camp, perhaps best captured by one of Vives' sisters, who said: "Lo que no entiendo es cómo los presos, viendo que tenían que morir igualmente, no se vengaban de sus torturadores" (Roig, "Una generación romántica" 37).[80] This comment revealed a pro-found misunderstanding of the Nazis' pathological violence, starvation tactics, and wholesale repression of their captives in the atmosphere of the concentration camps. Vengeance was not a survival strategy.

Roig's basic questions about Mauthausen began to correct some of these widespread erroneous assumptions. Thousands of Spaniards experienced the French internment camps after the Spanish Civil War, and many survived. These camps were essentially refugee centres; although the conditions were inhumane, there were no mechanisms of extermination or systematic abuse. This was not the case with Nazi con-centration camps. More than 10,000 Spaniards were imprisoned in Nazi camps, and fewer than half survived: some 65 per cent of the Spaniards in Mauthausen died. In this context, Roig's question about the differ-ence between the French internment camps and the Nazi concentration camps was key. Pagès replied that "[e]n Mauthausen todos estábamos condenados a morir. Lo que pasa es que se podía tardar más o menos. Unos morían de inanición; otros, por enfermedad; otros, fusilados, otros, por una paliza, otros en la cámara de gas ... " (Roig, "Una generación romántica" 35).[81] Given these circumstances, Roig asked how the two survivors carried on, physically and mentally. Pagès and Amat-Piniella credited the system of solidarity and resistance in the camps among the Spaniards with their survival. They protected the youngest Spanish prisoners from the depravity of the SS, and individuals such as Francesc Boix attempted acts of resistance that would help to indict Nazis during the postwar trials. But Pagès clarified that the fate of the Spaniards was much different than that of the Jews: "ellos eran los únicos destinados a desaparecer en un plazo muy corto" (37).[82] In subsequent decades, the question of whether Spaniards in Mauthausen had suffered a genocide tantamount to the murder of Jews in the Holocaust has become a topic of debate. Roig's interview established that the Spanish experience of the Nazi camp was inherently distinct from the Nazi policy of genocide against the Jews, albeit still deadly.

Another line of questioning from Roig traced the curiosity of the uninformed reader when she asked whether the townspeople of Mauthausen knew what was going on in the concentration camp, and if anyone had helped the prisoners. This was a particularly incisive question, given that debates over bystander guilt in Germany were still years from heating up. The survivors Roig interviewed were convinced that Mauthausen was impossible to ignore, given that the townspeople could see the flames from the crematory smokestack. Moreover, Amat-Piniella said, "[e]l olor de la carne quemada de los crematorios se olía desde la ciudad de Linz, a vientisiete kilómetros de Mauthausen" (Roig, "Una generación romántica" 36).[83] The survivors acknowledged that some townspeople did try to help, but that many others collaborated with the Nazis. The fate of the Spaniards in Mauthausen – along with all the other prisoners there – was serially ignored by bystanders near and far.

The final questions Roig posed to the survivors in this article revealed a hidden trauma within the already hidden trauma of the Holocaust. When Roig asked if the SS were homosexuals, Pagès and Amat-Piniella agreed that the majority were, but pointed out the apparent hypocrisy of Nazis who sexually abused their male captives while punishing homosexuals as part of the Nazi agenda. This skewed notion of sexuality and hypocrisy in Mauthausen extended to another curious admission the two survivors made to Roig. When Pagès and Amat-Piniella discussed the prostitutes housed in Mauthausen – female prisoners of different nationalities (though not Spanish) forced into sexual slavery by the Nazis, who normally killed the women after their term of service – they bragged that "[u]na de las primeras luchas 'políticas' de los españoles fue el reconocimiento de nuestros derechos a poder acostarnos con ellas. Y lo conseguimos" (Roig, "Una generación romántica" 37).[84] There was a double standard in the minds of these two concentration camp survivors in which heterosexuality and masculinity were traits that retained some minimal sense of power and superiority. Within a Nazi power structure that left the concentration camp prisoners at the very bottom of the hierarchy, prostitutes and homosexuals occupied the lowest rung.

Roig's questioning of the survivors on the topic of sexuality anticipated new avenues of Holocaust study that only emerged decades later.

Roig pushed against the confines of late-dictatorship Spain in this article, gathering a group of people personally touched by the indisputable existence of Spaniards in Nazi concentration camps. Within the contours of the interview, she also juxtaposed the experiences of the Spanish survivors of Mauthausen with the experiences of the Jews and the SS, giving the reader a larger frame of reference and a shocking comparative perspective. Roig, moreover, asked the reader to trust the testimony of the victims – a contentious confidence in the survivor's words over the historian's authority. Yet in 1972 there were no objective Spanish historical accounts of Spaniards in Nazi concentration camps or in the Second World War. Antonio Sinca Vendrell's historiography was decidedly subjective; Mariano Constante and Eduardo Pons Prades' equally subjective volumes were still a year or two away; and the Spanish translation of the Pappaletteras's book did not mention Spaniards in Mauthausen. Survivor testimony in this context may be judged as biased, but it was the only historical record available.

Over the next five years, Roig published additional articles on the Spaniards in Mauthausen, Spanish survivors of other Nazi camps, and the cultural reverberations of the Holocaust in Spain.[85] The information and emotions Roig exposed in these pieces were preparation for her groundbreaking historiographic work, *Els catalans als camps nazis*. With the benefit of hindsight, it is apparent that Roig's articles and subsequent book inaugurated an investigative wave of Spanish historians and survivors who delved into the topic of Spaniards deported to Mauthausen and other camps. Roig's articles rediscovered this decades-old historical event. She located Mauthausen survivors and published interviews with Pagès, Amat-Piniella, Casimir Climent, and others, allowing these individuals to provide a counternarrative to the historical falsities so entrenched in Franco's Spain. After Franco's death, Roig continued to publish myth-breaking journalism about conceptions of the Holocaust in Spain.[86] After a frustrating encounter in 1976 with Ramón Serrano Suñer, Franco's brother-in-law and minister of Foreign Affairs during the Second World War, while she was writing *Els catalans als camps nazis*, Roig went on the attack. Her open letter to Serrano Suñer caused a stir when it was published in *El País* in 1979. Roig accused Serrano Suñer – and by extension, the late dictator – of being complicit in the deportation and murder of thousands of Spaniards in Nazi camps, despite his public denials of any knowledge of the Spanish concentration camp prisoners. This article opened a new debate in Spain about the Spanish government's collaboration with the Nazis.

Roig's unrelenting questioning of a status quo that accepted that Spain had no part in the Holocaust and left Spanish Mauthausen survivors isolated in oblivion was a catalyst. As a Catalan woman, Roig wrote from the geographic and social margins of late-dictatorship Spanish society, holding Spain to account for a dark period in its past and pressing for social justice for the Spanish victims of the Nazi camps. These exposés and editorials published at the cusp of Spain's transition to democracy began what would become a surge of renegotiations with Spain's collective memory at the turn of the twenty-first century. Yet for Roig, they were efforts "simplemente para que este país empiece a reconciliarse consigo mismo" (*La lluita contra l'oblit* 127).[87] Roig began a dialogue profoundly necessary to understanding Spain's past.

Els catalans als camps nazis changed the course of history for the Spanish deportees and their families. Roig devoted three years to tracking down, interviewing, and publicizing the experiences of Catalans in Nazi camps. In this way, *Els catalans als camps nazis* represents a moment of discovery: of the Spanish presence in Nazi concentration camps, of the individual Catalans who lived and died in those camps, of the difference between the Nazi genocide of Jews and the persecution of Spanish Republicans, and of the complacency of Franco's government towards its ill-fated countrymen. Roig brought these threads together into a single volume: she discovered Mauthausen as a site of collective memory for a new generation of Spaniards, bringing ghosts back from the dead. Not without its flaws, *Els catalans als camps nazis* nevertheless broke new ground in the organization and dissemination of first-person testimony of Spanish Nazi concentration camp survivors, in the commitment of a non-survivor and journalist to recount the story of Spaniards in Mauthausen, and in the creation of a narrative that gave Catalans in particular a voice and an authority to tell their experience of the Nazi concentration camps.

In the introduction to *Els catalans als camps nazis*, Roig wrote that even after working on the book for three years, "no sé què és un camp d'extermini nazi. És impossible de fer-se'n una idea" (*Els catalans* 26).[88] Nevertheless, this volume was as close a confrontation with the horrors of the Third Reich as most Spaniards would ever encounter. Roig lived inside the memories and testimonies of dozens of Catalan survivors of Nazi camps. As she relayed to Artur London, the International

Brigadist who was one of the book's early champions, she was totally absorbed by the immediacy of the survivors' tales, even though she herself was not a victim of a Nazi camp:

> 'Estic tan immergida en l'univers dels camps de concentració, que descobreixo que m'és impossible d'abstreure-me'n. Menjo, m'adormo amb vosaltres, allà … sento els crits dels SS, els cops, els lladrucs dels gossos… sento l'olor del podrimener, l'olor de la fumera que s'escapa dels forns crematoris… amb els ulls oberts, continuo vivint deins un malson sens fi!' (6)[89]

What to Roig was a "nightmare," was, to the ex-deportees and their families, the embodiment of their spectral identities in post-Franco Spain. As Roig showed, they and their stories were far too real. Through the first-person testimony that formed the foundation of this text, Roig brought the reader into the sordid world of the concentration camp. Unlike Constante's potboiler memoirs, however, Roig laboured to keep melodrama at bay: her primary interest was capturing every aspect of the experiences of the Catalans who were victimized by the Nazis in concentration camps during the Second World War. In this way, her text began to return a corporeality to the Spanish bodies who had suffered in Mauthausen but who had become ghosts in Spanish society.[90]

Though *Els catalans als camps nazis* was the work of a journalist and novelist who concentrated primarily on the firsthand testimony of Catalan deportees, it has become a central historical source text in the ever-growing bibliography on the subject of the Spanish experience of Nazi camps.[91] Praise for Roig's tireless effort has extended throughout the decades. In a review soon after its publication, Luís Permanyer wrote in *La Vanguardia* that Roig's book stood as "el mejor monumento que cabría levantar a la memoria de los catalanes que sufrieron el terror nazi" (78).[92] Thirty-eight years later, in a lecture on the Spanish deportees in 2015, Alfons Aragoneses called Roig's book the first database of survivors, a formidable work considering the limitations of the era ("Deportados españoles"). By the time the Spanish translation of the book was published in 1978, a representative of Spain's King Juan Carlos had made an official visit to Mauthausen. Although we can only speculate that Roig's book pushed the king to act, his acknowledgment brought legitimacy to a cause that only a year earlier had been anathema to Spain's transition-era government.

At the time of its original publication, however, some found fault with Roig's narrow focus. A number of survivors in exile in France criticized

Roig's decision to limit her book to Catalan deportees as opposed to all Spaniards victimized by the Nazis; others were unhappy with what they viewed as the book's favourable treatment of communists. In a letter to the head of the Spanish organization of deportees and political prisoners, FEDIP, Roig defended her decisions, writing that her intentions were to answer to "l'obligació moral de parlar d'una part de la història recent que ens havien amagat amb tota la mala fe. Restituir la vostra història, exemplar i heroica per a la nostra memòria col·lectiva. Vosaltres us mereixieu un nom ben gros en la nostra història recent i jo hi volia contribuir amb l'únic que podia: escrivint-ho" ("Letter to Josep Ester").[93] Above all, Roig recognized that without the collaboration and willingness of the survivors whose testimony appeared in and influenced this book to share their innermost experiences and secrets, she would not have been able to recreate the Nazi concentrationary world to the extent she did. Although Roig's volume was a subjective encounter with a fraction of the experiences of a select few Catalans who were deported to Nazi camps and survived, it was nevertheless a book that changed the course of Spain's collective memory of the Second World War, just as the author set out to do.

Hundreds of pages long, with dozens of black and white photographs, drawings, maps, the testimony of more than 40 Nazi concentration camp survivors, and a substantial appendix listing Catalans who died at Mauthausen or its *Kommandos* or were sent to other Nazi concentration camps, *Els catalans als camps nazis* was the most extensive study of the Spanish deportees to date. Although Roig limited herself to Catalan victims, she clarified that "[n]o hi ha, però, cap intenció de distinguir el comportament d'aquests amb els ex-deportats de la resta de l'Estat espanyol" (*Els catalans* 15).[94] Subsequent historical studies of Spaniards in Nazi camps have demonstrated that Roig's micro-community of Catalans did, in fact, share the broad strokes of their experiences with the macro-community of most if not all Spanish deportees to Nazi camps. It was the author's prerogative to limit herself to a population to which she felt a particular kinship, to "una parcel·la boirosa de la nostra història recent" (15).[95] Indeed, Roig's identification with the men and women whose stories she relayed in these pages – "els nostres deportats" ("our deportees," 17 and throughout), as she called them – betrayed the subjectivity with which she approached this slice of history. In particular, the author's friendships with Amat-Piniella, in whose tired eyes "més coses em van saber dir del què havia significat l'infern nazi" (14), and Climent, whom she visited in a psychiatric facility until his death, were particularly close.[96] Moreover, her association with the Partido Comunista de España (PCE or Spanish Communist Party) tended to colour the narrative with a bias that emphasized the influence of the Spanish clandestine resistance group inside the camp, formed initially by members of the PCE. Although this volume was a history of the Catalan deportees, it was also Roig's history, a history that became entangled with the author's novels, journalism, political beliefs, and personal life.

Roig captured this subjectivity in terms of her drive to recover a history that had been silenced in Spain:

> El silenci que han fet planar per damunt dels catalans, dels republicans, dels vençuts de la guerra, m'ha semblat, tot sovint, que era un silenci que volien fer planar per damunt dels meus i de mi mateixa. Veia que si no retornàvem la paraula als qui l'havien de tenir quen els pertocava, nosaltres no la tindríem mai en la seva totalitat. (11).[97]

Restoring the voices of those who were denied a stake in Spain's history was paramount to the restoration of what Roig called "la nostra salut històrica" ("our historical health," 11). As a member of a generation of Spaniards whose access to their collective past was severely limited, Roig felt it was her duty to write this book. Roig brought the stories of the Catalans in Nazi camps to bear on her 1980 novel *L'hora violeta* (*The Violet Hour*);[98] she continued to write about and interview Catalan concentration camp survivors in newspapers and on television;[99] she became so identified with the collective memory of the deportees that in 2001 the Amical de Mauthausen honoured her, on the tenth anniversary of her death, with a homage at the Palau de la Música Catalana in Barcelona.[100] Despite – or perhaps because of – the personal relationships the author maintained with the deportees she interviewed, *Els catalans als camps nazis* crossed over from a strictly historical volume to a work of historiographic testimony that expressly sought to correct the omissions of the Franco era. Ultimately, the author herself was one of these testimonial voices: instead of bearing witness to the concentration camps, Roig bore witness to the struggles of a group of aging, outcast ex-deportees as they attempted to come to terms with the memories of their persecution by the Nazis and their place (or lack thereof) in Spain's contemporary history.

Understanding *Els catalans als camps nazis* as a complex convergence of history, testimony, and subjective narration allows an examination of the book on its own terms. It was not, as the author herself allowed, a decisive historical work; or at least, it was not solely a historical work. Although Roig encouraged "algun historiador," after reading her volume, to "fes el llibre decisiu des del punt de vista historiogràfic" (*Els catalans* 15), no subsequent work on the deportees has come close to matching the breadth and vision of *Els catalans*.[101] This was in part due to Roig's timing: she was able to contact dozens of Catalan and Spanish concentration camp survivors while they were still lucid and eager to divulge their stories. Although the author also encountered some resistance to her project – survivors who told her not to trust anything their compatriots told her, who doubted their own memories, who argued that what they suffered paled in comparison to the global suffering of millions, or who simply refused to participate in the project (16) – she gained incredible access to men and women who were often recounting their experiences for the first time, to the first person outside their immediate community of family members and fellow ex-deportees who showed the slightest interest in their memories. To this end, Roig's interviews captured the intimate nature of the interlocutor-witness relationship prevalent in oral histories of Holocaust survivors.[102] Franco's death in 1975 also meant that *Els catalans als camps nazis* was among the vanguard of publications to test the boundaries of free expression during the years of the Spanish transition to democracy, a time when historical memory was in vogue and the Spanish reading public was receptive to visiting a past about which they had no knowledge.[103]

By the same token, Roig wrote this volume before subsequent efforts to contact, count, and catalogue Spanish deportees to Nazi camps. In the 1970s, Spanish historians had not yet worked to corroborate survivor testimony; many Spanish state archives were decades from existence. The argument can be made, however, that Roig's efforts in *Els catalans als camps nazis* paved the way for these future endeavours: before the book was published, the Amical de Mauthausen was an illegal organization, no Spanish official had acknowledged the presence of Spaniards in Nazi camps, and no list of Spaniards killed in Mauthausen or any other Nazi camp had been made public. Given the limitations of the era, Roig was exacting about comparing details with the historical volumes she cited in her bibliography, which are mainly French sources.[104] She also worked to corroborate survivor testimony: if one witness remembered an event differently than another, Roig made these contradictions explicit in the text. Roig allowed survivors who did not want their identities revealed to remain anonymous. She included controversial topics that languished on the margins of Holocaust studies, such as homosexuality, prostitution, and prisoners who collaborated with the Nazis. She was, in short, as rigorous and exacting as any other respected Holocaust historian without undermining her own presence as interlocutor in the narrative.

Quoting liberally from her interview subjects, Roig began *Els catalans als camps nazis* by unravelling their trajectories from Catalonia, into exile, and to the concentration camps. The deportees came mainly from working-class and agricultural backgrounds; most were politically active for the Republic before and during the Spanish Civil War. Landing in different French internment camps once they fled Spain, the deportees agreed on the horrible conditions and futile attempts by the French to convince them to return. As Francesc Teix put it: "'els francesos et matavan de fam i els nazis ho feien directament" (*Els catalans* 56).[105] Although some deportees were fortunate to be released from the French camps to go into exile elsewhere, many others joined work companies to escape the camps and to continue the fight against fascism, while others joined the French Resistance. As pressure from Germany mounted, these men were captured and sent to *Stalags*. Many of the survivors who testified to their experience in the *Stalags* drew a distinction between the German soldiers in these POW camps and the SS in the concentration camps. Miquel Serra i Grabolosa, for one, said that "el tracte dels soldats de la Werhmacht, que ens vigilaven [en el *Stalag*], no tenia res a veure amb la crueltat que després trobaríem en els SS del camp de Mauthausen" (182).[106] This foundational information answered the misconceptions and conflations rampant in a Spanish population that considered "the camps" a unified body. Through the testimony of these witnesses, Roig explicitly differentiated the French internment camps from the German prisoner of war camps from the Nazi concentration camps. She also implicitly distanced Franco's penitentiary colonies inside Spain from the Nazi camps. The reader of *Els catalans als camps nazis* started to comprehend the complexities of wartime deportation and detention seemingly as it dawned on the survivors themselves what their ultimate fate held.

As Roig began to delve into the presence of Catalans in Nazi concentration camps, the reader came to know a number of survivors whose testimony formed the cornerstone of the narration: Pagès, Climent, Amat-Piniella, and de Diego become familiar names. Although the author interviewed Catalan survivors of Buchenwald, Dachau, Sachsenhausen, and Ravensbrück, the majority of the deportees – including these four men – were survivors of Mauthausen. The operation, hygiene, discipline, *Kommandos*, prisoner-*Kapos*, means of execution, and prisoner resistance movement at this camp was the primary focus of *Els catalans als camps nazis*. The testimony of Mauthausen survivors, coupled with Roig's contextualizing and at times editorializing narration, provided the reader with an in-depth introduction to the camp: it seemed as though no detail was too insignificant to be recorded.

As page after page of survivors discussed the nightmare they endured, Roig's comment that "[n]omés la memòria humana, la voluntat de memòria i el record viu dels qui ho patiren, pot reconstruir tot un món que sembla inversemblant" (*Els catalans* 201) became patently clear.[107] The deportees relied on the vagaries of memory to recreate this unimaginable universe: there was no other way. Serra i Grabilosa warned Roig that "'tinc moltes dificultats a recordar detalls lligats als actes que he viscut (...) Però el que diré serà cert, indiscutible. Diré la veritat, el que no vol pas dir TOTA la veritat, ja que no 'inventaré' res'" (18).[108] Witness testimony is subjective: individuals remember events differently, some points may be exaggerated, others forgotten or omitted. Yet from the first recorded Holocaust testimonies to efforts to capture the impressions of the very last survivors, witness testimony is the only way for non-survivors to experience secondhand what occurred inside Nazi concentration camps.[109] The readers filter this testimony through their belief systems and gut reactions; Roig also checked her historical sources to weed out testimony that seemed incongruous or unreliable.[110] In the end, the author, reader, and fellow survivors can only trust that some version of the actual events has been transmitted when individual survivors remembered what happened to them in the camps.[111] There is no one authoritative story of the Nazi genocide: there are millions. Only a fraction can ever be told.

The men who testified about Mauthausen to Roig recalled a place of great deprivation, struggle, hunger, and solidarity. Although they arrived on different transports, in different seasons, during the day or at night, the men remembered a common series of events upon entering Mauthausen. Members of the SS received the deportees at the Mauthausen train station with blows and shouts; the prisoners were herded into formation; their clothing removed; ushered into showers; given warnings of what was to come. Teix remembered a German interpreter telling his convoy: "'Suïcideu-vos, és el millor que podeu fer. Si no, morireu d'una altra manera, com els qui hi ha per terra'"

(*Els catalans* 226).[112] He then realized that he was standing on blood-soaked ground. Another survivor, Josep Escoda, recalled an Austrian member of the International Brigades who told his convoy, "'Pobres! D'aquí només se surt per la xemeneia del crematori'" (227).[113] These two accounts captured Roig's methodology in the collection of survivor testimony: she worked with threads that were common to the memories of multiple deportees, allowing their voices to extract the nuanced differences and commonalities in their experiences. The deportees remembered events differently, but they shared a communal outline of their imprisonment in Mauthausen.

The section on "Un camp: Mauthausen" ("One Camp: Mauthausen") begins with the incongruous statement that "[e]ls qui hi han estat, diuen que Mauthausen és un lloc meravellós" (*Els catalans* 214).[114] Of course, throughout the book, survivors described a place that was anything but "marvelous." From this point of entry, Roig's text followed the Catalan deportees through their daily routines in Mauthausen. By delving into their day-to-day existence, Roig and the deportees who provided their testimony portrayed Mauthausen as both a site of survival and of annihilation. Life and death coexisted in Mauthausen; these survivors were a testament to both.

Miquel Maydeu Pallerola, the first Catalan who died in Mauthausen, arrived on 15 August 1940, and died less than a month later, on 13 September, an indication of the lifespan of a Spanish deportee during the earliest years in the camp (*Els catalans* 267). Roig identified many ways that a Spanish prisoner could perish in a Nazi camp:

> durant el treball, o 'en curs d'evasió' i en realitat llançat a les filferrades, podies deixar-t'hi morir o podies suïcidar-te, podies morir executat, ofegat a l'aigua ... També podies morir per haver estat conillet d'Índies a les experiències pseudo-científiques dels metges SS ... [o] bé sota les tortures del Kapos, o per una injecció de benzina al cor ... o a Hartheim ... (267)[115]

But a violent death was not the only way to die in the camp, "[a]mb els estralls que feia la fem, i el fred i la set, ja n'hi havia prou ... També podies morir per esgotament físic a causa de la duresa dels treballs forçats ... Podies morir-hi pel tifus, per les diarrees, per pulmonia, etcètera" (Roig, *Els catalans* 268).[116] Roig's use of the second person gives the narration immediacy, highlighting that these kinds of horrible deaths could have happened to any of us, had we, like these Catalan deportees, found ourselves on the wrong side of history.

By highlighting the moments when the Spanish Republicans interacted or overlapped with Jews in the camps, Roig expanded her purview in order to invite the reader to consider the Spanish presence in the Second World War in a new light. These episodes confirmed that Spaniards in Mauthausen were witnesses to the Holocaust, however physically and emotionally removed from the Jews they were. The Catalans who Roig interviewed saw the extermination of Jews in Mauthausen: "Els nostres deportats republicans van haver de presenciar com els nazis portaven a terme la mort, sistemàtica, ordenada, precisa, contra els ciutadans de la raça jueva" (*Els catalans* 215).[117] But the Catalan survivors maintained a complicated relationship to the Jews in Mauthausen that dispels any myth of heroic resistance. Roig explained that the Spaniards' wellbeing was predicated on the extermination of the Jews in Mauthausen: "Quan els nazis feien una 'ofensiva' contra els jueus, els presos repiraven alleujats, perquè potser aquell dia no rebrien ells."(266).[118] That the state of the Spanish prisoners was seemingly connected to the extermination of the Jews presents a paradox that the author admitted was difficult to confront. Yet Roig asked the reader to withhold judgment, arguing that our (and her) distance from the subject matter meant that we simply could not understand the circumstances: "Això, vist des de fora, ens pot semblar terriblement inhumà. Però, com ho podem jutjar si no estem avesats a conviure diàriament amb la mort com ells?" (266).[119] In this and other curious moments in *Els catalans als camps nazis*, Roig both encouraged and discouraged the reader from identifying with her subjects. Non-survivors were, in essence, held at arm's length from the complex set of human emotions so central to the survivors' ordeal.

According to Roig, while Catalans in Mauthausen witnessed the atrocities perpetrated against the Jews, they were not mere bystanders. The riskiest form of solidarity for the Spaniards was aiding Jews. Although Roig did not provide examples of specific actions in Mauthausen on behalf of Jewish prisoners, she did delve into moments of animosity between Catalans and Jews in the camp. One witness recalled seeing a Valencian man steal gold teeth, almost certainly removed from Jews who were exterminated upon their arrival in Mauthausen (*Els catalans* 437). Joan Tarragó watched as a fellow deportee killed Jews by drowning them in puddles of water: "Els agafava pel cap, els enfonsava, els tornava a treure i, en acabat, els premia amb una rascleta."(437).[120] He told Roig that this nameless man "deia que els jueus tenien la culpa que els republicans haguessin perdut la guerra d'Espanya" (437).[121] The characterization of the Catalan deportees as dispassionate observers or willing participants in the victimization and murder of Jews disappeared almost entirely from later accounts of the Spaniards in Mauthausen. As such, Roig's willingness to wade into testimony that cast Spanish deportees in a harsh light regarding Jews was one of the author's unique contributions to the history of the Spanish presence at the margins of the Holocaust.

Indeed, this volume is a testament to Roig's efforts to capture Mauthausen through historical data, which she examined with the benefit of contemporary sources. She was the first author to systematically analyse and publish identifying information for the thousands of Catalans who were deported to Nazi camps, extracted from original lists she obtained through the Amicale de Mauthausen in Paris, Climent, conversations with survivors, and the historian Josep Benet.[122] Benet served as Roig's benefactor during the years she spent researching *Els catalans*. He closely observed the dedication with which Roig confronted the subject matter, calling her work "un dels més rigorosos documents europeus concebuts sobre aquella tètrica tragèdia, un document bàsic i imprescindible sobre uns horrors que la Montserrat no va parar, salvant diferents menes d'obstacles, fins a descobrir-los" (Benet i Jornet 151).[123] Indeed, the book was an all-absorbing project, a life's work that succeeded in becoming a foundational text for the study of the history of Spaniards in Mauthausen and the representation of that experience.

Above all, *Els catalans als camps nazis* was an opportunity for survivors to tell their stories. Although Roig was indeed a presence as narrator in this volume, she allowed the testimony of the survivors to stand on its own in the majority of the volume. She presented historical context or summarized what some survivors told her, quoting liberally from the extensive interviews she conducted with Spanish ex-deportees.[124] The uninterrupted testimony of witnesses constituted a sensory window into the sights, sounds, smells, and emotions of life and death inside a Nazi concentration camp. The scenes that survivors described provided jarring juxtapositions of violence and relative normality, as when Climent recounted the howling of prisoners confined to their cells while he watched a camp boxing match: "'Udolaven de fam i de set i de por. S'estaven a les fosques i no els donaven res per a menjar i per a beure. Al cap de deu dies encara en quedaven de vius que s'enterraven entre els morts per tal d'escalfar-se'" (*Els catalans* 240).[125] They were startlingly intimate portrayals of death, such as Miquel Serra's description of carting the destroyed bodies of prisoners murdered by the SS while constructing Mauthausen: "'transportava una part dels morts de la jornada i que hi vaig veure cervells, fetges, i l'anatomia interna barrejada amb draps, fang, cabells, tot ple de sang'" (331).[126] They showed flashes of humour and humanity, such as Tarragó's description of the risks he and other Spaniards took to steal bread from the SS and redistribute it to starving prisoners: "'Moltes vegades escolàvem els pans a través dels filferrats; aprofitàvem els dies que no hi havie corrent'" (484–5).[127] The voices of the survivors themselves is the unifying factor in a volume saturated with detailed personal recollections of destruction, agony, and resistance. Roig's "discovery" of Catalans deported to Nazi concentration camps was actually the survivors' own discovery of the power of their memories and agency in finally telling their own stories.

Arriving precisely in the middle of our timeline of Spanish Mauthausen representations between 1940 and 2015, Roig's volume was a turning point. It exposed previously unseen information about the Spanish deportation to Nazi concentration camps, including the identities and personal stories of survivors. Roig took a confrontational stance on the issue by researching and publishing this volume: with it, she argued that the Catalans – and by extension, the Spaniards – deported to Nazi camps should be afforded a stake in Spain's twentieth-century history. She openly demanded accountability from the Spanish government for its responsibility in the initial deportation and abandonment of the Spaniards to their fate in the Nazi camps and also in the subsequent decades of willful neglect of the survivors and their families. She individualized a mass of humanity who died at the hands of the SS or lingered forgotten in postwar France, returning names and identities to the dead and the living, reinvigorating the nameless bodies Franco would have preferred to leave in unmarked graves. Yet Roig's volume was not the beginning of a groundswell of interest in the Spaniards in Mauthausen; if anything, it was a formative yet isolated attempt to move the topic of the deportation of Spanish Republicans to the top of a Spanish agenda. The two-decade period that followed the publication of Roig's book swept the stories of the Spaniards in Mauthausen and other Nazi camps back under the rug. Although *Els catalans als camps nazis* and its Spanish translation *Noche y niebla: los catalanes en los campos nazis* momentarily stirred the public's interest, it would take another twenty years for the story to regain its lost ground among historians and to awaken Spain's imagination once again.

4 Memories Unleashed: Mauthausen after Franco, 1980–2015

After a first wave of survivor memoirs and histories during the 1970s, Spanish representations of Mauthausen tapered off in the 1980s and the first half of the 1990s. Not since the 1950s when the censorship and oppression of the early years of the Franco dictatorship stifled Spanish Mauthausen representations for more than a decade, had the Spanish experience of the camp disappeared completely from view. Although the Spanish memory of Mauthausen continued through other means – the activities of the Amical de Mauthausen in Barcelona and organizations of ex-deportees in France, commemorations at Mauthausen and private gatherings of survivors, and periodicals dedicated to the memory of Nazi concentration camp deportees endured[1] – there were no published books by Spanish Mauthausen deportees, and very few by authors with no direct connection to the camp, during this decade and a half.[2] This lull can be explained by Spain's changing political landscape, the public's historical-memory fatigue, and a so-called pact of silence that also quieted the collective memory of the Spanish Civil War during the same period.

But the story of the Spaniards in Mauthausen was not doomed to obscurity. A second wave of Mauthausen survivor memoirs began in 1995 with José de Dios Amill's *La verdad sobre Mauthausen* (*The Truth about Mauthausen*). The pace of Mauthausen survivor memoirs picked up precipitously by 2001 and continued through the first decade of the twenty-first century. Written by an array of now-elderly Mauthausen survivors, these books recorded personal and collective memories of the concentration camp. Moving beyond the more visible survivors who held privileged positions in Mauthausen and whose names dominated in accounts published in previous decades, these new efforts offered the personal thoughts and impressions of men who had never before had a public presence on the topic of their concentration camp ordeal. They offered idiosyncratic and individualized approaches to remembering the past during the twilight years of the last remaining Spanish survivors of Mauthausen.

By the year 2000, twenty years had passed since the limited release of the first and only Spanish Mauthausen documentary, Llorenç Soler's *Sobrevivir en Mauthausen*. This year saw a surge in visual representations of Mauthausen with the release of the first of a decade's worth of films about the Spanish experience of the camp. Appearing on Spanish television, these documentaries attained a wide viewership, effectively reinvigorating the public's interest in and knowledge of Spaniards who were victims of Nazi aggression. Although they varied in quality and depth, these films introduced a chapter in Spain's history to a viewership largely unfamiliar with the topic, and recorded the voices and images of survivors for posterity.

By the end of the decade, a new generation of writers, artists, and journalists were assuming the mantle of representation of the Spanish experience of Mauthausen. Although some counted Mauthausen victims among their relatives, others maintained no family tie to the deportees. This "postmemory," as Marianne Hirsch has called it, of the Spanish Mauthausen experience, brought unique perspectives to a subject that had been solely the provenance of survivors and historians. Hirsch characterizes postmemory as "the relationship that the 'generation after' bears to the personal, collective and cultural trauma of those who came before" (5). Although the descendants of these victims do not remember the Holocaust, they experience the memories of their family members to such a degree that they *"seem to constitute memories in their own right"* (Hirsch 5; emphasis in the original). A second- or third-generation Mauthausen survivor who edited a relative's memoirs or wrote a fictionalized version of a family member's experience practiced what Hirsch labels "postmemorial work ... [which] strives to *reactivate* and *re-embody* more distant political and cultural memorial structures by reinvesting them with resonant individual and familial forms of mediation and aesthetic expression" (33; emphasis in the original). Although Hirsch's theory of postmemory privileges the immediacy of the memories of descendants of victims, she also includes the "affiliative postmemory" (36) of individuals who have no familial tie to the Holocaust.[3] As such, we can think of a generation of relatives of Mauthausen victims as well as non-descendants as sharing in a postmemory archive of the Spanish experience of the camp. The resulting varied array of representations "reactivate and re-embody" what might seem to be a remote historical event with immediacy and relevance for new generations and audiences.

By the seventieth anniversary of the liberation of Mauthausen, the camp had taken on a different meaning to a new Spanish public, inspiring a diverse collection of creative endeavours: novels, comics, a play, and a serialized Twitter account. As these materials have created interest among Spaniards with perhaps only a tangential connection to the Spanish Mauthausen prisoners, they have ushered the history and postmemory of the camp into the realm of popular culture. These works present their share of complications as they transform history into forms of entertainment that may or may not educate the public. Nevertheless, they mark a moment of evolution as Mauthausen is solidified into part of the country's current popular imagination, beyond the influence of survivors whose numbers are now dwindling. The "post-Holocaust generations" who look to television and the internet for society's norms and values may, according to Andreas Huyssen, "find their way toward testimony, documentary and historical treatise precisely via a fictionalized and emotionalized Holocaust" created for mass media (*Twilight Memories* 256). As representations of Mauthausen mature, the understanding of the Spanish presence in the camp has evolved beyond the unique memories of the people who lived through it towards a collective memory of resistance and survival that resonates with a generation of audiences accustomed to using contemporary media for their engagement with the past.

Unimposed Silence: The Absence of Mauthausen Representations during the Spanish Transition, 1980–1995

Thousands of people were killed and buried in unmarked mass graves during the Spanish Civil War. These individuals – almost all, without exception, men and women who fought for or supported the Republic and were killed by Nationalist forces – were never properly buried, yet their relatives and community members kept track of their gravesites during the thirty-six years of Franco's dictatorship. The period after Franco's death in 1975 brought sweeping political and cultural changes as the country transitioned from a dictatorship to a parliamentary monarchy. As the political situation in Spain evolved, families in certain regions of the country started to search for the remains of their relatives. Numerous mass graves from La Rioja to Extremadura were opened between 1978 and 1981. In particular, the election of the first leftist municipal governments in 1979 signalled a definitive shift for many Spaniards: they were able to excavate without fear of retribution (Silva 131–2). Yet the political tensions that were mounting within Spain's coalition government also affected these disinterrments. The editor who oversaw the exhumation coverage for the magazine *Interviú* in the late 1970s noted that he was subject to denunciations from private and political sources alike: even the newly legal Spanish Communist Party (PCE) told him he was "'provoca[ndo] la represión de nuevo'" (qtd in Ferrándiz 163).[4]

The takeover of the Spanish Parliament by members of the military on 23 February 1981 quickly put an end to these ad hoc exhumations (Silva 132). Although the attempted coup was foiled, it resurrected fears associated with the Franco regime. The niece of a man who was shot in La Rioja during the Spanish Civil War attested to this quelling effect: "'Claro, hubo el golpe de estado, vieron a Franco otra vez, y sí, fue paralizarse la cosa'" (qtd in Hristova 31).[5] By the summer of 1981, these private exhumations had all but stopped (Hristova 31).

But in 2000, after an almost twenty-year lapse, the exhumations resumed. That year, Emilio Silva disinterred his grandfather's remains from a mass grave in the town of Priaranza del Bierzo. Soon after, he formed the Asociación para la Recuperación de la Memoria Histórica, which would aid in hundreds of excavations of mass graves in the next decade. The Law of Historical Memory, passed in 2007, further promoted the state's financial underwriting of these exhumations, and they have continued to the present day.[6] These events heralded a new era for memories of the Spanish Civil War: a memory boom that was accompanied by countless histories, novels, films, and works of art treating the Civil War and its aftermath.

Spanish representations of Mauthausen underwent a similar multi-year lapse followed by a resurgence. Spain headed into the last two decades of the twentieth century with what seemed like momentum to right the historical omission of the Spaniards in Nazi concentration camps. The years immediately after Franco's death brought rapid changes to the landscape of the country's historical memory of Mauthausen. The publication of Montserrat Roig's *Els catalans als camps nazis* in Catalan in 1977 and in Spanish the next year sparked a subdued movement of historical recuperation. Family members who were ignorant of the fate of loved ones who had crossed the border into France in 1939 learned of their deaths in Nazi concentration camps from Roig's book. During a state visit to Austria in 1978, King Juan Carlos I sent two representatives to Mauthausen. They laid a wreath on the monument to Spaniards killed in the camp with the inscription, "El Rey de España a los españoles muertos fuera de su Patria" (Alférez), making the king the first Spanish official to acknowledge the presence of Spaniards in Mauthausen.[7] That same year, the Amical de Mauthausen, an organization of survivors and their families that had operated illegally since its founding in 1962, was legalized. A wave of publications continued through the end of the 1970s: from Mariano Constante's memoirs, to Eduardo Pons Prades' testimonial histories, to Amadeo Sinca Vendrell's personalized history. Sinca Vendrell's book, originally published in France in 1946, capped off this post-Franco burst of activity with its publication in Spain in 1980. Like the rush to exhume mass graves from the Civil War during the Spanish transition, all indications were that the history of the Spaniards in Mauthausen would continue to gain visibility through the next decade.

But the Spanish experience of Mauthausen slipped back into the shadows in the 1980s and 1990s. Fifteen years elapsed before a Spanish Mauthausen survivor released a new publication. The correlation with the lapse in exhumations of mass graves from the Spanish Civil War is not a coincidence. In both cases, an early movement to confront a contentious era in Spain's history ended abruptly at the beginning of the 1980s. In the case of the Spaniards in Mauthausen, there is no documentation that ties the end of the movement's first wave to the attempted coup in 1981.[8] Nevertheless, it stands to reason that the fear that spread through the families who were opening up mass graves – who were literally digging up the past – would have also spread through the survivors who had begun to publicize the plight of the Spaniards victimized in the Nazi camps. Although many of these ex-deportees continued to live in France after Franco's death, others lived in Spain and would have been attuned to these changing political tides. Some wrote letters to their local newspapers publicizing the continued willful ignorance about Spaniards deported to Nazi camps, only to be barraged with death threats, including from members of their regional governments (Toran, *Amical de Mauthausen* 34–5). Others may have attempted to tell their stories, but found friends and family members in disbelief at the magnitude of the oppression they had confronted in the camp. This was the case for Mauthausen survivors like Francisco Batiste Baila, who told an oral historian in 2002, "'Me habrían tomado por un alienado, era imposible contar estas atrocidades, estuvimos en el silencio hasta que los cineastas, los media, gente como ustedes ...'" (Vilanova, *Mauthausen, después* 132).[9] Perhaps sensing that their moment was over, these survivors largely kept their stories to themselves during the last two decades of the twentieth century.

Moreover, Spain became absorbed in its transition from Franco's dictatorship to a democratic system of governance. Many have identified a pact of silence in the transition government's enactment of an Amnesty Law in 1977 and decision not to enter into recriminations about the Civil War and dictatorship. Although discussions of the country's divided past continued in private, public attention to Spain's twentieth-century history largely disappeared. Thus, after an intense period of scrutiny of the country's past during the 1970s, it seemed that Spain had reached a saturation point, encouraged by a government that, by omission, had put an end to public discussions of the past. A few tentative attempts to reinvigorate the memories of the Spaniards in Mauthausen emerged in the mid-1990s. This movement would reap the benefits of the collective memory boom of the first decade of the 2000s, when a second and final wave of Mauthausen survivor memoirs began to appear. The "people like you" to whom Batiste Baila refers to were the historians, filmmakers, and journalists who exhumed the story of the Spaniards in Mauthausen at the turn of the century.

**Life Narratives of Mauthausen Survivors:
The Second Wave of Accounts, 1995–2012**

Spanish survivors of Mauthausen authored or co-authored more than two dozen memoirs published in Spain between 1995 and 2012, in the last significant wave of Spanish testimonial writing by witnesses to the Holocaust.[10]

The majority of these texts are autobiographical, written by an individual survivor decades after his imprisonment in Mauthausen. Others, written by non-survivors, blur the lines between testimony and biography. As the remaining number of Spanish survivors of Mauthausen grows ever smaller, first-person accounts have given way to books that

Life Narratives of Mauthausen Survivors, 1995–2012

Year	Title	Author or Editor	Mauthausen Survivor/ Subject of Memoir	Publication Information
1995	La verdad sobre Mauthausen (The Truth about Mauthausen)	José de Dios Amill	José de Dios Amill	Barcelona: Sírius
1997	El precio del paraíso. De un campo de exterminio al Amazonas (The Price of Paradise. From an Extermination Camp to the Amazon)	Manuel Leguineche	Antonio García Barón	Madrid: Espasa Calpe
1997	Sobrevivir a Mauthaussen[11] (Surviving Mauthausen)	Agapito Martín Romaní	Agapito Martín Romaní	Self-published
1997	Mauthausen, fin de trayecto: un anarquista en los campos de la muerte (Mauthausen, End of the Line: An Anarchist in the Death Camps)	Lope Massaguer with María Ángeles García-Maroto	Lope Massaguer	Madrid: Fundación Anselmo Lorenzo
1999	El sol se extinguió en Mauthausen: vinarocenses en el infierno nazi (The Sun Was Extinguished in Mauthausen: People from Vinaròs in the Nazi Hell)	Francisco Batiste Baila	Francisco Batiste Baila	Vinaròs: Antinea
2001	Manresa-Mauthausen-Gusen: deportació i retorn d'un home compromès amb la llibertat (Manresa-Mauthausen-Gusen: Deportation and Return of a Man Committed to Liberty)	Jacint Carrió i Vilaseca	Jacint Carrió i Vilaseca	Manresa: Centre d'Estudis del Bages
2001	Un català a Mauthausen: el testimoni de Francesc Comellas (A Catalan in Mauthausen: The Testimony of Francesc Comellas)	David Serrano i Blanquer	Francesc Comellas	Barcelona: Pòrtic
2002	La colina de la muerte: basado en la narración de Fermín Arce, prisionero en Mauthausen, No 4.051 (The Hill of Death: Based on the Narration of Fermín Arce, Prisoner Number 4051 in Mauthausen)	Oscar Luengo	Fermín Arce	Self-published
2002	Sobrevivir al infierno: memorias de una víctima del nazismo (Surviving Hell: Memories of a Victim of Nazism)	Galo Ramos	Galo Ramos	Avilés: Foto Angelín

(Continued)

(Continued)

Year	Title	Author or Editor	Mauthausen Survivor/ Subject of Memoir	Publication Information
2003	*Republicanos españoles en Mauthausen-Gusen (Spanish Republicans in Mauthausen-Gusen)*	Enrique Calcerrada Guijarro with Florencio Pavón Mariblanca	Enrique Calcerrada Guijarro	Benalmádena: Caligrama
2003	*Mauthausen 90.009: la historia de un español en los campos nazis (Mauthausen 90009: The Story of a Spaniard in the Nazi Camps)*	Enmanuel Camacho and Ana Torregrosa	Antonio Muñoz Zamora	Sevilla: Centro Andaluz del Libro
2003	*K.L. Mauthausen 5894*	José Egea Pujante	José Egea Pujante	Barberà del Vallès: Tabelaria
2003	*Un clam de llibertat: vivències de Josep Simon i Mill, exdeportat de Mauthausen (4.929) (A Cry for Liberty: The Life of Josep Simon i Mill, Ex-Mauthausen Deportee [4929])*	Ramon Salvadó i Valentines	Josep Simon i Mill	Saldes: Abadia Editors
2005	*Mi vida en los campos de la muerte nazis (My Life in the Nazi Death Camps)*	Prisciliano García Gaitero with José Luis Gavilanes Laso	Prisciliano García Gaitero	León: Edilesa
2006	*Nacianceno Mata, un canario en Mauthausen: memorias de un superviviente del holocausto nazi (Nacianceno Mata, a Man from the Canary Islands in Mauthausen: Memories of a Nazi Holocaust Survivor)*	Nacianceno Mata with Ricardo A. Guerra Palmero and Oliver Quintero Sánchez	Nacianceno Mata	La Laguna: Centro de la Cultura Popular Canaria
2006	*De Calaceite a Mauthausen: memorias de Raimundo Suñer (From Calaceite to Mauthausen: Raimundo Suñer's Memories)*	Raimundo Suñer Aguas with Miguel Blanc Grau	Raimundo Suñer Aguas	Alcañiz: Centro de Estudios Bajoaragoneses
2006	*Records d'un moianès a Mauthausen (Memories of a Man from Moià in Mauthausen)*	Joan Vilalta i Prat with Raül González Carrasco	Joan Vilalta i Prat	Moià: Associació Cultural Modilianum

Year	Title			
2007	*De Barcelona a Mauthausen: diez años de mi vida (1936–1945)* (From Barcelona to Mauthausen: Ten Years of My Life [1939–1945])	Manuel Alfonso Ortells	Manuel Alfonso Ortells	Móstoles: Memoria Viva
2007	*Mauthausen: memorias de un republicano español en el holocausto* (Mauthausen: Memories of a Spanish Republican in the Holocaust)	Ignacio Mata Maeso	Alfonso Maeso	Barcelona: Ediciones B
2008	*Eusebi Pérez Martín: recordar per viure, viure per recordar* (Eusebi Pérez Martín: Remember to Live, Live to Remember)	Ramon Arnabat Mata and Rosa Toran Belver	Eusebi Pérez Martín	Vilafranca del Penedés: Ajuntament de Vilafranca del Penedés
2008	*Memòria d'exilis i retorns* (Memory of Exiles and Returns)	Josep San Martín Boncompte	Manolo San Martín	Lleida: Pagès Editors
2009	*Testimoniatges i memòries (1936–1945): una nit tan llarga* (Testimonies and Memories [1936–1945]: Such a Long Night)	Marcial Mayans	Marcial Mayans	Valls: Cossetània Edicions
2010	*Amanece en París* (Dawn in Paris)	Paloma Sanz	Ramiro Santisteban	Madrid: Ediciones Planeta
2010	*Un cadáver en el espejo: la odisea de Juan Camacho: Gádor, Mauthausen, Montevideo* (A Cadaver in the Mirror: The Odyssey of Juan Camacho: Gádor, Mauthausen, Montevideo)	David Serrano i Blanquer	José Camacho	Sabadell: Fundació Ars
2011	*Luis Montero Álvarez Sabugo: en los abismos de la historia: vida y muerte de un comunista* (Luis Montero Álvarez "Sabugo": In the Abyss of History: Life and Death of a Communist)	Silvia Ribelles de la Vega	Luis Montero Álvarez	Oviedo: Pentalfa Ediciones
2012	*Francisco Aura Boronat: resistència i dignitat enfront de la desmemòria* (Francisco Aura Boronat: Resistance and Dignity Against Forgetting)	Àngel Beneito Lloris,Francesc-X. Blay Meseguer and Natxo Lara Jornet	Francisco Aura Boronat	Alcoi: Associació Cultural l'Alcoià-Comtat i Cubicat Edicions

represent the memories of survivors filtered through the lens of a family member, historian, or journalist who edited or otherwise curated the text.[12] In both types of life story, the subjects were not public figures.[13]

Decades after their liberation from the concentration camp, the survivors remained on the margins of the movement to recover Spain's historical memory. Although these memoirs have held relatively little sway in the Spanish popular imagination, they nonetheless constitute important source material for Spain's ongoing confrontation with its historical legacy through the country's tradition of life writing. Particularly in the nineteenth and twentieth centuries, Spanish writers developed life writing as an integral part of the country's representation of the self.[14] Carlos Rodríguez del Risco inaugurated the genre for Spanish Mauthausen survivors (chapter 1). Approaching these late-twentieth- and early-twenty-first-century publications as a cohesive body of life writing by and about Spanish survivors of Mauthausen and noting their contribution to the form allows us to consider their commonalities and differences as variations on a theme.

What distinguished these men from thousands of their fellow Spaniards in Mauthausen was, foremost, that they survived. Primo Levi wrote that "we the survivors, are not the true witnesses": the "true witnesses" of the Holocaust "have not returned to tell about it" (*The Drowned and the Saved* 83). To this end, the Spaniards who wrote memoirs of their years in a Nazi concentration camp were a self-selecting group: they survived to liberation, and also had the presence of mind to record their memories of the camp. Survival in Mauthausen for the Spaniards often meant some form of collaboration with the Nazis, mainly as prisoners with privileged working conditions. The thousands of anonymous Spaniards who died in the quarry, from starvation or disease, or were shot by the SS – the "true witnesses," in Levi's estimation – were never able to record their starkly different experience of the camp.

"When we study life writing as a source for cultural memory," Max Saunders writes, "our conclusions will also be literary-critical ones: interpretations of the ways in which memory was produced, constructed, written, and circulated" (323). Saunders's observation captures the significance of the contemporary Spanish life writing that has come about in reaction to the Holocaust. These texts not only provide access to the collective memories of an often-overlooked population of Spanish witnesses to the Holocaust, but their construction, publication, and marketing (or lack thereof) reveal how they interact with the cultural memory of Spain's past. As "Autobiograph[ies] of Those Who Do

Not Write," in Philippe Lejeune's words (185), these texts were composed either by non-professional writers who were both the authors and subjects of their accounts, or with the collaborative efforts of editors who gathered, organized, and distributed the survivor's testimony.

All of these life narratives are subjective accounts of a Mauthausen survivor's individual memory of his personal experience in the camp. Although each text represents how one survivor – or his biographer – viewed his imprisonment in Mauthausen, they neither represent all Spanish Mauthausen survivors nor can they be read as unfiltered historical treatments of the camp. After as many as sixty years of hindsight, these authors' memories have at times degraded or been influenced by other sources, including the memoirs of fellow Mauthausen survivors, histories, and documentary films on the camp. Moreover, the cultural production and examination of the Holocaust that at times has dominated international media coverage over the decades has coloured the survivors' own sense of their experience. Yet this coverage mainly focused on the treatment of Jews in other Nazi camps who had a deadlier trajectory than the Spaniards in Mauthausen. For instance, some Spanish ex-deportees staunchly argued that Mauthausen was an extermination camp, although we know it was not.[15] This cross-pollinization from other sources as well as the vagaries of a survivor's memory account for uncertain details, omissions, and factual errors. Although the process of forgetting is natural and in most cases not intentional, as a result we must read these life narratives as constructed texts. That is, they are the products of diverse influences that cannot be constrained solely by the survivor's firsthand experiences. Errors, exaggerations, and lacunae are endemic to the life narrative, as is historically accurate information. The Mauthausen survivors' written testimony exists in the balance between these two extremes.

The accounts authored solely by a Mauthausen survivor are generally narrated in the first person. In memoirs that have been constructed with the aid of editors or co-authors, a third-person narration or interview format is standard. The majority of these texts were published by small, regional Spanish publishing houses with limited distribution; others were self-published by the authors. In either scenario, these books are by and large available only to a small Spanish readership.[16] The authors and subjects were Aragoneses, Andaluces, and Canarios, from Calaceite, Manresa, Vinaròs, and dozens of other regions and towns in Spain. Titles such as *Vinarocenses en el infierno nazi* (*People from Vinaròs in the Nazi Hell*),

Un canario en Mauthausen (*A Man from the Canary Islands in Mauthausen*), and *Records d'un moianès a Mauthausen* (*Memories of a Man from Moià in Mauthausen*) attest to this regional affiliation. A quarter of the survivor memoirs were written in Catalan and have not been translated into Castilian, the primary language of Spain. This local positioning is integral both to the texts and to the identities of the Mauthausen survivors. During the years they spent in exile and in the camp, these men encountered fellow exiles from their hometowns: they depended on their regional identity to be able to form a community outside of Spain. After liberation, they steadfastly maintained contact with other survivors from their regions of Spain. The authors of these memoirs considered it their responsibility to record the collective memory of the deportees from their home region who would not live to tell their own story; many included lists of compatriots who died in the camp in an appendix to their memoirs.[17] The Spaniards in Mauthausen were forced to renounce their homeland when they fled Spain. Furthermore, they were considered stateless by the Spanish government and displaced by the Nazis. By recovering an identity that grounded them in their native region as opposed to their Spanish nationality, they returned their stories to the locality where their family and friends kept their memories alive, as opposed to recognizing a government that did not recognize them.

The publication of these memoirs by regional publishing houses, often affiliated with municipal governments or cultural institutions, further emphasizes the need to associate the survivors with their particular corner of Spain. Their stories are not only integral to a larger historical record but also to a local Spanish pride in their survival and in their willingness to speak out. The majority of the life narratives of Spanish Mauthausen survivors would never have been published were it not for the editorial and financial support of these regional cultural institutions. Indeed, these efforts demonstrate an ongoing grassroots collective-memory movement, kept alive regionally despite the central Spanish government's defunding of similar efforts at the national level. However, this heightened regional identity further isolates the Spanish experience of the Nazi camp into a separate category from other populations of non-Jewish survivors of Nazi aggression. Even within the body of Spanish representations of Mauthausen, these texts remain on the margins.

For some of these memoirs, the author or editor of the account was a family member – such as a nephew or great-nephew – who collected or transcribed his relative's story, creating a work of postmemory. In the case of the postmemory of Spanish deportees to concentration camps, the second or third generation was central to the publication of the survivor's memoirs, which often reached book form only after the survivor himself had died.[18] These descendants of Spanish Mauthausen victims "share a legacy of trauma" with their uncles and great-uncles, "and thus the curiosity, the urgency, the frustrated *need* to know about a traumatic past" (Hirsch, *Generation of Postmemory* 35; emphasis in the original). Yet the intervention of a non-survivor also complicates the immediacy of the subject's reactions to his experiences in the camp.

Raimundo Suñer's memoirs were extensive but incomplete when he died in 1976. The author's son, Manolo Suñer, presented two notebooks' worth of his father's manuscripts to Miguel Blanc Grau, the nephew of another Mauthausen survivor, in 1990 (Suñer Aguas 13). Blanc Grau described the process of editing the manuscript in his introduction to *De Calaceite a Mauthausen: Memorias de Raimundo Suñer* (*From Calaceite to Mauthausen: Raimundo Suñer's Memories*). He typed, rearranged, and cut portions of the manuscript for various reasons, including to omit some familial details that he felt had little relevance to the author's story. Blanc Grau's draft was subsequently edited again by Manolo Suñer, "quien creyó conveniente atenuar diversas opiniones de su padre sobre adversarios políticos, suprimir nombres de personas comprometidas y rebajar o anular adjetivos (asesino, matón, etc.) con los que, en principio, el autor matizaba algunos personajes" (14).[19] Although the author's original language was compromised, these collaborative memoirs often read more coherently than self-published or self-edited survivor's accounts in that they provided context, detail, and narrative style to the author's original manuscript. Nevertheless, the collaborative efforts of editors disturb the "autobiographical pact," in Lejeune's definition, that the reader maintains with the survivor, inserting distance from the testimonial account as well as doubt that the intentions of the author are the same as the intentions of the editor (14). Ultimately, it is up to the reader to judge whether each individual Mauthausen memoir is faithful to the survivor's interpretation of his experience. As Saunders has observed, however, the audience may gain a better understanding of cultural memory when it reads these accounts as a means of mediating the past as opposed to a means of providing accurate representations of history (323). Still, the symbolic control of the story remains with the name on the title page, as Lejeune has argued (11). Whether that name appears as the author, co-author, or in the title of the text itself does not challenge this control.

Although they can be understood broadly as life writing, these accounts also conform to Sidonie Smith and Julia Watson's definition of memoir. They focus on a particular moment in the life of the subject that has proven consequential for that individual's sense of self (Smith and Watson 3–4). In this case, that memory consisted of the period during the Second World War when the subject was imprisoned in Mauthausen. Dios Amill's 1995 publication inaugurated this late-twentieth- and early-twenty-first-century mini-boom in Mauthausen memoirs. Like the majority of these texts, Dios Amill's now out-of-print memoir was published by a small publishing house and is available at only a few libraries in Spain. *La verdad sobre Mauthausen* (*The Truth about Mauthausen*) is a first-person narrative that begins in the middle of Dios Amill's life, when he was stationed with the 86th *Compagnies de travailleurs étrangers* (CTE) in France and the Germans were approaching. Dios Amill wrote about his experiences supporting the Republic as a cultural advisor in Fraga, Spain; being deported to Mauthausen in January 1940; surviving five years of imprisonment, hard labour, and abuse; and returning to Spain thanks to a bureaucratic connection in 1947. His book was the first published Mauthausen survivor account in Spain since 1980.[20] The Mauthausen memoirs published over the course of the next decade and a half more or less follow Dios Amill's account in form and function.

Although these stories are each unique accounts, narrative patterns emerge across the genre of the Mauthausen memoir. Constructed almost entirely chronologically, the text begins either with a brief overview of the survivor's childhood in Spain or with his military or political actions for the Republic during the Spanish Civil War. The memoirists described how they were forced into exile, crossing into France as the Spanish Civil War ended and their prospects in their native country darkened. Once in France, the majority were immediately herded into internment camps along the shore: Argelès-sur-Mer, Barcarès, Saint Cyprien, Agde, Septfonds, or, in the cases of the younger ex-deportees, to the town of Angoulême.[21] In the fetid, overcrowded internment camps, the survivors had no means by which to support themselves nor possibilities to escape their barbed-wire enclosure. They "voluntarily" joined one of the CTEs, which many of the Mauthausen memoirists called "Compañías de trabajadores españoles," in that they were composed almost entirely of Spaniards. They inevitably ended up working on military fortifications along the Maginot Line while German troops advanced through Germany, Luxembourg, and Belgium. Other deportees, again coerced and facing deportation back to Spain, joined the French Army or the Foreign Legion in their efforts to push back Hitler.

As the Nazis advanced, the survivor described his eventual capture by German troops. At this point, the deportees were sent to a *Stalag* or prisoner-of-war camp. Some memoirists described the conditions in the *Stalags* as relatively more humane, in hindsight, than what the survivor later encountered in Mauthausen. After months in the *Stalag* or in Angoulême with other exiled Spaniards, the surviving Spaniards were packed into cattle wagons. They wrote about being transported in train convoys under brutal conditions, whether in summer or winter, across Europe to the Mauthausen train station. They expressed a universal lack of knowledge about their destination, but in retrospect they interpreted the Mauthausen sign at the station as an ominous indication of the miserable existence that awaited them.

Most of the memoirists arrived at Mauthausen in 1940 or 1941, along with the majority of the Spaniards.[22] The deportees' first introductions to Mauthausen were strikingly similar, attesting both to the Nazis' desire for uniformity and the relatively communal experience of the Spaniards of Mauthausen. They were greeted by an interpreter who told them some version of the same warning: that the only way out of the camp was through the crematory smoke or that they should throw themselves on the electric fence to avoid a more painful death. They were forced to remove their clothes and turn over their possessions. After a cold shower, the shaving of their body hair left them bloodied. Next, the deportees were assigned an ill-fitting prisoner uniform and a blue triangle. They came to understand the uniform and the triangle as the mark of the Spanish political prisoner. Unified now by their shaved heads and baggy, striped clothing, the men completed their transformation from individual to subhuman with the assignment of their prisoner number, stitched onto their uniform, which they were required to memorize immediately and pronounce in German upon demand (Salvadó i Valentines 94). Although dehumanizing, these numbers became something of a badge of honour for the ex-deportees who wrote their memoirs: they were proof of an ordeal that only a lucky few survived. To that end, most of these memoirists included photos, identity documents, and letters in the text with the aim of attesting to the historical truth of their accounts, that they were where they said they were.[23] But in their various states of conservation and decay, these relics also demonstrated an agency to save the material forming the survivor's sole link with the outside world.

From this point the prisoners' experiences diverged, depending on whether they arrived while the camp was still under construction or when it was more or less finished, on what work *Kommando* and barracks they were assigned to, on their health and age when they entered the camp, on the other prisoners with whom they associated in the camp, and on pure luck. Some were sent to Gusen or Ebensee to work in the tunnels, narrowly avoiding the deaths that were common in those two subsidiary camps, while others remained in the main camp, working in the quarry. Some were transferred to work *Kommandos* outside the camp under the control of the SS guards or prisoner-*Kapos*, suffering through austere conditions for years. Still others, like Suñer, who worked in the garages, or Manuel Alfonso Ortells, who worked drafting maps, described the privileged positions they attained in the Mauthausen main camp. They witnessed elements of the *Lager* that others were not permitted to see: Suñer glimpsed the inside of the so-called *coche fantasma* (ghost car) and Alfonso saw the maps of the surrounding countryside and the Nazi propaganda he copied for the SS. Those who survived Gusen, Enrique Calcerrada Guijarro and Jacint Carrió i Vilaseca among them, were able to recount the particularly desperate conditions in this nearby Mauthausen subcamp to which very few Spaniards lived to bear witness.

The accounts converged again on 5 May 1945. All of the Mauthausen memoirists provided a narrative of the exhilarating, chaotic, and desperate days leading up to and following the liberation of the camp. Many memoirs also traced the survivor's movements after the camp's liberation, as he returned to exile in France, began to re-establish his life, married, had children, and forged a career after his long hiatus in the concentration camp. Others moved even farther away from Spain, going into exile in Latin America.[24] Dios Amill was among the few who returned to Spain shortly after the end of the war, risking severe repercussions from the Franco government for his involvement in the Civil War and his exile. For these Mauthausen memoirists, their adopted home was as much a part of their survival story as the years they spent in the concentration camp.

Encouraged by anniversaries of liberation and their need to come to terms with their imprisonment, many of the survivors who wrote their accounts returned to Mauthausen decades later. Indeed, revisiting the site of their years of suffering was in many cases what prompted them to record their memories of the camp. Photos of some survivors posing before the monument to the Spaniards killed in Mauthausen and walking through the now-empty Appellplatz illustrate a number of these publications. The impetus to describe their brushes with death and their will to survive is another thread that runs throughout these memoirs. Marcial Mayans began his account by celebrating its publication, recognizing that "[a]ra estic segur que els meus records passaran a la Història de la Humanitat" (16).[25] Like many of his fellow memoirists, Francisco Batiste dedicated his account to his fallen comrades and their families: "Para cuantos fueron inmolados mi eterno recuerdo. Para sus familiares que jamás serán resarcidos por la pérdida de sus seres queridos, mi solidaridad y respeto" (*El sol se extinguió en Mauthausen* 227).[26] There was a sense for some of these authors, whether realistic or not, that their story was now destined to be incorporated into a European culture of memory of the Holocaust.

The survivors were not historians, but often composed a basic background about the war and the concentration camps. While imprisoned in Mauthausen, the Spanish deportees knew very little about other Nazi concentration camps or the movements of the Allies and Axis powers. In the years after 1945, however, this historical background was required knowledge for the ex-deportees to be able to contextualize their years of absence with the experiences of family, friends, and compatriots in Spain during the same period. Yet these contextualizing personal and historical anecdotes also complicated the testimonial quality of the memoirs in that the survivor often provided opinions about episodes that he did not witness. Distinct from the early survivor accounts that emerged in the late 1940s, these contemporary memoirs strove to prove their historical merit. By including discussions of events related to the Second World War, the Nazi camps, and the Holocaust to which they were not privy, having heard about them via word of mouth or from documented texts, the authors underlined the relevance of their experiences to historical events on a world stage while at the same time sacrificing their grounding in firsthand testimony.

Major events in Mauthausen such as the public hanging of the Austrian prisoner Hans Bonarewitz, who attempted to escape the camp hidden in a box; the day-long general disinfections; or the arrival of transports of evacuees from other concentration camps as the war was ending were shared experiences in which the entire camp participated. The many memoirists who wrote about these occurrences were all witnesses. However, other events or actions that only a select few saw firsthand nevertheless were common knowledge to other prisoners who did not watch them happen. Middle-of-the-night escape attempts, Russians and Jews who were set upon by the SS dogs, and the work that Joan de Diego, Casimir Climent, Francesc Boix, and Antoni García performed within the camp offices and photography laboratory found their way into many of these personal accounts, despite the fact that their authors were not witnesses. Other episodes have attained a level of notoriety such that a number of memoirists recounted them as if they had seen the events as they happened. The escape attempt of four Spaniards who were subsequently caught and returned to the camp, the arrival of prostitutes from other camps, and the Spanish women transported from Ravensbrück in 1945 became fodder for anecdotes that stretched beyond what any one prisoner saw firsthand. The majority of the Spanish prisoners did not follow the route and capture of the Spaniards who escaped, come into contact with the prostitutes, nor see the arrival of the Spanish women. Yet through the telling and retelling in the camp of these episodes, many of the survivors were at least aware of these events, and some related them in great detail. This, in essence, is the process of collectivizing the memories that only some possess as individual memory. By intermingling individual with collective memories, the Mauthausen memoirists at once diluted the testimonial nature of their accounts and expanded their view of Mauthausen beyond what their two eyes actually ascertained. These accounts must be read, therefore, not as historical treatises on the Spaniards in Mauthausen, but as individual attempts to capture the overarching experience of the camp.

Despite these forays into Mauthausen lore, however, the memoirists tended to concentrate on their day-to-day existence. Details that commonly get lost in more historically minded accounts become foundational information in these memoirs: the measly rations, the squalid barracks, the cruel punishments exacted by the SS, the incessant work regimen in the quarry, the harsh Austrian weather, the prisoner-*Kapos* to whose control and power the rest of the prisoners were subjected, and the interactions with other international prisoners in the camp. In the spirit of Primo Levi, who devoted sections of *If This Is a Man* to how he and his fellow Auschwitz prisoners trimmed their nails with their teeth and polished their shoes with machine grease, no detail is too small.

Josep Simon i Mill described his daily routine in Mauthausen with precision: what time he got up, how he kept himself clean, how he washed his clothes, and what he did on Sundays (Salvadó i Valentines 119, 147, 152). Enrique Calcerrada Guijarro listed the daily nourishment he and his fellow Spanish prisoners were provided in Gusen. By his tally of centilitres, the SS allowed the prisoners just over a litre of food or liquid per day:

> Mañana: Café (especie de malta que casi nadie bebía) 10 cl.
> Mediodía: 1 litro de nabos cocidos, o espinacas, o patatas 362 cl.
> Tarde: 360 a 400 g. de pan negro 791 cl.
>   25 a 30 g. de salchicha 40 cl.
> Domingos: una cucharada de mermelada (65 cl.), que repartida entre los 7 días de la semana tocan a 10 cl.
> Total persona/día 1.213 cl (Calcerrada Guijarro and Pavón Mariblanca 140)[27]

Fermín Arce recalled an outbreak of fleas in the barracks at a moment when it had been nearly nine weeks since the Spaniards had been afforded a change in underwear. The two general disinfections that followed in June 1941 allowed the SS to humiliate the prisoners as they suffered the cold and heat of over 12 hours of continuous exposure naked (Luengo 231–6). During another disinfection in 1944, after a snowfall, Mayans watched as men died "gelats als nostres peus" ("frozen at our feet" 155). Batiste faulted certain Spanish *Kapos* for the mistreatment of their compatriots, singling out those he considered traitors for selling themselves to the SS as "destacados verdugos" ("distinguished executioners" *El sol se extinguió en Mauthausen* 79). Other Spanish *Kapos*, whom he also named, were forced to collaborate with the Nazis but redeemed themselves as "salvadores de muchas vidas de sus camaradas" (Batiste Baila, *El sol se extinguió en Mauthausen* 79).[28] Juan Camacho also discussed the Spaniards who collaborated with the SS, including Flor de Lis, who was killed by a group of Spaniards after liberation while waiting for a train (Serrano i Blanquer, *Un cadáver en el espejo* 66). Although Camacho revealed that he knew Flor de Lis' killer, he refused to identify that person by name.

Some survivors took the opportunity to set the record straight on matters that had been debated by their fellow ex-deportees. Eusebi Pérez Martín took exception to the claim that the Spaniards in Mauthausen were all politically united in the clandestine resistance organization: "Cal insister ... en les diverses percepcions del que succeïa dins del camp, a redós de les circumstàncies de cada internat, pel que fa al seu destí, barracot i relacions personals, a més de les adscripcions polítiques i sindicals i del les trajectòries després de l'alliberament" (Arnabat Mata and Toran Belver 110).[29] Pérez also questioned the notion presented by Mariano Constante and others that the Spaniards were armed and fought the SS in the days just before and after their liberation. The historians who curated his life narrative wrote that "L'Eusebi Pérez, pel contrari, negava, de manera reiterada, l'existència d'una organització armada preparada i cohesionada en la darrera fase de Mauthausen" (112–13).[30] Pérez even disputed Boix's magnanimity in the days after Mauthausen's liberation, recounting that Boix refused to take a photo of Pérez and his friends, claiming he didn't have any film (101).[31] Antonio Muñoz Zamora, who arrived in Mauthausen in 1944, after years in Dachau, had a somewhat different experience than other Spanish deportees in the camp. For one, he recalled, "Yo nunca pasé por esas filas en las que el republicano catalán Amat daba la bienvenida a los españoles" (Camacho and Torregrosa 205).[32] The Mauthausen memoirs are opportunities for individual survivors to differentiate their experiences from the similar, but not exact, experiences of their fellow countrymen.

Without fail, these memoirists recorded the unrelenting violence and death that surrounded them. Every survivor described in chilling detail the SS killings they witnessed.[33] Such are the number of deaths the Spanish memoirists related that a reader can just about open a page at random to find an example. Massaguer recounted vicious attacks by the SS dogs that left a prisoner ripped to pieces and lacking his genitals (Massaguer and García-Maroto 131). Mayans watched as an SS commander shot at a formation of prisoners, killing one of the deportee's friends before his eyes (157). Fermín Arce described how an SS guard dislocated the shoulders of a prisoner strung up with his arms behind his back by standing on him until he lost consciousness and died (Luengo 112). The sheer depravity of the Nazis is evident on virtually every page of these survivor memoirs. The memoirists felt compelled to describe with sickening precision the murders they and their compatriots saw: it remains largely unsaid that the fate of any one of these murdered fellow prisoners could have been their own.

As a whole, the Mauthausen memoirists grappled with how their experiences fit into the larger framework of the Holocaust. Although they had limited direct contact with the camp's Jewish population, many survivors acknowledged the substantial difference between the Spanish and Jewish experience of Mauthausen. Perhaps more directly than any of his contemporary ex-deportee memoirists, Dios Amill argued that the fates of the Spanish and other non-Jewish deportees had been unjustly ignored in light of the millions of Jews who died in concentration camps: "Sobre el holocausto nazi hay un sinfín de libros que describen la persecución del mundo hebreo pero se ha escrito muy poco, y gran parte del mundo lo ignora, sobre los millones de personas no judías que también perecieron en los campos de concentración" (58–9).[34] Nevertheless, the author admitted that the Spaniards benefited from the Nazis' obsession with the extermination of the Jews in Mauthausen: "no dejaba de considerar, de una manera un tanto egoista, que con su llegada [de los judíos] al campo habían dado al traste con mi buena situación pero ellos no tenían culpa de mi destino ni de que éste fuera bueno o malo" (118).[35] Dios Amill's sentiments about the attention given to the Spaniards deported to Mauthausen versus the Jews was mitigated by the admission that the two groups faced very different, albeit interrelated, fates. Other Mauthausen memoirists also emphasized this distinction. Massaguer wrote that "[s]er *Rotspanier* (rojo español) en Mauthausen era estar dispuesto a los más atroces castigos, ser *Juden* (judío) era todavía peor, significaba la peor de las muertes" (Massaguer and García-Maroto 151; emphasis in the original).[36]

Some Spaniards were afforded fleeting glimpses of the Jews in Mauthausen, allowing them to draw conclusions about their treatment. Among the many tortures he witnessed in Mauthausen, Massaguer described an SS officer forcing a group of Jews to jump into freezing water, holding their heads under until they were almost to the point of asphyxiation, then ordering them back to the quarry. Massaguer knew "por experiencia que la mayoría de aquellos hombres dejarían de existir a los pocos días" (Massaguer and García-Maroto 152).[37] Camacho remembered that whereas the Spaniards wore wooden-soled shoes, the Jews who worked alongside him did not have shoes, and their feet were a bloody mess (Serrano i Blanquer, *Un cadáver en el espejo* 62). Suñer witnessed the arrival of a transport of some 200 Jews from the garages where he worked in October 1942. He wrote that he saw this group of Jews, naked and arranged in three lines, marching towards the wash room. Suñer overheard their cries as the SS beat them, and noticed that by the next day, they were all gone: "Después de las nueve de la noche se oían gritos y ruidos, y es que los SS se divertían con ellos con palos, vergajos y hasta con los picos. A la mañana siguiente no quedaba ninguno vivo y cuando salimos al trabajo ya estaba todo limpio" (Suñer Aguas 249).[38] By remembering just one instance of the millions of murders of Jews throughout the Nazi concentration camp empire, Suñer was a witness to the Holocaust.[39]

Suñer also provided chilling details of the so-called "autocar de la muerte" or "coche fantasma" ("automobile of death" or "ghost car") that the SS used to gas prisoners. Because he was assigned to the garages, Suñer could verify the identities of the SS drivers. He described a gruesome scene in the interior of the car after it had been used: "Dentro encontraba señales de las personas: vello, sangre, trozos de ropa y hasta sesos" (Suñer Aguas 250).[40] Alfonso Mata Maeso also bore witness to the murders that happened daily in Mauthausen. He recounted being ordered to stay inside the barracks with the windows shut as transports of Yugoslavs, including women and children, arrived and were taken directly to the gas chamber and exterminated. Mata said that he could never forget their cries, and that because of those terrible memories, "hubo un tiempo en que decidí no hablar de mi experiencia en Mauthausen" (100).[41] When he drafted his memoir, however, he realized that his memories could help the next generation never forget this horrific past. Mata's cognition about the importance of his individual story, recounted more than sixty years after the end of the Second World War, illustrates the pressing need for this type of life writing. The Mauthausen survivors captured traces of the Holocaust that would have otherwise accompanied them to their graves.

Given the present-day resurgence in interest in Spain's historical memory, one might imagine that the subjects of these life stories would have piqued the Spanish public's imagination as the amateur equivalent of Primo Levi and Jorge Semprún. Yet in fact these memoirs as a body are a virtually unknown manifestation of life writing in Spain. This absence can be explained in part by their limited distribution, regional specificity, idiosyncratic composition, and lack of national publicity. As the Spanish concentration camp survivors near extinction, their earnest life stories have been supplanted in the cultural sphere by more marketable versions of survivors' stories. Biographies, documentary films, graphic novels, and historical fiction dealing with the Spaniards in Mauthausen have emerged in the past fifteen years as dynamic new representations of a story that at one point seemed to have run its course in the country's consciousness. These updated entries in the body of representations of the Spanish experience of Mauthausen were not written by survivors, yet clearly depended on the life narratives of survivors for their historical depth and detail. Despite the popularity and aesthetics of these more professional endeavours, the Mauthausen memoirs constitute a raw, emotional telling of a dramatic episode central to Spain's past that cannot so easily be relegated to obscurity.

Smith and Watson write that authority in autobiography "neither confirms nor invalidates notions of objective truth; rather it tracks the previously uncharted truths of particular lives" (16). The body of Mauthausen life writing attests to the importance of reporting for the historical record the existence of the concentration camp and the fact that Spaniards were among the prisoner population there, and including specific details and images that implicitly argue for the veracity of the author's narrative. Yet these life stories are not works of historiography, and as such the "uncharted truths" that Mauthausen survivors communicate take the reader behind the walls of silence left by those who did not survive the Nazi genocide, into the depths of lives lived in tandem with history. How these memoirs are uncovered, read, and remembered is central to the legacy they leave for continued efforts to unravel Spain's – and humanity's – collective memory of its past traumas.

Mauthausen Onscreen: Documentary Films on Spanish Television, 2000–2005

By 2000, Spanish Mauthausen survivors were publishing life narratives at the rate of one per year. Their voices could be heard in the pages of these memoirs. But they were still a relatively silent contingent, an anonymous group with no real collective identity in Spain's eye. Who were these elderly survivors? What did they look like and how did they sound? Although Llorenç Soler's 1975 documentary *Sobrevivir en Mauthausen* covertly inaugurated a contemporary way of visualizing the camp and its Spanish victims (chapter 3), there would be no other cinematic representation of Mauthausen until the turn of the twenty-first century. Beginning in the year 2000, a succession of documentary films on the Spanish experience of Nazi policies and practices began to appear.[42] Though none would find wide release in Spanish cinemas, these documentaries were shown on Spanish television and at a few international film festivals. Following a standard narrative pattern of combining the testimony of Mauthausen survivors with archival and contemporary footage of the camp, these films brought visual acuity to a topic that had previously only been portrayed in print and black and white still images. Although the artistic merit of these Mauthausen documentaries varies, they largely succeeded in putting faces and names to the last remaining Mauthausen survivors. By preserving their voices and memories, these films gave Spanish victims a visible identity and the last word.

Over the past two decades, Spanish documentary film has matured into a widely popular medium, particularly on television. Although a national cinema award for documentaries was only established in 2002, autonomous television stations like Televisió de Catalunya and the subscription channel Canal Plus have underwritten and broadcast hundreds of homegrown non-fiction films over the past fifteen years. Spain's state-run station, Televisión Española (TVE), also contributed to the new wave of Spanish documentaries, despite repeated allegations of partisanship (Estrada, *El documental cinematográfico* 37). The genre has become particularly associated with the movement to recover the collective memories of the Spanish Civil War and Franco's dictatorship. However, historical documentaries on Spanish television have also brought lesser-known chapters from the country's history into its living rooms.

Isabel Estrada writes that digital technology has "democratized" the Spanish documentary, "facilita[ndo] la producción de documentales independientes que se realizan con bajísimos presupuestos" (*El documental cinematográfico* 13–14).[43] Although the low production costs of some of these documentary films has inhibited their wider release beyond Spain, they have had an impact inside the country on the population's grasp of its recent past. In the case of the victims of the Spanish Civil War, Estrada argues that by the 1990s, "el documental es la única producción cultural que responde directamente al interés por la perspectiva de la víctima" (15).[44] This observation rings true for documentaries that confront the Spanish legacy of Mauthausen as well. Taking advantage of the relative ease and mobility of digital production, filmmakers sought out Spain's elderly concentration camp survivors in their homes and retirement centres.[45] Many of these victims were unknown, not having participated in other testimony collections undertaken by journalists in Spain; others, like Mariano Constante, appeared repeatedly on Spanish television talk shows, becoming the faces of the deportation of Spaniards to Mauthausen. Onscreen, the advanced age and fragile health of the few ex-deportees who were able to communicate their accounts to the filmmakers made their stories that much more urgent. The digital filmmaking revolution arrived just in time to record the ingrained memories of Mauthausen's last living Spanish survivors.

Four films released between 2000 and 2005 are central to the creation of a visual narrative of the experiences of the Spaniards in Mauthausen. The first three were broadcast to coincide with the fifty-fifth anniversary of the end of the Second World War in 2000, and the fourth arrived four years later. Considered together, they capture the panorama of methods filmmakers have used to transform decades-old events into stories that are relevant to contemporary audiences. *Cerca del Danubio* (*Near the Danube*), a documentary short directed by Felipe Vega, was shown on Canal Plus in April 2000. *Francisco Boix, un fotógrafo en el infierno* (*Francisco Boix, a Photographer in Hell*) directed by Llorenç Soler, now a mainstream director, followed on Canal Plus in May of the same year. And *Mauthausen, el deber de recordar* (*Mauthausen, the Duty to Remember*), directed by Joan Sella and Cesc Tomás, appeared on the state-run TVE 2 station in three instalments in September 2000. Although each of these films has a slightly different purpose, they all give priority to the voices of Mauthausen survivors in the creation of the narrative. However, they vary as to the historical information they relay, and in particular how they characterize Franco's role in the deportation of Spaniards to Nazi camps.

A number of additional documentaries on the Spanish experience of Mauthausen were produced throughout the first decade of the 2000s, some of which appeared on Spanish television.[46] But it was Montse Armengou and Richard Belis's *El comboi dels 927* (*The Convoy of the 927*), first shown on Televisió de Catalunya in 2004, that became the most successful and widely known of the Spanish Mauthausen documentaries. By altering the standard narrative to include the stories of women and children who were deported on the notorious convoy from Angoulême, France, to Mauthausen, Armengou and Belis widen the perspective of their film beyond the typical heroic testimony of male survivors. At the same time, their film contains the most damning evidence to date implicating Franco's government in the conscious decision to send Spanish refugees to their deaths in Nazi concentration camps. *El comboi dels 927* tells a dramatic story that leaves no doubt that Spain maintains its own horrifying connection to the Holocaust.

Like the Spanish Mauthausen memoirs, however, these films present a subjective narrative that focuses on particular aspects of the overall history of the Spaniards in the camp. Although they contain historically accurate information and details common to a collective of Spanish Mauthausen prisoners, they also construct a particular perspective of the camp dependent on the memories of just a few survivors. The filmmaker(s), identities of the survivors interviewed, and means of distribution all contribute to the vantage point relayed onscreen. Although documentary film gives the appearance of historical transparency, the process of selecting, editing, juxtaposing, and narrating the footage creates subtle subtexts that communicate a particular message to the viewer. Historical context is distilled into sound bites that value entertainment over education; dramatic tension and conflict are inserted in the interest of creating a sensationalist storyline. For instance, interviews with Mauthausen survivors who were members of the Spanish communist clandestine organization group pivot three of these films towards accounts of heroic resistance. This narrative builds to a crescendo around the famous photo of the Spaniards welcoming the American liberators to the camp in *Francisco Boix, un fotógrafo en el infierno*; *Mauthausen, el deber de recordar*; and *El comboi dels 927*. The focus on the iconic photo of a group of Spanish survivors gathered before the Mauthausen main gate punctuates a dramatic arc in these three documentaries that communicates in words and images the central role of the Spanish population in the camp's liberation. Although the Spaniards were indeed front and centre for liberation, these films create a tunnel vision that excludes any other possible narrative. *Cerca del Danubio*, the only one of these four documentaries that does not use period photographs and footage, presents a slightly different, though no less subjective, perspective.

Cerca del Danubio is the most self-consciously artistic of the three Mauthausen documentaries from 2000. The director, Felipe Vega, juxtaposes seemingly disconnected images and abruptly cuts from one scene to another in this twenty-five-minute short. Although Vega provides a schematic context for the film's storyline, only after the viewer has seen the entire short is it possible to grasp how the visual strands of the narrative come together. Vega identifies Antonio Muñoz Zamora and Joaquín Masegosa Rodríguez in credits appearing before the film's title, but their status as Mauthausen survivors must be inferred from the film's context and the men's testimony. Interviewed in their homes in Almería, Spain, they recall elements of their imprisonment in the camp. Among the film's opening shots are scenes of a monument in Almería dedicated to Spaniards deported to Nazi camps. With no contextual information, however, an uninformed spectator could not be expected to identify the significance of this monument or the events and individuals it commemorates. Only at the film's end does a title card appear to explain that some 7,000 Spaniards were deported to Mauthausen, including 142 from Almería. Vega provides no other explicit historical information.

Unlike the typical narrative chronology that has become familiar in Mauthausen survivor memoirs, Muñoz Zamora and Masegosa Rodríguez begin by reflecting on their dreams while in the camp. Only then does the filmmaker backtrack to their descriptions of entering the camp. Vega cuts between images of the survivors' homes – songbirds in a cage, a crackling fire in the fireplace, family photos on the walls – and these two elderly men speaking, at times overcome by emotion, about their memories of Mauthausen. In medium shots taken with a handheld camera, Muñoz Zamora and Masegosa Rodríguez describe the everyday existence in the camp: their uniforms, lack of food or eating utensils, the blows of the SS guards, the interminable formations. While Masegosa Rodríguez sits outside his home in the sun, the rolling hills of Almería behind him, he describes being forced to perform "salto al rana" ("leapfrog") exercises on the frozen tundra of the Appellplatz as men collapsing from exhaustion were marched to the gas chamber. Vega creates a striking contrast between the survivors' descriptions of Nazi crimes and their bucolic surroundings. Only when Masegosa Rodríguez admits that he has never returned to the camp do the film's images converge with the spaces the survivors describe.

The second half of *Cerca del Danubio* transports the viewer to Mauthausen and the surrounding countryside. Dark and subdued in early spring, with snow still on the ground, Vega includes video of the camp devoid of any human presence. The camera pans around the Appellplatz, enters the gas chamber and the prisoner barracks, and films the quarry, accompanied by a booming non-diegetic classical soundtrack. The short ends with the two survivors reading a section of Primo Levi's poem "If This Is a Man" translated into Spanish. As Levi's words capture the disconnect between those who lived "seguros en vuestras càsas caldeadas" and the man "quien muere por un sí o un no," the film closes on two survivors who knew both the warmth of home and the horror of the concentration camp.[47] Vega's short seeks to elicit an emotional reaction in the viewer, not through shocking images of violence or historical revelations, but by hinting at the struggle to survive mapped on the faces and voices of these two men. By rejecting a more historical retelling of the experience of the Spaniards in Mauthausen, Vega positions *Cerca del Danubio* as a subtle and suggestive film that, much like Levi's poem, aims to elicit a vague sadness in the audience. Yet by avoiding background context, *Cerca del Danubio* sidesteps a number of important details, such as what these two survivors' backgrounds were, why they – and not other survivors – were included in the film, and how their experiences differed or were consistent with those of other Spanish Mauthausen survivors. The two other Mauthausen documentaries released in 2000, though also highly selective with the information they provide, take a much more direct route.

Francisco Boix, un fotógrafo en el infierno begins with the testimony of another Spanish Mauthausen survivor in a wholly different context: archival footage of Boix's deposition at Nuremberg in January 1946. The deep voice of the narrator outlines the film's intention to understand the mysterious life of its protagonist, counting on the recollections of "los últimos protagonistas y testigos del mayor genocidio de los tiempos modernos."[48] Because he died in 1951, the fractured memories of these aged Spanish Mauthausen survivors are the spectator's only link to Boix's life story. It is clear that the filmmaker depends on drama and suspense to elicit an immediate reaction in his audience: outrage and disgust at the actions of the Nazis melded with admiration and pity for the heroic and long-gone Boix. If *Cerca del Danubio* was a quiet homage to two Mauthausen survivors, *Francisco Boix* is a glossy melodrama told with urgency.

The historian Benito Bermejo's book *Francisco Boix, el fotógrafo de Mauthausen* (*Francisco Boix, the Mauthausen Photographer*) is the primary source material for the film.[49] As such, director Llorenç Soler and executive producer Oriol Porta ground the film in historical information and generally avoid any ongoing doubts about Boix's legacy (chapter 1). Over quick cuts between black and white filmstrips and images, Soler weaves together scenes from Boix's childhood and the rapidly ending Spanish Civil War. He emphasizes Franco's friendly relationship with Hitler with footage from Spanish newsreels from the 1940s documenting the meeting of the two dictators. Soler implicates the Franco government in the deportation of Spanish Republicans to Nazi camps, as the voice-over narration states: "Serrano Suñer negocia con Hitler anular la condición de ciudadanos españoles de todos los republicanos hechos prisioneros por los alemanes en Francia. Dicho de otro modo: se trataba de negociar su exterminio."[50] As the camera pans over typed documents in German, the filmmaker draws a direct connection between the meeting Serrano Suñer, Franco's minister of foreign affairs, had in Germany with Hitler and the Führer's 25 September 1940 decree ordering the Spaniards to be turned over to the Gestapo and deported to concentration camps. Although this was not the first time Franco and his government were accused of colluding in the deportation of the Spanish Republicans to Nazi camps, it was the first time this collaboration was spelled out in unmistakable words and images in a Spanish television documentary. The shocking accusation that Serrano Suñer "negotiated the extermination" of the Spanish prisoners of war in Soler's film would be further dramatized in *El comboi dels 927*.

Given its protagonist's death at a young age, *Francisco Boix* relies on the filmed testimony of other Mauthausen survivors in its recreation of Boix's experience of the camp. Eleven elderly survivors appear onscreen speaking not only about their experiences in the camp, but also about their interactions with Boix.[51] They were chosen selectively for their affinity with Boix as fellow members of the clandestine communist organization in Mauthausen, former Poschacher *Kommando* workers, or contemporaries of Boix's after liberation. Filmed in medium shots, these men are interviewed in their homes describing a litany of starvation, abuses, and killings in the camp.[52] Unlike in *Cerca del Danubio*, however, the voice-over narration contextualizes what the elderly Mauthausen survivors recount with additional historical background, illustrated with black and white filmstrips and photographs. A number of survivors emphasize the privilege certain Spaniards attained in the Mauthausen offices. The voice-over narration asks whether the men who enjoyed better working conditions and the solidarity of their fellow prisoners survived because of luck, or because they were more calculating than their compatriots. This commentary establishes a dramatic tension in the film that absorbs Boix, who survived in part because he obtained a privileged position in the photographic laboratory. It is one of the few moments when the film hints at the existence of a counterstory to the dominant narrative that characterizes Boix as a hero.

Nevertheless, the Spaniards' resistance efforts are the narrative core of the film, with Boix's actions at the forefront. The documentary relies not only on the voices of the survivors to tell his story, but also on the photographic images that became Boix's legacy. After claiming one of the SS Leica cameras after the camp's liberation, the voice-over narrates, "la cámara fotográfica será su arma de lucha, su herramienta de militante comunista" until the end of Boix's life.[53] Positioning his camera as equivalent to a weapon further emphasizes Soler's core message of Boix's almost mythical heroism. These photographs, the spectator is reminded, became definitive proof in postwar trials against the Nazis. Thus Boix attained both military and legal prowess. The photos that Boix took after liberation attested to the humanity of the prisoners, both the dead and the living. He recorded the first open meeting of the Spanish Communist Party, eight days after the camp's liberation, as well as Franz Ziereis during his deathbed confession. The cascading archival still images Soler uses in the film illustrate the breadth of Boix's photographic eye as well as his seeming omniscience.

Boix's return to Paris and the continuation of his political activities after liberation bring a new subtext to the film: Boix dominated the public imagination of Mauthausen even after the war ended. The documentary returns to Boix's testimony at Nuremberg, the centrepiece of his postwar influence. This original footage, in which Boix speaks clearly in French before a room full of Nazis, prosecutors, translators, and witnesses, is a film within a film. This was the only postwar footage of a Spanish Mauthausen survivor actively accusing the Nazis of their crimes. No other Spaniard participated in the Nuremberg trials. Subtitled in Spanish, Soler allows Boix's testimony to speak for itself. Soler's dependence on this archival footage as well as the photographs Boix took and rescued is itself an argument for visual imagery as a central medium in the creation of a contemporary Mauthausen narrative. Soler's documentary, like Boix's photos, is a visual testament to the Spanish experience of Mauthausen. By including photos Boix took and saved – as all the Mauthausen documentaries do – as well as Boix's filmed testimony at Nuremberg, Soler implicitly argues for the central function of still and moving images in the recreation of this experience. Boix's use of photographs to illustrate his Nuremberg testimony and Soler's reappropriation of them to illustrate this film aim to solidify the photographer's centrality in exposing the crimes of the Nazis. *Francisco Boix* provides a seductive argument for securing Boix's legacy. However, the filmmaker's skill at convincing his audience of Boix's martyrdom excludes all other narratives, heroic and otherwise, of the Spanish experience of the camp.

Soler was responsible for the first documentary film to establish a visual record of Mauthausen in the Spanish imagination with *Sobrevivir en Mauthausen*. In his earlier film, he interviewed Mauthausen survivors who had never spoken on camera: the underground vanguard of survivor testimony. The director's second documentary on the same subject matter continues to prioritize the testimony of survivors, but builds a visual record of Boix without the man himself. Although it relies on melodrama, *Francisco Boix* is a landmark Mauthausen documentary.[54] The figure of Boix continues to elicit great interest among new generations of Spaniards, plucked from relative obscurity to become the emblem of the Spanish deportees.[55] This interest can be attributed in part to the ability of the photographic images he saved and authored to communicate essential truths about the Holocaust. But Boix also fills a void in the Spanish imagination of Mauthausen as a selfless hero who died young, leaving a tangible legacy. Soler's film does not focus on the Spaniards' collective struggle to survive or provide an understated historical recounting of the Spaniards in Mauthausen so much as a focal point for an appealing tale: one man who, against all odds, survived a Nazi camp and exposed its inner workings to the world.

A few months after Soler's documentary appeared on Canal Plus, Spanish television followed with a Mauthausen documentary of its own. The news program *Línea 900* (*900 Line*) first aired *Mauthausen, el deber de recordar* on TVE 2 over three nights in August and September 2000. The directors Joan Sella and Cesc Tomás sought to distill fundamental information about the Spanish experience of Mauthausen into a 75-minute report. They underscored the didactic objective of the film with a recurring scene: the survivor Antonio Roig's presentation to a classroom of elementary school students in Sitges. The children pepper Roig with questions: Did you only eat soup? Were you tortured? Was there an escape plan? Does it hurt to remember all of this? They are young and innocent interlocutors for this aged survivor; their questions arise from an understandable ignorance of the history of the Nazi concentration camps. Sella and Tomás allow the children's inquiries to represent the audience's shared doubts: the spectator is tantamount to a Spanish schoolchild for whom this page of Spain's history is unknown and unimaginable. Consequently, the film is a simplification of the diverse trajectories that constituted the Spanish passage through Mauthausen.

Along with Roig, the documentary relies on the filmed testimony of seven other survivors, some of whom also participated in *Francisco Boix*.[56] Most of these men are interviewed in their homes, with photos or drawings of the camp visible just behind them. Francesc Comellas, however, addresses the camera from the barracks and quarry of the wintery Mauthausen camp. As Comellas wanders through the empty camp, he describes the memories Mauthausen's installations have awakened in him. The sight of a former prisoner freely walking through the camp, remembering its sinister past, is a unique addition to the film.

The filmmakers explore a subtle subtext with Comellas's return to Mauthausen, now free of Nazi officials and SS personnel: the survivor has outlasted his torturers. Although Comellas speaks freely, he appears at times to be following the filmmakers' script. This disquieting and unacknowledged construction of a survivor's testimony throws the origin of the other survivors' interventions into doubt. Comellas's return to Mauthausen, however, also reminds the viewer that without the firsthand recollections of survivors to actualize the camp's past, it is an empty space inherently devoid of meaning.

In *Mauthausen, el deber de recordar*, Sella and Tomás assemble a chronological account that begins with Hitler's rise to power and the Spaniards' deportation to Mauthausen. Unlike *Francisco Boix*, this film is not as forthright about Franco's role in the deportation of the Spaniards. Providing a brief historical overview for Spanish schoolchildren, Roig describes the meeting Franco and Hitler had in Hendaye to discuss the fate of the ten thousand Spaniards who were in France fighting against the Nazis. Roig explains to the students that Franco "dijo que fuera de España no había españoles, entonces aquel grupo de españoles nos quedamos todos sin patria."[57] The voice-over narration clarifies that these men were "abandonados a su suerte" ("abandoned to their own luck") in Germany, insinuating that although Franco had negated the citizenship of the Spanish exiles he did not explicitly agree to their deportation to Nazi camps. The source of this imprecise perspective is difficult to pinpoint. The filmmakers may have chosen not to make an allegation that, in 2000, was still not widely known in Spain. Alternately, Televisión Española under the conservative government of José María Aznar may not have permitted such an overt statement to be aired. In either scenario, the film glosses over a more complete recognition of the Franco government's role in the deportation of Spaniards to Nazi concentration camps.

Nevertheless, *Mauthausen, el deber de recordar* remains largely true to the historical record. The filmmakers intercalate the survivors' testimony with black and white photos and film from Mauthausen, contemporary colour footage of the camp, and a female voice-over narration that provides context. Period film from the archives, including a rarely seen Czech clip of prisoners carting stone up the Mauthausen quarry steps, footage shot by the US Army Signal Corps of the camp just after liberation, and film of Boix's testimony before the International Military Tribunal at Nuremberg root the documentary in visual evidence of the Nazis' crimes. The survivors recount events that are common to many of the Mauthausen life narratives as well: the formation of the clandestine communist organization during the camp's general disinfection in 1941; the slaughter of the thousands of Russians who entered the camp beginning in 1941, consequently improving the Spaniards' chances of survival; and Boix and the Poschacher *Kommando* boys' operation to save the black and white photos that the directors used to illustrate the documentary. These oft-repeated episodes form the core narrative of the film, implicitly positing them as the "main" storylines of the Spanish experience of Mauthausen. As such, they push other, lesser-known details and events to the margins. *Mauthausen, el deber de recordar*, unlike *Cerca de Danubio*, does not seek to add a novel way of imagining the camp to the canon of documentary films on the subject. Rather, it reiterates and repeats what has come to be an agreed-upon and simplified narrative of the Spaniards in Mauthausen.

As with all of the Mauthausen documentary filmmakers, Sella and Tomás do not hesitate to create emotional tension as a way of resonating with their audience. In a carefully edited montage, a number of the survivors remember the music that was played to accompany the public hanging of the would-be escapist Hans Bonarewitz. As the song slowly builds on the soundtrack, Comellas, then Joan de Diego, Francisco Batiste Baila, and Ramón Milá all sing snippets of "J'attendrei." Accompanied by the survivors' descriptions of the grotesque spectacle and photos that clearly show Spaniards in the front row forced to watch the hanging, this moment in the documentary demonstrates the immediacy of memory, even of a song the men heard six decades ago. It is also a calculated way to pull on the heartstrings of the spectator.

Although *Mauthausen, el deber de recordar* is not as overtly political as *Francisco Boix* or *El comboi dels 927*, the directors allow the survivors to express their outrage at their treatment by the Nazis and Spain's governments. As Josep Egea angrily puts it: "¿En España? No había un gobierno que levante un dedo – un dedo – para defender los intereses de los deportados españoles que quedan. Ni uno."[58] The film ends with Comellas, in the fading Mauthausen twilight, standing before the monument to the Spanish Republicans. The narrator has explained that this monument, unlike those erected by the governments of other nations to honour their Mauthausen victims, was paid for by "subscripción popular" ("popular subscription"). As he lays two stones from the Mauthausen quarry at the base of the monument, Comellas recites a dedication to "mis compañeros asesinados por los fascistas alemanes, en complacencia de los fascistas españoles."[59] Reminding the spectator that these elderly Mauthausen survivors would never forget their years of suffering in the concentration camp – and as Roig patiently explains to the Spanish schoolchildren, neither should the rest of us, so that humanity does not repeat its past mistakes – the film fades to black to the strains of "J'attendrei." Although the Nazis used the song as a not-so-subtle metaphor that they would always be waiting for their enemies, the filmmakers align the tune with the memories of the Spanish Mauthausen survivors. They would continue to wait – for recognition from the Spanish government, for opportunities to tell their stories, and for the next generation to continue the fight against injustice. This takeaway message transforms the film into a plea for justice for the Spanish survivors of Mauthausen, for whom the spectator feels more pity than identification. As *Mauthausen, el deber de recordar* has been re-aired on TVE 2,[60] its simplified narrative and familiar imagery have supplanted more complex and diverse approaches to the deportation of Spaniards to Nazi camps. Yet the purpose of all of these television documentaries is, in essence, just this: to give the viewer a quick and easy way to grasp this period in Spain's history, meet a small subsection of its protagonists, and learn the basic information behind its historical context.

Although *Cerca del Danubio, Francisco Boix, un fotógrafo en el infierno,* and *Mauthausen, el deber de recordar* inaugurated the genre of Spanish television documentaries on Mauthausen, Montse Armengou and Richard Belis's film had the farthest reach. *El comboi dels 927* joined a series of documentaries directed by Armengou and Belis unveiling Francoist crimes produced for the newsmagazine series *30 minuts* (*30 Minutes*) on Televisió de Catalunya.[61] Some 664,000 viewers watched *El comboi dels 927* when it was first broadcast in its original Catalan on 7 March 2004, a 22 per cent share of the spectatorship and the third most seen program on Catalan television that night (Baget Herms). The documentary was translated into Spanish and broadcast nationally on TVE 2 on 6 February 2005. A third translation into English allowed the film to be distributed to television channels in Ireland, Slovenia, Sweden, and Poland (Herrmann, "Documentary's Labour of Law" 207, note 4).[62] Like many of the Mauthausen documentaries, it has had a second life on YouTube, where it has been viewed thousands of times.

El comboi dels 927 distinguishes itself from its contemporary Mauthausen documentaries on multiple levels. For one, the film's subject matter encompasses a wider breadth than its peers and a more specific episode from the deportation of Spanish Republicans that had not been studied in detail. Through a focus on a single train convoy of 927 exiled Spaniards, Armengou and Belis examine the experiences of Spanish men, women, and children in exile; explore official correspondence between Spain and Germany during the Second World War; and find relevance to the historical memory movement in Spain. To be able to incorporate such a wealth of material, the filmmakers include extensive archival documentation and interviews with Spaniards who remained in France in exile, survived Mauthausen, or were deported back to Spain. The film is so thoroughly documented that Armengou and Belis published a companion volume in Catalan and Spanish in 2005 with additional reporting and complete source material.[63] The story of these 927 individuals is a microcosm of the political retribution Spanish Republicans suffered inside Spain under Franco, in France in exile, and in Austria in a Nazi concentration camp.

However, a second factor in the film's popularity mitigates the careful documentation and composition: the directors position it as an unabashedly subjective and sensationalist exclusive report. Armengou admits that she is sympathetic to the plight of the Spanish Republicans and that, although her documentaries rely on historical source material, she is first and foremost a journalist looking for a scoop (Herrmann, "Entrevista" 218). As a consequence, the film claims multiple revelations, introducing new information even to the small segment of its viewership already familiar with the background story of Spaniards in Mauthausen. Although these "exclusives" had been in the public record since the publication of Montserrat Roig's *Els catalans als camps nazis* in 1977, this was the first time they found a large audience on Spanish television. This dramatization achieves the same goal as the previous three documentaries: a palatable and simplified retelling of the Spanish deportation that sticks in the viewer's memory, to the exclusion of more complete and accurate histories of these events.

Last, *El comboi dels 927* does not solely allow the survivors the final word, but rather, as Gina Herrmann has explored, turns them into witnesses for the prosecution of the absent Franco government ("Documentary's Labour of Law" 200–3). This a priori legal hearing casts the spectators as judge and jury, allowing viewers to participate as central figures in the film. As Armengou explains, the combination of a documentary on an incendiary topic still present in Spain's memory and its airing on public television elicited a strong reaction among the film's spectators: "'Si lo decía la televisión, era que ya se podía hablar, que ya no había peligro'" (Herrmann, "Entrevista" 216).[64] By turning the Spanish experience of Mauthausen into a de facto trial, Armengou and Belis's reporting appeals to an audience eager to participate in distant moments in Spain's history.

The film's structure does not stray far from what the three Mauthausen documentaries from 2000 established. The testimony of survivors is central to the narrative; they are filmed in medium closeup shots before a plain dropcloth. The advanced age of these witnesses is particularly evident in *El comboi*: one survivor breathes through an oxygen machine. These men and women speak directly to the camera, their eyes watering and lips quivering as they describe witnessing the primal suffering and deaths of their compatriots. Unlike the other documentaries, Armengou is present just off camera, interjecting or clarifying what her elderly interview subjects recounted. She does not, however, act as a critical voice in the film by correcting any inaccuracies or inconsistencies the survivors may recall. As with all of the nonfiction Mauthausen films, interspersing black and white photographs, documents, and archival film footage illustrates a topic well removed from the present day. Contemporary video of trains, tracks, and the Mauthausen camp today allow the viewer to imagine scenes that were never captured on film. Some of this footage is washed in black and white and dubbed with sounds: dogs barking, men yelling in German, and train wheels grinding on the tracks. These kitschy visual and auditory details lessen the authority of the documentary. Despite the filmmakers' attempt to uncover an unknown chapter from the story of the Spanish deportation, they still fall victim to clichéd modes of repetition and visual storytelling present in this and the other Mauthausen documentaries.

Yet the focus on a single convoy of Spaniards differentiates Armengou and Belis's film. The basic outline of the particular episode becomes clear at the outset of *El comboi dels 927*, as men and women describe being packed into cattle cars and sent across France with no idea of their destination. The voice-over explains that 927 Spanish men, women, and children were deported on 20 August 1940 from the Alliers refugee camp in Angoulême, France, where they had been exiled after their defeat in the Spanish Civil War. They arrived four days later at the Mauthausen train station, where the men and boys were forced into the concentration camp. The women and younger children remained on the train, which wound its way through Europe, returning them to Spain two weeks later. The narrator explains: "Són els integrants del primer comboi que regata famílies senceres amb destinació a un camp d'extermini.

Ells inauguren aquestos transports de la mort que dos anys després els jueus farien tristament famosos."[65] Two years before the Nazis began rounding up entire Jewish families from France and deporting them to concentration camps across Germany, a trainload of Spanish Republican families was en route to their deaths in Mauthausen.

The Spanish women and children, unlike their Jewish counterparts two years later, did not enter the concentration camp. Only the Spanish men and boys on the trains from Angoulême faced death in Mauthausen. The film does not make this distinction, however. Instead, *El comboi dels 927* explicitly compares the treatment of Jews under the Nazis with the treatment of Spaniards under Franco. Jesús Tello recalls that, as a child on the convoy, he and the others who returned to Spain were "marcados como si fuéramos los judíos con la estrella de David."[66] Although they were treated with cruelty – including having their heads shaved, being sent to prisons, or shot – the defeated Spanish Republicans who remained in the camp or who returned to Spain after the Civil War were not all rounded up, deported to concentration camps, and gassed as Jews were during the Holocaust. Jesús Ramos calls the treatment of exiles who were returned to Spain "otro martirio" ("another ordeal") after the Spanish Civil War. Moreover, as Ramos remembers his childhood in Barcelona, he describes the ubiquity of German fighter pilots during the Civil War: "Alemanes. Todos los aviones que bombardearon en España eran alemanes. Quien destruyó Guernica eran alemanes."[67] In these at times misleading juxtapositions of the Spaniards and the Jews as well as of Franco and Hitler, the convoy survivors and the directors overlay a Holocaust narrative on a Spanish experience of the concentration camp that was inherently different.

Nevertheless, the film's inclusion of women in the traditionally masculine story of Spaniards in Mauthausen emphasizes a dehumanization that targeted both genders. The men were imprisoned and killed at Mauthausen and the women and children were sent back to a Spain overtly hostile to them and their defeated cause. The question of gender is present from the outset of the film, as the Mauthausen survivor Pablo Escribano comments that the Spaniards who fought against Franco in Spain "han guardado la cosa de un hombre. En Mauthausen, no."[68] The degradation suffered in Mauthausen, which erased what Escribano called the essence of a man, eliminated any distinction between the genders. The women interviewed in the documentary also speak about the dehumanization they suffered inside the train cars and then in Spain. Luisa Ramos describes starving in cattle wagons for 18 days and nights on the convoy's circuitous return voyage. After crossing the border into Spain, Ramos remembers that the women and children were left for dead: "nos dejaron en el vagón y nadie nos abría. Nadie sabía ni que estamos allí."[69] When they were eventually released from the trains, they were treated like criminals in Francoist Spain.

Of the 430 men and boys from the Angoulême convoy who remained in Mauthausen, the voice-over explains, 357 died there. The film turns to exploring why a group of Spaniards were deported to a Nazi concentration camp in the first place. Over archival film stock of Franco and Serrano Suñer meeting with Nazi officials and overseeing fascist ceremonies in Spain, the filmmakers focus on who was ultimately responsible for the deportation of exiled Spaniards to Nazi camps. As pages of yellowing correspondence flash across the screen, the voice-over describes how the German embassy in Madrid and the Spanish embassy in Paris sent multiple requests to Serrano Suñer's Office of the Foreign Ministry for clarification on what to do with the Spanish refugees in France. The final assessment that emerged from the Foreign Minister's office provides the film's stunning climax. Almost a year after the convoy from Angoulême began its voyage, a handwritten commentary in the margins of a memo from the Spanish embassy in Berlin cemented the deportees' fate. The typewritten letter informing Serrano Suñer's office that the Spanish refugees from Angoulême were deported to Mauthausen appears onscreen. The camera zooms in on a penciled note in the left margin, reading, in part: "[P]uesto que no parece oportuno hacer nada en favor de los internos, archívese."[70] As the voice-over narration clarifies, "aquesto 'archívese' és la condemna a mort d'aquells espanyols del comboi dels 927."[71] The film's argument remains clear: this handwritten note by a functionary in Serrano Suñer's office is definitive proof that the foreign minister was aware and complicit in the deportation of an entire convoy of Spanish families to Mauthausen.

As if this documentation were not enough evidence, Armengou and Belis track down one of the Spaniards on the Angoulême convoy who was quickly released from Mauthausen. Exploiting her connections in the Franco government, Francisco Pindado's mother wrote to Serrano Suñer to ask that her son be released from the concentration camp and returned to Spain. Pindado admits to the filmmakers that "los alemanes me dijeron que no hablara del campo de concentración" in Spain.[72] He complied, fearing that Gestapo spies in Spain would take retribution on him or his family. The order to repatriate the young Spanish deportee came directly from Serrano Suñer's office. *El comboi dels 927* argues for an unambiguous interpretation of Spain's role in the Holocaust: Franco's government left Spaniards it considered enemies in the hands of the Nazis, fully aware that they would be sent to die in concentration camps.

The reactions of the elderly survivors of the convoy – the majority of whom had family members who were killed in Mauthausen – seals the critical narrative of the film. One after another, they blame Franco, his government, and his supporters for sending these Spaniards to their deaths. Jesús Ramos wags his finger as he says, "Franco no levantó un dedo, ni un sólo dedo, a favor de los republicanos españoles ... y la iglesia menos."[73] Others add their words of condemnation, but none want vengeance: only justice. His eyes watering with emotion, Escribano describes how the lack of official recognition for the Spanish survivors of Mauthausen left him devoid of his nation: "He combatido por un ideal de libertad y de justicia, y yo no vuelvo a España. Yo he perdido todo. Todo, todo, todo. Mi familia, mi bienestar, y la libertad, perder a España. Es terrible. No se pueden ustedes imaginar."[74] As the survivors challenge the viewer to imagine what their suffering entailed, the filmmakers aim to elicit a lasting emotional response.

The desire to be recognized by the Spanish government for their part in combating Francoism motivated these survivors and their families to appear before Armengou and Belis's cameras. Manuel Huerta was the child of Spanish refugees in Angoulême who lived in fear of being deported after the infamous convoy departed. He tells Armengou, his voice breaking, "cuando hay un silencio es que nadie habla. Por eso he venido, por eso he venido a verla, para participar."[75] *El comboi dels 927* combines the voices of those who lived through the saga of this convoy of Spaniards with official documents that illustrate the callous motivations of the Spanish government. Armengou and Belis invite individuals from all facets of this traumatic episode, including Franco and Serrano Suñer in absentia, to participate in the reconstruction of their collective past. Given this evidence and testimony, the viewer is expected to arrive at the same judgment as the filmmakers: that the destiny of these 927 Spaniards was written by Franco's government. This takeaway simplifies what was a much more tangled history of exile, deportations, and returns. However, Armengou and Belis saved this more complex history for the print version of their film: onscreen, the directors wanted an immediate emotional response that the spectator would remember more than the historical context.

Raising the images and voices of Mauthausen survivors as their primary weapon, these four documentaries capture the visceral emotion, political beliefs, and ongoing suffering of the individuals who lived through this chapter of Spain's history. They argue for Spain's inclusion in the list of countries affected by the Holocaust. Moreover, they attach voices and faces to stories that until then had primarily been told in memoirs and history books. These television documentaries reached hundreds of thousands of viewers, likely the largest audience of any of the Mauthausen narratives to date. In them, the Spanish Republican exile, the Second World War, and five years of imprisonment and death in Mauthausen are condensed into an hour's worth of dramatic imagery. This historical reduction simplifies what was without question a much more complex and fraught period than could possibly have been portrayed in a documentary film. One could argue that these documentaries ultimately do a disservice to the memory of the Spaniards in Mauthausen: of the more than two thousand survivors, only a handful appeared onscreen. They recount the same isolated incidents, over and over, at times working against the precision of the historical record. Yet by transporting contemporary viewers to a Nazi concentration camp in Austria during the early 1940s via the popular medium of the television documentary, the essence of the story of the Spaniards in Mauthausen found relevance in the 2000s. The broadcast of these films allowed the casual viewer to encounter an episode from the annals of Spain's history that may have been new to them. As such, *Cerca del Danubio*; *Francisco Boix, un fotógrafo en el infierno*; *Mauthausen, el deber de recordar*; and *El comboi dels 927* attempt to ensure that successive generations are exposed to the history of Spanish Republicans deported to Nazi camps. In that these films have garnered hundreds of thousands of viewers in Spain, as well as spectators abroad through rebroadcasts and online media services, they achieved their goal. In the years after the release of these films, the stories of the Spaniards in Mauthausen have been absorbed by more diverse forms of mass media in even more polemical ways as the survivors' voices have faded into silence.

**Reframing Mauthausen: The Camp in Spain's
Popular Imagination, 2008–2015**

In the mid-1980s, Art Spiegelman was shopping a graphic novel around to publishers. The simplistic metaphor of the Holocaust as a game of cat and mouse in *Maus* belied a complex story of memory, family, artistic representation, and history. Rejections poured in. The prospect of publishing a comic version of the Holocaust was just too risky, too unknown, and too trite at a time when stories of the Shoah were dominated by more traditional narrative forms. One editor wrote that "'the contrast between the seriousness of the subject and the apparent frivolity which 'a cartoon with Jews as mice and Nazis as cats' inspires is so great that I had in several cases to talk for 5 minutes just to convince someone to even read the book'" (Spiegelman 78). The transition from a world where poetry after Auschwitz was barbaric to a world where a comic book became one of the most successful, wide-reaching, and canonical works of literature on the Holocaust occurred over the span of just a few decades. The two volumes that comprise *Maus* have been translated into more than thirty languages, were bestsellers in the United States, and are taught in countless college courses (152). Today, virtually every artistic genre and medium has been used as a means to capture the Nazi era and the Holocaust. We have reached, in Andreas Huyssen's words, "a globalization of Holocaust discourse" (*Present Pasts* 13). So too has the history of Spaniards in Mauthausen begun to move beyond more traditional narratives in the last decade. A field once dominated by survivor memoirs and historiographies now includes fiction, graphic novel, drama, and social media. Yet these new narrative forms challenge the reader to discern the historical truth often hidden behind a veil of creative engineering. Fresh forms of representation may attract new audiences to the story of the Spaniards in Mauthausen, but they also pose a risk to historical accuracy.

Scholars of the Holocaust have had to work through the dilemma of whether to accept these kinds of new narratives into the corpus of "serious" Holocaust representation. The underlying question, as Hayden White puts it, is whether "Nazism and the Final Solution belong to a special class of events such that ... they must be viewed as manifesting only one story, as being emplottable in one way only, and as signifying only one kind of meaning" (28). For Berel Lang, this "one way" of giving meaning to the events of the Holocaust is through nonfiction alone: "documentary and historical writings about the genocide have been more adequate and more compelling – in sum, more *valuable* – than the imaginative writings about the subject" (140; emphasis in the original). Lang, among others, believes that fictional approaches to the Holocaust falsify the events. The further they move from "historical authenticity," the more they risk amorality: "*no* imaginative representation of the Nazi genocide escapes these risks of the likelihood of failure, no matter how original or compelling it otherwise is" (Lang 149; emphasis in the original). Yet the facts alone – as contentious as they may be – cannot always capture the essence of the Holocaust. As Paul Ricoeur wrote, "it is an illusion to believe that factual statements can satisfy the idea of the unrepresentable, as though facts could through the virtue of their literal presentation be dissociated from their representation in the form of events in a history; events, history, plot all go together on the plane of figuration" (257). This "figurative plane" mingles fact and fiction, capturing the Holocaust in different, and at times startling, ways.

Maus, Roberto Benigni's film *Life is Beautiful*, or Nathan Englander's short story "What We Talk About When We Talk About Anne Frank" are Holocaust narratives that cross between high and low art, humour and severity, and truth and imagination in order to tell a story about the Nazi period. *Maus*, in particular, self-consciously straddles a line between fiction and nonfiction, a strategy its author defends as grounded in historical accuracy: "Reality is too complex to be threaded out into the narrow channels and confines of narrative and *Maus*, like all other narrative work including memoir, biography and history presented in narrative form, is streamlined and, at least on that level, a fiction ... that usefully steer[s] you back directly to reality ..." (Spiegelman 150). To some, these semi- or whole fictions may be offensive or otherwise unacceptable ways to approach the Nazi genocide, but to others they make the history of the Holocaust accessible and relatable to different and oftentimes younger audiences. "[H]istory," Spiegelman writes, "was far too important to leave solely to historians" (100). In this spirit, representations of the Holocaust and the Nazi period have flourished outside the boundaries of traditional historical narratives. What White calls "antinarrative nonstories" break with traditional storytelling, are "less fetishizing," and feature "stylistic innovations" (82) in the interest of crafting a communal whole story from the sum of the Holocaust's parts.

Once again these theoretical guideposts from Holocaust scholarship aid in understanding an analogous process at work in the representations of the Nazi era that encompass the stories of Spaniards in Mauthausen. As we have seen, fictional representations of Mauthausen such as Mercè Rodoreda's short story "Nit i boira" and Joaquim Amat-Piniella's novel *K.L. Reich* entered the cultural milieu soon after the end of the Second World War (chapter 2). They joined a decades-long corpus of historical narratives, survivor memoirs, and documentary films that sought to portray the Spanish experience of the camp accurately, albeit subjectively. Yet at the turn of the twenty-first century, a different type of text has emerged in Spain that rejects the fact-based foundations of its predecessors to take a more imaginative approach to Mauthausen. These postmemory narratives move towards a retelling that is divorced from direct contact with a Mauthausen survivor and, as such, from the original events themselves. To this end, these texts are ripe for the type of denunciation that has plagued mass media representations of the Holocaust: that they promote the banalization of the suffering of victims and commercialize the Holocaust. Although to a certain extent valid, this criticism overlooks the contribution these narratives have made to the development of Spain's collective memory over the last decade. They are comparable to "[p]opularizing representations and historical comparisons" – from Jonathan Safran Foer's *Everything Is Illuminated*, to Steven Spielberg's *Schindler's List*, to Anthony Doerr's *All the Light We Cannot See* – that are now "ineradicably part of a Holocaust memory which has become multiply fractured and layered" (Huyssen, *Twilight Memories* 256). These examples of American portrayals of the Holocaust have profited from history while also becoming new entries in a popular canon of Holocaust representation: they, like many of the Spanish authors in this section, cannot be cast aside for their so-called memory opportunism because they have laid claim to a Holocaust consciousness among new populations of readers and spectators.

There is a twenty-five-year gap between the appearance of the first graphic novel to depict the Holocaust – the first volume of *Maus* was published in 1986 – and the 2011 publication of the first graphic novel to depict the deportation of Spaniards to Mauthausen. This lag underlines the fact that Spain is still in the process of working through its ties to the Holocaust and interrogating its body of representations of the deportation of Spaniards to Nazi camps. The six texts discussed in this section – a fictionalized memoir, two popular historical novels, a graphic novel, a play, and a narrative on social media – have begun the process of reframing Mauthausen in the Spanish imagination. They can be situated alongside a larger body of increasingly prevalent commercial Holocaust and the Second World War fiction and fictional cinema. It largely remains to be seen how these mass-market fictions will transform the spectre of Mauthausen in the Spanish eye, but there can be no doubt that they have and will continue to affect the culture of memory in Spain.

Perhaps the most visible and contentious text published over the past decade regarding the Spanish deportees is Javier Cercas's "relato real" about Enric Marco, the false survivor who rose to head the Amical de Mauthausen in the early 2000s before being unmasked as a fraud by the historian Benito Bermejo in 2005.[76] In *El impostor* (*The Imposter*, 2014), Cercas confronts the dilemma of treating a subject who, despite raising the ire of Spanish concentration camp survivors, their families, and representatives, became a highly visible champion of the collective memory of these same survivors.[77] In his decision to write about Marco – instead of one of the thousands of stories of actual Spanish victims of concentration camps – Cercas rankled scholars in Spain and abroad who bristled at his characterization of Spain's "industria de la memoria [que] resultó letal para la memoria" (*El impostor* 307).[78] Yet *El impostor*, in tracing Marco's real and imagined movements through Western Europe from the Spanish Civil War through the sixtieth anniversary of the end of the Second World War, has had real implications for the current state of Europe's culture of memory.[79]

Cercas attacks Spain's historical-memory boom, which he eulogizes by saying that "ya pocos se acuerdan de la llamada memória histórica" (*El impostor* 306).[80] As he wades into the very same memory landscape with the slippery figure of Marco, his efforts reflect the current state of popular representations of Mauthausen in Spain.[81] Like Marco and *El impostor*, these contemporary texts are at once fiction and non-fiction, tales "based on a true story." They mediate the intimate experiences of an unfortunate few through the lenses of popular culture, postmemory, and commercialization. They by turns indict and profit from their predecessors, leaving a confusing trail of memory crumbs behind them. Nevertheless, the Mauthausen narratives under examination in this section, along with the continued efforts of scholars and activists, contradict Cercas's edict that Spain's historical memory movement is dead. The movement may have shifted from the purview of state-mandated programs to grassroots campaigns, but confrontations with Spain's past are alive and well in the second decade of the twenty-first century.

In these six narratives, Mauthausen is less a concrete space than a romanticized point of departure. The camp resides in the Spanish imagination as a significant site of memory, but is now portrayed in broader strokes. Mauthausen in the past ten years has become a literary trope that sparks identifiable but frequently imprecise connections to Spain's history: it conjures up the exile and deportation of Spanish Republicans,

Nazi concentration camps, the Second World War, and the Holocaust in the minds of the audience. However, juxtapositions between the treatment of Jews and Spaniards that were common in previous survivor narratives have all but disappeared in these twenty-first-century texts. Now that most Spanish survivors of Mauthausen have died, the first-person testimonials and memoiristic accounts of the previous decade have given way to new vantage points. With the fading of these first-hand accounts, the specificity and emotional core of the narratives of survivors has been lost. These new entries in the body of narratives representing the Spaniards in Mauthausen raise a host of contingent dilemmas. How does one recreate Mauthausen without the aid of the testimony of a survivor? Is it possible to bring a fresh perspective to a subject that has been explored in myriad ways for more than sixty years? Can Mauthausen's importance in the Spanish imagination continue to evolve without being subject to a process of dehistoricization? Are these authors capitalizing on an international trend that exploits the Second World War and the Holocaust for commercial gain? As Mauthausen transitions from a lived space of memory for the survivors to a symbolic place of postmemory for their children, grandchildren, and Spaniards who have no personal connection to the camp, it veers into uncharted representational territory.

Fictionalized Memoir: Joanna Maria Melenchón i Xamena's *Mauthausen des de l'oblit (2008)*

Joanna Maria Melenchón i Xamena's 2008 book *Mauthausen des de l'oblit* (*Mauthausen from Obscurity*) is a novel disguised as a Mauthausen memoir. It begins its flirtations with history and autobiography in the first few pages. Àngels, the narrator whose name coincides with the author's, wants to understand the story of her Uncle Rafel.[82] Among her family's archives, she finds a postcard sent from a German POW camp, which is reproduced in the pages of the book. Dated 22 March 1941, the postcard was signed "Rafael Xamena," bore the return address of "Stalag XII-D, Trier," and was stamped "CENSURA MILITAR, PALMA DE MALLORCA" (Melenchón i Xamena 15).[83] Frustrated with the lack of concrete information she has been able to find about her uncle, Àngels looks to another source. By consulting the appendix of Montserrat Roig's *Els catalans als camps nazis*, the narrator confirms that Rafel Xamena Moll (or "Rafael Chamena," in the Castilian spelling) passed through German *Stalag*s as prisoner number 39044, was deported to

Mauthausen on 3 April 1941 with the number 3896, and died in Gusen on 6 January 1942 (Melenchón i Xamena 19; Roig, *Els catalans* 703). Àngels writes that "[a]questa petita informació ens confirmava allò que tots ja ens havíem imaginat."(20).[84] She decides that she will "treure l'entrellat de la seva vida," rescuing her uncle from existing "a mig camí entre enlloc i l'oblit" (20).[85]

Àngels is the fictional embodiment of the many family members of Spanish Mauthausen deportees who were only able to confirm the fate of their loved ones by consulting Roig's historiography.[86] But from the very beginning of Melenchón i Xamena's novel, the boundaries between fiction and history blur. The basic fact that the narrator's uncle – who is the author's uncle – died in Mauthausen is verifiable.[87] But it is unclear what portion of the rest of the story is true and what is invention. The narrator's aunt, Rafel's sister Eulària, captures the novel's central motif when, asked in the past by her young niece for a story, she would respond: "Què vols, la de veritat o l'altra?" (9).[88] In this fictionalized memoir, the reader is not given the choice between the true story or "the other one"; they have been combined into one.

At first blush, *Mauthausen, des de l'oblit* appears to be Rafel Xamena Moll's life narrative, written and researched by his niece, following the narrative conventions of the many other Mauthausen memoirs published in the 1990s and the first decade of the 2000s. Àngels investigates her uncle's past, interviews elderly members of her family, and transcribes their oral testimony into the pages of this book. She includes Rafel Xamena's postcard: a fragment of realia identical to the *Stalag* postcards that appeared in histories of the Spanish deportation and the Mauthausen memoirs of other ex-deportees. Yet *Mauthausen, des de l'oblit* is not a memoir: it is the story of Àngels more than the story of her uncle. Written in Mallorquin, the author intermingles a search for details about a man deported to a Nazi camp with the narrator's search for meaning in her own life. Influenced by historical narratives of the Spanish deportation, the book nevertheless veers away from recounting the last days of Rafel Xamena's life in Mauthausen towards an at times melodramatic family tale of young love, mistaken identities, deception, and death. Although the reader encounters tidbits of historical accuracy in *Mauthausen, des de l'oblit*, it is a novel written to entertain, not enlighten. Only a reader with a detailed background in the history of the Spaniards in Mauthausen would emerge with a clear sense of what is truth and what is fiction. The novel engages with history as a narrative, not a didactic, strategy. It privileges the vantage point of the second-generation survivor over the actual witnesses of the Nazi camps.

The novel's plot turns on Àngels' central quest to discover what happened to her uncle in Mauthausen. A young couple separated by extreme circumstances, a newborn baby removed from his mother for his own safety, an intentionally swapped identity, an imposter, and the eventual untangling of these confused family lines form the core retrospective narrative of the book. Meanwhile, in the novel's present, the narrator's dissatisfaction with her life as a childless divorcée, her family's insistence that she delve into their tangled past, a terrorist attack, and an unexpected pregnancy conspire to draw connections to an otherwise remote past. These thematic resonances link the outer framework of the novel, consisting of the narrator's existential crisis, with the novel-within-a-novel, consisting of her family's story in the years surrounding the Second World War. In one instance, after a particularly difficult day, Àngels feels "com si hagu[é] picat pedra tot el dia" (59),[89] a heavy-handed metaphor that associates her work trying to sort through her family's history with the daily struggle of the Spanish prisoner population of Mauthausen in the camp's quarry to survive.

Mauthausen, des de l'oblit is the story of three women searching for answers to their own life struggles through the collective memory of Rafel and his compatriots. Although its premise and title focus on Mauthausen, the lives of those outside the camp's walls is more prominent in the novel than the Spaniards who were inside them. The reader learns very little through the narrative about the camp itself. Rafel's story only emerges in the novel's climactic moment, through an apocryphal missive he inscribed on his clothing before he died in Gusen. Discovered by his family decades after his death, Rafel's secret letter was an aspirational voice from beyond the grave: the last word that so many family members of Spaniards who perished in Mauthausen and Gusen wished they could have heard. In his letter Rafel asked, "'Quin mal tan horrible hem fet tots plegats?'" (120): a question that represents an imagined collective bafflement at the plight of the Spaniards in Mauthausen.[90] Rafel's letter envisions the astonishment the Spaniards in Mauthausen must have felt to have been imprisoned, violated, and killed by the Nazis. Melenchón i Xamena's fictional foray into the inner thoughts of a Mauthausen victim attempts to tell a story that cannot be told in any other way.

Not unlike the many Mauthausen memoirs it mimics, *Mauthausen, des de l'oblit* was published by a small regional press in Spain. The novel was a finalist for a local literary prize, but has not been translated into Spanish and thus has had little impact beyond the Catalan-speaking world.[91] Melenchón i Xamena's first novel does, however, represent a fictional turn in the portrayal of the Spaniards in Mauthausen that anticipates other, higher-profile publications yet to come. As a second-generation Mauthausen survivor who references the genre of life narrative in composing her uncle's story, the author has not fully rejected the reality-based accounts of her first-generation predecessors. Instead, she works in the terrain of postmemory, remotely affected by her uncle's primary trauma, but, in a typically Generation X–style narrative perspective, is more focused on her own problems than those of others. Most subsequent Mauthausen narratives further break with the individual experiences and memories of actual Mauthausen victims and survivors. Melenchón i Xamena's direct, personal link between author and Spanish Mauthausen victim is severed by two popular historical novelists in books published on the heels of this fictionalized memoir.

Historical Novels: Andrés Pérez Domínguez's El violinista de Mauthausen *(2009) and Clara Sánchez's* Lo que esconde tu nombre *(2010)*

A decade before Javier Cercas's takedown of Spain's historical memory movement with the labyrinthine tale of a fake Spanish concentration camp deportee in *El impostor*, Antonio Muñoz Molina elicited a wave of criticism for another novel that constructed a Holocaust façade. *Sefarad* (*Sepharad*, 2001) combines disparate historical events of the twentieth century with real and imagined individuals in its approximation of the Holocaust. Soon after the book was published, the Austrian Hispanist and Holocaust scholar Erick Hackl debated Muñoz Molina in the pages of a Spanish magazine. Muñoz Molina's inaccuracies – misspelling the name of the Bergen-Belsen concentration camp and imprecisely characterizing the Holocaust victims Victor Klemperer and Jean Améry as forgotten, among many others – rankled Hackl's sensibilities. Hackl found "[e]l caso de *Sefarad* ... más deplorable ya que su autor trata de personas de carne y hueso, con nombre y apellidos, lo que significa asumir un alto grado de responsabilidad" (29).[92] Muñoz Molina defended himself, reminding Hackl that the great names in Holocaust studies elicited almost no recognition inside Spain. He also chastised Hackl for confusing the author with his narrator, arguing, as Cercas does, in favour of the author's literary license to combine the real and the invented in the creation of characters and a story: "Así se han creado siempre los personajes literarios, que en mi libro se cruzan a veces con personajes históricos, pero no se confunden con ellos" (Muñoz Molina, "El caso Hackl" 7).[93] Hackl and Muñoz Molina's debate, alongside Cercas and the so-called "Caso Marco," capture the provocations that arise when aspects of the deportation of Spanish Republicans to Nazi concentration camps enter the sphere of fictionalized mass entertainment in Spain.

Although the topic of the Spaniards of Mauthausen has not inspired as much popular literature as the Holocaust in Spain, two bestselling novels by well-known Spanish authors have broached the subject.[94] Andrés Pérez Domínguez and Clara Sánchez are highly visible and active writers fluent in the art of self-promotion.[95] Taking full advantage of what Muñoz Molina identifies as the author's right to make fictional characters cross the paths of actual historical figures, Pérez Domínguez and Sánchez situate the plots of their respective novels against a backdrop of Mauthausen, the Nazi era, and its aftermath. They integrate details, characters, and events from the concentration camp and the Second World War into melodramatic tales of intrigue, lost love, and violence. With *El violinista de Mauthausen* (*The Mauthausen Violinist*) and *Lo que esconde tu nombre* (*What Your Name Hides*),[96] the two authors reject an accurate portrayal of the Spaniards in Mauthausen in favour of fictional creations that draft Mauthausen as another character in the story. Unlike Melenchón i Xamena's fictionalized memoir, Pérez Domínguez and Sánchez have little interest in integrating the trappings of the oral historian into their narratives: their novels are works of historical fiction divorced from the direct influence of the recollections of their countrymen and women who actually passed through Mauthausen's gates. *El violinista de Mauthausen* and *Lo que esconde tu nombre* embark on an experiment never before seen in representations of the Spaniards in Mauthausen: stories told without the intervention of an actual survivor.

Such a gap between historical reality and fantasy in a popular historical novel makes it an unreliable way for a reader to gather verifiable information. This slippage between empirical truth and imagination allows the author of the historical novel a great deal of latitude. As Marthe Robert wrote, "[t]he degree of reality of a novel is not something quantifiable; it depends on the amount of illusion the writer chooses to activate" (61). Nevertheless, in practice, the historical backdrop that serves as scenery in works of historical fiction may be interpreted – even unconsciously – as an underlying truth by an uninformed or suggestible reader. The reader's "horizon of expectations" (22), in Hans Jauss's term, shifts as the audience becomes further removed from the events at hand. This dilemma begs the question as to what, if anything, a reader would learn about the Spanish experience of Mauthausen from *El violinista de Mauthausen* or *Lo que esconde tu nombre*. Whether these novels are responsible for informing or misinforming a reading public about this hidden period in Spain's history determines whether or not Pérez Domínguez and Sánchez have contributed to a revisionist history. A comparison of the fictional aspects of the novels to the events that inspired them allows us to understand how these mass market texts have piqued the interest of a generation of readers who have been chronically underexposed to the history of the Spanish deportation.

The universe of popular Holocaust fiction has expanded exponentially in the first decade of the twenty-first century while steadily moving towards commercially successful yet highly inaccurate portrayals of the Shoah. These two novels follow this commercial trend, though because Spain has seen little popular fiction addressing the deportation of Spaniards to Nazi camps, one must be cautious when grouping them together with other creations on the popular Holocaust bandwagon. While these two novels afford a broad understanding of the historical moment and consequences, they also lead audiences astray from the nuanced knowledge that only survivors and historians have been able to provide thus far. Although it is counterproductive to juxtapose more "serious" efforts to reconstruct the past with these types of mass media ventures, as Huyssen suggests, "we must in principle be open to many different possibilities of representing the real and its memories" (*Present Pasts* 19) in the terrain of both the Holocaust and the Spanish experience of Mauthausen.

As one of the protagonists of *El violinista de Mauthausen* emerges liberated from the concentration camp in the opening lines of Pérez Domínguez's novel, his "second death" sounds familiar: "Cuando Rubén Castro llega a París ya está muerto, pero aún no sabe que habrá de morir otra vez..." (13).[97] After spending five years in Mauthausen, Rubén Castro's first death is the figurative death of his spirit. His second death is also figurative: it occurs when he learns that his fiancée abandoned and betrayed him while he was in the camp. Employing a tantalizing opening gambit that leaves the main character both dead and alive at the same time, Pérez Domínguez also drops a subtle clue that points towards his inspirations for this novel. One is Montserrat Roig's foundational historiography *Els catalans als camps nazis*: Roig described Joaquim Amat-Piniella's second death in 1974 after his first spiritual death in the concentration camp in her opening pages (*Els catalans* 13). The other is *Sefarad*, quoted in the novel's epigraph: Muñoz Molina's narrator describes a survivor of an extermination camp who returned to the same unchanged room he left three years earlier and imagined that nothing would be different had he actually perished in the camp. These two allusions capture the schism between the two faces of Pérez Domínguez's novel. On the one hand, the author incorporates an accurate historical background, episodes recounted by survivors, and nuanced observations related to the Nazi era and the Spanish experience of Mauthausen into his novel. On the other hand, *El violinista de Mauthausen* embellishes, dramatizes, and disfigures these details while inventing others, making it impossible for the novel to be considered a historical reference.

Weaving together the strands of a love triangle and espionage ring set during and just after the Second World War, Pérez Domínguez alternates among coincidences uniting the four main characters. A German violinist, Franz Müller, casually played a waltz for Rubén and his French fiancée in the Luxembourg Garden in Paris before the war. Astonishingly, Müller turns up years later playing the same waltz for the SS inside Mauthausen, where Rubén overhears him. In another amazing set of circumstances, the violinist saves a prisoner – perhaps Rubén – from throwing himself to his death over the quarry precipice and later becomes involved with Rubén's erstwhile fiancée. These melodramatic qualities are right at home in the novel, a page-turner that does not disappoint readers eager for a historical thriller. Yet the blending of fact with fiction results in a portrayal of the Spanish deportation that is likely to mislead readers interested in the actual historical underpinnings.

Although the novel includes no footnotes, bibliography, or acknowledgment of historical sources, the author researched histories of Spanish Republican exiles during and just after the Second World War as well as Spanish survivors' memoirs of Mauthausen. In his descriptions of the concentration camp, Pérez Domínguez availed himself of details that are available through myriad historical documents, working in mentions of the central role of the Spaniards in constructing the camp, the quarry's 186 steps and its steep cliff, the interminable formations on the Appellplatz, the repeated warnings that prisoners should kill themselves, the division and cruel treatment of the Russians and the Jews, the public hangings, the liberation of the camp by a division of the US Army, the inverted blue triangles worn by the Spaniards, and the identity of camp commander Franz Ziereis. The author even includes a reference to the convoy of 927 Spaniards who were among the first to arrive at Mauthausen, with details gleaned from Montse Armengou and Richard Belis's 2004 documentary *El comboi dels 927*.

But there are other, more imaginative scenes in *El violinista de Mauthausen* that collapse the realities of the concentration camp into allegory. Müller is hired to play in a string quartet for a child's birthday party inside the camp. Once inside Mauthausen, he witnesses a full range of atrocities: the stacks of bodies loaded onto carts, the starving prisoners, and a German boy taking aim at prisoners on the Appellplatz with a borrowed SS Luger pistol.[98] He secretly passes Rubén a pair of apples, leading to the discovery of the novel's central coincidence between the two characters.[99] These and other scenes in *El violinista de Mauthausen* distill through Müller a series of stories that survivors and witnesses have told about Mauthausen over the years. The connection between the German and the Spaniard, the senseless violence, and Müller's selfless act are symbols of the camp's perverse morality mitigated by a flash of international regard for humanity. The author is less concerned with accurate portrayals of the camp than he is with these overarching themes.

Without the direct input of a Spanish Mauthausen survivor, *El violinista de Mauthausen* avails itself mainly of familiar Holocaust tropes, secondary sources, or primary sources cited in secondary sources. Pérez Domínguez describes researching the novel by reading "todos los libros sobre este tema que cayeron en mis manos" (Cerezo).[100] In its removal from the voices of the survivors themselves, however, the author creates a gulf between the fictional narrative and historical reality. In an interview, he recognized that his is a work of pure fiction that uses history in the interest of crafting a compelling narrative: "Yo escribo ficción ... lo que he hecho es construir una novela documentada, no un documental novelado. La documentación me ha servido para sustentar la obra con solidez y diseñar una trama atractiva" (Cerezo).[101] Pérez Domínguez's goal is to entertain his readers, not educate them. Still, the novel is a highly visible means of encountering the story of the Spaniards in Mauthausen. The author's attempt to distance his novel from the historical documentation from which it sprung does not mean that in the reader's eyes *El violinista de Mauthausen* is divorced from historical reality. It may, indeed, serve as a first and only encounter with the Spanish experience of Mauthausen for a host of readers.

The novel has had a measure of success in Spain unseen by previous representations of the Spaniards in Mauthausen.[102] It can even be found on a shelf devoted to Spanish-language books at the Mauthausen Memorial bookshop at the camp in Austria, lending it an air of authority in the effort to capture one nation's concentration camp experience. *El violinista de Mauthausen* was the first attempt to bring the story of the Spanish experience of Mauthausen into the world of mass-market fiction. Pérez Domínguez's book conflates the diverse realities of the Spanish Mauthausen deportees before, during, and after their incarceration into one sprawling potboiler. Yet, at the very least, the novel is a way for readers to discover the basic fact that Spaniards participated in the Second World War and died in Mauthausen.[103]

As the protagonist in Clara Sánchez's *Lo que esconde tu nombre*, Sandra embodies a contemporary generation ignorant of Spain's connection to a Nazi past. Unlike *El violinista de Mauthausen*, Sanchez's novel is set in the present day and deals with how the past returns to haunt the living. A community of Nazis, former concentration camp SS personnel and their wives, live out their golden years in Alicante, hiding in plain sight while they enjoy the sun and sand of Spain. Meanwhile, a community of Spanish concentration camp survivors share the same streets. Julián, a Mauthausen ex-deportee, considers this convergence: "habíamos llegado al mismo punto, unos por el camino de los verdugos y otros por el camino de las víctimas" (Sánchez 334).[104] This quasi-concentration camp retirement village returns victims and their persecutors to the same space, creating an eerie post-Mauthausen on the eastern coast of Spain. Sebastian, a former Mauthausen SS guard, tells Julián that they were both part of an unbreakable system: "Yo iba con el uniforme de las SS y vosotros con el uniforme de rayas de los prisioneros. Estábamos dentro de un orden establecido, imposible de romper. No había nada que pensar. Habíamos conseguido un equilibro, ¿comprendes?" (382).[105] Sánchez's novel explores the boundaries of this equilibrium, asking whether the past can ever truly be relegated to the history books, or if it is just as likely to continue to walk our streets and threaten our daily lives.

Lo que esconde tu nombre provides furtive glances inside Mauthausen and other concentration camps via the nostalgia of the aging Nazis and the nightmares of the elderly Spanish survivors. The novel takes Franco and Hitler's friendly collaboration as a baseline fact, one that has produced this strange offsite settlement of Nazis and their victims fifty years later. Sánchez pulls together these opposing sides through Sandra, a pregnant and vulnerable young woman taken in by a Nazi couple. Through Julián, an elderly Mauthausen survivor who returned to Spain from exile to hunt Nazis, Sandra – and by extension, the reader – begins to comprehend the nefarious ways of these seemingly innocuous retirees. Julían is a heroic force who reclaims a sense of agency in righting historical wrongs. Like his fellow ex-deportees, though, he does not consider himself a hero: "No nos sentíamos como héroes, sino más bien como unos apestados. Éramos víctimas, y nadie quiere a las víctimas ni a los perdedores. Otros no tuvieron más remedio que callar y sufrir el miedo, la vergüenza y la culpa de los supervivientes, pero nosotros nos convertimos en cazadores ..." (Sánchez 11).[106] Though he is not interested in bringing the Nazis in Alicante to justice, Julián wants them to be aware that their past atrocities will remain etched in the country's collective memory so long as others know who they are and what they have done.

The presence of Nazis who fled to Spain after the end of the Second World War creating so-called werewolf groups engaged in covert activity is documented, as is their continued engagement with neo-Nazi groups during the postwar years (Messenger 63, 168). Nazi hunters like Simon Wiesenthal pursued those who fled to Spain and other countries after the war. *Lo que esconde tu nombre*, like *El violinista de Mauthausen*, is clearly informed by these historical antecedents, though any source material remains uncredited by the author. Nevertheless, the novel's characters and situations are largely inventions.[107] Julián describes seeing his future wife for the first time the moment she passed through the Mauthausen gates. The narrative does not clarify whether Raquel is a Jew or a Spaniard, but in either scenario this romantic encounter is pure fiction. Even a detail as minimal as the number of quarry stairs leads the novel into the terrain of historical revisionism: Julián describes 189 quarry stairs when in actuality there were (and still are) 186 quarry stairs (Sánchez 199). *Lo que esconde tu nombre* won the prestigous Premio Nadal prize in 2010, garnering the novel considerable attention in the Spanish media, and sales and translations abroad. Like *El violinista de Mauthausen*, it has elicited little scholarly study or critical consideration. Both novels have enjoyed a popular success unmarred by the kind of critical backlash that Muñoz Molina encountered.[108] Yet *Lo que esconde tu nombre* and *El violinista de Mauthausen* are also guilty of dehistoricizing a chapter in Spain's history that was obscure to begin with.

As witnesses disappear and contemporary historical knowledge becomes ever more diluted, Pérez Domínguez and Sánchez's novels have contributed to Spain's collective memory about Spaniards in Mauthausen while at the same time cashing in on it. The uncritical reader who takes either of these novels at face value may emerge understanding the basic fact that Spaniards were deported to Nazi camps, but will miss any real sense of why they were there, what they experienced, how they survived, and what happened to them as a community after liberation. *Lo que esconde tu nombre* and *El violinista de Mauthausen* undermine historical knowledge with fictional constructs, which is a dangerous game with even the most well-known historical events. The popular fictionalization of the history of Spaniards in Mauthausen risks supplanting any fact-based awareness of this historical moment in the public's consciousness with a partial and sensationalized version of events. These two novels are apocryphal variations on the Holocaust that at once trivialize and popularize the historical event for a mass market.

Graphic Novel: Toni Carbos and Javier Cosnava's
Prisionero en Mauthausen *(2011)*

The process of dehistoricization that the history of Spaniards in Mauthausen has undergone through its depiction in the popular media in the first decade and a half of the 2000s arguably finds its apex in Spain's first graphic novel on the subject. *Prisionero en Mauthausen* (*Prisoner in Mauthausen*), though influenced by the tradition of the Holocaust graphic novel developed by Art Spiegelman, is a far cry from *Maus*. Created without the direct input of a Spanish Mauthausen survivor, *Prisionero en Mauthausen*, like *El violinista de Mauthausen* and *Lo que esconde tu nombre*, has nevertheless benefited from historical and testimonial sources on the topic. As a fictional interpretation of the concentration camp, the authors do not cite or make reference to these documents directly. They dance between a grounding in history and a splashy, violent dramatization based on – but not always true to – historical events. *Prisionero en Mauthausen* is a graphic creation that sensationalizes the Spanish ordeal in Mauthausen without lending it or the Nazi era any of the artistic and emotional nuance seen in *Maus*. Toni Carbos and Javier Cosnava's effort introduces Mauthausen to a new audience at the cost of removing the story of the Spanish deportees from its historical moorings.

With text by Cosnava and artwork by Carbos, *Prisionero en Mauthausen* offers a complex narrative timeline rendered in monochromatic tones, cartoonish drawings, and a range of frame sizes. The protagonist, Juan Placambó, narrates his story with flashbacks to his imprisonment in Mauthausen, punctuated by ersatz memoranda and communiqués between Nazi officials. Juan, drawn by Carbos as a tall, slender figure with sunken eyes, recalls the sordid timeline of his existence from an uncertain present in which he is wracked with guilt. Living at the centre of history, Juan fought against fascism for the Spanish Republic but later switched sides by becoming a Mauthausen *Kapo* in thrall to the Nazis who abused his fellow Spaniards. In the graphic novel's opening scenes, Juan aims his gun not at the Nazi, Paul Winzer, but at his comrade Miguel, who yells: "Si no acabamos con Winzer y su pandilla de Nazis habrá campos de concentración en España" (Carbos and Cosnava n.p.).[109] Hingeing the Franco dictatorship's involvement with the Nazis on this singular moment, the novel positions Juan as an agent who changed the course of history. From this beginning, *Prisionero en Mauthausen* demonstrates its imaginative disregard for historical accuracy in the interest of a lurid tale of moral transgression, treason, and violence.

Placambó arrives in Mauthausen on a cattle wagon from a German *Stalag*, experiencing a visual transformation in Carbos's drawings from a Nazi informant rendered in shades of grey, and with a full head of hair just before the Second World War, to a cartoonish and stubble-headed prisoner wearing a striped uniform and blue-triangle insignia in Mauthausen. As a *Kapo*, he alternates between his tenuous loyalty to his Spanish compatriots and his service to the Nazi regime. The Nazis keep Juan alive – secreting him chocolate as he toils in the quarry – while they manipulate him into sacrificing his fellow Spanish prisoners to save himself. This apocryphal experiment, compared to Dr Mengele's notoriously deadly Nazi medical tests in the text, underlines *Prisionero en Mauthausen*'s central message: that the concentration camps were ultimately all perverse moral experiments. In the present-day narrative frames, Juan agonizes over the nature of his guilt on the spectrum of evil that surrounded him in the camp: "Juan Placambó fue algo mucho peor que un Nazi: yo era un Kapo... [L]a culpa me pesa como un yugo imaginario formado por la osamenta de una legión de cadáveres" (Carbos and Cosnava n.p.).[110] Nevertheless, Juan survives Mauthausen and changes his identity to evade retribution by his fellow Spaniards.

Prisionero en Mauthausen contains a glimmer of verifiable historical background, though it is fictionalized to suit the narrative. Hartheim

Castle appears in full-page detail, as Carbos underlines its function by adding a murder of crows encircling it. Juan's antagonist Faust – the originator of Juan's "experiment" – is a fictional embodiment of Franz Ziereis, the Mauthausen commandant, while Paul Winzer, a Gestapo officer stationed in Spain throughout the Second World War, appears as a version of himself. The graphic novel also emphasizes the Spaniards' role in constructing the camp and toiling in the quarry, depicting cadaverous men cutting and hauling stone while subject to the blows of the SS. However, *Prisionero en Mauthausen* also blatantly tinkers with history in its construction of a crude tale. The graphic exploration of the moral weakness of a Spanish *Kapo* in *Prisionero en Mauthausen* veers into a fictional realm with the imaginary memos sent between high-ranking Nazis focused on the manipulation of this "español subhumano" ("subhuman Spaniard," Carbos and Cosnava n.p.) and Winzer's postwar transformation into a homicidal Austrian priest. Cosnava and Carbos's novel moves beyond the benign dehistoricization of Mauthausen towards a more explicitly deformed counterhistory.

There is no doubt that a reader new to the history of the Spaniards in Mauthausen would come away from *Prisionero en Mauthausen* with a warped impression of the historical era, one in which conspiracy and subterfuge reigned not only between the Nazis and their victims, but among the Spanish deportees themselves. The visual representation of the Spaniards as simplistic caricatures superimposed on a monochromatic Mauthausen metaphorically illustrates this historical deformation. As the history of the Spaniards in Mauthausen moves into ever more popular forms of mass media, some audiences may be irretrievably influenced by this counterfactual representation. *Prisionero en Mauthausen* opens the door to a type of fictional construction that, unhinged from first-person testimony, may ultimately skew a faithful collective memory of the experiences of the Spaniards in Mauthausen, trivializing their role as witnesses to the Holocaust.

Drama: Mariano Llorente and Laila Ripoll's
El triángulo azul *(2014)*

In the opening moments of *El triángulo azul* (*The Blue Triangle*), Mariano Llorente and Laila Ripoll's theatrical production about the Spanish experience of Mauthausen, a bearded man, dressed in a sports jacket and plaid bow tie, sits alone onstage, listening to the radio and speaking into a tape recorder. It is 1965, and Paul Ricken – a former SS squad leader described in the stage directions as *"un hombre roto, acabado"* (Llorente and Ripoll 17; emphasis in the original)[111] – contemplates the course of his life in service to the Nazi party. In his opening monologue, he articulates: "Sacrifiqué mi moral en beneficio del bien común. Sacrifiqué mis ideas, mi integridad, mi pureza. Sacrifiqué todo lo que de bueno y noble había en mí" (19).[112] Llorente and Ripoll's play begins and ends with Ricken, who supervised the Mauthausen photography laboratory, where the Spanish prisoners Antoni García and Francesc Boix worked, from 1940 to 1943.[113] The authors of this dramatic representation of the Spanish deportation to Mauthausen return to a literary recourse last seen in Joaquim Amat-Piniella's *K.L. Reich*: a top-down examination of the universe of the camp, from high-ranking Nazi officers to the most expendable of prisoners. By placing the play's omniscient narration in the hands of an SS officer, Llorente and Ripoll offer a sympathetic portrayal of Ricken. In a departure from the many contemporary Spanish Mauthausen representations, from memoirs to documentary films to fictional texts, that filter the story through the perspective of a Spanish prisoner, the playwrights ask the audience to empathize with the guilt and grief of a Nazi officer as an individual, instead of as a faceless torturer at the behest of Hitler.

El triángulo azul was first staged at Madrid's Teatro Valle Inclán in 2014 and won Spain's Premio Nacional de Literatura for a dramatic work the following year. As the first theatrical production to tackle the subject of the Spaniards in Mauthausen, it offers the spectator a compact visualization of five years of imprisonment over the course of a little more than two hours, focusing on the camp's Spanish population and the conflicts in the photography laboratory. The play moves among Ricken's narration, dramatized scenes from the history of Mauthausen, and vignettes with a trio of musicians and a chorus of uniformed Spanish prisoners. Llorente and Ripoll incorporate real names and specific episodes from Mauthausen's history into the action: the public hanging of Hans Bonarewitz; the minute of silence the Spaniards observed for José Marfil, the first Spaniard to die in Mauthausen; and the risky participation of the young members of the Poschacher *Kommando* in the clandestine photography smuggling ring. Moreover, two of the protagonists, Toni and Paco, are multidimensional incarnations of the severe García and the jocular Boix. Intermingling these real people and scenes with farcical musical numbers and fictional conversations challenges the casual spectator to discern the lines between fact and fiction and between homage and spectacle in the darkened theatre.

El triángulo azul imagines perhaps the most noted accomplishment of the Spanish prisoners of Mauthausen: the conversations, threats, deals, and blackmail behind Boix and García's secret preservation of photographic evidence of Nazi violence (chapter 1). In a metatextual wink, the playwrights project some of these photographs on the back wall of the theatre over the course of the play: the iconic photo of Spanish survivors before the Mauthausen gates welcoming their liberators illustrates the final scene.[114] Although Llorente and Ripoll do not directly credit David Wingeate Pike's *Spaniards in the Holocaust* or Benito Bermejo's *Francisco Boix, el fotógrafo de Mauthausen*, these two historiographic volumes are clearly sources for the dramatized interactions among Ricken, García, and Boix. In his book, Pike argued that Ricken was not as cruel and ideologically driven as many of the other Nazi officers in Mauthausen: in the play, the SS official treats Toni and Paco benignly and is anguished by his actions on behalf of the Nazis. Both Pike and Bermejo wrote about fraught interactions between García and Boix that are dramatized in the play. *El triángulo azul* succeeds in melding history with fiction where other fictional representations have failed: it bestows a nuanced literary interpretation of the historical moment in question. Although Ripoll has clarified that "[n]o pretendíamos hacer un documental, porque eso ya está y no somos historiadores" (Díaz Sande),[115] *El triángulo azul* resides in the blank space between the real and the imagined, dramatizing episodes that only Mauthausen prisoners and guards saw firsthand and entering into the thought processes and emotions of anonymous individuals who would never bear witness in a public forum. These imagined scenarios work in tandem with the recorded history of the camp to actualize for audiences what life might have been like for the Spanish prisoners, in all its tragicomic absurdity.

Indeed, musical theatre is both an appropriate and disquieting genre through which to display the contradictions of the Spaniards in Mauthausen. The playwrights weave Spanish *pasodobles, chotis,* and other song forms sung by the prisoners, the strains of an "orquestra gitana" ("gypsy orchestra," Llorente and Ripoll 36) and traditional Sephardic verse into the action. Given their subject matter and the comic actualization the actors offer onstage, these musical interludes are particularly divisive. With titles like "Canción de la cantera de Wienergraben" ("Ay, me muero, / que la diño, que me muero, / por la gracia del Caudillo"), "Canción de la alambrada electrificada," ("Yo soy la electrocución, / yo soy la alta tensión, / tu cuerpo en ebullición. / Trecientos ochenta voltios, / listo para el crematorio"), and "Canción de la supremacía de la raza aria" ("Una aria es / para asear / la más activa. / En higienizar / sin duda es / la preferida"), the songs imbue the play with fanciful elements while relating serious aspects of the camp's deadly agenda (49, 113, 79).[116] Watching as a prisoner with a coil of barbed wire atop his head sings about deadly electric shocks next to an actor miming electrocution, or hearing a blond-wigged prisoner drawl out the word "gaaaaaaaaaaaaaaaaaaaaas" is designed to provide comic relief between sadistic encounters while potentially offending spectators' sensibilities (80). They are echoed in the playwrights' interpretation of Paco as a voyeur of the Nazi crimes who engages in gallows humour: this representation challenges other one-dimensional portrayals of Boix as a pure hero.[117] Llorente and Ripoll's interest in moving beyond a simplistic retelling of the solidarity and will to survive of the Spanish deportees sets *El triángulo azul* apart from the prevailing narrative recounted, in particular, in the Mauthausen documentaries.

Llorente and Ripoll include a number of other details that emphasize the play's metatheatrical qualities. A group of prisoners pays oblique homage to Francisco de Quevedo's "El sueño de la muerte" ("The Dream of Death") when Death – Hitler himself, in a long black leather coat, black gloves, black Nazi military hat, and distinctive moustache – discusses the "[t]rienta y cinco maneras de morir en Mauthausen" (Llorente and Ripoll 30).[118] When the Spanish prisoners stage a traditional *zarzuela* (Spanish operetta) inside the camp, Ricken reacts with amazement: "¡Un espectáculo de variedades en medio de aquel horror! ... Y, por encima de todo, aire fresco, diversión, moral para aquella tropa de hombres deshechos, diezmados, recentados, que sabían que la dignidad y la moral era lo único que les podía mantener con vida," (54).[119] Ricken's observations underline the Spaniards' physical and spiritual fight to survive that made way for such seemingly absurd phenomena as musical theatre, soccer matches, and greeting cards inside a category-three Nazi concentration camp. Ricken's comments also capture the contradictions inherent in *El triángulo azul*: a farcical musical variety show – a "vodevil" ("vaudeville") as one reviewer called it (Morales) – that seeks to represent the deadly ordeal suffered by more than seven thousand Spaniards.

The rich visual and auditory ambiance created in *El triángulo azul* distinguishes this fictionalization of the Spanish experience of Mauthausen from other one-dimensional representations. The play offers the audience a portal inside Mauthausen and invites them to empathize with a diverse population of prisoners and Nazis. While dressed alike in their tattered striped prisoner uniforms, some of the Spanish deportees in *El triángulo azul* are cruel collaborators with the Nazis, others are innocent children unaffiliated with political parties, and others are heroes who nevertheless put their compatriots at great risk. From Oana, the Roma prostitute who is unceremoniously shot at the end of the play, to Brettmeier (aka Georg Bachmayer, Mauthausen's second-in-command), who shoots her, the play dramatizes the Nazi universe of victims and victimizers. There are, however, no Jews in this version of Mauthausen, an omission also noted in many of the other texts that have emerged in the past decade and a half. The absence of Jewish prisoners on stage is tantamount to their absence in the Spanish prisoners' daily lives in Mauthausen. Although the play has not been performed outside of Spain, one imagines that this absence would particularly rankle Holocaust scholars who argue against the "banalization" of the genocide of Jews. As a dramatization of a long-ignored chapter of Spain's contemporary history, however, *El triángulo azul* chooses to fill a representational void by devoting the play to non-Jewish prisoners in the camp.

In the play's closing moments, Ricken describes how the photographs of Mauthausen that Paco smuggled out of the camp with the help of one of the Poschacher boys inculpated the Nazis: "Gracias a esos negativos que los españoles sacaron del campo se pudo demostrar nuestra culpabilidad" (Llorente and Ripoll 123).[120] He laments that he and the Nazis as a whole will never be held accountable for the Holocaust writ large: "Y aun así no pagaré, no pagaremos."(124).[121] In the joyous moments of liberation, the Spanish prisoners dance to the strains of a *pasodoble* and form a conga line around the boundaries of the stage. One Spaniard tells Ricken that the legacy of the Nazis will fade to black, while their victims will be afforded a rekindled future: "Para ustedes la noche. Para nosotros, el día" (124).[122] Ricken's suicide at the end of *El triángulo azul*, while the product of the playwrights' imaginations, presents a more Manichean outcome than the moral uncertainties foretold throughout the drama. Taking advantage of the variety of representation and symbolic meaning available in a dramatic form, *El triángulo azul* pushes the boundaries of the theatre to arrive at a thoughtful contemporary Mauthausen representation. Llorente and Ripoll do not shy away from the discomfort, humour, humanity, and sadism that are integral not only to the original experience of the Spaniards in Mauthausen but also to the collective memory that seeks to reinvigorate their ordeal for new generations of Spaniards.

Social Media: Carlos Hernández's "@deportado4443" (2015)

Antonio Hernández Marín was deported to Mauthausen on 25 January 1941 as prisoner number 4443. His friend from the *Compagnies de travailleurs étrangers*, Antonio Cebrián Calero, entered with him and was assigned number 4442. Although Cebrián died in Gusen in November 1941, Hernández survived to see Mauthausen's liberation on 5 May 1945 (Bermejo and Checa, *Libro memorial* 197, 441). Hernández remained in exile in France for the rest of his life, although he was reunited with his family during a visit to Murcia in the 1960s. He died in 1992 in Ivry, France, suffering from Alzheimer's during the last years of his life (Hernández de Miguel, "Ferroviario").

Antonio Hernández was reborn on 21 January 2015. Beginning with his first communiqué – "Me encuentro en el campo de prisioneros de guerra de Trier, Alemania. Somos unos 700 españoles. Los nazis nos mantienen separados del resto" – Antonio became the subject of the first narrative on social media devoted to one Spanish deportee's experience of Mauthausen (Hernández de Miguel, "Me encuentro en el campo").[123] As the narrator and protagonist of this unique text, Antonio's story unfolded in 140-character bursts on the social media platform Twitter over three months. Users who followed "@deportee4443" were thus transported back to events that had occurred more than seventy years earlier. Antonio's narrative culminated on 8 May 1945, as he recounted the exhilarating and emotional days after his liberation from Mauthausen. In the final entries that constituted this ex-deportee's story, 8 May 1945 converges with 8 May 2015: the original event becomes one with its commemoration decades later.

The "@deportado4443" Twitter narrative is the brainchild of journalist Carlos Hernández de Miguel, whose uncle, Antonio Hernández, survived Mauthausen. Much like Melenchón i Xamena's postmemory of her uncle in fictionalized memoir form, Hernández de Miguel recreated his uncle's life story through social media and the lens of postmemory. Thus, the Mauthausen survivor who died in 1992 became the main character in a story that sits halfway between history and fiction. Hernández de Miguel began this Twitter narrative *en medias res*, as Antonio was deported from a German *Stalag* to Mauthausen. Antonio's account developed over more than eight hundred individual entries posted from January to May, 2015.[124] It adhered to the conventions of this social media platform, through which anyone on the internet can read and respond to short missives ("tweets" in English or "tuits" in Spanish) that are updated as a feed in real time and available in perpetuity online. The "@deportado4443" handle – denoting the title, locator, and protagonist of this serialized narrative on the Twitter website – also spawned the truncated story of Antonio Cebrián: "@deportado4442." This subsidiary Twitter feed links directly to the primary source of "@deportado4443," contributing a brief serialized narrative about Mauthausen's subcamp Gusen and Cebrián's death there in 1941.

In his biography on the Twitter website, Antonio Hernández is described as having been born on "24/08/1907 en Molina de Segura (Murcia). Carabinero durante la guerra. Exiliado en Francia y deportado a Mauthausen por los nazis. Esta es mi historia real" (Hernández de Miguel, "@deportado4443").[125] But the "real" of Twitter is not the "real" of a historical account: virtually every aspect of "@deportado4443" was a construction of its author, Hernández de Miguel, who posted entries in the voice of his long-departed uncle. Marianne Hirsch, in her theorization of postmemories of the Holocaust, accounts for second-generation survivors who "*re-embody* more distant political and cultural memorial structures" in their aesthetic endeavours (33; emphasis in the original). Hernández de Miguel "'remember[s]' only by means of the stories, images, and behaviours among which [he] grew up" the experiences of the Spaniards in Mauthausen (Hirsch, *Generation of Postmemory* 5). Adopting the voice, persona, and life trajectory of his uncle as his own on Twitter, then, constitutes postmemorial work for the social media age.

The "@deportado4443" narrative arc melded the format of an intimate diary with the immediacy of social media. Although the real Antonio Hernández spent more than four years in Mauthausen, the Antonio of "@deportado4443" consolidated this long imprisonment into three months' worth of short descriptions, observations, questions, and documentation. The author composed this Twitter narrative in the form of a serialized novel, updating Antonio's story six to ten times daily. As a Spanish Mauthausen representation, "@deportado4443" brought the form into the world of social media while at the same time returning it to the kind of serialized narration that Carlos Rodríguez del Risco had initiated some seventy years earlier. In this sense, "@deportado4443" is at once innovative and imitative, a unique way of capturing a new audience while echoing Rodríguez del Risco's harrowing blow-by-blow account of his survival of Mauthausen.

Antonio Hernández never wrote his memoirs. Hernández de Miguel used the outlines of his uncle's story and the scattered writings he left behind, embellished with experiences that are common to all of the Spanish Mauthausen deportees to construct this narrative. In the course of adapting the story to Twitter, Hernández de Miguel took advantage of social media's ability to stretch into multiple formats at once: Antonio's tweets included links, photos, and YouTube videos resurrected from the archives.[126] In one tweet published on the seventieth anniversary of Mauthausen's liberation, Antonio used the demarcator "#RotSpanier" (Hernández de Miguel, "Durante casi 5 años"). The Twitter hashtag is a means of cataloguing individual posts: "RotSpanier" effectively links "@deportado4443" to other Twitter users who posted comments in homage to the Spanish deportees, who were referred to as *Rotspanier* (Spanish red) by the Nazis. The hyperlinks that pepper "@deportado4443" brought twenty-first-century media to bear on a mid-twentieth-century tale, a disconnect that in practice actualized the stories of the Spaniards in Mauthausen for online audiences.

By the conclusion of Antonio's story on 8 May 2015, "@deportado4443" had tens of thousands of Twitter users subscribing to its regularly updated feed.[127] Virtually every entry in the narrative, every tweet, was retweeted and favourited – signs of approval from other Twitter subscribers – at least fifty times, and sometimes as many as three hundred times. But this give-and-take between other Twitter users and the narrator of "@deportado4443" over the course of the primary narrative only travelled one way. As he recounted his Mauthausen existence, Antonio did not interact with other Twitter users or entities: he was entirely isolated from this contemporary world and his followers. Thus, although "@deportado4443" took advantage of the succinct storytelling format and illustrative possibilities available on Twitter, the account laboured to recreate its narrator's isolation from the world outside Mauthausen. Given that the narrator of "@deportado4443" did not publish or respond to the comments of his followers, he essentially narrated his story into a void, not cognizant of his larger audience. Perhaps unconsciously, then, Hernández de Miguel echoed the sense of futility many Spanish Mauthausen prisoners felt while they were trapped inside the camp: like messages in a bottle from a desert island, any non-sanctioned communication they managed to send to the outside world wound up in an unknown limbo. But Hernández de Miguel ruptured this metaphor when Antonio interacted with "@deportado4442": Antonio "favourited" five of the tweets that Cebrián wrote, ostensibly from Gusen. In the real world of Mauthausen, once Cebrián was sent to Gusen, he had no additional personal contact with his compatriots in Mauthausen.

To narrate a story that took place from 1941 to 1945 in the social media world of 2015, Hernández de Miguel took additional liberties with historical accuracy. Much like the Mauthausen memoirists who wrote their accounts decades after their liberation from the camp, "@deportado4443" described events that the narrator did not witness, published photographs of scenes that a Spanish prisoner would never have seen, and made commentaries that betrayed Hernández de Miguel's cognizance of the contemporary importance of certain occurrences in the camp. When Antonio reported that the Nazis had repatriated a Spanish prisoner with connections to Franco, he realized: "Que los SS hayan soltado a Pindado significa que Franco sabe que estamos aquí encerrados" (Hernández de Miguel, "Deberíamos estar durmiendo").[128] Similarly, in a tweet posted on 2 May 2015, Antonio pondered why the SS cut the prisoners' rations: "Tengo una sensación extraña. Algo planean" (Hernández de Miguel "¡No traen la comida!").[129] The author heightened the tension of the narrative with messages that transcended the wartime setting. As a consequence, informed readers are able to fill in details about which Antonio could only conjecture: that Franco's government was complicit in the deportation of Spaniards to Mauthausen; that by early May 1945, liberation was around the corner. Antonio posted SS photographs, reproduced pages from the lists of dead prisoners and quotes from his fellow Spanish deportees, all material that has only been available in photo collections, archives, and memoirs released during the postwar period. To this end, Hernández de Miguel benefited from the oral testimonies and memoirs of Spanish Mauthausen survivors he compiled for his book, *Los últimos españoles de Mauthausen* (*The Last Spaniards of Mauthausen*), quoting liberally from these sources in the course of "@deportado4443."[130] As a result, many episodes familiar to all Spanish deportees to Mauthausen – the public hanging of Hans Bonarewitz, the presence of a black man from Barcelona in the camp, the establishment of the prostitutes' barracks – are integrated into Antonio's story. Intermingling Antonio's sense of his presence in a larger narrative with verifiable historical details may encourage readers who are unfamiliar with the history of the Spanish Mauthausen deportees to conflate fact and imagination, to come to the erroneous conclusion that the deportees were more aware of their fate and historical circumstances than they actually were.

Yet other aspects of publicizing the plight of the Spaniards in Mauthausen on this social media platform would be impossible in more traditional forms of media. More than forty thousand Twitter users followed

"@deportado4443" over the course of Antonio's primary narrative: young Spaniards, Spanish journalists, international groups dedicated to the preservation of collective memory related to Nazi concentration camp prisoners (such as the Amical de Mauthausen and the Gusen Memorial Committee), and Spanish speakers from other countries all watched Antonio's story unfold, sharing aspects of it with their own followers. The immediacy of Twitter affects a wider, if not larger, audience than other contemporary Spanish representations of Mauthausen. In addition, through the author's separate personal Twitter account, Hernández de Miguel interacted with his readers without breaking the rhythm and isolation of his creation. As Twitter users read and responded to the posts from "@deportado4443," Hernández de Miguel retweeted and replied to their thoughts: through the author's Twitter account, the audience for "@deportado4443" became even more concrete and imaginable. The author was able, in this way, to correct factual errors and interact with detractors, another dimension to social media that, for better or for worse, is not possible with traditional media.[131]

As the "@deportado4443" narrative approached 5 May 1945, other Twitter users sent words of encouragement and motivation to the fictionalized Spanish deportee whose ordeal they had followed for months. In anticipation of liberation day, one Twitter user replied to "@deportado4443" that "El martes es el día de la liberación, ánimo queda poco pero con estos salvajes es una eternidad" (lumipife).[132] On the same day, another Twitter user wrote: "Tres días Antonio! Tres días!!!" (Blanco).[133] These interactions allowed other Twitter users not only to share in the experiences of the fictional Antonio Hernández, but also, in their own way, to become a part of his story some seven decades after the original historical moment. For many of the followers of "@deportado4443," this was their only exposure to the history of Spaniards in Mauthausen; for others, it continues to be a more active way to engage with the history of the deportees than through fleeting references in history books, documentaries, or Wikipedia pages. By bringing the story of one deportee into the realm of social media, Hernández de Miguel demonstrated that the Spanish victims of Mauthausen may be kept alive even after all of the remaining survivors have died. Recreating the story of a Spanish Mauthausen survivor at a remove of seventy years – "re-embodying" Antonio Hernández – requires a modicum of invention, but the underlying experience is a fresh approach rooted in historical fact and poised to usher the stories of the Spanish deportation to Nazi camps towards unique forms of representation.

The six authors in this chapter guided the story of the Spaniards in Mauthausen through a period of intense evolution, yet in the end these new forms of mass-media representation are not as radically different as they may seem from earlier published accounts of the camp. Melenchón i Xamena's invented memoir of her uncle captures the immediacy and sense of collaboration seen in the life narratives of Mauthausen survivors from Mariano Constante to Ramiro Santisteban. Pérez Domínguez and Sánchez's page-turners fictionalize a history and characters that captured the Spanish imagination in Antonio Sinca Vendrell's florid historiography. Carbos and Cosnava's sensationalist graphic novel works in a lurid terrain of fiction not dissimilar to Mercè Rodoreda's violent short story. Ripoll and Llorente's literary dramatization of a cross section of Mauthausen calls back to Joaquim Amat-Piniella's sensitive novel cataloguing the camp's diverse population. And Hernández de Miguel's foray into new media suggests Carlos Rodríguez del Risco's appropriation of the timeless serialized account to craft an adventure story of the most harrowing kind.

As representations of the Spanish experience of Mauthausen continue to evolve, they have eclipsed the first-person survivor narratives that attempted to document lived experience. Individual memory must necessarily look to collective memory to remember the Spanish deportation, its human and psychic toll. Meanwhile, audiences seek out modes of storytelling that appeal to their contemporary tastes. Lived experience told through oral histories becomes imagined experience told through comics, novels, and social media. The underlying history remains constant: more than seven thousand Spaniards deported to Mauthausen during the Second World War, with just a little more than two thousand surviving to the end. The smell of the crematorium smoke, the taste of the malt "coffee," the sensation of an SS boot to the torso or a gunshot to the head, the rigid bunks in fetid barracks, the fourteen hours daily of punishing hard labour, all must now be recreated by authors, artists, and audiences who could never truly imagine such traumas. All the while a distance grows between truth and fiction, but without these fictions the truth might disappear entirely. A compromise emerges between what, in the interest of knowing the truth, we most desire – a Mauthausen survivor before us, relaying the most intimate details of his imprisonment, sharing his fallen compatriots' names, their stories, their struggles – and the reality for which we must settle. Contemporary accounts mine the recorded stories, the voices of survivors who are long gone, and the archival research of historians to find a balance between fact and fiction. Some of these creations are more fictional, some more historical. Whether it is preferable to know the truth or to keep the story alive in the hearts and minds of the public is subjective. These contemporary creations implicitly argue that even through a fog of imagination and the lure of commercialization, understanding some semblance of the story of the Spaniards in Mauthausen is better than knowing nothing at all.

5 Mauthausen Today

A Spanish Memorial in Austria: Commemoration and Legacy

With diverse histories and cultures, and distinct languages and geography, Spain and Austria are seemingly worlds apart. Although the Hapsburg line ruled Spain and constructed what is known as the "Madrid de los Austrias" during the sixteenth and seventeenth centuries, in modern times the two countries are outwardly connected only by a common currency and a contentious membership in the European Union.[1] Yet in the 1930s, Austria and Spain began a tandem trajectory that would leave both nations in thrall to fascist dictators. The fraught process of coming to terms with this uneasy history, symbolized by the transformation of the Nazi concentration camp in Austria where Spaniards were condemned to death into a site of memory, has united these two countries.

Hitler annexed Austria, his homeland, into the Third Reich in 1938. The country was ruled by the Nazis until the end of the Second World War, though Austria signed an agreement with the Allies in 1943 that rebranded it "neutral" during the conflict. Austria's absolution of its responsibility in the war became "that nation's founding myth" (Young, *Texture of Memory* 92) by the postwar years. This "amnesia in Austrian collective memory" was then the basis for a "dramatic awakening" (Diner, "Resolution and Memory" 38) at the end of the Cold War, when Austrians were confronted with the truth of their country's collaboration with the Nazis. Austria has since faced its role in the Second World War and the Holocaust through the same types of memorial structures – both tangible and conceptual – built in the rest of Europe.[2] One of these "sites of memory," in Pierre Nora's parlance, is Mauthausen: rebuilt from a Nazi concentration camp to a memorial and museum grounds in the green hills of the Danube River Valley.

The same year that Germany annexed Austria, the German Nazi Party was bombing Spanish towns and providing munitions to support a Nationalist victory in the Spanish Civil War. Franco's rise to power was only helped by the rise of Hitler and National Socialism in Germany. Spain, though officially "non-belligerent" in the Second World War, was solidly in Hitler's corner until 1943, when Franco began to court the Allies. Consequently, Franco made sure that his hyperbolic tale of "saving" countless European Jews was written into Spain's postwar myth. The country's actual role in the Second World War and the Holocaust was suppressed for decades, only emerging in fits and starts in the 1970s, after the dictator's death. Spain, like Austria, was "never held to account for its past" (Young, *Texture of Memory* 92), a situation that disabled sustained attempts to delve into the country's past until the beginning of the twenty-first century. Mauthausen – where thousands of Spaniards were deported at the implicit behest of Franco in the 1940s and where survivors and their families return to actively maintain a collective memory of this traumatic period – is symbolically and literally where the contemporary histories of Austria and Spain converge.

The Mauthausen concentration camp – which James Young has called "the pastoral memorial" (*Texture of Memory* 92) – is located atop a hill about four kilometres from the train station in the town of Mauthausen. Although prisoners arriving at the station from 1938 to 1945 were forced to march up the hill to the camp, today visitors arrive by car, bus, bicycle, or on foot via a picturesque pedestrian path. Past the town's quaint centre and postwar homes, beyond the rolling farmland and stands of trees, what is now the Mauthausen Memorial appears on the crest of a hill. The camp is unmistakable: it dominates the top of the rise and affords a commanding view of the surrounding countryside, the Danube River, and snow-capped mountains. "Transformed from a hellish scar on the landscape," the camp is now "a clean, beautifully maintained state memorial" (93). Given its imposing presence just beyond the residential areas of the town, Mauthausen is now – and was during its years of operation as a concentration camp – difficult to ignore.[3]

Nora observes that "[m]emory attaches itself to sites, whereas history attaches itself to events" (22). The gruesome events that unfolded at Mauthausen between 1938 and 1945 have been inscribed into what remains of the built form of the concentration camp. The camp serves as memorial, monument, and museum to the memory of the thousands of victims of the Nazis whose blood was absorbed by the earth inside this walled fortress. Interpreted as a collective site of memory, Mauthausen illustrates that "[b]oundaries between the museum, the memorial and the monument have indeed become fluid in the past decade in ways that render obsolete the old critique of the museum as a fortress for the few and the monument as a medium of reification and forgetting" (Huyssen, *Twilight Memories* 254). Mauthausen is a living memorial, actualized by a steady stream of visitors and commemorations that bring thousands of "tourists of history" seeking "a cathartic 'experience' of history" (Sturken 9) to its gates annually. Although Mauthausen's transformation from concentration camp to memorial site has not escaped controversy, it endures as an ongoing effort to warn against the perils of history and to preserve the memory of the victims for new generations.

Holocaust memorials can be at once tangible and intangible sites of memory whose aim, according to Young, "is not to call attention to their own presence so much as to past events *because* they are no longer present" (*Texture of Memory* 12; emphasis in the original). The entirety of the Mauthausen grounds as well as the camp's conceptual framework constitute a memorial whose foundation is, counterintuitively, the absence of Mauthausen as a concentration camp. Indeed, the postwar shift in Mauthausen's name – from the Mauthausen Concentration Camp to the Mauthausen Memorial – underscores how the site has transitioned from a space dominated by the violence of history to one devoted to the contradictory task of making memory, which is by definition invisible and remote, into something visible and immediate.

The visual panorama of Mauthausen today is marked by presence and absence. The solid stone walls and guard towers stand as lasting vestiges of the Nazis' mindful construction and the brutal labour of the prisoners. Just beyond the SS swimming pool, the gate that opens towards the SS garages remains, although it is devoid of the Nazi iron eagle that once stood atop its arch, which former prisoners ripped down after liberation. Through the gatehouse into the main camp, the Appellplatz is paved where once it was packed earth that the prisoners kept smoothed and maintained. Only three of the wood-frame prisoner barracks are preserved, though stone foundations and stairs outline a grid where additional barracks once stood. The Russian camp, where the infirm were sent to die, and the Jewish tent camp on the northeastern edge of the Mauthausen complex are also gone, though barbed wire and electric insulators still trace the camp's perimeter. The crematory

5.1 Mauthausen SS gate, May 2011. Photographed by the author.

smokestack rises above barracks that once housed the gas chamber, the camp prison, and the infirmary, mostly stripped of signs of their original functions. Although overgrown with vegetation, the Wienergraben quarry is still just outside the camp walls, its steep 186 steps and ominous Parachute Jump precipice intact. Young has called this "staircase of death ... its own best monument" (*Texture of Memory* 97).

Within the Mauthausen Memorial grounds, dozens of monuments were installed after the war, from towering carved stone statuary dedicated to the diverse national groups who perished en masse in the camp to small plaques in honour of both named and anonymous victims. These monuments are public art, built forms, or "plastic objects" (Young, *Texture of Memory* 4) that join the concentration camp's original installations in their effort to memorialize the camp's

5.2 Mauthausen Wienergraben stairs, May 2011. Photographed by the author.

history and keep the individual and collective memory of Mauthausen alive. The sculptures and plaques are, in turn, dotted with flowers and small stones that represent fleeting memorializations by visitors: temporary and abstract displays that connect the viewer to the permanent monuments, personalizing what is otherwise a more formal and distant structure. As multilingual as the camp's brochures and audio guides, these monuments remind visitors of the sheer number of people and nations affected by the Nazi regime in Mauthausen. The stones and flowers tell of their continued place in national imaginations and the connection visitors feel to their own long-dead countrymen. "Together," Young observes, the monuments at Mauthausen "suggest the essential plurality of memory, nation by nation" (94). The placement of these memorials – on the Wailing Wall where prisoners faced the cruelty of SS tortures, beatings, and executions upon first entering the camp; deep within the labyrinth of the gas chamber and crematory ovens; and in the dedicated memorial park where the SS barracks and recreational areas once stood between the main camp and the quarry – is another constant reminder of the human toll of Mauthausen, spread out over the entirety of its grounds. These monuments, appended with the ephemera of visitors, look back at a historical moment while also looking forward towards how the past will be remembered via its concrete memorialization.

Viewing these visible and invisible spaces, a contemporary visitor is afforded a sense of the vast area ruled by the Nazis inside the Mauthausen walls, analogous to the vast territory claimed by the Third Reich in Europe during its reign. Mauthausen's transformation from a space of death and violence to a site of remembrance has played out over the decades. After the war, Austrians were reluctant to support the conversion of the concentration camp into a memorial. By 1949, when Mauthausen was first declared an official memorial site and the sarcophagus at the centre of the Appellplatz was dedicated, "voices were raised in open opposition to the proposal of preserving the main camp at Mauthausen as a memorial and warning for present and future generations" (Horwitz 169). Townspeople had dismantled portions of the main camp's fortifications, barracks, and other installations at the satellite camps were absorbed into the local landscape as private homes and event spaces, and bodies had been exhumed in the interest of "recovering" land lost to the Nazis (171–2). Originally confrontational and political, at its inception the memorial assumed as its central message that Mauthausen was "a cradle of political resistance and ... evidence for the thesis that Austria was the first victim of National Socialist expansionist politics" (Perz and Skriebeleit 14). Yet the development of the Mauthausen Memorial also began to reflect changing attitudes towards Austria's involvement in the Second World War and increasingly welcomed the intervention of survivor groups in the conceptualization of the camp as a site of memory. For years, Manuel García Barrado, a Spanish survivor who settled in the town of Mauthausen after the camp's liberation, was the decommissioned camp's de facto tour guide and administrator. When a small museum space opened in the former Mauthausen infirmary building in 1970, it became the first "permanent exhibition devoted to the topic of National Socialism" in the country (13). A visitor's centre was constructed in 2003 as a space for interactive and pedagogical programming. The museum's expansion and redesign in 2013 sought to update Austria's role not just as victim but as perpetrator of the Nazi genocide as well (14). This contemporary rethinking of the Mauthausen Memorial is in line with the larger-scale project of transforming Europe's concentration and death camp memorials into memory sites that unify a common cultural memory of the Holocaust and continue to maintain their relevance well into the twenty-first century.

Yet efforts to construct and preserve a lasting conceptual and built space dedicated to the victims at the Mauthausen Memorial labour against the fog of forgetting that threatens to envelope the Holocaust globally. They also play into criticisms of the appropriation of sites of genocide as tourist attractions ultimately interested in financial gain over a nuanced exploration of history.[4] The Auschwitz survivor Ruth Klüger has questioned the capacity of other memorial sites, such as Dachau, to capture the essence of the concentration camp:

> The missing ingredients are the odor of fear emanating from human bodies, the concentrated aggression, the reduced minds. I didn't see the ghosts of the so-called *Muselmänner* (Muslims) who dragged themselves zombie-like through the long, evil hours, having lost the energy and the will to live. Sure, the signs and the documentation and the films help us to understand. But the concentration camp a memorial site? (67)[5]

Visitors who walk along the uneven paving stones and climb the quarry steps may imagine a physical connection to prisoners who climbed the same stairs and stumbled along the same uneven ground. Yet what is lacking in the modern-day tourist's experience of Mauthausen is evidence of the camp's human costs. Without 50-kilogram stones lashed to their backs, wearing tennis shoes instead of wooden-soled clogs, stepping around puddles instead of slipping on wet ground, visitors can only glean a fraction of the experience of the prisoners in Mauthausen. Photos and audio guides cannot recreate the constant sense of dread, the shouts of the SS guards, and the acrid smell of burning flesh that the Mauthausen prisoners suffered daily. Viewing the fenced-off Parachute Jump or the gas chambers denuded of their killing apparatus is not tantamount to being pushed off the precipice or suffering the agony induced by canisters of Zyclon B. A decades-old crust of bread on display in the museum does not capture what it felt like to starve. The plaques on the Wailing Wall fail to communicate the pain of being beaten or shot to death. Every visitor to the camp who is not a Mauthausen survivor will face the impossibility of understanding with any depth what being imprisoned in Mauthausen was like. And by virtue of having lived through their imprisonment, the few remaining Mauthausen survivors cannot describe how it felt to die at the hands of the Nazis in the camp. Investing symbolic value in Holocaust memorials may allow visitors to feel they have achieved a deeper understanding of the concentration camp experience, but, contradictorily, the visitor also has "divested [themselves] of the obligation to remember ... [because these] monuments may relieve viewers of their memory burden" (Young, *Texture of Memory* 5). One way to counteract an expiration date stamped on the memory of the concentration camps, Young argues, is through regular social rituals that take place within these memory sites: "once ritualized, remembering together becomes an event in itself that is to be shared and remembered" (7). The annual commemoration events at Mauthausen are social memory acts, and while they cannot resurrect the past lives they seek to memorialize, they prevent history from actively forgetting the victims of Nazism.

Every year, on the first Sunday following 5 May, the Mauthausen Memorial holds commemoration activities to coincide with the anniversary of the camp's liberation. These events are at once a spectacle and a homage, performance and quiet contemplation, concentration camp tourism and a collective effort at cultural memory. What the scholar Jan Assmann defines as "cultural memory" is mediated by social rituals and requires certain moments "when the community comes together for a celebration" (112): the ritualized set of acts at Mauthausen celebrate and preserve the memories of victims of the Nazis. Yearly visitors to Mauthausen become, in turn, "tourists of history" who make a pilgramage to the concentration camp site "in order to pay tribute to the dead and to feel transformed in some way in relation to that place" (Sturken 11). Attendees will inevitably come away both moved and perturbed by what they have witnessed: the Mauthausen commemorations distill the private suffering of hundreds of thousands into busloads of international visitors, vigorous flag-waving, and picnics on sacred ground. Yet where this annual gathering fails to coax nuance out of Mauthausen's history and built environment, it succeeds at ensuring that thousands will become new witnesses to the existence of the camp. Nora writes that sites of memory require deliberate archives, celebrations, and anniversaries: "the truth of *lieux de mémorie* [is] that without commemorative vigilance, history would soon sweep them away" (12). Mauthausen survivor groups and, indeed, survivors, witnesses, and scholars worldwide actively participate in the "commemorative vigilance" that preserves a cultural memory of the Holocaust through these intentional social gatherings and rituals.

More than twenty-five international delegations of survivors, their families, students, and interested others participate in Mauthausen's commemoration activities, which are broadcast live on Austrian national television.[6] The day-long commemorations begin with national survivor groups gathered at their respective monuments in the Memorial Park area of the Mauthausen Memorial. Delegations from one national group deliver flowers and wreaths to other national groups for which they feel a certain affinity. These rituals underscore Mauthausen's unique position as a Nazi concentration camp with an international prisoner population. The ceremony culminates in a parade of nations and groups (such as homosexuals and Roma) representing the panoply of Mauthausen prisoners. Flanked by spectators, a small orchestra and chorus, and news media, each delegation marches through the entrance gate into the Appellplatz, offering flowers or a wreath to the sarcophagus situated at the centre of the main plaza. The commemorative tomb is marked with the flag of Mauthausen – an inverted red triangle bearing the years of the camp's existence, "1938–1945," in white lettering – under which these diverse contingents are united.

The identities on display during the commemoration activities are at once divisive and unifying. They foster the notion of a Mauthausen divided by nationality: a camp where the Russians and Jews were greeted more violently than the Spaniards, for instance. Yet these national groups gather together in the singular geographic site of the Mauthausen Memorial, under the Mauthausen flag, as one body of

5.3 Mauthausen sarcophagus at the center of the Appellplatz surrounded by offerings, May 2015. Photographed by the author.

people touched by the Nazis' inhumanity. This union symbolizes the collective struggle for survival that all of the prisoners in Mauthausen, regardless of nationality, faced. Above all, it is the reclaimed space of the concentration camp that unites diverse groups during these rituals. The Memorial Park, located in the former space of the SS barracks and recreation yards, symbolically demonstrates that those who were dominated have assumed the physical place of the dominators and raised their voices above any vestige of a Nazi past. Moreover, the final international parade reaches its climax in the Appellplatz, where all prisoners were unified decades earlier in their common suffering and death under the abuses and humiliations of the Nazis. This plaza is reappropriated as a victim's space where all nations, all cultures, all individuals, and all religions are equally respected. Here, visitors are afforded a moment to grieve for those lost while celebrating an ultimate triumph over Nazi hatred that affected not only the victims, but also the survivors, their families, and their national brethren. Although this triumph over the past is a common thread, the anniversary commemorations also emphasize the ongoing fight against extremism and intolerance. The Mauthausen commemoration activities are peaceful and political, a reminder that divergent beliefs and origins can in fact coexist in a global society. They look towards the victims' common history to remind the world of humanity's burden to remember so as not to repeat past atrocities.

Never forgetting the Jewish and non-Jewish victims of the Nazis is the underlying message of the commemoration ceremonies, a message that grows in importance as fewer and fewer Mauthausen survivors remain.[7] The children and adolescents who take part in the ceremonies communicate, at times explicitly, that a new generation will soon be responsible for making sure the atrocities that occurred at Mauthausen and those who suffered them are not forgotten. The ceremonies also emphasize a national identity that, in the case of the Spaniards, is not absolute. Silvia Cueto, the head of the Association of Spanish Republicans from Austria and the daughter of a survivor, pointed out the irony inherent in the Spaniards' inverted triangle: it symbolizes the "Rotspanier" as political prisoners representing Spain and also as stateless individuals.[8] This blurred national identity continues to mark the Spanish participation in the anniversary commemorations, as Spanish survivors and their families who have remained in France tend to participate with the Amicale de Mauthausen from Paris instead of the Spanish delegation. There remains a lingering rivalry – some years a full-blown animosity – among the survivor groups that seek to represent the Spaniards in Mauthausen.[9] Nevertheless, over seventy years after the liberation of Mauthausen, the task of remembering and honouring the memory of Spanish victims now largely falls to a second, third, and fourth generation of individuals committed to these yearly memorial events.

"Mauthausen" has become a relatively common point of reference in Spanish newspapers and on television as shorthand for the role Spaniards played in the Second World War and the Holocaust. However, Mauthausen as a physical space continues to be elusive for the majority of the population: most will never make the pilgrimage to see the camp. For those who know what and where Mauthausen is, their understanding may be cursory by virtue of mass-media representations of the camp and the Holocaust that have supplanted historical information or actual lived experience over time. As more representations of Mauthausen stray from historical accounts and survivor testimony, they veer towards the kind of popular representations seen in *Prisionero de Mauthausen* and *El violinista de Mauthausen* (chapter 4).[10] As a consequence, the Spanish public's understanding of Mauthausen and its significance will become diluted and based primarily on the secondhand knowledge contained in these fictional retellings.

For those Spaniards who do maintain a firsthand knowledge of the space of Mauthausen – survivors, their children and grandchildren, and the high school students who attend the commemorations – the camp is a combination of the black and white photos on display in the museum and the physical surroundings that they see with their own eyes. Much of what constitutes Mauthausen today is empty: negative space where barracks once stood, where tent camps were once located, and where the SS pool was once filled with water. These absent sites demand the active imagination if not memory of the spectator to repopulate and refill them. Mauthausen's transformation from a Nazi concentration camp to a memorial site encourages the visitor to face the camp as it is now, missing crucial parts of its physical history as a concentration camp, but also to grasp its contemporary utility as a place of remembrance and memorialization.

Today Mauthausen maintains these symbolic meanings while also encapsulating political controversies and ongoing polemics surrounding historical memory in Spain. Different groups jockey to represent the Spanish survivors. They quibble over territory ceded to the French organizations and the presence of government officials from Madrid at the commemorations. They express disgust at the lack of state support and official recognition of Mauthausen survivors and their associations in Spain. Alongside young Polish men in polished military uniforms holding national standards, a ragtag band of supporters waves flags of the Spanish Republic and the Catalan independence movement attached to long sticks. All the while, the question of how to best represent the Spanish experience of Mauthausen in an uncertain future remains open. As the Spanish Mauthausen survivors disappear, groups like the Amical de Mauthausen must reinvent themselves as associations akin to the empty foundations of the barracks in Mauthausen. They exist to tell the stories of men and women who are now gone. The foundational narrative of the Spaniards in Mauthausen is their cornerstone, their reason to exist, but the intimate knowledge and understanding of the camp that can only be provided by those who were there will be lost.

Testimony and the Archive: Recording the Last Survivors

International attempts to record and preserve the oral histories of Holocaust survivors before their stories and voices are lost forever have been ongoing worldwide. "The seduction of the archive and its trove of stories of human achievement and suffering," Andreas Huyssen writes, "has never been greater" (*Present Pasts* 5). From David P. Boder's first systematic attempts to interview survivors in 1946, the need to record and collect the individual strands of the story of the Holocaust has become ever more urgent with each passing decade. Nora writes that "[e]ven as traditional memory disappears, we feel obliged assiduously to collect remains, testimonies, documents, images, speeches, any visible signs of what has been, as if this burgeoning dossier were to be called upon to furnish some proof to who knows what tribunal of history" (13–14). In Spain, this "tribunal of history" is the public's consciousness, maintained in a state of semi-ignorance for decades. For a population that has been as willfully ignored as the Spaniards in Mauthausen, gathering the materials for this memory archive, collecting the testimony and the documents that corroborate the validity of their claims, is of paramount importance. Both the subjectivity of the interview subject and the selectivity of the archive itself must be taken into consideration when trying to revisit the past through the words of someone who lived it (A. Assmann 337).

Although historians may agree that the overarching goal of survivor testimony "is the richest (most inclusive, detailed, and nuanced) possible representation of what different survivors have to convey" (Hayes and Roth 419), there is little agreement on the methodology by which to arrive at this ideal testimony. The advantage that video and oral histories have over the memoir or written life narrative, however, is the ability to experience "that point at which memory is transformed into language, often for the first time." (Young, *Writing and Rewriting* 161). As the survivor enunciates his or her memories, "the process of remembrance, of construction, of editing, of formulating ideas, and the search for order" (161) is laid bare in a way simply not possible in a literary text. The listener is presented with unmediated recollections in all their complexity that may run counter to historical acuracy. The interlocutor is also part of the process: the interviewer will naturally bring his or her implicit bias and subjectivity, for better or worse, to bear on the formation of the testimony (*Writing and Rewriting* 166–9; Felman and Laub 85; Baer, *El testimonio audiovisual* 201–12). This confluence of memories, lapses, voices, and, in some cases, visual cues provides a valuable window into the survivor experience that cannot be obtained in any other way. As survivors disappear, the collection of audio and video testimony has become even more urgent.

Efforts to record the testimonies of the last remaining Spanish survivors of Mauthausen, however, have come piecemeal. Inside Spain, journalists have been primarily responsible for contacting and interviewing Spanish Mauthausen survivors, a trend that dates to Montserrat Roig's efforts in the 1970s. Most of these projects are written testimonies, though one journalist has also spearheaded an effort to film short oral testimonies of Spanish survivors. Outside the country, Spanish Mauthausen survivors have been included in only a handful of oral history projects. Although not Holocaust survivors, the Spaniards in Mauthausen, as we have seen, were victims and witnesses to the Holocaust who suffered and died as a result of the Nazi cause. Many of the most prominent Holocaust oral history projects include other non-Jewish victims of the Nazis in their archives.[11] However, none of these projects include the testimony of Spanish survivors of Nazi camps. Spain has no large-scale oral history project of its own. The USC Shoah Foundation's Visual History Archive, the largest digital collection of the recorded testimony of Holocaust survivors and witnesses in the world, includes only one Spanish survivor of Mauthausen. Of the almost nine hundred Mauthausen Survivor Documentation Project interviews recorded for the Mauthausen Memorial in Austria, twenty-eight are of Spanish survivors. Grouped together, these twenty-nine oral histories tell only a fragment of the more than two thousand individual stories that belong to the collective of Spanish Mauthausen survivors.

Two journalists inside Spain have recently contacted and published excerpts from the testimony of the last remaining Spanish Mauthausen survivors. Montserrat Llor interviewed nineteen Spanish witnesses to the Holocaust for her 2014 book *Vivos en el averno nazi* (*Alive in the Nazi Inferno*), fourteen of whom are Mauthausen survivors. Carlos Hernández de Miguel interviewed fourteen Mauthausen survivors for his book, *Los últimos españoles de Mauthausen* (*The Last Spaniards of Mauthausen*).[12] These works are mediated presentations of Mauthausen survivors: the authors have self-consciously embarked on an effort to capture survivors' last words on their ordeal. Both projects face the reality of an elderly and much-diminished population of Spanish Mauthausen survivors. To that end, Llor and Hernández de Miguel interview many of the same individuals, draw extensively from previously published source material, and selectively edit the survivors' testimony.[13] The self-selection of individuals willing and able to give their oral histories almost seven decades after their liberation from Mauthausen means that often the same memories and experiences are repeated from interview to interview. At this stage in the recuperation of the collective memory of the Spanish experience of Mauthausen, there is little new to discover, yet every intervention counts.

The strength of the last Spanish Mauthausen survivors to contribute to these oral history projects cannot be discounted: these octo- and nonagenarians – as well as some who are still bearing witness after reaching one hundred years of age – remain committed to the cause of keeping alive the memory of their experiences and those of their fallen compatriots. Given the absence of any systematic drive in Spain to film or record oral histories from the Spanish deportation, these smaller-scale individual efforts become steeped with significance and urgency. However, the interviews Llor and Hernández de Miguel undertook are not published in their entirety: rather, the authors quote from the transcripts or paraphrase the words of their interview subjects.[14] This manner of curating their interviews – a technique Roig also used in *Els catalans als camps nazis*, though in a less heavy-handed way – leaves potentially significant details on the cutting room floor. Recorded oral histories, though less accessible to the public, capture the survivors' memories in a more organic fashion.

The only Spanish survivor of Mauthausen to figure in the USC Shoah Foundation Visual History Archive achieves this type of uncensored oral history. Eulogio Garijo was interviewed at his home in Argentina on 14 December 1997. Over the course of two hours and 48 minutes of conversation with an off-screen and anonymous interviewer, Garijo recalled going into hiding during the Spanish Civil War, escaping to France, and being imprisoned in Mauthausen and Gusen. Garijo spoke haltingly at first, lapsing into silences. As the interview went on, however, his memories flowed more fluently, and he was animated to narrate more about his experience. At times, Garijo had trouble remembering details, becoming frustrated, for instance, when he forgot his brother's name. Eighty-two at the time of the interview, Garijo's memory lapses became part of the intangible quality of the oral history, as did the light-blue button-down shirt he wore and the vase of roses at his side. It is in this confluence of sound and image that the listener "perceive[s] traces of a story the survivor is not telling" (Young, *Writing and Rewriting* 162), communicated solely through movement and vocal register.

Although Garijo's life history is not radically different from the trajectories of many of his compatriots, elements of his testimony underline the fact that each Spanish Mauthausen survivor has a distinct story to tell. Garijo repeatedly emphasized to the interviewer that he was never involved in politics: not in Spain during the Civil War, not in Mauthausen later. Garijo mused that among Spanish Civil War veterans in the camp there may have been solidarity, but emphasized that the influence of the Spanish communist organization inside the camp had been greatly exaggerated. According to Garijo, there were many Spaniards like him who did not get special treatment from the Nazis or the Spanish clandestine organization. This perspective is one of the most valuable aspects of Garijo's oral history, as it tells a counternarrative to the stories told by numerous Spanish Mauthausen survivors. Given the solidarity of the Spanish communists, many of them lived to liberation and have since become dominant voices within the body of Spanish Mauthausen survivor narratives. Garijo's assertion demonstrates that the Spaniards in Mauthausen were each individuals. When the Shoah Foundation interviewer asked Garijo what he knew about Franco's relationship with the Nazis, he responded that he knew that the Nazis aided Franco, but that he was unaware of Hitler until after the end of the Second World War. Though the interviewer took pains to pinpoint Garijo's historical understanding, this oral history is rooted in the subject's personal experience of events that only in retrospect can be judged for their historical significance.

Garijo displayed a range of emotions as he described his liberation from Gusen on the afternoon of 5 May 1945. In the video, Garijo first smiled and laughed, then cried as he recalled his feelings on that day: "La alegría ... la más grande del mundo fue aquello" ("The happiness ... that was the best feeling in the world"). The interviewer asked Garijo, "¿Por qué cree que se salvó?" ("Why do you think you were saved?"), a question that required the subject to ascribe cause and effect to his survival. Garijo mused that perhaps God, perhaps a magical presence, or perhaps his efforts to remain optimistic allowed him to survive. After nearly three hours of solo testimony, Garijo proudly introduced his wife and children to the camera. His children's presence as second-generation witnesses to Garijo's testimony underlines the fundamental importance of this type of oral history in the formation of postmemory. This Shoah Foundation video, one of thousands archived and available to the public at various research sites around the world, is a lasting testament that only Eulogio Garijo could provide to his life and ordeal in Mauthausen. It is unfortunate, then, that his is the only oral history collected from a Spaniard who had been in Mauthausen. The many other faces, voices, and stories of these survivors have mostly been lost to the passage of time.

The Mauthausen Survivors Documentation Project (MSDP), sponsored by the Austrian government, aimed to collect oral histories from a cross section of the Mauthausen prisoner community. The result are 859 recorded and filmed testimonies in various languages preserved at the Archiv der KZ-Gedenkstätte Mauthausen (AMM) in Vienna and folded into the multimedia exhibitions located at the Mauthausen Memorial. This collection of audio recordings includes 28 Spanish survivors of Mauthausen interviewed between May and November, 2002.[15] Mercedes Vilanova was the interlocutor for 26 oral histories in Spanish, Catalan, and Valenciano.[16] Depending on their willingness to speak, Vilanova either guided the interview with open-ended questions, or removed herself, allowing the subject free rein. This technique produced mixed results: Manuel García Barrado was eager to end his testimony after about 40 minutes, while Marcial Mayans Costa spoke freely for more than four hours. Vilanova's subsequent reflections on the interview process add an extra layer of self-reflection to this oral history project.

As with any oral testimony, the caprices of the survivors' memories made for some unusual revelations. Some details the witnesses recalled have not been corroborated by other survivors or historians, leaving room for doubt. Vilanova at times expressed surprise at her interview subjects' unique perspective, though she rarely corrected them. This complicated the truth value of these testimonies, a complication that must return the listener to the essential subjectivity of these stories. Life narratives, whether written or oral, are one of many ways of gathering historical evidence. They are not, however, measures of historical accuracy. Manuel Azaustre recalled in his interview that everyone in the quarry wore boots. Emiliano Pérez remembered the Spanish *Kapo* César Orquín as crueler than the SS. Luis Balleno swore that his Mauthausen convoy arrived in a passenger train. Joaquín López-Raymundo reminisced about strolling around Mauthausen at night while Francesc Boix played the harmonica.[17] These memories diverged from the commonly accepted narrative of Spanish survivors of Mauthausen, most of whom attested that everyone wore wooden clogs or were barefoot in the quarry, that César Orquín was a saviour of many Spaniards, that their convoys were packed into cattle wagons, and that there was no time, energy, or permission to stroll the camp grounds playing music at night.[18] Sorting out the apocryphal information from the verifiable memories is, indeed, a difficult undertaking. Unfortunately, in part because of a reluctance to question the memories of survivors that is endemic to oral history projects, one imposter was included among the original twenty-nine Spaniards interviewed for the MSDP.[19]

Nevertheless, Vilanova later second-guessed her questions, wondering "¿Por qué no les había preguntado más y mejor? ¿Por qué no había protestado por sus tópicos y anécdotas mil veces repetidas, copiadas, trasnochadas?" (*Mauthausen, después* 30).[20] The testimony of these Mauthausen survivors, many of whom had spoken or written at length previously about their experiences, may indeed ring stale or seem imitative. Vilanova thought that she could have done more to elicit new details from her interviewees, a desire that may have been more aspirational than practical. She saw the lapses or omissions in the survivors' memories as "el silencio que quiso derrotarme."[21] Instead of what they revealed to her, "fue lo que callaron, lo que ocultaron y que ni ellos sabían o habían olvidado, bloqueado," that had the biggest impact on her (Vilanova, *Mauthausen, después* 28).[22] Vilanova's reflections provide the unspoken perspective in the pairing of interviewer and interviewee, illustrating the give and take that Holocaust scholars see as central to the oral history process.

Like Garijo, a number of the Spanish Mauthausen survivors interviewed for the MSDP emphasized their distance from the clandestine activities of their compatriots in the camp. When asked what he knew about the resistance movement while he was in the camp, Jaume Álvarez Navarro replied: "Jo sabia que havia una resistència, jo sabia que havia un comitè fet de resistens, però no mes que això, no sabia ni que era ni que no era."[23] Only in retrospect, after liberation, did Álvarez Navarro realize the extent of the Spanish resistance inside the camp. Francisco Aura Boronat concurred that in Mauthausen "predominava el pres" ("the prisoners predominated"): the common prisoners were more prominent than those involved in the resistance. Although he benefited from working as a mechanic in the camp, Aura Boronat said that he wasn't one of the privileged "enchufats" ("well positioned") nor was he involved in the resistance movement. These testimonies, like the Mauthausen life narratives written in the early 2000s, offer a counternarrative, particularly to Mariano Constante and Montserrat Roig's publications from the 1970s that emphasized the role of the Spanish clandestine organization in the survival of Spanish Mauthausen deportees. Although not mutually exclusive interpretations, the availability of both versions – that the solidarity of the Spanish committee and the fortitude of individual Spaniards were crucial in assuring the survival of a relatively large community of Spaniards throughout the camp system – enriches our understanding of what went on behind Mauthausen's walls. The plurality of voices in these oral histories democratizes any unilateral "story" to emerge from the Spanish experience of Mauthausen.

As efforts to interview Spanish survivors of Mauthausen have of necessity come to an end, work on counting and cataloguing the Spanish deportees continues through the country's shifting political tides. Online databases, which can be continuously updated, provide a new way of tracking the history of the Spanish deportation to Mauthausen. Alfons Aragoneses has called Roig's interviews and lists in *Els catalans als camps nazis* the first database of the Spanish deportation to Nazi camps: a formidable effort considering the limitations of the era ("Deportados españoles"). It would take another thirty years for Benito Bermejo and Sandra Checa's *Libro Memorial: Españoles deportados a los campos nazis (1940–1945)* (*Memorial Book: Spaniards Deported to the Nazi Camps [1940–1945]*) to revisit the census. Sponsored by Spain's Ministry of Culture under José María Rodríguez Zapatero's socialist government, *Libro Memorial* predated the passage of the Law of Historical Memory by a year. Bermejo and Checa's register benefited from state interest and funding during the first decade of the 2000s to memorialize, catalogue, and record Spain's divisive history during the Civil War and Franco dictatorship.[24]

The even more recent "Censo de deportados españoles a campos nazis" ("Census of Spaniards Deported to Nazi Camps"), created by a cooperative of academic and governmental institutions in 2010, has suffered from a political swing in the opposite direction. Directed by Aragoneses, the "Censo de deportados" counts the Universitat Pompeu Fabra and the Amical de Mauthausen in Barcelona among its collaborators and was financed by the Generalitat de Catalunya. Based on an array of archival sources in Spain and Germany, as of this writing the database has fallen victim to political differences among its collaborators and an absence of funding and is no longer accessible to researchers.

Although protracted and at times hampered by the changing Spanish political landscape, these attempts to account for all of the Spaniards deported to Nazi camps demonstrate a continued commitment inside

Spain to recuperating a history that was long ignored. The fact that it took seventy years to ignite this interest has not escaped the notice of some of the ex-deportees. As Marcel·li Garriga, a Catalan Buchenwald survivor, noted, "'Han pasado sesenta años y nadie ha querido saber nada ni se ha hablado, y ahora, de pronto, sale en todas partes: diarios, revistas, universidades'" (Vilanova, *Mauthausen, después* 53).[25] It is debatable whether it has been better late than never for the Spanish survivors of Mauthausen.

Mauthausen Tomorrow: A Symbol of Spanish Memory

In a way that had not been apparent since the sixtieth anniversary of liberation, when Spain's Prime Minister José Luís Rodríguez Zapatero attended the commemorations mere hours after the Amical de Mauthausen's president Enric Marco was unveiled as a fraud, attention turned again to the Spanish experience of Mauthausen for the seventieth anniversary of the camp's liberation in 2015. Mainstream Spanish newspapers such as *El País* and *La Vanguardia* as well as Spanish state television and radio covered the events in Mauthausen. This time, the occasion was marked by another first: a member of the conservative Popular Party government attended the activities in Austria for the first time. José Manuel García-Margallo, Minister of Foreign Relations under Prime Minister Mariano Rajoy, elicited deep-seated emotions from the ranks of the Spanish survivor associations. His presence brought both welcome attention to the day's proceedings and angry resentment that the Spanish government continues to officially ignore the Spaniards in Mauthausen. For his part, Margallo publicly defended his presence at the commemorations. He struck a defensive tone, seeking to claim space for the political right in the efforts to remember Spanish victims of Franco and honour difference in all its forms. Ironically, Margallo's voice – recorded for posterity by the Spanish television crew present – did not rise above the background noise. Waving flags and handmade signs calling for judicial recognition of the Spanish victims of Mauthausen, the Spanish delegation in attendance could not hear him.

Just two days after the seventieth anniversary commemorations, the Spanish Parliament voted on a resolution that would officially recognise the Spaniards deported to Mauthausen. The motion, presented by Joan Tardà of the leftist Esquerra Republicana de Catalunya party, sought an apology from King Felipe VI on behalf of Spain for the deportation of

5.4 Spanish delegation gathered around Spanish Republican monument at Mauthausen Memorial, 10 May 2015. José Manuel García-Margallo, Minister of Foreign Relations, at centre in beige coat. Photographer: Eric R. Danton.

thousands of Spaniards to Nazi camps. The resolution would honour the last remaining survivors of Mauthausen and pave the way for their families to seek economic reparations from the state. After a strenuous debate in Congress on the evening of 12 May 2015, however, the motion was solidly rejected (Torrús). It would seem that Margallo's attendance at the Mauthausen commemorations, two weeks before municipal elections in Spain, was mainly a publicity stunt. Politicians on both sides of Spain's ideological aisle continue to ignore the human cost of Franco's damning decision to allow the Nazis to deport Spanish Republicans to Mauthausen. While Germany, Austria, and France have taken significant steps to recognize their culpability for the millions killed during the Holocaust, Spain continues to fall behind.

In the days and weeks after the buzz of the seventieth anniversary and the Spanish government's brief flirtation with honouring the victims, Mauthausen once again receded from the headlines. Fewer than two dozen Spanish survivors remain; they are the last link to firsthand memories of the camp. Non-survivors who have visited Mauthausen will retain their own experience of the camp, based on memories of the commemoration ceremonies and their relationship to the Spanish victims. But most of the Spaniards who encounter Mauthausen today will do so via a television documentary, a graphic novel, or a fleeting reference on social media. Now that the story of Mauthausen has been told and retold – in memoirs, in history books, in fiction, in documentaries, on the news, on Twitter – it remains to be seen what direction representations of the Spanish experience of the camp will take in the future.

As one of the hundreds of concentration camps where the Nazis targeted the "racially impure," Mauthausen is integral to our understanding of the Holocaust. The camp continues to be of particular significance to Spain. The events surrounding the deportation of Spaniards to Mauthausen have captured Spain's imagination during the last decade in a way that was impossible during Franco's dictatorship and difficult during the silence of Spain's transition to democracy. Only now, as the last Spanish survivors of the camp are disappearing, has Mauthausen claimed a stake in Spain's cultural capital. Mauthausen's symbolic power will no doubt continue its transformation in the decades to come as the landscape of Spain's collective memory continues to shift. Whether Mauthausen will become a flashpoint for Spain's quest to recover aspects of its historical memory lost to the passage of time and the repression of dictatorship, as the Spanish Civil War has become, remains to be seen. Nevertheless, the Spanish experience of Mauthausen has expanded from the memories of its 2,000 or so survivors to capture the attention of a growing segment of the population. Mauthausen will cease to exist as a concentration camp as firsthand memories of it are lost, but as an imagined space the camp will become more visible as Spaniards continue to encounter its diverse representations. The Spaniards who lived and died in Mauthausen deserve to be remembered in perpetuity. Their victimization is the tangible evidence of Spain's dark allegiance with the Nazis. Their driving will to fight against fascism and survive in the face of evil is their legacy. They are, now and forever, part of the history of the Second World War and the Nazi genocide.

Notes

Introduction: Memory and Legacy

1 "There are a great many books about the Nazi Holocaust that describe
the persecution of the Hebrew world but very little has been written
about, and much of the world ignores, the millions of non-Jewish people
who also perished in the concentration camps. On the part of all nations,
except Israel, there has been a desire to silence or minimize the reality of
these six million beings who were also exterminated, just like the Jews."
Except where otherwise noted, all translations are mine.

2 James Young clarifies that the term "holocaust" did not come to represent
the "murder of European Jews" until about 1957–9 (*Writing and
Rewriting* 87).

3 The total number of Spaniards who were imprisoned in Nazi
concentration camps varies according to different historians. David
Wingeate Pike cited Antonio Vilanova's estimate of 15,000 (Vilanova *Los
olvidados* 147) but clarified that "Vilanova tends to inflate his figures"
(Pike *Spaniards in the Holocaust* 316, Ch. 2, note 2). Montserrat Roig
estimated 10,000 (*Els catalans* 201). Benito Bermejo and Sandra Checa
listed approximately 8,700 (*Libro memorial* 21). The census of Spaniards
deported to Nazi camps coordinated by Alfons Aragoneses totaled
11,147 ("Censo de deportados"). These discrepancies are undoubtedly
due to the dependence on clandestine prisoner counts to determine the
number of Spanish nationals entering each camp. Nevertheless, records
for Mauthausen are more complete and precise than records from other
concentration camps, in part because of the role of Spaniards as camp
clerks. Although "7000 republicanos españoles muertos" appears on
one plaque at Mauthausen to commemorate the Spanish dead, this is

most likely an exaggeration. Rosa Toran has estimated the total number of Spaniards to perish at Mauthausen is closer to between 4,800 and 4,900 (*Vida i mort* 167). Roig, based on the survivor Casimir Climent's clandestinely kept records, calculated a total of 4,815 Spanish dead at Mauthausen, its subcamps, and Hartheim Castle (*Els catalans* 200). At least another 200 died in other Nazi concentration camps as well (Vilanova, *Los olvidados* 200–1).

4 A small number of the Spaniards deported to Nazi camps were Jews born elsewhere who were subsequently naturalized as Spanish citizens (Aragoneses, "Història i memòria").

5 Many Holocaust scholars have taken issue with Hilberg's essential distinctions in *Perpetrators, Victims, Bystanders* over the years, including Michael Berenbaum and John M. Cox, who add rescuers and resisters to Hilberg's essential categories (Friedman 315–36).

6 Joseph Halow, a court reporter, would later question the legality of the trials against the four Spanish *Kapos* accused at Dachau. Halow wrote that "[w]hether [one of the Spaniards] was selected to be a kapo or whether he volunteered for the job should not have been the basis for establishing his guilt or innocence" (227), given that the Spaniards were unjustly imprisoned in Mauthausen and thus obliged to follow Nazi orders or be punished themselves.

7 As Marianne Hirsch explores in her work, the concept of survivor may also extend to subsequent generations: "descendants of victim survivors as well as of perpetrators and of bystanders who witnessed massive traumatic events connect so deeply to the previous generation's remembrances of the past that they identify that connection as a form of *memory*, and that, in certain extreme circumstances, memory *can* be transferred to those who were not actually there to live an event" (3; emphasis in the original). This mechanism of memory transference operates to a certain extent among Spanish victims and their families, descendants of Spanish Mauthausen victims, who can be considered second- or third-generation survivors.

8 Although James Young defines the genre in his introduction to *Reference Guide to Holocaust Literature* as "consist[ing] of all the literary responses to the destruction of European Jewry and other peoples by the German Nazi state and its collaborators during World War II" (Riggs xxxi), only Jorge Semprún is included in this volume as an example of a Spanish Holocaust writer.

9 This movement was arguably inaugurated with Emilio Silva's excavation of his grandfather's mass grave in Priaranza de Bierzo and subsequent

foundation of the Asociación para la Recuperación de la Memoria ("Association for the Recuperation/Recovery of Historical Memory"), both in 2000. The movement gained governmental sanction with the 2007 passage of the so-called Law of Historical Memory under Prime Minister José Luis Rodríguez Zapatero (*Ley 52/2007*).

10 "Can there be a culture of Holocaust memory when there is not a culture of memory of the Spanish tragedy?"

11 For a full accounting of the Spanish refugees in France, see Dreyfus-Armand and Soo.

12 Such was the number of Spanish "volunteer" workers in the CTEs that they became known colloquially as *Compañías de trabajadores españoles* (Companies of Spanish Workers).

13 "It is necessary to insist that it was Ramón Serrano Suñer, Franco's brother-in-law and government minister, who incited, on his trip to Berlin in September 1940, the German authorities to maximize their cruelty with the trapped Spanish Republicans."

14 "You hold in your hands part of the key to our history, and at this point you cannot evade all responsibility" ("Open letter to Serrano Suñer"). During the last years of his life, Serrano Suñer was under investigation by the Comisión Española de Investigación del Oro Nazi (Spanish Investigative Commission on Nazi Gold), and had been served with a lawsuit by a French organization of ex-deportees (Armengou and Belis, *El convoy de los 927* 287). He was protected in part by the Spanish Amnesty Law of 1977, and died before he might have been extradited to France to stand trial (288).

15 The *División Azul* was Franco's one concrete concession to Hitler. Franco sent some 47,000 men, Nationalists who had fought in the Spanish Civil War, to the Russian front in 1941 to fight alongside Hitler's army there (Núñez Seixas, *Camarada invierno* 12). Franco sold the mission to these "volunteer" forces by labeling it a battle against communism on the Soviet front.

16 Isabelle Rohr traces the Spanish political right's anti-Semitism to the late-nineteenth-century movement of philosephardism, which promoted the country's reconciliation with its Spanish-speaking Sephardic Jews in order to staunch the "'degeneration of the Spanish race'" (10). Graciela Ben-Dror details the Spanish Catholic Church's support of Nazi anti-Semitism from the pulpit and in the Spanish press during Hitler's rise to power and the Second World War (57–113).

17 "in the Spanish legislation there exists no discrimination in relation to the Jews who reside in Spain."

18 Preston has shown that Franco subscribed to anti-Semitic literature in the 1930s (*Spanish Holocaust* 38), though Payne argues that the dictator was not as anti-Semitic as Hitler (214).

19 For more on the role of Spanish diplomats in providing safe passage to Jews, see Avni; Baer and Israel Garzón; Carcedo; Lisbona; Rother *Franco y el Holocausto*.

20 The other was Flossenbürg in Germany.

21 In fact, the Spaniards built the steps: when they arrived in the camp, there were 139 or 140 uneven stone stairs (Sinca Vendrell, *Lo que Dante no pudo imaginar* 92; Amat-Piniella, *K.L. Reich* 69 [1963a]).

22 Marc Buggeln has concluded that the type of slave labour performed in the Mauthausen subcamps also determined the prisoners' chance of survival: the Mauthausen subcamps devoted to construction had a mortality rate that was six times higher than the subcamps devoted to the production of wartime materials (89).

23 In this volume general references made to Mauthausen also encompass its 40 subcamps established by the Nazis and located throughout Austria. Many of these satellite camps were formed as exterior work *Kommandos* dedicated to the production of armaments and war materials. The vast majority of the Spaniards who died in Mauthausen actually died in Gusen, a subcamp located about four kilometres from the main camp.

24 Some Spanish Mauthausen survivors have insisted that, given the presence of the gas chamber, Mauthausen was an extermination camp. Although the camp did exterminate groups of prisoners, Mauthausen, unlike Auschwitz or Chelmo, did not exist for the sole purpose of efficiently exterminating large numbers of Jews.

25 Of the 197,464 prisoners who entered Mauthausen, some 95,000 died in the camp system. Of these, approximately, 14,000 were Jews (USHMM "Mauthausen"). The monthly rate of death for Jews in Mauthausen from November 1942 to December 1943, for instance, was 100 per cent (Goldhagen 312).

26 Literally "Night and Fog," an expression borrowed from Goethe, this was a codename established by Hitler's decree in December 1941 that demanded the "disappearance" of these prisoners (USHMM "Night and Fog"). They would remain cut off from military due process, families, and the outside world at Mauthausen.

27 Beyond Mauthausen, Spaniards could be found throughout the *Konzentrationslager* system, primarily, as survivors have attested, in Buchenwald, Ravensbrück, and Dachau. However, smaller numbers of Spaniards were also imprisoned and killed in Bergen-Belsen,

Flossenbürg, Neuengamme, Sachsenhausen-Oranienburg, Natzweiler-Struthof, Auschwitz-Birkenau, Stutthof, and Treblinka, among others. See Pons Prades and Constante 39, 171, 277–8; Bermejo and Checa, *Libro memorial* 20; Toran, *Vida i mort* 170.

28 There is disagreement as to the number and identities of the Spanish women who were transferred to Mauthausen. The five women listed in the Joan de Diego archive are Alfonsina Ester, Angela Martinez [*sic*], Herminia Martorell, Rosita da Silva [*sic*], and Carmen Zapater ("Trasladadas de Ravensbrück a Mauthausen"). Hans Marsálek agrees that there were five Spanish women as of the SS count on 31 March 1945 (169). Mariano Constante, however, lists seven Spanish Republicans and one "Polish-Spaniard" by their given names: "Carlota García 'Charlie,' responsable del grupo de españolas, Angelines, Herminia, Carmen, Dolores, Feliciana, Alfonsina y una polaca-española llamada Estucha" ("Carlota García 'Charlie,' responsable for the group of Spanish women, Angelines, Herminia, Carmen, Dolores, Feliciana, Alfonsina and a Spanish-Pole named Estucha," Pons Prades and Constante 248). Carlos Hernández de Miguel, based on Constante's information, provides a more specific accounting of these seven native-born and one "honorary" Spanish Republican women: "Carlota García, Angelines Martínez, Feliciana Pintos, Herminia Martorell, Carmen Zapater, Rosita de Silva y Alfonsina Bueno ... [y] la brigadista polaca Estucha Zilberberg, a la que todas llamaban Juanita" ("Carlota García, Angelines Martínez, Feliciana Pintos, Herminia Martorell, Carmen Zapater, Rosita de Silva and Alfonsina Bueno…[and] the Polish brigadist Estucha Zilberberg, whom everyone called Juanita," Hernández de Miguel, *Los últimos españoles* 451–2).

29 Hans Marsálek, an Austrian Mauthausen prisoner who held a role as a camp clerk similar to Climent, arrived at 7,189 total male Spaniards deported to Mauthausen and 2,187 Spanish survivors as of the last official Nazi count on 31 March 1945 (237; 161). José Bailina Silba, who worked with Climent in the Politische Abteilung, calculated 2,184 survivors (15).

30 Adding to this naming confusion, titles in Spanish are not capitalized, leaving one to wonder whether Armengou and Belis intended to reference the Holocaust (proper noun) or a holocaust (common noun).

31 Preston adds that "unknown numbers of men, women and children" were killed in bombings, in prisons, and Francoist concentration camps (*The Spanish Holocaust* xi), a number still definitively less than the 11 million total from the Holocaust.

32 "a very Spanish interpretation of the Holocaust."

33 "in Spain the Holocaust continued to be a topic 'of Jews and of Germans.'"

34 Andreas Huyssen has also identified this trend, in which the Holocaust "function[s] as a metaphor for other traumatic histories and memories" (*Present Pasts* 14).

35 As Pike explains, Spaniards who worked on the construction of the Mauthausen gas chamber were unaware of its intended use (*Spaniards in the Holocaust* 88). Four hundred forty-nine Spaniards died in gas chambers, according to one list in the Joan de Diego archive ("Muertos en cámara de gas") which Vilanova also cited (*Los olvidados* 178). Roig, using Climent's data, specified 499 Spaniards gassed at Hartheim Castle (*Els catalans* 200). These Spaniards were most likely gassed in the so-called *coche fantasma* (ghost car) transport truck en route to Hartheim Castle, or in the gas chamber of the castle itself, not in the gas chamber constructed at the main Mauthausen camp.

36 In his book on non-Jewish victims of the Holocaust, Berenbaum claims that "[f]or the first time, in *A Mosaic of Victims* all major groups victimized by the Nazis are represented in one work" (2). This statement argues that Spaniards were not a "major group" victimized by the Nazis, because they do not merit a chapter (unlike Poles, Jehovah's Witnesses, pacifists, homosexuals, and Roma). Who constitutes a major group of Holocaust victims is, of course, entirely relative.

37 Among deportations, the passage of refugees, and collaboration, the Holocaust stretched across southern Europe, to the Americas, and into Asia.

38 See, for instance, Henry Friedlander's *The Origins of Nazi Genocide* and Michael Burleigh's *Death and Deliverance* on the euthanasia of the handicapped; Dagmar Herzog's *Sex after Fascism* on sexuality under the Third Reich; Heinz Heger's *The Men with the Pink Triangle* for an account of a homosexual man in a Nazi camp; and János Bársony and Ágnes Daróczi's *Pharrajimos* as well as Radu Ioanid's *The Holocaust in Romania* on the Nazi persecution of Roma.

39 Małgorzata Pakier and Bo Stråth define this project as working "towards the construction of European collective memories in the plural, which strive for a growing understanding of diversity" (13). Levy and Sznaider describe it as "shared memories of the Holocaust ... [that] provide the foundations for a new cosmopolitan memory. It is a memory that harbors the possiblity of transcending ethnic and national boundaries" (4).

40 Semprún was not only a survivor of Buchenwald, but also served as
   Spain's Minister of Culture from 1988–91 under Prime Minister Felipe
   González.

41 This word is understood as a "coming to terms with the past" that
   occured in postwar Germany. Although one can argue that Spain
   has seen a recuperation of historical memory, that movement has
   not spread to all corners of the Spanish culture and consciousness,
   as it did in Germany. What is more, attempts to investigate Francoist
   crimes by the prominent judge Baltazar Garzón and others have been
   met with hostility and indictments by Spanish authorities.

42 Gunter Demnig installed the first five Stolpersteine plaques in Spain on
   9 April 2015. These five "stumbling blocks," honouring five Catalans
   deported from Navàs, Catalonia, to Mauthausen, were a genuine attempt
   to address this absence of national referents to Spain's relevance to the
   Holocaust ("Projecte Stolpersteine a Navàs").

43 For an overview of the contemporary Spanish thinking on collective and
   historical memory as it pertains to the Spanish Civil War and postwar, see
   Brenneis 9–12.

44 For discussions of the contemporary manifestations of anti-Semitism in
   Spain, see Baer "Memoria de Auschwitz" 115–17 and Álvarez Chillida
   461–88.

45 "The Spanish Republicans deported to the Nazi concentration camps
   have been represented and one of the six candles has been lit in their
   memory and honour."

46 Underlined on a daily basis with the obituaries of prominent survivors
   and figures involved in the Spanish Civil War and the Second World
   War in Spanish newspapers: Ramón Serrano Suñer, who died in 2003 at
   101 years of age, and Manuel García Barrado, the Spanish survivor of
   Mauthausen who ran the camp's museum and died in 2009, are only two
   such examples.

47 A term that may have been coined or developed by Saul Friedländer in
   Reflections of Nazism.

48 "Postmemory" is a term developed by Marianne Hirsch to characterize the
   relationship that successive generations of Holocaust survivors have to the
   first generation's firsthand memory. This concept will be further explored
   in Chapter Four.

49 The documentary A Film Unfinished, using extra film reels recorded
   inside the Warsaw Ghetto, attests to the ways scenes and individuals
   were manipulated for the benefit of the audience and/or author(s) of
   the original Nazi-era film (Hersonski).

50 Adorno's original statement was published in a 1949 commemorative
   publication (*festschrift*) in German, and translated to English in the 1967
   volume *Prisms*. He walked it back somewhat in a 1973 publication, writing
   that "it may have been wrong to say that after Auschwitz you could no
   longer write poems" (Adorno, *Negative Dialectics* 362).
51 "the so-called historical memory."
52 "the memory industry turned out to be lethal for memory."

1. The View from Inside

1 Between one and nine transports of Spanish Republicans arrived at
   Mauthausen every month between August 1940 and February 1942, with
   anywhere from 1 to 1,506 Spanish prisoners on each transport (Marsálek
   138–42).
2 "we had absolutely no idea what it all was."
3 In the Nazis' system of categorization, Mauthausen was regarded as
   second only to Auschwitz in terms of its brutality. Being transferred to
   Mauthausen from another camp was commonly regarded as a severe
   punishment (Le Chêne 36). Our contemporary understanding of the
   camps, however, distinguishes Mauthausen from Auschwitz as a
   concentration camp, not a death or extermination camp.
4 "the Spaniards, without any protection, occupied the lowest rung on
   the concentration camp ladder and they ended up with the hardest
   Kommandos, subject to the hostility of the deportees with more power."
5 Some 6,690 Spaniards entered Mauthausen between 1940 and 1941 (94.9 per
   cent of the total number of Spaniards who eventually arrived at the
   camp), but by the winter of 1942, only 3,000 were still alive (Toran, *Vida i
   mort* 165).
6 "without losing sight of the reason for their internment and without
   forgetting that the attainment and conservation of the position was
   not the fruit of the condescension of the Nazi officers but of the daily
   struggle."
7 "the spelling of the last names of these people, the system of the double
   Spanish surname, the names of their place of origin."
8 "ambassador of the Spaniards."
9 Climent's name and its variations illustrates one of the unique difficulties
   posed by these Spanish names. Although his full name in Catalan is
   Casimir Climent i Sarrión, the "i" was frequently dropped when referring
   to him in Castilian. Moreover, in English translations, he was often
   referred to as "Casimiro." In the War Crimes Tribunal Cohen Report, he

was variously referred to as "Casimiro Climent" and "Climent Casimiro" (Cohen 222–5).

10 "everything that had to do with the Spaniards here" (original translation by Jack R. Nowitz, Cohen 222). The original typewritten Spanish transcript lacks accentuation.

11 "a certain personality because [he was] in the office ... it gave you an authority that no other prisoner in the camp had."

12 "it allowed me to know that there were gas chambers." Despite de Diego referring to multiple "chambers," there was, in fact, only one gas chamber in the Mauthausen main camp, although it consisted of a series of small rooms.

13 There are conflicting accounts in Pike and Roig as to whether the German prisoner Gerhard Kanthack, who worked with de Diego in the camp administrative office, originally secreted away the Unnatural Deaths book. In either case, Joan de Diego appears to have had the book in his possession upon liberation.

14 "to maintain order inside their general ranks [via the main index file] and finally I was put in charge of things referring to the women imprisoned in the camp," (Cohen 222, trans. Nowitz).

15 Climent clarifies that prisoners who were slated for immediate execution were marked with the letter K on the camp registry, and that when he arrived in the Gestapo office, "'el full extraviat amb la K, havien d'ésser destruïdes totes les fitxes i esborrats els seus noms de tots els registres, de l'oficina política, de la del camp i de l'oficina que controlava tota la mà d'obra'" ("'the separate sheet with the K and all of the index cards had to be destroyed and their names had to be erased from all the registries in the political office of the camp and from the office that controlled all the prisoner labor,'" Roig, *Els catalans* 303–4). This accounts for some discrepancy between Climent's calculations of the Spanish prisoners killed in Mauthausen and actual estimates that include these doomed "K" prisoners.

16 "such a brave man, so patient and so careful that ... he was the hero who made it possible to know the names and dates of all of the Spaniards who died in Mauthausen and their *Kommandos*."

17 The Museu d'Història de Catalunya's staggering collection of correspondence, identification materials, and ephemera tracks de Diego's singular experience of Mauthausen and a post-liberation life dedicated to disseminating information about his former Mauthausen compatriots.

18 "Like all of those who lived in the camp I can testify to the executions – often innumerable – as many women as men, many not very advanced

in age. I can say that the sodistic [*sic*] acts were endless from the number of those shot, killed in rooms full of poison gas, abandoned to die from hunger, shut up in places where men of all sorts died," (Cohen 222, trans. Nowitz).

19 "three key names"; "particularly complete." Bailina wrote a detailed article for the ex-deportee periodical *Hispania* in 1972 that specified the work he performed in Mauthausen in the *Politische Abteilung* and after liberation with the aid of other survivors to catalogue the Spanish presence in the camp. This article, Bailina admitted, was written "ante la insistencia de varios amigos" ("at the insistence of various friends" 16). Otherwise, Bailina was not as visible a presence in postwar accounts of the Spaniards of Mauthausen. Unlike Climent and de Diego, for instance, he was not interviewed for Roig's *Els catalans als camps nazis*, which likely was Bailina's and not Roig's decision (see Roig "Letter to Josep Ester").

20 "sometimes I made drawings secretly to celebrate friends' birthdays; I made postcards that I later signed and this made a good keepsake."

21 In Blatter and Milton's footnote, they clarify that "The name Manuel Alfonso is signed at the bottom of what appears to be the draft of a greeting card found in Mauthausen" (240). This was one of only three works of concentration camp art by a Spaniard to appear in their *Art and the Holocaust* volume. The authors had no further information about Alfonso.

22 Another version of this drawing, with colour accents and a dedication to "Salvador Ruiz" appears in Alfonso Ortells 106.

23 This work seems to be inspired by a number of situations in the camp. Mariano Constante quotes the Spanish deportee Julio Casabona, who acted as veterinarian to Ziereis's pigs, as saying that "'En Mauthausen vale más ser un cerdo del comandante que una persona humana'" ("'In Mauthausen you were better off being a commandant's pig than a human being,'" *Republicanos aragoneses* 199). According to Constante, Ziereis also called the Spaniards in Mauthasen "mis cerdos" ("my pigs," Pons Prades and Constante 13–14). The original caption on Alfonso's drawing enigmatically reads "C. Cabeza"; a later caption in the author's autobiography clarifies the reference to Constante: "Se ha escrito un libro 'Los cerdos del Comandante' de M. Constante" ("The book *The Commandant's Pigs* has been written by M. Constante," Alfonso Ortells appendix). Thus the drawing also points to the complex relationship fellow survivors maintained with Constante (chapter 3).

24 Alfonso is one of the few Spanish Mauthausen survivors to admit to having used the services of one of these prostitutes, although it is

common knowledge that other Spaniards did as well (Hernández de Miguel, *Los últimos españoles* 417).

25 "Drawing saved my life in Mauthausen. Thanks to that, I saved myself."

26 "We pay you an effusive homage, hopeful for the quick disappearance of the small ball."

27 One of Milá's postwar creations illustrated the cover of Mariano Constante's book, *Yo fui ordenanza de los SS* (chapter 3). Milá also exhibited some of his drawings in the 2000 documentary *Mauthausen, el deber de recordar* (chapter 4).

28 Rodoreda's story is almost certainly based on Mauthausen (chapter 2). The illustrations that accompany the story's initial publication also depict Mauthausen and may have been created by Pere Vives i Clavé, who is the only Spaniard with the "Clavé" surname deported to a Nazi camp (Aragoneses, "Censo de deportados").

29 This is according to Boix's testimony at the Mauthausen trial as well as Bermejo's analysis of the recollections of other Mauthausen survivors. García claims that Boix did not begin working in the photo lab until the end of 1942 (Pike, *Spaniards in the Holocaust* 139). García's oftentimes contradictory information can in part be attributed to a general animosity between the two men during their time in Mauthausen.

30 According to Pike, Spaniards were photographed in the *Stalags* from which they were transferred to Mauthausen, and so did not merit new identity photographs (*Spaniards in the Holocaust* 135).

31 Ricken testified to the work performed in the photo lab at Mauthausen during his trial before the American military's War Crimes Branch in Dachau in 1947 (Bermejo, *El fotògraf de l'horror* 107).

32 However, SS photographic documentation did survive a number of other Nazi camps. For instance, Auschwitz prisoners saved some 40,000 photos documenting the camp (Didi-Huberman 24).

33 In a now iconic photograph of Boix in the days after liberation, he is pictured smiling, with a Leica camera strung around his neck and a homemade white armband reading "Spanish War Reporter – War Photographer."

34 As both Herrmann and Bermejo have pointed out, and Pike has acknowledged in retrospect, García's version of these events presented a biased viewpoint tainted by García's general animosity towards Boix. It was also coloured by García's (unsubstantiated) accusation that Boix was under the thumb of the SS and held up by the Spanish communist party as a "fals heroi" ("false hero"); (Bermejo, *El fotògraf de l'horror* 133, note 19; Herrmann, "Camera Caedens" 123; Pike, *Españoles en el holocausto* 23).

García was able to present his version of events to Pike, Le Chène, and possibly Vilanova before his death in 2000. Boix's version of events, in that he died in 1951, must be recreated through his statements to the American War Crimes authorities, his testimonies at Nuremberg and Dachau, and scattered correspondence with other Spanish Mauthausen survivors. Ultimately, the historical record sides with Boix's central role in saving the Mauthausen photographs, though not without continuing contention (Pike, *Spaniards in the Holocaust* 301–12; Pike, *Españoles en el holocausto* 22–4; Bermejo, *El fotògraf de l'horror* 131–45).

35 "Boix's affair. García and I did nothing more than watch, listen and keep quiet."

36 Laila Ripoll and Mariano Llorente dramatize the disagreements and conflicts between Boix and García in the photo lab in their 2014 play *El triángulo azul* (chapter 4).

37 José Alcubierre Pérez, Jesús Tello Gómez, and Ramiro Santisteban Castillo, interviewed by Montserrat Llor, all served as character witnesses for Boix. The survivors interviewed for Lorenç Soler's 2002 documentary *Francisco Boix, un fotógrafo en el infierno* also attested to Boix's central role in the clandestine organization of the camp (chapter 4).

38 Poschacher Industries continues to maintain a presence in Mauthausen, Austria. The current Poschacher building is visible from the pedestrian route between the Mauthausen train station and the entrance to the Mauthausen Memorial complex, site of the concentration camp.

39 Estimates of the total number of negatives and prints vary between about 1,000 to the 20,000 Boix claimed at the Mauthausen trial to have saved (*Boix Testimony* 3439). Bermejo gave credit to Ramón Bargueño for hiding a packet of negatives and to Jacinto Cortés García for smuggling the negatives out of the camp and establishing contact with Anna Pointner (Bermejo, *El fotògraf de l'horror* 124, 128). José Alcubierre Pérez took credit for smuggling some of the negatives and contacting Pointner in Montserrat Llor's interview with him (121). Mariano Constante provided conflicting accounts of his involvement in smuggling out the negatives in two of his autobiographies (*Yo fui ordenanza* 22–3; *Tras Mauthausen* 37–42; chapter 3).

40 "everyone [in the Poschacher *Kommando*] kept quiet and thanks to this silence [the operation] could be carried out."

41 "SS photos saved by the clandestine organizations of the PCE (Spanish Communist Party) and JSU (Unified Socialist Youth) in Mauthausen."

42 In this instance, however, these individuals have not been positively identified. This photo resembles Ricken's image of the hanging of Hans

Bonarewitz, in which Joan de Diego can be seen looking directly at the camera "fend[ing] off the controlling Nazi gaze," in Gina Herrmann's analysis ("Camera Caedens" 127).

43 Some of these photos of liberation were actually images of a re-enactment of the American troops' arrival in Mauthausen staged on 7 May 1945 (AMM 140–1).

44 One such example is the iconic photo of prisoners pulling down the Nazi eagle positioned over Mauthausen's main gate on 5 May, attributed to the US Signal Corps in *The Visible Past* (139) and to Boix in Bermejo *Francesc Boix* (173).

45 Unable to return to Spain, where the Communist Party was illegal, the newly liberated Spaniards ironically had more freedom of political assembly in the decommissioned Nazi camp than they would have had in their own country.

46 The photo-article in the 1 July 1945 issue of *Regards* includes a number of SS photos that Boix and others saved. This article also incorporates a pen and ink drawing by "Lalo," Eduardo Muñoz Orts (Bermejo, *El fotògraf de l'horror* 180).

47 Many of the photos in the Museum's archives were donated by the Amical de Mauthausen in Barcelona (Toran and Sala 80).

48 The photography archives at the Archiv der KZ-Gedenkstätte Mauthausen in Vienna, Austria, also maintain reproductions of photos and documents on loan from Antoni García's family; post-liberation photos and French newspaper clippings about Boix from José Perlado Camaño's family; and post-liberation photos from the family of "Claude García" (who is perhaps Claudio Gómez García). The National Archives Records Administration in Maryland also holds a collection of Mauthausen SS photographs as well as Boix-authored photographs. Most of these prints were given to Lieutenant Jack Taylor – an American POW who was imprisoned in and liberated from Mauthausen alongside the Spanish deportees – by Boix himself or submitted as evidence at either Nuremberg or Dachau (Schmidt and Loehrer 16–18).

49 There were some exceptions to this policy of isolation. For instance, Jacint Carrió received a letter from his sister in early 1941 after the death of their mother. He was not permitted to reply (Roig, *Els catalans* 253).

50 Roig speculates that there may have been some intervention from the Spanish government that allowed the Nazis to restrict the Spaniards' ability to correspond with families from home even though they were not officially NN prisoners (*Els catalans* 251).

51 Vives was one of the inspirations for Bartra's novel *Crist de 200.000 braços*, originally titled *Xabola*, written from Mexico as Vives lay dying in Mauthausen (Vives i Clavé 11; Bartra).

52 Vives was not permitted to write his family from Mauthausen in 1941, following the strict isolation of all of the Spaniards in Mauthausen that year.

53 "a spiritual richness, human interest, and a desire to document our times."

54 "And also Amat!!! the one who came over to study with Colominas and the others, just as intelligent and sensible as always."

55 "Why don't you write me?"

56 "[s]uffering during this long ordeal, I learned many skills that I would have always ignored."

57 "He was sick when he left Agde. Arriving at Mauthausen was fatal. Do you understand? In an extermination camp it is not possible to continue any sort of treatment. An injection ended it all. The friend assured us that he did not suspect anything. A new cure, he thought. Apparently, that's all, it seems. But what spiral of thoughts, of mental suffering that we will never know, precipitated it and overpowered him?"

58 "Pere died at Mauthausen all alone."

59 "My morale is excellent ... I would not be a man if I feared uncomfortable states."

60 Roig's 1972 articles on Spaniards in the Holocaust for the Barcelona periodicals *Tele/eXprés* and *Triunfo* include meditations on Vives' plight and an interview with two of his sisters ("Una historia provisional," "Una generación romántica"; chapter 3).

61 "To Pere Vives i Clavé, killed by the Nazis on 31 October 1941, in remembrance of a brotherly friendship."

62 "after three years we were practically without any correspondence from our families."

63 "I am well. Send package. Kisses and hugs."

64 After Francisco Aura Boronat wrote a short missive to his family in 1943, they took the postcard to the business where their son had worked before the war to show his former co-workers that he was still alive. However, the British workers there understood that Aura Boronat, though alive, was in a Nazi concentration camp. Aura Boronat explained that, "'[e]ls anglesos tenien molta més informació que els espanyoles, perquè formaven part del bàndol aliat'" ("'The English had much more information than the Spaniards, because they were with the Allies,'" Beneito Lloris, Blay Meseguer, and Lara Jornet 56).

65 "I do not doubt that there are many families who would allow tears of
   remembrance to escape their eyes for their loved ones who, beneath a
   foreign sky, wait for human passion to be reintegrated into the cause of
   peace and return to them their former happiness."

66 Reproductions of these two postcards, dated "Para la navidad de
   1943" ("For Christmas 1943") and "12–3–44" ("12 March 1944") are
   included in the Joan de Diego Archive at the Museu d'Història de
   Catalunya.

67 "my health and situation could not be better but they will be even
   more so when I can hold you in my arms and tell you how the distance
   heightens my fondness."

68 "the Bolsheviks have managed to reach the Suchau-Andrichau-
   Auschwitz line, where they were detained."

69 "As to the persecution of the Jews, [...] His Holiness's herald, Monsignor
   Angelo Rotta, and the Legation of Spain made great efforts to stem the
   violence against them."

70 On the role of Spanish diplomats in saving Jews, see Avni; Baer and Israel
   Garzón 39–59; Carcedo; Lisbona. On the myth created by the Franco
   government regarding its intervention on behalf of the Jews, see Rother
   Myth and Fact and Rohr.

71 "thousands of political prisoners of diverse nationalities, including
   Germans, suffered torment and death." The documentary filmmaker
   Basilio Martín Patino used images from this No-Do of a camp identified
   only as "un campo alemán" ("a German camp") in the narration, to stand
   in for Mauthausen in *Canciones para después de una guerra* (*Songs for After
   a War*, 1976). The camp shown was most likely Bergen-Belsen, however,
   as there were no images of Mauthausen in the Spanish press from this
   period. As Barbie Zelizer writes, this was a common practice even at the
   end of the war: photos were used somewhat indiscriminately, such that
   "a Buchenwald picture illustrated a Mauthausen story" in the Western
   press, for instance (98).

72 "Everything is so tragic that it brushes against the grotesque."

73 "The U.S. Third Army has found, to the east of Salzburg, a concentration
   camp which reduces those of Buchenwald and Dachau to the level of a
   child's game, in the words of a U.S. Army colonel to a delegation of the U.S.
   press. The colonel added that this camp was intended for political prisoners
   who were forced to work in limestone mines 'for hours and hours, without
   more food than a scoop of potato soup per day" (Pike, *Franco and the Axis
   Stigma* 131). Pike identified the colonel quoted in the article as Richard R.
   Seibel (*Franco y el eje* 290, note 120).

2. Postwar Impressions

1 See Antelme *L'espèce humaine* (*The Human Race*, 1947), Lengyel *Souvenirs de l'au-delà* (*Five Chimneys*, 1946), Levi *Se questo è un uomo* (*If This is a Man*, 1947), Rousset *L'univers concentrationnaire* (*A World Apart*, 1946) and Szpilman *Śmierć miasta* (*The Pianist*, 1946).

2 None of these Spanish authors are included in anthologies of Holocaust writing that include other non-Jewish writers. See, for instance, Kremer, as well as Roskies and Diamant.

3 The definition provided by Roskies and Diamant upholds this understanding of "Holocaust literature" as comprising "all forms of writing, both documentary and discursive, and in any language, that have shaped the public memory of the Holocaust and been shaped by it" (2).

4 "Catholic by conviction, I am a soldier of the Church; fervent Spaniard, I will always be a loyal servant of my Country. And my Country is now, whether or not the communists and renegades like it, unanimously represented by Franco, a man providentially chosen to liberate it from the most tremendous loss of life of all time." Citations of Rodríguez del Risco's articles are identified by the original publication date of the article in the series followed by the page number in *Arriba* where the quote is found.

5 This assessment is based on my investigation and evaluation of the available Spanish texts published since 1945 on the topic of Mauthausen.

6 The critical attention paid to Jorge Semprún's contributions to the genre of Holocaust literature is the exception that proves this rule: Semprún, an exiled Spaniard and Franco detractor, wrote his narrative accounts of Buchenwald in French and published them first in France. He is commonly the only Spaniard included as an author of Holocaust literature, including in Kremer.

7 Juan Ferreras defines these general characteristics of the *novela por entregas* in Spain while also emphasizing that the popular serialized novel is always founded on "acción o aventura siempre personal o individualizada" ("always personalized or individualized action or adventure" 252).

8 In correspondence with the author, Bermejo affirmed that he was able to communicate with members of Rodríguez del Risco's family and confirm the outline of Rodríguez del Risco's journey through German *Stalags* and Mauthausen (Bermejo "Re: Información viaje.doc").

9 "When on the first of February we arrived from our respite in the town of Base-Ham, its inhabitants, upon seeing the Nazi flag that we fluttered as

a 'great war trophy,' made us the object of extended ovations. *Our heroism was confirmed.*"

10 Rodríguez del Risco stated that he arrived in *Stalag* XI-B on 6 August 1940. Aragoneses recorded this precise date in "Censo de deportados."

11 The date of entry appears in Rodríguez del Risco, "Yo he estado en Mauthausen," 2 May 1946, 4; the prisoner number in the 3 May 1946, third instalment. Bermejo and Checa (299) and Aragoneses "Censo de deportados" corroborate both pieces of information.

12 Bermejo and Checa (299) and Aragoneses "Censo de deportados" confirm Rodríguez del Risco's movements through Gusen and Steyr, which the author described throughout "Yo he estado en Mauthausen."

13 Aragoneses "Censo de deportados" confirms the date of Rodríguez del Risco's liberation, but records that he was liberated from the Steyr work camp. Bermejo and Checa corroborate the Gusen II liberation site (299).

14 "'prestige of the Nation, or of the Regime, obstruct[ed] the Government's labour in the new State or sow[ed] pernicious ideas among the intellectually weak.'"

15 The Franco regime's publications became an exercise in duplicity, matched only by the regime's changing allegiances, as Justino Sinova describes: "La Prensa controlada fue un espejo de la adaptación del Gobierno español a la evolución de la Segunda Guerra Mundial. La censura tuvo a los periódicos sujetos mediante unas estrictas consignas que les hicieron ser neutrales en un primer momento para pasar a estar sometidos a las indicaciones llegadas de Berlín después y para acabar, finalmente, argumentando que España, por supuesto, siempre había mantenido buenas relaciones con los países aliados, triunfadores de la guerra" ("The controlled press was a mirror of the Spanish government's adaptation to the evolution of the Second World War. The censorship office held newspapers to account through strict instructions that forced them to be neutral at first, only to afterward become subjected to directions arriving from Berlin and to wind up, finally, arguing that Spain, of course, had always maintained good relations with the Allied countries, victors of the War," 255).

16 *Arriba* was one of a number of Falangist movement papers that together reached more than 400,000 daily readers in 1946 (de las Heras Pedrosa 253).

17 By the post-Spanish-Civil-War era, Spanish conversion narratives had grown beyond these ideological boundaries to encompass the political conversions of such authors as the communist-turned-anti-Marxist Ramón J. Sender, and Franco's former chief of propaganda-turned-opposition Dionisio Ridruejo. For accounts of Spanish authors who

narrated their conversion to or disillusion with communism during and after the Spanish Civil War, see Herrmann, *Written in Red* 54–83.

18 "I contemplated, sometimes with bitterness, sometimes happily, the land of my Spain, where, if before the war it had produced enormous scars, it now lived in peace and tranquility while the world bled to death in the chaos of the war."

19 "on the path to defeat, it was not only a demoralized population, but also divided, semi-bolshevik."

20 "They showed special interest and kindness for Spain and they assured us with the utmost sincerity that second to the German soldier, the Spanish soldier was the best on the planet."

21 However, in some memoirs from the 1990s and 2000s, other Spanish Mauthausen survivors agree that their treatment in the German POW camps was better than in the Nazi concentration camp. See Chapter Four.

22 Adolf Hitler provided munitions for the Nationalist side in the Spanish Civil War, sending German war planes to bomb Guernica. Franco's government and in particular his brother-in-law and minister of foreign relations, Ramón Serrano Suñer, were complicit in the deportation of Spaniards to Nazi concentration camps (Introduction).

23 Although Rodríguez del Risco cites 16 August 1940 as the date the convoy from Angoulême arrived in Mauthausen (6 May 1940, 3), most sources agree that the convoy arrived on 24 August 1940 (Sinca Vendrell, *Lo que Dante no pudo imaginar* 93; Pike, *Spaniards in the Holocaust* 64; Toran, *Vida i mort* 160).

24 "Astonishment, anger and terror gained control of all of them, but all of the protests they formulated ended up being useless. They made the men and boys over ten years of age get off the train, and despite the desperation of the women, mothers, sisters and wives who stayed on the train, they were imprisoned in Mauthausen."

25 This episode explicitly connecting Spain to the Third Reich forms the central event in Montse Armengou and Richard Belis's documentary film *El comboi dels 927*, widely viewed on Spanish television in 2005 (chapter 4). It is also reported in Sinca Vendrell, *Lo que Dante no pudo imaginar* 93; Vilanova, *Los olvidados* 132; Pike, *Spaniards in the Holocaust* 64.

26 "a true patriot [who] feels the pressing need to work for the resurgence of his country ... elevating the nation well above those who humiliated it with military victories ... [T]his man, without a doubt extraordinary, was incapable and could never – to my mind – have known the true and sad reality of the Dantesque horrors in the concentration camps."

27 "the largest number [of deaths] must be attributed to the barrack bosses, the *Kapos* and the well-positioned; prisoners who were all like their victims, but who were induced by the SS with more or less violent methods."

28 "hypocrites, fakes and egotists, and a little more or less food would result in scenes of a son beating his own father."

29 "Nevertheless, their torment exceeded the limits of what is humanly conceivable."

30 Although the author alluded to the unavoidable fate of Jewish prisoners in Mauthausen, the term "Holocaust," only commonly used years later, does not appear in the text.

31 Rodríguez del Risco referred to dozens of individuals by name, including Mauthausen's second-in-command, Capitan Bachmayer (whom he called, phonetically, "Balmeyer"), Franz Steyr (the SS overseer of the Steyr work commando), the SS Knosppe Franz, and Enriquito (a notorious Spanish *Kapo*), among many others.

32 "in Mauthausen – we are told – the 'gas chamber' has been installed."

33 Francesc Boix was the only Spanish survivor of Mauthausen who testified at the Nuremberg trials (chapter 1). Spain has never held Truth and Reconciliation trials of its own.

34 Vilanova describes Largo Caballero as an honest and upstanding citizen, contradicting Rodríguez del Risco's characterization (*Los olvidados* 148).

35 The Mauthausen survivor Enrique Calcerrada Guijarro contradicted Rodríguez del Risco's assessment, calling the camp coffee an "especie de malta que casi nadie bebía" ("a kind of malt that almost no one drank," Calcerrada Guijarro and Pavón Mariblanca 140).

36 These interruptions are fissures in the flow of the narrative and chronology "that serve to disrupt the text," following Eaglestone's taxonomy of Holocaust testimony (59). In the case of Rodríguez del Risco, the narrative interruptions are the most propagandistic moments in the text.

37 "stained their hands with blood"; "frightful tragedy of Mauthausen"; "as hard and inflexible as the justice that our Motherland may impose on us, we maintained a ray of hope based on the Christian charity of the Generalísimo [Franco]."

38 This volume was originally published under a common misspelling of the author's surname: Cinca Vendrell.

39 "Other books have been written about what the extermination camps in Germany were. Other survivors have described the torment and the thousand walking dead. But this book has the merit of being the first that

was written." Sinca Vendrell repeats this assertion in his prologue to the 1980 edition, self-promoting "el primer libro sobre la deportación titulado *Lo que Dante no pudo imaginar*, salido en 1946 y éditado en St. Girons" ("the first book about the deportation titled *Lo que Dante no pudo imaginar* [*What Dante Could Not Imagine*] came out in 1946 and was edited in St. Girons," *Lo que Dante no pudo imaginar* 29).

40 Aragoneses "Censo de deportados" and Bermejo and Checa 281 confirm the dates and locations of Sinca Vendrell's entry into Mauthausen and liberation from Gusen II.

41 "Thousands of Spaniards from other camps in France, we were concentrated on a great plain surrounded by barbed wire and guarded like prisoners of war, even though our only crime (if it can be qualified as such) was nobly defending, with arms in our hands and a firm countenance, our country's liberties that the traitor Franco, sold to the tyrants of Germany and Italy, snatched away from us after 32 months of fighting."

42 Indeed, *Lo que Dante no pudo imaginar* did not include a bibliography, but rather acknowledged a number of other Spanish Mauthausen survivors and collaborators.

43 "It is only us (like me) one of the survivors who were the first to arrive at the MAUTHAUSEN and Gusen camp who suffered and know truthfully the catastrophe that occurred there during the five years lived in these camps that we have never forgotten."

44 "Concentration camps." This is an early example of what Isabel Estrada has identified as an imprecise use of Holocaust vocabulary by Spaniards ("To Mauthausen and Back" 41–2).

45 Sinca Vendrell focused in particular on the cruelty of the Germans toward British soldiers who were forced to bury German dead found along the route (*Lo que Dante no pudo imaginar* 73–4).

46 "Hunger began to wreak havoc on our flaccid stomachs, covered with the blanket of night in the thick mist; the headlights of the cars that passed along the highway swam like a cloud, giving off a bluish glare, fleeting and frightened of illuminating our miserable bodies."

47 Only a year later, Primo Levi included a similar motif in *Se questo è un uomo*, when he attempted to teach a *Kapo*'s assistant Italian using Dante's *Inferno* as his source text, ultimately acting as guide to the Inferno that was Auschwitz.

48 "in the twilight of a precipice without end."

49 "the famous imperial eagles, creation of the monstrous hitlerian spirit, [that] presided over the dismal premises."

50 Given the fact that Hitler never visited Mauthausen, his physical absence
   yet spiritual presence – as Führer – was historically accurate.
51 "A dense stench spread across the exterior of the camp, rarefying the
   atmosphere and preventing respiration, producing in our stomachs
   nauseating effects."
52 "a sinister ghost; cries of pain ... guttural groaning and pleading."
53 "My impression was so intense that I imagined the interior of the camp
   as if it were Dante's inferno."
54 "reality rapidly corroborated this vision, contemplating how our starving
   bodies were instruments of the criminal sadism enshrined by the German
   Nazi-Fascist system."
55 "Spaniards, surely you have never heard Mauthausen spoken of until
   the present day ... ! Mauthausen is the Camp of Death. Here to disobey
   orders means paying with your life." This explicit warning, delivered by
   a Spanish or Spanish-speaking *Kapo* (who appeared to have arrived in the
   camp before the first major transport of Spaniards) upon the deportees'
   arrival in Mauthausen, is corroborated in many Spanish accounts of the
   camp. See, for example, Roig, *Els catalans* 226. "Enrique" (also referred to
   pejoratively as "Enriqueta") is identified as a notorious *Kapo* in various
   historical accounts, including Roig, *Els catalans* 406 and Toran, *Vida i mort*
   216.
56 "skeletal beings, decomposed figures with an air of madness, poorly
   dressed and ragged, with a repugnant aspect that produced a double
   contrast of pain and fear."
57 "describing so much misery is difficult."
58 "In these conditions, dear reader, open a parenthesis in your thinking in
   order to pause on the painful scene that thousands of faces reflect after
   such grandiose suffering."
59 "Gusen, there is not a pen that can describe it. There is no graphic
   expression that one can use to signal the reality of the Gusen camp."
60 "I write this narration and affirm having witnessed it."
61 "Their procedures, rooted in crime, disgrace, and forced labour, exceeded
   the era of the Inquisition and all that humanity had suffered through its
   resistance."
62 "I well know that the fateful names of Mauthausen and Gusen will pass
   unnoticed among the body of extermination camps."
63 "Not a groan, nor a cry of pain, ever left the chests of these men so vilely
   killed."
64 By 1980, after watching the broadcast of the American mini-series
   Holocaust, Sinca Vendrell lamented the focus on the persecution of the

Jews to the exclusion of Spaniards from the show's storyline. In his prologue to the 1980 edition of *Lo que Dante no pudo imaginar* published in Spain, he wrote: "aunque refiere la verdad, no hay que olvidar que la deportación fue para todas aquellas nacionalidades que cayeron bajo las garras del nazismo, sufriendo todas las nacionalidades las graves consecuencias: castigos, persecuciones, fusilamientos, etc., para nosotros jamás olvidados" ("although it communicates the truth, one cannot forget that the deportation was aimed at all of those nationalities that fell beneath the talons of Nazism, all nationalities that suffered grave consequences: punishments, persecution, shootings, etc. that for us are never forgotten," Sinca Vendrell, *Lo que Dante no pudo imaginar* 37).

65 "About the expedition from Angoulême, one must highlight a meaningful fact full of cruelty. The Spaniards ... arrived at the Mauthausen station with women and young children."

66 "Where are you taking our husbands and sons?"

67 "We expressed our pain unanimously." This is an episode first reported in Rodríguez del Risco's account (6 May 1946, 3) and corroborated in other survivor accounts. José Marfil Peralta claimed his father, José Marfil Escalona, was the Spaniard killed in Mauthausen for whom the SS allowed the Spaniards to observe a moment of silence (Llor 276–7). In Sinca Vendrell's account, the first Spanish prisoner to die in Mauthausen was the elder Flordelís. Llorente and Ripoll dramatize this singular moment of silence in their 2014 play, *El triángulo azul* (chapter 4).

68 "unnatural vices ... of amoral disturbance ... were very rare among the Spaniards who lived together in the camp."

69 "our interventions in the infirmary, in the camp hygiene, in the work in the quarry, in the administrative offices, in the kitchen, and in the general routine and treatment in the camp were intense and beneficial for everyone."

70 "to liberate Spain and avenge our brothers, no matter the nationality, killed vilely in Germany"

71 "if I was to escape with my life, I would fight for justice. A promise that I, as one of the survivors, try to carry out remembering my brothers in captivity, honouring their memory and firmly maintaining my word."

72 "This entire painful process dedicated to the dead, this promise that I keep, ideally will fill out the terrible Nuremberg dossier."

73 This assessment is based on the letters Sinca Vendrell wrote and provided to José Sedano Moreno from 1981–3. The author continued to consider his deportation and incarceration in Mauthausen and Gusen in the context of postwar advances in Europe and stagnation in Spain in his self-published pamphlet "Mis 20 artículos."

74 Sinca Vendrell's original 1946 publication (attributed to "Cinca Vendrell")
   appears in the bibliographies to Pons Prades 219, Pike 421, and Vilanova
   511.

75 "They dragged me out of my cell, then returned me. They took me out
   to beat me and sent me back to recover, so they could beat me again"
   (Rodoreda, *Selected Stories* 190)

76 "I was playing a game: I wanted to see what the fish would do. I didn't
   want it to die" (190).

77 "here in the camp I was so glad I didn't have a white spot" (190).

78 "had cut her life into two irreconcilable halves."

79 Although Spaniards inside Spain received little news about the
   liberation of the concentration camps and the Nuremberg trials,
   this was not the case for Spaniards exiled in France. In addition to
   news reports about the camps and the trials, the left-wing French
   publications *Regards* and *Ce Soir* published illustrated issues dedicated
   to the plight of prisoners in Mauthausen in the summer of 1945.
   Francesc Boix's photos were the centrepiece of both publications,
   which presumably would have been available to Rodoreda.

80 "'During my exile I didn't write anything because I had another job
   trying to survive. Writing in Catalan, abroad, is wanting flowers to bloom
   at the North Pole.'"

81 Rodoreda sent "Nit i boira" to Mexico on 5 June 1946, along with four other
   stories that depict wartime Europe: "Orleans, 3 quilòmetres," "El bitllet de
   mil," "Nocturn," and "Mort de Lisa Sperling" (Rodoreda and Murià 73).

82 On the range of interpretations of Adorno's statement since its initial
   publication, see Rothberg *Traumatic Realism*, Chapter One.

83 "play dead," "[be] a shadow" (Rodoreda, *Selected Stories* 189); "Be
   invisible. Invisible like an object" (195).

84 "The first two blows are the ones that hurt. If they hit you on the head,
   sometimes only the first hurts. Hide your face" (194).

85 "Get out: why? Some want out so they can continue. If I were part of
   the resistance or a communist ... But I'm not a communist; I've never
   done anything. I haven't helped blow up a train or delivered any secret
   password. Maybe I don't even hate them" (194).

86 "infinite, serene marsh" (195).

87 "To return to the womb, doubled up, drowsy, enveloped in warmth"
   (195). Tennent's translation follows the convention of interpreting
   "ventre" as "womb."

88 Various sources count between four and seven Spanish women who
   were transported from Ravensbrück to Mauthausen in March 1945

("Trasladadas de Ravensbrück a Mauthausen"; Pons Prades and Constante 248).

89 "If all of us here could return to the womb, half would be trampled to death by those who fight to get in first. A womb is warm, dark, enclosed…" (Rodoreda *Selected Stories* 189).

90 "The more deaths that occur here, the better I feel" (189).

91 "if everyone would just stay still"; "'reserve your strength'" (190).

92 "then I'd be left alone. And the guards would spot me. I'd be visible" (191)

93 "When I arrived, the camp seemed like paradise. The tall, wide door and the watch towers made it look like a fortress, but inside … By the entrance, around a little square, stood some wooden huts, a fresh green colour, with flower boxes. They weren't for us, of course" (191).

94 This passage also describes the exterior gate and SS barracks in Mauthausen.

95 "the soft snow muffled the sound of their footsteps" (Rodoreda, *Selected Stories* 191).

96 "the following morning seven were still alive. A frozen corpse is quite pretty. Clean" (191).

97 Thirty years after Rodoreda's story, the survivor Mariano Constante described a group of prisoners from Auschwitz who were killed in the same way upon their arrival to Mauthausen in the winter of 1944–5. In his version, Constante levied a judgment that condemns the actions of the Nazis and lauded the resistance of the prisoners rather than reaching an aesthetic evaluation of them as Rodoreda's narrator did: "Eran duchados con agua fría, luego los hacían salir desnudos de las duchas y forma en el *appellplatz*, a 30 grados bajo cero. Después los bajaban de nuevo a los sótanos, les daban otra ducha y volvían a salir … Hubo hombre que, durante treinta y seis horas, aguantaron aquel martirio antes de convertirse en bloques de hielo. Hecho espantoso que da una idea de la resistencia del cuerpo humano" ("They were showered with cold water, then they made them get out of the showers naked and get into formation in the Appellplatz, at 30 degrees below zero. Then they took them back down to the basement rooms, gave them another shower, and took them out again … There were men who, over the course of 36 hours, withstood this ordeal before becoming blocks of ice. A terrifying fact that gives one an idea of the human body's capacity to resist") (*Yo fui ordenanza* 286). A monument to an anonymous prisoner frozen in this way stands just outside the main prisoner gate of Mauthausen today.

98 "freezing shower, boiling shower" (Rodoreda, *Selected Stories* 191).

99 "It's hard to hate a man if you've never seen his face" (194).

100 In the letters and archives available at the Fundació Mercè Rodoreda in Barcelona, Rodoreda does not clarify which concentration camp or camps serve as the model for "Nit i boira."

101 "Once arrived in Roissy, we all soon knew the names of his friends in the concentration camp: Vives, Puig, above all Vives. They had had very long conversations and exchanged long letters."

102 Given that he died in 1941, the protagonist of Rodoreda's story is not a literal embodiment of Vives. Rather, the story could have been influenced by Vives' experience.

103 This experience was represented in the short story "Orleans, 3 quilòmetres," also eventually published in Spain in *Semblava de seda*.

104 The Nazis forced prisoners to build tunnels near the Mauthausen subcamps of Gusen and Ebensee where the prisoners worked on war munitions.

105 Roig published *Els catalans als camps nazis* in 1977. Spanish Mauthausen survivor accounts were published or circulated in manuscript form in France in the 1960s, and by the 1970s Vives, Amat-Piniella, and Constante's accounts had been published in Spain.

106 "Nit i boira" alluded to the plight of Jews in the Holocaust through the Jewish surnames of the only two named characters in the story (Meier and Staub), and the mention of "Jahvé" ("Yahweh," Rodoreda, "Nit i boira" 232), the Hebrew name of God.

107 For more in-depth accountings of Spanish women in Nazi concentration camps, see Armengou and Belis *Ravensbrück, el infierno de las mujeres*; Català; Serrano i Blanquer *Les dones als camps nazi*.

108 "You say that you're tired of America; I am disgusted with France. You never know if tomorrow you will eat. Life is hard and disagreeable."

109 "'If I get out of here alive, what will I be like? I'll always feel like I'm transporting a stream of corpses'" (Rodoreda, *Selected Stories* 193).

110 "a mass of men and women from all races, all religions, and all ideologies, a mass that has given everything of themselves without complaint, a mass ignorant of the value of their own sacrifice, a sacrifice that is the deepest heartbeat of the world" (Amat-Piniella, *K.L. Reich* 234 [2014]). Unless otherwise noted, all in-text quotations originate from the second published edition of *K.L. Reich* in the original Catalan from October 1963. English quotations from the novel are from Robert Finley and Marta Marín-Dòmine's 2014 translation of this original Catalan edition of the novel.

111 "The astronomical figures for the Jews ... Russians, Poles, the French, Czechs, etc., who died in Nazi camps do not diminish the importance of the Catalan and Spanish portion of that overwhelming carnage" (5).

112 "ought to be taken into account in the measure of the Peninsular effort in the cause of liberating Europe" (5)

113 Amat-Piniella made only passing distinctions between Catalans and prisoners from other regions of Spain in the novel. A Catalan collective memory in *K.L. Reich* is evident in the novel's original language and primary focus on characters of Catalan origins (distinguished by their Catalan names).

114 In an interview with Montserrat Roig, Amat-Piniella identified the man who intervened as "Arnal" (Amat-Piniella, "Entrevista" 14). A pen and ink drawing of a prisoner hauling a cart full of stone that accompanied the author's publication of "La fam" was also credited to Arnal.

115 "the idea of leaving with my life, and then being able to explain it all."

116 Amat-Piniella was also an active writer while he was in Mauthausen: he wrote the 71 poems that comprised *Les llunyanies, poems de l'exili (1940–1946) (The Distances, Exile Poems [1940–1946])* clandestinely while he was imprisoned in the camp (Amat-Piniella, *K.L. Reich* 8–9 [2005]). This volume was published posthumously, in 1999.

117 "what almost nobody knows of these events is that, among the millions of people from all nationalities who met their deaths in Hilter's camps, there were ... Catalan[s and Spaniards]" (Amat-Piniella, *K.L. Reich* 5 [2014]).

118 As David Serrano i Blanquer describes, Amat-Piniella edited his manuscript of *K.L. Reich* numerous times over the course of the 1940s and 1950s in an effort to conform to Francoist censorship regulations. Although the manuscript circulated among a group of fellow Catalan writers, it would have to wait seventeen years for publication (Serrano i Blanquer, "Edició i recepció" 91–2).

119 "Vicenç was condemned and he knew it, but before dying he defended himself like a besieged beast."

120 "*Anthology* wants to offer a panoramic outlook, from which Catalonia may watch Europe, steeping itself in authentic universality, through which its own national personality, in contrast, will strengthen and grow robust."

121 "Of the seven thousand Spaniards who have passed through the German concentration camp Mauthausen, scarcely one thousand eight hundred survived. The author is one of these survivors and, about his memories of his four and a half years of captivity, he has written a novelized report with the title 'K.L. Reich,' still unpublished, and from which we now publish a chapter."

122 "Death does not frighten me, because it is, in a certain way, a compensation for those of us who have always fought against our killers. In killing us they give us a reason, they justify our effort."

123 "without him, the continuation of life in the camp, the defeat of the
    Germans, and even the end of the war became incomprehensible."

124 "No ... No ... They're taking me to kill me! I know it, they want to kill
    me!"

125 "I am an idiot, he thought; there is nothing real about any of this! Not the
    doctors, not the tables, not the lamp shades, not even me!"

126 "you will improve with this treatment. Don't be afraid!"

127 Benzene is a component of gasoline.

128 The publication of a Castilian translation as the first edition of the
    novel constituted the censorship of the original language. In 1961,
    Barral wrote to Amat-Piniella that the original Catalan manuscript,
    counterintuitively, "por efecto de este convenio, [será] considerado a
    todos los efectos como una traducción" ("by virtue of this agreement,
    will be considered for all intents and purposes a translation") (qtd in
    Stanley, "'Parlo ...'" 73).

129 The fact that the novel was published some seventeen years after it was
    originally written has allowed for some ambiguity about its immediacy.
    For instance, General Omar N. Bradley – one of the American officers
    who liberated Mauthausen, to whom the author dedicates (along
    with Pere Vives i Clavé) *K.L. Reich* – commends Amat-Piniella for his
    dedication in recording his story. In a letter dated 1 July 1963, and
    included in the Catalan edition of the book, General Bradley comments
    that "[i]t must have been difficult to undertake this task after the lapse
    of so many years, for surely it meant reliving that regrettable period of
    imprisonment in German concentration camps" (Amat-Piniella, *K.L.
    Reich* 11 [1963b]). Clearly, General Bradley, like many readers of the 1963
    editions of *K.L. Reich*, was unaware that Amat-Piniella had written the
    book in 1946 when the memories of his experiences in Mauthausen were
    fresh in the author's mind.

130 "the contemptuous references to the German character, their anti-
    Semitism, as well as explicit symbols of a leftist nature or the Spanish
    dedication to Republican liberties." There are four additional episodes
    in this re-edited 2002 edition that were omitted in the original, including
    a description of 40 Yugoslavs killed, a Jewish lawyer who kills himself
    rather than suffer any longer, the hungry Frenchman, and the fights
    between the communists and the "libertarios en el *Kommando* de August"
    ("Libertarians in August's *Kommando*," Amat-Piniella, *K.L. Reich* 12–13
    [2002]), a Spanish *Kapo*, that were not present in the 1963 editions.

131 "the only book I know of that describes the lives and deaths of Spaniards
    in a German concentration camp."

132 "treats the subject in a novelized form, with figurative names and where many of the episodes related do not correspond, wholly or partially, to reality. And this is not writing history, nor does it serve historial ends."

133 "offer a determined moral perspective ... a genre that allows it to arrive at the essence by means of symbolism and synthesis."

134 "constructed after the annexation of Austria into the Greater German Reich, overlooking the waters of the 'beautiful Blue Danube'" (Amat-Piniella, *K.L. Reich* 71 [2014])

135 "a young Spaniard had left the camp, repatriated as a minor" (126).

136 "Apart from the Danube ... no other point of reference could be made out" (183).

137 This is the abbreviation of the non-specific "Konzentrations Lager Reich" or "Concentration Camp Reich."

138 This character is one of the few whose name changes slightly between editions: Vicent in the original Catalan; Vicenç in the Castilian translation.

139 "Vicent knew nothing, understood nothing, remembered nothing. All he had was hunger" (Amat-Piniella, *K.L. Reich* 56 [2014]).

140 "there were so many cases like his in the camp!" (56).

141 Based on the 1945 publication date of "La fam," which the author incorporated verbatim into Chapter Three of *K.L. Reich*.

142 "strange fascination of the blood and the torture" (Amat-Piniella, *K.L. Reich* 95 [2014]).

143 "I can't do it!" (96)

144 Emili's eventual promotion to the camp's photo laboratory allowed the author to incorporate details from the story of Francesc Boix and the photographic evidence smuggled out of the camp into the novel (chapter 1).

145 "thought it would be better to get all the Spaniards together"; "'People are apathetic and selfish. No one thinks it's worth the effort to try'" (Amat-Piniella, *K.L. Reich* 64; 106 [2014]).

146 The Spaniards in Mauthausen, among other concentration camp prisoners, euphemistically referred to stealing food as "organizing" food.

147 "'With so many among the privileged we are on the verge of reaching our initial goal, that no Spaniard go hungry ... we need everybody working together for what comes next'" (Amat-Piniella, *K.L. Reich* 165 [2014])

148 "The Spaniards in the camp, who had become more and more interested in moral reform so as to make a good impression as a collective, openly repudiated Ernest's conduct" (166).

149 As Emili and Francesc entered the camp, August was the first person they encountered, described as "un pres alemany que parlava castellà

amb entonació efeminada. Era l'intèrpret oficial del camp" (Amat-Piniella, *K.L. Reich* 25 [1963b]) ("a German prisoner who spoke an effeminate Castilian. He was the official interpreter of the camp") (Amat-Piniella, *K.L. Reich* 16 [2014]). August was later revealed to be a Valencian who spoke Spanish and German fluently. Montserrat Roig identified "August" as a representation of Cèsar Orquín, from Valencia (*Els catalans* 438).

150 "'coup d'état'"; "new dictator," (Amat-Piniella, *K.L. Reich* 172 [2014]).

151 "With the relative abundance being shared among the Spaniards, political infighting between communists and anti-communists reached an unprecedented intensity ... They had discovered that generosity towards the weak could be turned, with time, to political advantage. And so it ceased to be generosity ... Leaders and followers alike were passionate in their search for converts, as if the future of their homeland and of the whole world depended on the hegemony of the Spaniards in the camp. The undecided, the neutral and the self-serving took advantage of this rivalry and could sell themselves to one side or another just as they liked" (173).

152 "left just after his comrades, without a trace. His enemies would not have the pleasure of bringing him to account" (207).

153 As Robert Finley and Marta Marín-Dòmine explain, the Spaniard on whom August was based, Cesar Orquín Serra, also disappeared – perhaps to Argentina – after Mauthausen's liberation, spared any reprisals from the other Spaniards in the camp (245–6, note 47).

154 "Each rank and every decoration would have meant hundreds of lives sacrificed on the altar of 'Greater Germany.' This flamboyant *Obersturmführer* of the SS had acquired his hero's laurels through the murder of Jews and communists" (39).

155 "'The Jews he slaughtered with an axe didn't particularly move him ...'" (210).

156 Georg Bachmayer is commonly mentioned as sympathetic to the Spaniards, including in Rodríguez del Risco 2 May 1946, 3 and throughout (identified by the phonetic variation "Balmayer") and Sinca Vendrell (who misspells his surname as "Bachmeyer"), among other texts.

157 "'In ancient civilizations, cremation was a ceremony carried out with grandeur. Here they burn the dead to erase any trace of their murder'" (Amat-Piniella, *K.L. Reich* 140 [2014]).

158 "women were just machines to make children for the Fatherland, believing that nudity and sports were not only a path, but also an aim ... A perfect climate for every kind of aberration!" (125).

159 "'I am crying from rage, do you understand?'" (139).
160 See, for instance Dios Amill 43; Roig, *Els catalans* 252 and elsewhere;
     Constante, *Los años rojos* 117 (1974).
161 Two Jews in the narration who are afforded some modicum of
     individuality include the man whom Francesc witnessed being
     beaten by an SS guard and the Jewish boy Francesc encountered in
     the infirmary. None of the Jews in the novel were identified by name,
     however.
162 "The hundreds of Dutch Jews who had just arrived inaugurated the
     season of the great slaughters. Hans Gupper's camp ... had begun to
     welcome the Gestapo's favourite victims" (Amat-Piniella, *K.L. Reich* 71
     [2014]).
163 "'Their death is certain, more so than ours. At least, more immediate'" (83).
164 "A world of spectres shifted behind his closed eyes through a silence
     even more shrill than the howls of terror a little while before" (123).
165 "it seemed monstrous, this law that said so many had to die so that just a
     few could survive" (185).
166 "The few Jews lucky enough to have made it through to the end,
     hunched over and dragging their feet ... took everything in, sharp-eyed,
     saying not a word" (225).
167 "a peace that is not passive, that is not founded on resignation, but is
     instead an active moral condition, like a state of grace" (234).
168 "Behind is a past of horrors; in front opens a future full of hope" (235).

3. Transitions: Early Accounts of Mauthausen

1 These groups included the Amicale de Mauthausen, the primarily
   anarchist Federación Española de Deportados e Internados Políticos
   (FEDIP, Spanish Federation of Deportees and Political Prisoners), and
   the communist Federación Nacional de Deportats i Resistents Patriotes
   (FNDIRP, National Federation of Deportees and Resistant Patriots)
   (Toran, *Vida i mort* 274).
2 The truth value of the resulting text is, however, ultimately determined
   by the reader (Brenneis 27–9).
3 According to Roig, this unexpected interview took place in June 1976,
   when she was seated next to Serrano Suñer during a coffee reception at
   the home of Rafael Borràs, the director of the Planeta publishing house
   (Roig, *Els catalans* 21).
4 "the book acquires on occasion levels of unsubstantial epic poetry, almost
   of adventure story, buoyed by reality."

5 "a stimulating book because it shows that, in the most extreme, dogged situations, human dignity brings an extraordinary force and is capable of becoming a factor in historical change."

6 Art Spiegelman displays his collection of mass-market Holocaust paperbacks in *Metamaus* 44–5.

7 "This story was written based on my and my mother's memories, and from notes taken in 1945. I have placed everything in chronological order. I am not a writer."

8 The memoirs encompass *Les années rouge/Los años rojos* (1971/1974), *Yo fui ordenanza de los SS* (1976), and *Tras Mauthausen* (2007); the co-written volumes are *Triangle bleu/Triángulo azul* (1969/1979) with Manuel Razola and *Los cerdos del comandante* (1978) with Eduardo Pons Prades; and the collection of memories is *Republicanos aragoneses en los campos nazis* (2000). Constante published a number of other volumes and articles on the Spanish Civil War as well.

9 Constante's terminology from this 2000 volume reflects the imprecision at work in Spanish designations of the Holocaust (Introduction).

10 "I never sought out being a 'bigwig' nor a 'brownnose' in order to obtain direct orders that made my positions and responsibilities stand out. In Spain, and outside Spain, I had the luck, the honour it would be more justly put, that my companions always chose me to direct organizations, both military and civil, clandestine and legal, to defend our ideals, our battles, our tasks, and our moral and physical rights. Did I obtain notoriety because of this? I didn't seek it out."

11 "It's not because of vanity that I have combined personal activities with those of my Asturian companions; it's only in this way that certain very difficult and almost incredible situations can be understood. I consider my participation at all times necessary to lend heightened credibility to all of these matters."

12 "excessive protagonism on his part, in which he seems to have been everywhere (and sometimes, he explicitly claims to have been)"

13 "To say that this surprised the Spaniards would be a lie. Without being strategists or professional politicians, for some time we had anticipated that the policy of aggression of Hitler's Germany would develop in such a way that, one day or another, it would go after the nations who called themselves 'defenders of liberty.'"

14 "told me my life story with more details than I was capable of remembering."

15 See Toran *Vida i mort*; Pike *Spaniards in the Holocaust*; Roig *Els catalans*; Armengou and Belis *El convoy de los 927*.

16 "that they would not have been able to obtain without the collaboration of the Spanish authorities."

17 "had our differences, of course, but, faced with a common enemy, our unity was much stronger than it was in Spain."

18 "I was surprised to see the dignity with which our compatriots confronted adversity ... And the solidarity was admirable. We were fortified until the end by those who continued to endure."

19 Taking advantage of a prolonged separation from his countrymen when he fell ill in the *Stalag* and was sent to the infirmary, Constante wrote that this was when he taught himself German (*Los años rojos* 92 [1974]).

20 "spider's web that found itself to have quite an extension."

21 "safeguarded by the members of the Spanish organization."

22 See Joan Pagès' assertion in Roig, "Una generación romántica" 37.

23 "The difference of the Jews with respect to us was that our extermination was done slowly, methodically, taking advantage of our labour, while theirs was complete and rapid."

24 "the book makes our hair stand on end and reminds us to what extremes human cruelty can go."

25 "the young Mariano Constante sees himself carried along by the great flood of historical events, but just like them he acts motivated by voluntary impulse, by a candid and frightened desire to join a fight that he considers just."

26 "not even the left thought that the history of the Second World War, the Holocaust, and the Nazi camps formed part of Spanish history."

27 "philosopher's stone for everyone who wants to know something about the wanderings of our Republican brothers who were objects of the Nazi insanity."

28 This drawing is credited to Ramón Milá, whose postwar artwork focuses on provocative depictions of Nazi brutalities (chapter 1).

29 "it does abound in details and nuances about the inhumane conditions of life in the camp and in the twists and turns and strategies that one had to draw from to be able to gain a position as porter or servant to the SS, and in this way to be able to survive."

30 "the same inner workings of the Nazi organization that created and exploited the German concentrationary hell"; "the Spanish national group."

31 "excluding the Jews – who were all exterminated – we were, next to the Soviets, the most punished national group owing to the fact that we were the first political deportees from Western Europe who entered into that concentrationary universe and suffered extermination methods during the first years of Nazi victories."

32 "Impressions about the mentality and activities of the SS."

33 "were entirely distanced from any human reality."

34 "at the margin of all principles established for and by mankind."

35 "I could never comprehend [the reactions of] the SS."

36 "The Spanish Reds who know how to speak German step out of the lines and present yourselves before me!"

37 "Spanish Red number 4,584 from block 13, present yourself here immediately!"

38 "Had they figured out that I was one of the directors of the Spanish clandestine organization?"

39 "The plates [negatives] that would one day serve as historical testimony, and that had been extracted from the SS precisely by Boix and García, on the former's initiative."

40 "the porter who moved by their sides 16 hours a day, carried sewn into the lining of his jacket the irrefutable proof of their crimes."

41 Bermejo writes in 2001 that Constante had some 300 photo negatives in his possession from the collection that Boix either saved or took himself in Mauthausen (*El fotògraf de l'horror* 122). Some photos included with *The Concentration Camp Mauthausen 1938–1945* are credited to "Mariano Constante Collection" (Holzinger and Kranebitter 127 and throughout).

42 Constante characterized Boix as a thief in *Tras Mauthausen*: the author claimed that Boix stole the negatives from the Spanish Communist Party to publish them in postwar pulp magazines in which Boix himself was "presentado como único protagonista – héroe solitario" ("presented as the only protagonist – solitary hero," *Tras Mauthausen* 39).

43 "The liars and historical falsifiers ought to have more modesty and shame and not invent stories full of tall tales!"

44 "They were able to raise the morale of a dead man!"

45 "'well connected'"; "like a big octopus: a body, the clandestine organization, with tentacles, each one of us, that started to gain access everywhere."

46 "you Spaniards are the best 'bandits' in the camp. You Spaniards are capable of stealing a shirt right off another man's back!"

47 "Much has been discussed about the clandestine political activity inside the extermination camps. It's true that they existed but they had very little influence over the day to day lives of the majority. The ideological discussions were the stuff of well-fed prisoners situated in key places."

48 "I don't insist on the number of the ones who passed through and were murdered in the [camp], what's important is having demonstrated

with proof the crimes committed by the SS, without forgetting the complicity of the Franco regime."

49 "habitual silence"; "completely imaginary, if not false."

50 "Constante writes books in which he presents himself as the example, and in which he says that he did everything in the camp and that he served as a jack of all trades. Unfortunately it's true, he did everything, including something that the majority of us Spaniards have not done."

51 Rosa Toran provides a detailed account of the infighting among Spanish Mauthausen survivors in the 1970s, dwelling on the polemics that Constante's publications inspired (*Joan de Diego* 277–89).

52 "his personal relationship with Boix wasn't as good as some of his writings would have us believe."

53 "began to crush my fingers, mashing them with his steeltoed boots, as if he were crushing a reptile. At the same time as I recalled this I seemed to feel this past pain once again and looking at my fingers I could confirm that it wasn't simply a bad dream: they were deformed forever on that sad day in the winter of 1941 ..."

   Constante narrated this attack in *Los años rojos* as well, writing that he suffered permanent damage to his hands: "mis manos quedaron deformes para siempre debido a los golpes recibidos" ("my hands became deformed forever because of the blows I received" 133 [1974]).

54 "It's sad that Mariano Constante, who could have made a useful contribution to the history of Mauthausen, opted for distortion and falsehood, granting for himself the roles of others, with the result that many of his compatriots, who knew quite well that the history of Mauthausen demanded a flat telling, without adornments, look at his writing with disdain."

55 In other respects, Constante's contradictory and inflated accounts share some similarities with those of Enric Marco, the false survivor who claimed he had been imprisoned in the Flossenbürg Nazi camp. The first published instance of Marco's false claim was, coincidentally, in Constante and Pons Prades' volume *Los cerdos del comandante* 88–9.

56 Constante's personal narratives would continue to flavour representations of Mauthausen well into the twenty-first century. In Aitor Fernández Pacheco's 2007 documentary *Mauthausen: una mirada española*, for instance, he claimed to have been the one to steal six bed sheets from the SS to serve as the banner welcoming the Americans as they liberated Mauthausen.

57 As Joshua Francis Hirsch explains, newsreel footage and compilation films of the Nazi ascent and concentration camps predate *Nuit et brouillard*, but have not had the lasting impact of Resnais' film (*Afterimage* 32).

58 Jean Cayrol, a French Mauthausen survivor, provided the film's text and perhaps some influence over which camps were visually emphasized (Hirsch, *Afterimage* 30).

59 "Three thousand Spaniards died building these steps leading to the Mauthausen quarry."

60 It is not unreasonable to imagine that Soler would have seen *Nuit et brouillard* in Barcelona, particularly given his association with Joan Pagès and the Amical de Mauthausen.

61 "At the very end of the Second World War, the concentration camp Mauthausen is the last to be liberated by the Allied troops. In this place, 127,000 deportees belonging to diverse nationalities died – officially – , victims of Nazi barbarism, among them some 7,000 ex-combatants of the Spanish Republican Army."

62 "was taboo, and as a consequence, the majority of Spaniards were totally ignorant of it."

63 "a marginal, semi-clandestine documentary filmed with scarce resources and challenging the severity of the Francoist censorship, condemned by it to an uncertain and subterranean existence."

64 "That group of survivors were marginalized and lived in obscurity."

65 Pagès detailed his route to Mauthausen, his date of entry (24 January 1941) and his prisoner number (4238) in his filmed testimony. Although today this information would clearly corroborate Pagès' identity, at the time it would have been almost entirely meaningless as a way of identifying the Spanish ex-deportee.

66 The detail of the cigarette Pagès held between his fingers made a subtle reference to the "cigarette trade" in Mauthausen, which another survivor in the film mentioned as one of the ways the clandestine resistance organization aided Spanish prisoners.

67 Pagès participated in many other efforts to revive the testimony of Spanish Mauthausen survivors until his death in 1978, including Roig's *Els catalans als camps nazis* (Toran, *Amical de Mauthausen* 11–57).

68 The five survivors interviewed are identified as Pagès, Alfonso López Yañez, Amadeo López Arias, José Sugrañes Boix, and Saturnino Martínez in the credits.

69 No identifying information as to the date, director, or theatre where this production was staged is given in the film.

70 "A toned-down vision of that barbarity. But today survivors still exist who suffered the barbarity on their own flesh. Their testimony is indispensable to be able to understand the truth of the events." In another reference to the performative nature of the camp, Pagès described the organization

of soccer games, boxing matches, and theatrical productions as part of
the Spaniards' "moral victory" over their captors: "[E]ran para nosotros
una verdadera victoria sobre la SS. En primer lugar una victoria moral.
En segundo lugar una victoria de nuestro sentimiento solidario. Era una
victoria de nuestra organización clandestina" ("They were, for us, a true
victory over the SS. In the first place, a moral victory. In the second place,
a victory for our feeling of solidarity. It was a victory for our clandestine
organization" Soler *Sobrevivir en Mauthausen*).

71 "personality annulment, humiliations, physical and moral tortures,
surrender, and sadism."

72 "But will there be a tribunal in history capable of judging the collective
crime of these people in all its magnitude? Is there sufficient evidence
against them?"

73 "became incorporated into clandestine distribution channels." No further
specific information about where the film was screened is available.

74 Indeed, *Sobrevivir en Mauthausen* is difficult to find in libraries and archives
in Spain. I wish to thank the director for providing me with a copy.

75 "encounter that was the point of departure for Roig's monumental
work."

76 "Then I realized that Nazism wasn't just a thing from movies and history
books for us, nothing more than the 'Jewish question' or the resistance of
the occupied countries during the war, rather Nazism had persecuted our
people, people who spoke my language."

77 In 1970, she figured among a group of Catalan intellectuals who occupied
the Montserrat monastery outside of Barcelona to protest the death
sentences of 16 ETA members in the so-called Proceso de Burgos.

78 "a typical Austrian town, from a picturesque postcard, it is situated in the
Danube Valley, among fir tree forests and fields."

79 "Some 130,000 men died, among them about 5,500 Spaniards."

80 "What I don't understand is how the prisoners, seeing that they were
going to die anyway, didn't seek revenge on their torturers."

81 "in Mauthausen we were all condemned to die. What happened was that it
could take longer or shorter lengths of time. Some died of starvation; others,
of sickness; others, shot, others, beaten, others in the gas chamber ..."

82 "they were the only ones destined to disappear in a short period of time."

83 "you could smell the stench of burning flesh from the crematories from
the city of Linz, 27 kilometres away from Mauthausen." In *In the Shadow
of Death: Living Outside the Gates of Mauthausen*, Gordon J. Horwitz
corroborates that the townspeople of Mauthausen were well aware of the
neighbouring concentration camp and its function.

84 "one of the first Spanish 'political' fights was the recognition of our right to be able to sleep with them. And we achieved it." When the same topic arises in *Els catalans*, Roig quoted Pagès again, this time anonymously. She wrote that other Spanish witnesses she spoke with tried to explain away the use of prostitutes as another dehumanizing aspect of Mauthausen, or denied ever having gone to the camp brothels. Nevertheless, it is clear in the narrative that some Spaniards did visit the brothels and were aware of what happened to the prostitutes after their "term of service" ended (Roig, *Els catalans* 468–70).

85 These articles were gathered in a posthumous collection edited by the Amical de Mauthausen: *La lluita contra l'oblit: escrits sobre la deportació* (*The Fight Against Oblivion: Writings About the Deportation*). Roig also delved into this topic in her television journalism.

86 A number of these articles were inspired by the broadcast of the *Holocaust* mini-series on Spanish television in the summer of 1979.

87 "simply for this country to begin to reconcile with itself."

88 "I don't know what a Nazi concentration camp is. It's impossible to give oneself an idea."

89 "I am so immersed in the universe of the concentration camps, that I have discovered that it's impossible for me to separate myself from them. I eat, I sleep with you all, back there ... I hear the shouts of the SS, the blows, the barking of the dogs ... I sense the smell of filth, the stench of the smoke that escapes from the crematory ovens ... with my eyes open, I continue to live inside an endless nightmare!"

90 Roig made this metaphor explicit by titling the section on the day-to-day experiences of the Spaniards in the camps "Un món d'espectres" ("A World of Spectres").

91 It is, indeed, listed in the bibliography of every successive comprehensive historical study of the Spanish deportation to Nazi camps.

92 "the best monument that it would be possible to erect in honour of the memory of the Catalans who suffered the Nazi terror."

93 "the moral obligation to talk about a part of recent history that you have all hidden away in betrayal. To restore your exemplary and heroic history for our collective memory. You deserve a prominent name in our recent history and I wanted to contribute the only way I could: by writing it."

94 "there is not, however, an intention to distinguish the behaviour of these men from the ex-deportees of the rest of the Spanish state."

95 "a foggy plot of land in our recent history."

96 "told me the most about what the Nazi hell meant."

97 "The silence that has covered over the Catalans, the Republicans, those who lost the war, seems to me to have been a silence that they wanted to

use to cover over my people and myself. I saw that if we didn't return a voice to those who needed it when it was their turn to speak, we would never again have a voice."

98 For further analysis of the overlapping nature of *L'hora violeta* and *Els catalans als camps nazis*, see Brenneis 47–86.

99 Her interview with the Ravensbrück survivor Neus Català in 1978 for the Catalan program *Personatges* (*Characters*) and her 1984 interview with Joan de Diego for the TV2 program *Los padres de nuestros padres* (*The Fathers of Our Fathers*) are particularly important contributions to Spanish oral testimony about the Nazi camps.

100 This sentiment of respect and admiration for Roig continued: Roig's son Jordi was the invited speaker who appeared at the Amical de Mauthausen's annual trip to the Mauthausen commemorations in Austria in 2011.

101 "a historian ... write the decisive book from the historiographic point of view." Recent additions to the canon of histories of the deportees include books by the journalists Montserrat Llor and Carlos Hernández de Miguel. Llor and Hernández de Miguel contacted a much more limited number of elderly survivors, filtered their testimony through an even more remote lens – seventy years have passed since the end of the Second World War – and relied on previously published material to mount their narratives. As a consequence, their work is not as thorough or immediate as Roig's.

102 See Felman and Laub 85; Young, *Writing and Rewriting* 166–9; Baer, *El testimonio* 201–12.

103 Josep Maria Castellet, who was Roig's editor for many years at Edicions 62, revealed that *Els catalans als camps nazis* was slated to be published in Paris until Franco died, at which point the publisher decided to release it in Spain (Francés Díez 89).

104 Roig also included volumes by Alfaya, Amat Piniella, Constante (*Los años rojos*), Razola and Constante (*Triangle bleu*), and Vilanova among her Spanish source material.

105 "the French killed you from hunger and the Nazis did it directly."

106 "the treatment by the Werhmacht soldiers, who guarded us [in the *Stalag*], had nothing to do with the cruelty that we would later encounter with the SS in the Mauthausen camp."

107 "only human memory, the will of memory and recollection seen from those who suffered it, can reconstruct a whole world that appears improbable."

108 "'I have a lot of difficultly remembering details related to the acts I've seen (...) But what I will say will be true, indisputable. I will tell the truth, which means I won't tell ALL of the truth, but that I won't 'invent' anything.'"

109 The first systematic collection of oral histories of Holocaust survivors and Nazi victims was performed by the psychology professor David P. Boder in 1946.

110 David Wingeate Pike did the same when he asked Mariano Constante to prove that his hands were deformed.

111 That trust is broken when an individual makes the false claim that they have survived a Nazi concentration camp, as happened in the cases of Enric Marco and Antonio Pastor in Spain in the 2000s (chapter 4).

112 "'Kill yourselves, it's the best thing you can do. If you don't, you're going to die some other way, like the ones on the ground."

113 "Poor fools! You only leave here through the crematory chimney."

114 "those who have been there say that Mauthausen is a marvelous place."

115 "during work, in the 'course of an escape' or in reality thrown against the electric fence, you could let yourself die or you could kill yourself, you could die by execution, drowned in the water ... Also you could die having become a guinea pig for the pseudo-scientific experiments of the SS doctors ... [or] by the *Kapos'* tortures, or from a benzene injection to the heart, ... or at Hartheim ..."

116 "with the havoc that hunger, cold, and thirst wreaked, that would be enough ... Also you could die physically exhausted from the harshness of the forced labour ... You could die from typhus, diarrhea, pneumonia, etcetera."

117 "Our Republican deportees saw how the Nazis carried out a systematic, ordered, precise death against citizens of the Jewish race."

118 "When the Nazis carried out an 'offensive' against the Jews, the prisoners breathed easier, because that could mean that day they wouldn't receive it themselves."

119 "Seen from the outside, all of this could seem terribly inhumane. But, how can we judge them if we are not accustomed to living with death on a daily basis as they were?"

120 "He grabbed him by the head, he sank him in the water, he pulled him out again, and, finally, he rewarded him by wringing him out."

121 "said that the Jews were guilty of making the Republicans lose the Spanish war." Although Tarragó did not name the anti-Semitic deportee who perpetrated these acts, the man was, like Carlos Rodríguez del Risco, from Vilanova i la Geltrú. I can only speculate that these actions were performed by Rodríguez del Risco himself; Roig does not provide any additional information to corroborate this hypothesis.

122 At a presentation of Roig's book just days after its initial publication in 1977, Benet revealed that two people who stopped hearing from an exiled loved one in the 1940s were able to confirm that relative's death after

consulting *Els catalans* (Roig, *Noche y niebla* 9). Presumably other families have had similar experiences in the years since.

123 "one of the most rigorous European documents conceived about that dismal tragedy, a basic and indispensable document of the horrors. Montserrat [Roig], overcoming different kinds of obstacles, did not rest until she had uncovered them."

124 In this sense, Roig's work bears similarities to volumes of collected testimony of the Spanish Civil War, such as Ronald Fraser's *Blood of Spain* and Shirley Mangini's *Memories of Resistance*, to name only two examples.

125 "'They howled from hunger and thirst and fear. They were in the dark and they didn't give them anything to eat or drink. After ten days the ones who were still alive buried themselves between the dead ones to stay warm.'"

126 "I transported a part of the daily dead and saw brain, liver, and internal anatomy mixed up with cloth, mud, hair, all covered with blood."

127 "Oftentimes we squeezed the bread through the electric fence; we took advantage of the days that it wasn't electrified."

4. Memories Unleashed

1 *Hispania: Boletín interno de la Federación Española de Deportados* (*Hispania: Internal Bulletin of the Spanish Federation of Deportees*) was founded by FEDIP in 1961 and published continuously until 2000 in Paris. *Mauthausen: Bulletin intérieur de l'Amicale des déportés et familles de Mauthausen* (*Mauthausen: Internal Bulletin of the Society of Mauthausen Deportees and Families*) was founded by the Amicale de Mauthausen in 1967 and continues to publish in Paris. A number of articles by Mauthausen survivors printed in *Hispania* from the 1960s to the 1990s are collected in Salou Olivares *Los republicanos españoles*.

2 Mention of the Spanish deportees in Mauthausen appeared in historical studies from the 1980s and 1990s. However, no text by a Spanish author dedicated to the Spanish experience of Nazi concentration camps, nor Mauthausen specifically, was published in Spain during this period.

3 Hirsch focuses in particular on children and grandchildren of Holocaust victims. I would argue that direct descendants, particularly in the close-knit Spanish family structure, also include nieces and nephews. "Affiliative postmemory," Hirsch writes, "is thus no more than an extension of the loosened familial structured [*sic*] occasioned by war and persecution" (*Generation of Postmemory* 36).

4 "provoking the repression all over again."

5 "Of course, there was the coup d'etat, they saw Franco again, and yes, it paralyzed things."

6 Approximately 280 mass graves were opened between 2000 and 2012
   in Spain (Ferrándiz 14). The government's financial backing of these
   exhumations, however, ended with the election of Prime Minister
   Mariano Rajoy and Popular Party municipal governments in 2011. The
   limited state funding of exhumations allowed by the Law of Historical
   Memory was curtailed, although exhumations have continued on a more
   modest scale with private funding.

7 "From the King of Spain to the Spaniards who died outside their Country"

8 Unlike the interrupted process of exhumations in Spain, the publication
   of Mauthausen survivor memoirs has not been systematically studied,
   nor have survivors been asked why they did not publish their memoirs
   during the 1980s and 1990s.

9 "They would have taken me for mentally ill, it was impossible to speak
   about these atrocities, we were silent until the filmmakers, the media,
   people like you ..."

10 Additional memoirs were published in France by Spanish survivors.
    Given the present study's focus on texts published in Spain, they have
    not been included.

11 The apparent misspelling of "Mauthausen" in the title of Martín
    Romaní's autobiography is a graphic representation of the runic insignia
    used by the Nazis to symbolize the Schutzstaffel or SS.

12 For the purposes of this study, life narratives that are not authored by a
    Mauthausen survivor but that depend almost entirely on his written or oral
    testimony are considered examples of the genre of Mauthausen memoir.

13 The only Spanish Mauthausen survivor who could conceivably have
    been considered a prominent public figure throughout Spain was
    Mariano Constante, whose star faded in the 1980s (chapter 3).

14 In a tradition that began with Santa Teresa's sixteenth-century *Libro de la
    vida* (*Book of Her Life*), Angel Loureiro and James Fernández have explored
    significant Spanish autobiographical writers from the last two centuries.
    Additional twentieth century examples abound, such as Carlos Barral,
    Teresa Pàmies, Terenci Moix, Carmen Martín Gaite, and many others.

15 The Mauthausen survivor and life narrative subject Ramiro Santisteban was
    insistent on this point at a presentation in Barcelona in 2015 commemorating
    the seventieth anniversary of the liberation of the camp (Bermejo et al.).

16 The majority of these texts are currently out of print. Oftentimes, single
    copies are available exclusively in private regional collections or one
    of Spain's national libraries (the Biblioteca Nacional in Madrid or the
    Biblioteca de Catalunya in Barcelona).

17 Moreover, a number of publications focused exclusively on groups
    of deportees from single regions of Spain who were imprisoned in

Mauthausen. See Barrera Beitia; Calvo Gascón; Checa, del Río and Martín.

18 This is the case with Oscar Luengo's account of his uncle Fermín Arce, which was written in 1945 but only published in 2002. Raimundo Suñer's memoirs were published in 2006, thirty years after his death.

19 "who thought it convenient to tone down his father's diverse opinions about political adversaries, to eliminate the names of compromised people, and to reduce or excise adjectives (murderous, bullying, etc.) that, on principle, the author used to qualify some characters."

20 A number of these survivor memoirs were composed earlier but only edited and published in the 1990s or 2000s. José Luis Gavilanes Laso found Prisciliano García Gaitero's 1946 memoir in manuscript form in archives in Spain, editing and publishing them in 2005. Nacianceno Mata wrote his memoirs in Paris in 1971; they were curated and edited by Ricardo A. Guerra Palmero and Oliver Quintero Sánchez for publication in 2006. Many others were published posthumously by relatives of the author. These early manuscripts were inaccessible and as such had little impact in the chronology of Mauthausen representations until their later publication.

21 Eusebi Pérez Martín and Galo Ramos were both on the infamous convoy from Angoulême to Mauthausen (Arnabat Mata and Toran Belver).

22 The exceptions are Marcial Mayans, who arrived in 1942, and Antonio Muñoz Zamora, who arrived on one of the last transports of Spaniards to Mauthausen, in 1944 (Mayans; Camacho and Torregrosa).

23 Interventions in the community of Spanish Mauthausen survivors by the imposters Enric Marco and Antonio Pastor in the 2000s further underscored the need for hard evidence in these survivor memoirs.

24 Disappearing perhaps more effectively than any other deportee, Antonio García Barón went into hiding in the jungles of the Bolivian Amazon (Leguineche).

25 "I am now sure that my memories will pass on to the History of Humanity."

26 "For those who were sacrificed, my eternal recognition. For their families who will never be compensated for the loss of their loved ones, my solidarity and respect."

27 "Morning: Coffee (a kind of malt that almost no one drank) 10 cl.

Midday: 1 litre of cooked turnips, or spinach, or potatoes 362 cl.
Evening: 360 to 400 g. of black bread 791 cl.
25 to 30 g of sausage 40 cl.

> Sundays: a tablespoon of jam (65 cl.), which distributed over the
> 7 days of the week arrives at 10 cl.
> Total per person/day: 1,213 cl."

28 "saviours of many of the lives of their comrades"

29 "We must insist ... on the diverse perceptions of what happened inside the camp, in the shelter of the circumstances of each internee, with respect to his destiny, barracks, and personal relationships, in addition to his political and union affiliations and the trajectories after liberation."

30 "Eusebi Perez, on the contrary, negated, repeatedly, the existence of a prepared and cohesive armed organization in the last phase of Mauthausen."

31 Pérez Martín conjectures that he and his friends weren't photogenic enough for Boix to spend his limited film supply on (101).

32 "I never passed through those lines where the Catalan Republican Amat welcomed the Spaniards."

33 In his distillation of these survivor memoirs, Hernández de Miguel identifies more than twelve ways the SS killed Spaniards (*Los últimos españoles* 241–69).

34 "There are innumerable books about the Nazi Holocaust that describe the persecution of the Jewish world but very little has been written, and much of the world ignores it, about the millions of non-Jewish people who also perished in the concentration camps."

35 "I didn't overlook, in a somewhat egotistical manner, that with their arrival [of the Jews] in the camp they had put the kibosh on my situation, but whether my destiny was good or bad wasn't their fault."

36 "To be *Rotspanier* (Spanish Red) in Mauthausen was to be prepared for the most atrocious punishments, to be *Juden* (Jewish) was even worse, it meant the worst of deaths."

37 "from experience that the majority of those men would cease to exist in a few days."

38 "After nine at night, cries and noises could be heard, and what happened was that the SS were amusing themselves with them with sticks, whips, and even with picks. The next morning none of them were left alive and when we left for work everything was entirely clean."

39 Suñer also recounted that a Sephardic Jew was on this particular transport. Joan de Diego, identifying the man's Spanish surname as "López," was able to save him from the fate suffered by the rest of the Jews by virtue of his Spanish ancestry (Arnabat Mata and Toran Belver; Ramos).

40 "Inside you could find signs of people: hair, blood, pieces of clothing, and even brains."

41 "there was a time during which I decided not to speak of my experience in Mauthausen."

42 Spanish filmmakers have produced no popular fictional cinema depiciting the Spanish deportation and Nazi victimization in the past fifteen years, in contrast to a growing body of cinematic fictionalizations of the Spanish Civil War.

43 "facilitat[ing] the production of independent documentaries that were realized with very low budgets."

44 "the documentary is the only cultural production that responds directly to the interest in the victim's perspective."

45 The director Llorenç Soler describes the ease with which he was able to reduce his production staff to himself and the historian Benito Bermejo by virtue of using digital technology, thus putting the elderly subjects of *Francisco Boix, un fotógrafo en el infierno* at ease (*Los hilos secretos* 181).

46 Among these additional documentaries are Pedro Carvajal's *Exilio* (*Exile*, 2002), Pau Vergara's *Más allá de la alambrada, la memoria del horror. Mauthausen 1939–1945* (*Beyond the Barbed Wire, Memory of the Horror. Mauthausen 1939–1945*, [2005]), Lucía Meler and Victor Riverola's *Lágrimas rojas* (*Red Tears*, 2006), and Aitor Fernández Pacheco's *Mauthausen: una mirada española* (*Mauthausen: A Spanish Perspective*, 2007). Other documentaries on Mauthausen were produced during this decade in Spain as well, some of dubious historical value (Bermejo and Checa, "La construcción de una impostura" 75–8).

47 "safe / In your warm houses," "[w]ho dies because of a yes or a no" (Levi, *If This Is a Man/The Truce* 17).

48 "the last protagonists and witnesses to the greatest genocide of modern times."

49 Bermejo is credited as the main historical researcher in the film. His book was augmented and re-released in 2015 with the title *El fotògraf de l'horror: La història de Francesc Boix i les fotos robades als SS de Mauthausen* (*The Photographer of the Horror: The History of Francesc Boix and the Photos Stolen from the Mauthausen SS*).

50 "Serrano Suñer negotiates with Hitler to annul the Spanish citizenship of all of the Republicans taken prisoner by the Germans in France. In other words, he was negotiating their extermination."

51 Soler and Bermejo interviewed nine Spanish Mauthausen survivors onscreen (Agapito Martín, Mariano Constante, Manuel Azaustre, Joan de Diego, José Perlado, Manuel Alfonso, Jacinto Cortés, Francisco Comellas, and Joaquín López-Raimundo) as well as Pierre Daix and Hans Marsálek, French and German Mauthausen survivors, respectively.

52 According to Soler, Bermejo was the (unseen) interlocutor of these interviews (*Los hilos secretos* 181).

53 "the photographic camera will be his fighting arm, his tool as a militant communist."

54 The film enjoyed modest success in Spain and abroad: it was shown at festivals in Europe and the Americas, winning the grand prize at the Cinema et Histoire Festival in Pressac, France, and was nominated for an Emmy award in the United States in 2000 (Soler, *Los hilos secretos* 177).

55 The Museu d'Historia de Catalunya exhibit and catalogue, *Més enllà de Mauthausen: Francesc Boix, fotògraf* (*Beyond Mauthausen: Francesc Boix, Photographer*), the rerelease of Benito Bermejo's book on Boix, and the preparation of *El fotógrafo de Mauthausen* (*The Mauthausen Photographer*), a historical thriller based on Boix's exploits by the director Mar Targarona, all attest to this renewed interest in Boix.

56 The Mauthausen survivors interviewed onscreen are Antonio Roig, Joan de Diego, Francisco Batiste, Josep Egea, Ramón Milá, Mariano Constante, Francisco Comellas, and Manuel Alfonso.

57 "said that outside of Spain there were no Spaniards, so for that group of Spaniards we all were left without a country."

58 "In Spain? There was no government that lifted a finger – not a finger – to defend the interests of the Spanish deportees who were left. Not one."

59 "my companions killed by the German fascists, to the satisfaction of the Spanish fascists."

60 Most recently in 2013.

61 *Els nens perduts del franquisme* (*The Lost Children of Francoism*, 2002) and *Les fosses del silenci* (*The Graves of Silence*, 2003) were produced before *El comboi dels 927* (2004). Armengou and Belis also added *Ravensbrück. L'infern de les dones* (*Ravensbrück. The Women's Hell*) to this series in 2006.

62 Although it has primarily been seen on European television, *El comboi* also won the spectator's prize at the 2005 Festival Internacional de Derechos Humanos de Barcelona (Herrmann, "Entrevista" 213).

63 See Armengou and Belis *El convoy de los 927*. This is an added layer of documentation that the filmmakers have provided for their other projects as well as a way to solidify their credibility and journalistic capability.

64 "'If the television said it, that meant that one could talk about it, that there was no danger anymore,'"

65 "They are the internees of the first convoy that ferried entire families to the destination of an extermination camp. They inaugurate those death transports that two years later the Jews would sadly make famous."

66 "marked as though we were Jews with the Star of David."

67 "Germans. All the planes that bombed in Spain were German. The ones that destroyed Guernica were German."

68 "have kept the essence of a man. In Mauthausen, no."

69 "they left us in the train wagon and no one opened it. No one even knew that we were there."

70 "Since it does not appear to be beneficial to do anything on behalf of the prisoners, file it away."

71 "this 'file it away' is the condemnation to death of those Spaniards on the convoy of the 927."

72 "The Germans told me not to talk about the concentration camp,"

73 "Franco didn't lift a finger, not one finger, on behalf of the Spanish Republicans ... and the church did even less."

74 "I have fought for an ideal of liberty and justice, and I will not return to Spain. I have lost everything. Everything, everything, everything. My family, my wellbeing and liberty, losing Spain. It's terrible. You can't imagine."

75 "when there is a silence that means that no one speaks. That's why I have come, why I have come to see you, to participate."

76 "Relato real" is the term of art Cercas used in his canonical work *Soldados de Salamina* (*Soldiers of Salamis*, 2001), a way of defining the book as on the border between fiction and non-fiction, a "real story," as it were, that takes imaginative liberties with its historical subject matter. Maria Barbal's novel, *En la pell de l'altre* (*In the Skin of Another*, 2014), published earlier the same year, was also loosely based on the Marco case.

77 In the 2009 film *Ich Bin Enric Marco* (*I Am Enric Marco*), Marco told the filmmakers that if he had to apologize to the community of Spanish concentration camp survivors and their families for anything, "es haberles dicho que yo había estado en el campo de concentración," but he took credit for having brought more attention to the Spaniards in the camp ("it is for having told them that I had been in the concentration camp," Fillol and Vernal).

78 "memory industry [that] ended up being lethal for memory." See Faber, Aragoneses "El impostor," and Martín Alegre.

79 As of this writing, *El impostor* has been translated into Italian, French, Portuguese, and Chinese but not, significantly, English.

80 "now few remember the so-called historical memory."

81 Marco's claims to have survived the German concentration camp Flossenbürg began to surface in 1978, when he was included among the interview subjects in Eduardo Pons Prades and Mariano Constante's *Los cerdos del comandante*. Because Marco was not a concentration camp survivor and *El impostor* does not directly deal with Mauthausen, the

book has not been included among the contemporary representations analyzed in this chapter.

82 The narrator is referred to alternately as Joanna, Marieàngels, and Àngels: all forms of the author's name in Mallorquin.

83 "MILITARY CENSOR, PALMA DE MALLORCA"

84 "that small piece of information confirmed what we had all already imagined."

85 "sort out the mystery of his life," "half way between nowhere and forgetting."

86 This scenario was reported anecdotally after intial publication of Roig's volume in 1977. The novel suggests that Roig's book continued to be a groundbreaking source for the families of Spanish Mauthausen deportees well into the twenty-first century (chapter 3).

87 Bermejo and Checa also corroborate Chamena Moll's trajectory to Mauthausen and death in Gusen (*Libro memorial* 177).

88 "Which one do you want, the true one or the other one?"

89 "As if [I] had broken stone all day."

90 "What horrible evil had we all committed?"

91 I discovered this book in a small bookstore devoted to Mallorcan authors in Barcelona. Readers of Catalan can also read Mallorquín.

92 "the case of *Sefarad* ... more deplorable in that its author works with flesh and bone people, with first and last names, which means assuming a high level of responsibility."

93 "Literary characters have always been created this way, in my book they sometimes intersect with historical characters, but are not confused with them."

94 Aside from *Sefarad*, novels such as Maria Àngels Anglada's *El violí d'Auschwitz* (*The Violin of Auschwitz*, 1994), which shares some overlapping content with Perez Domínguez's novel, and Juana Salabert's *Velódromo del invierno* (*Winter Velodrome*, 2001), among others, have added to the body of Spanish Holocaust fiction.

95 Pérez Domínguez curates a blog and Twitter account that focus on his latest novels, while Sánchez has a promotional website and, like many popular Spanish novelists, is a columnist for the Spanish daily newspaper *El País*.

96 Clara Sánchez's book was published in English as *The Scent of Lemon Leaves* in 2012.

97 "When Rubén Castro arrives in Paris he is already dead, but he doesn't yet know that he will die again ..."

98 A similar scene, in which the son of an SS guard plays target practice with a concentration camp prisoner at a birthday party, appears in *Prisionero en Mauthausen*.

99 The trope of a civilian passing apples to a prisoner inside a concentration camp appeared in Herman Rosenblat's infamous false memoir (Rich and Berger).

100 "all the books about this topic that fell into my hands."

101 "I write fiction ... what I have done is construct a documented novel, not a novelized document. The documentation has allowed me to solidly support the work and design an attractive plot."

102 *El violinista de Mauthausen* won the 2009 Premio de Novela Ateneo de Sevilla and has been printed in ten editions.

103 A goal the author has stated explicitly in interviews ("Un idioma sin fronteras").

104 "we had arrived at the same place, some from the path of the executioners and other from the path of the victims."

105 "I wore the SS uniform and you all wore the striped prisoner uniform. We were inside an established order that was impossible to break. There was nothing to think about. We had reached an equilibrium, do you understand?"

106 "We didn't feel like heroes, rather more like plague victims. We were victims, and no one loves the victims or the losers. Others had no other choice but to be quiet and suffer the fear, the embarrassment and the guilt of the survivors, but we became hunters ..."

107 An exception is the author's inclusion of Aribert Heim, a notorious doctor who performed experiments on prisoners at Mauthausen, as a resident of this small Spanish town. Heim escaped to the Valencia region after the war (Messenger 168; Kulish and Souad).

108 Pérez Domínguez and Sánchez took liberties with the historical record that can be interpreted either as inaccuracies or as creative embellishments. To the extent that neither claimed to reinterpret the Holocaust, as Muñoz Molina did, nor are they as internationally known, they have thus far escaped any real criticism.

109 "If we don't finish off Winzer and his gang of Nazis there will be concentration camps in Spain." Miguel is a curious homage to the Republican poet Miguel Hernández.

110 "Juan Placambó was something much worse than a Nazi: I was a *Kapo* ... Guilt weighs on me like an imaginary yoke formed by the bones of a legion of cadavers."

111 *"a broken man, finished."*

112 "I sacrificed my morals to benefit the common good. I sacrificed my ideas, my integrity, my purity. I sacrificed everything good and noble in myself."

113 Ricken was tried at Dachau in 1947 and sentenced to life. He was paroled in 1954 (Schmidt and Loehrer 205–7).

114 In performances, the actors acknowledged the individuals gathered in the photo by gesturing toward it, as though the Spanish survivors of Mauthausen were the directors of the play.

115 "we weren't trying to make a documentary, because that already exists and we're not historians."

116 "The Wienergraben Quarry Song" ("Ay, I'm dying, / I'm kicking the bucket, I'm dying, / for the amusement of the Caudillo [Franco]"), "The Electrified Barbed Wire Song" ("I am electrocution, / I am high voltage, / your body at boiling. / Three hundred eighty volts, / ready for the crematory"), and "The Supremacy of the Aryan Race Song" ("An Aryan woman / tidies up / even the most active female. / Performing good hygiene / without a doubt is / preferred")

117 Seen, for instance, in Llorenç Soler's documentary.

118 "thirty-five ways to die in Mauthausen."

119 "A variety show in the midst of that horror! ... And, on top of it all, fresh air, diversion, morale for that troop of broken, decimated, reinvigorated men, who knew that dignity and morale were the only thing that could keep them alive"

120 "It is thanks to those negatives that the Spaniards smuggled out of the camp that our guilt was able to be demonstrated."

121 "Even so I won't pay, we won't pay."

122 "For you the night. For us, the day." Carlos Hernández de Miguel, in his Twitter narrative, credits Joan de Diego with delivering a version of this quote to Bachmayer ("Bachmayer dice").

123 "I find myself in the prisoner of war camp in Trier, Germany. There are about 700 of us Spaniards. The Nazis keep us separated from the rest."

124 As of this writing, Hernández de Miguel continues to contribute to this Twitter account, though he has completed the main narrative thread of his uncle's story. He now uses the account to draw attention to issues of Spain's historical memory circulating in the press and in public fora apocryphally through Antonio Hernández's voice. In 2017, he published a graphic novel, *Deportado 4443: Sus tuits ilustrados* (*Deportee 4443: His Illustrated Tweets*), that illustrated Antonio's collected tweets with black and white drawings by Ioannes Ensis.

125 "08/24/1907 in Molina de Segura (Murcia). Police officer during the war. Exiled in France and deported to Mauthausen by the Nazis. This is my real story."

126 Many of the short videos linked to "@deportado4443" are US Signal Corps films available online through the United States Holocaust Memorial Museum website.

127 This number would continue to grow in the following weeks, as Spain's newsmedia publicized Hernández de Miguel's project. By 12 May, the account had 45,000 followers.

128 "That the SS have let Pindado go means that Franco knows we are imprisoned here."
129 "I have a strange sensation. They're planning something."
130 Although these quotations are attributed to fellow deportees in the Twitter narrative, they are not cited in any other way. Footnoting and source citation is uncommon on Twitter.
131 Over the course of posting as "@deportado4443," Hernández commented on his personal Twitter account that he was attacked by internet trolls: anonymous users who inundated the author with negative feedback.
132 "Tuesday is liberation day, come on, there's only a few days left but with these savages it's an eternity."
133 "Three days Antonio! Three days!!!"

5. Mauthausen Today

1 A 2016 study found Spanish support for the EU in significant decline, down from 63 per cent in 2015 to 47 per cent in 2016 (Stokes). In Austria, the contested results of the country's 2016 presidential election and eventual defeat of Norbert Hofer of the far-right Freedom Party in the repeated runoff election highlighted the country's growing discontent with EU immigration and economic policies.
2 Including the installation of Stolpersteine and other monuments around the country, laws that prohibit Holocaust denial and Nazi glorification, and Holocaust memorial sites in Graz and Vienna, among other places (Young, *Texture of Memory* 97–112).
3 Indeed, a local farmer, Eleanore Gusenbauer, complained to the authorities about the atrocities committed in plain sight in 1941:

> In the Concentration Camp Mauthausen at the work site in [the] Vienna Ditch [quarry] inmates are being shot repeatedly; those badly struck live for yet some time, and so remain lying next to the dead for hours and even half a day long.
>
> My property lies upon an elevation next to the Vienna Ditch, and one is often an unwilling witness to such outrages.
>
> I am anyway sickly and such a sight makes such a demand on my nerves that in the long run I cannot bear this.
>
> I request that it be arranged that such inhuman deeds be discontinued, or else be done where one does not see it. (qtd in Horwitz 35)

4 See Sturken and Lennon and Foley.

5 Although translated as "Muslim" in the text, "Muselmänner" was a term commonly used by concentration camp prisoners to refer to fellow prisoners who, emaciated and nearly insentient, passed through the camp visibly on the brink of death.

6 The Mauthausen commemorations are sponsored by the Österreichische Lagergemeinschaft Mauthausen (Austria's Mauthausen Camp Community), the Mauthausen Komitee of Austria, and the Comité International de Mauthausen.

7 In 2011, the Spanish Mauthausen survivors Ramiro Santisteban and Alejandro Bermejo participated in the commemorations as members of the French Amicale de Mauthausen. In 2015, Cristóbal Soriano, 95, was the sole Spanish Mauthausen survivor to attend as a member of the French Amicale de Mauthausen.

8 Cueto made this remark during a speech at the Ebensee commemoration in Austria on 9 May 2015.

9 The Spanish delegation is composed of an amalgamation of survivors' groups, including the Amical de Mauthausen, from Barcelona; Triangle Blau, from Figueras; and the Association of Spanish Republicans, from Austria.

10 Both of these fictionalized treatises of Mauthausen are for sale in the Spanish-language section of the Mauthausen Memorial bookstore. Other, more factual accounts or survivor memoirs are not.

11 Including the United States Holocaust Memorial Museum oral history collection, the Yale Fortunoff Video Archive for Holocaust Testimonies, and the British Library Sound Archive.

12 Hernández del Miguel also interviewed Siegfried Meir, a German national who entered Mauthausen in 1945 as a boy and was "adopted" by a number of Spanish prisoners in the camp.

13 Manuel Alfonso Ortells, José Marfil Peralta, Lázaro Nates Gallo, Ramiro Santisteban Castillo, Esteban Pérez Pérez, and José Alcubierre Pérez appear in both journalists' volumes.

14 On a companion website to his book, *deportados.es*, Hernández de Miguel compiled video reports on these few remaining survivors. Although not full-length oral histories, these 10 to 20-minute edited clips allow the spectator to enter the homes of aged survivors, meet members of their families, see the artifacts they have saved for years, and hear their voices as they recount episodes from their pasts.

15 The director of the MSDP, Gerhard Botz, chose this number to represent the number of Spaniards in Mauthausen proportional to the rest of the prisoner population (Vilanova, *Mauthausen, después* 142).

16 Julia Montredon and Charlotte Pétrou performed two additional interviews with Pablo Escribano and Mariano Constante in French.

17 This detail is picked up in Llorente and Ripoll's dramatization *El triángulo azul*, in which the character based on Boix plays a harmonica while working in the photography lab (chapter 4).

18 Enric Gallart Vivé has examined the testimony of numerous Spanish Mauthausen survivors who claimed that César Orquín was an exception to the rule of brutal, power-hungry Spanish *Kapos*.

19 The testimony of Antonio Pastor Martínez, who invented his experience in Mauthausen, is still included in the AMM archive. See Bermejo and Checa, *La construcción de una impostura* 78–9 and Vilanova 143–5.

20 "Why didn't I ask them more and better questions? Why didn't I protest when they brought up topics and anecdotes that have been repeated, copied, and sleeplessly revisited a thousand times?"

21 "the silence that wanted to defeat me."

22 "it was what they kept quiet, what they hid, and what they didn't even know or had forgotten, blocked out."

23 "I knew that there was a resistance, I knew that they had formed a committee of resistors, but no more than that, I didn't know what it was or what it wasn't."

24 This state interest was evident also by the establishment of the Centro Documental de la Memoria Histórica in Salamanca and the Museu Memorial de l'Exili in La Jonquera, Cataluña, both in 2007. *Libro Memorial* is a reference text elaborated with the aid of survivor interviews and substantial archival research. It was published in 2006, accompanied by a searchable online database housed on the Ministry of Culture's website. Although ideological shifts in Spain's government are such that the Law of Historical Memorial is now defunded, the *Libro Memorial*'s companion database is still operational.

25 "Seventy years have gone by and no one wanted to know or talk about anything, and now, suddenly, it's coming out all over the place: newspapers, magazines, universities."

Works Cited

Adorno, Theodor. *Prisms*. Trans. Samuel and Shierry Weber. Cambridge, MA: MIT Press, 1967.

– *Negative Dialectics*. 1966. Trans. E.B. Ashton. New York: Seabury Press, 1973.

Agamben, Giorgio. *Homo Sacer: Sovereign Power and Bare Life*. Trans. Daniel Heller-Roazen. Stanford: Stanford UP, 1998.

Alakus, Baris, et al., eds. *Kunst und Kultur im Konzentrationslager Mauthausen 1938–1945: Katalog zur Ausstellung*. Vienna: Die Aussteller und Bundesministerium für Inneres, 2007.

Alfaya, Javier. *Españoles bajo el III Reich: Los recuerdos de un triángulo azul*. Madrid: Editorial Cuadernos para el Diálogo, 1970.

Alférez, Antonio. "Homenaje del Rey a los españoles muertos en Mauthausen." *ABC* 3 Feb. 1978: 5.

Alfonso Ortells, Manuel. *De Barcelona a Mauthausen: diez años de mi vida (1936–1945)*. Móstoles, Spain: Memoria Viva, 2007.

Álvarez Chillida, Gonzalo. *El antisemitismo en España: la imagen del judío, 1812–2002*. Madrid: Marcial Pons, 2002.

Álvarez Navarro, Jaume. Interview by Mercedes Vilanova. No. OH/ZP1/171. Vienna: Archiv der KZ-Gedenkstätte Mauthausen (AMM), 2002.

Amat-Piniella, Joaquim. "Eutanàsia." *Antologia dels fets, les idees i els homes d'occident*. Nov. 1947: 52–59.

– "La fam." *Per Catalunya: bulletin d'information des catalans en exil*. Aug. 1945: 3–4.

– Interview by Montserrat Roig. Manresa, Spain: Associació Memòria i Història de Manresa, 1973.

– *K.L. Reich*. Trans. Robert Finley and Marta Marín-Dòmine. Ontario, Canada: Wilfrid Laurier UP, 2014.

– *K.L. Reich*. 1963. Barcelona: Edicions 62, 2005.

– *K.L. Reich*. Trans. Antonio Padilla. Ed. David Serrano. Barcelona: El Aleph, 2002.
– *K.L. Reich: novel·la*. Barcelona: Club Editor, 1963b.
– *K.L. Reich: miles de españoles en los campos de Hitler*. Trans. Baltasar Porcel. Barcelona: Seix Barral, 1963a.
– *Les llunyanies: poemes de l'exili, 1940–1946*. Ed. David Serrano. Barcelona: Columna, 1999.
Anglada, Maria Àngels. *El violí d'Auschwitz*. Barcelona: Columna, 1994.
Antelme, Robert. *L'espèce humaine*. Paris: Éditions de la Cité Universelle, 1947.
"Antologia dels Fets, les Idees i els Homes d'Occident." Gran Enciclopèdia Catalana, 2015. Web.
"Los años rojos: Españoles en los campos nazis de Mariano Constante – Ed. Martínez Roca, B." *La Vanguardia Española* 12 Dec. 1974: 61.
Aragoneses, Alfons, ed. "Censo de deportados españoles a campos nazis." Barcelona: Universitat Pompeu Fabra; Generalitat de Catalunya, 2010. Database.
– "Deportados españoles en los campos nazis: Historia y memorias." Seminari d'Història de l'Institut Universitari d'Història Jaume Vicens i Vives, 17 Mar. 2015. Lecture.
– "Història i memòria dels jueus espanyols als camps nazis: lliçons per al segle XXI." *El palimpsest: Reflexions sobre el món d'ahir i d'avui*. Barcelona: Wordpress, 2011. Blog.
– "El impostor y la memoria democrática." *El Diario* 11 Nov. 2014.
– "Re: Censo sobre los deportados." Message to the author. 23 Jan. 2014. Email.
Archiv der KZ-Gedenkstätte Mauthausen (AMM). *The Visible Past: Photographs of Mauthausen Concentration Camp*. Vienna: Austrian Ministry of the Interior, 2005.
Armengou, Montse, and Ricard Belis. *El convoy de los 927*. Trans. Carles Mercadal. Barcelona: Random House Mondadori, 2005.
– *Las fosas del silencio: ¿Hay un holocausto español?* Barcelona: Plaza & Janés, 2004.
– *Ravensbrück, el infierno de las mujeres*. Barcelona: Belacqva, 2008.
Arnabat Mata, Ramon, and Rosa Toran Belver. *Eusebi Pérez Martín: recordar per viure, viure per recordar*. Vilafranca del Penedés, Spain: Ajuntament de Vilafranca del Penedés, 2008.
"Artistas y científicos españoles en Mauthausen." Ed. Amical de Mauthausen y otros campos y de todas las víctimas del nazismo de España. Barcelona: Amical de Mauthausen y otros campos, 2007.
Assmann, Aleida. "From 'Canon and Archive'." *The Collective Memory Reader*. Eds. Jeffrey K. Olick, Vered Vinitzky-Seroussi, and Daniel Levy. New York: Oxford UP, 2011. 334–7.

Assmann, Jan. "Communicative and Cultural Memory." *The Collective Memory Reader*. Eds. Jeffrey K. Olick, Vered Vinitzky-Seroussi, and Daniel Levy. New York: Oxford UP, 2011. 109–18.

Aura Boronat, Francisco. Interview by Mercedes Vilanova. No. OH/ZP1/174. Vienna: Archiv der KZ-Gedenkstätte Mauthausen (AMM), 2002.

Avni, Haim. *Spain, the Jews, and Franco*. Trans. Emanuel Shimoni. Philadelphia: Jewish Publication Society of America, 1982.

Aynat, Enrique. *El diario ABC y el holocausto*. Valencia: Diorama, 1990.

Aznar, Antonio. *Mauthausen: exterminio de los españoles*. Barcelona: Ediciones Petronio, 1976.

Baer, Alejandro. *Holocausto. Recuerdo y representación*. Madrid: Editorial Losada, 2006.

– "Memoria de Auschwitz y antisemitismo secundario ... y tres tesis sobre el prejuicio anti-judío en la España actual." *Constelaciones: Revista de Teoría Crítica* 4 (2012): 99–118.

– *El testimonio audiovisual: imagen y memoria del Holocausto*. Madrid: Centro de Investigaciones Sociológicas, 2005.

– "The Voids of Sepharad: The Memory of the Holocaust in Spain." *Journal of Spanish Cultural Studies* 12.1 (2011): 94–120.

Baer, Alejandro, and Jacobo Israel Garzón. *España y el Holocausto (1939–1945): Historia y testimonios*. Madrid: Federación de Comunidades Judías de España, Hebraica Ediciones, 2007.

Baget Herms, Josep M. "Mauthausen, última parada." *La Vanguardia* 9 Mar. 2004, sec. Vivir: 8.

Bailina, José. "Hace ya, 27 años." *Hispania* 42 (II época) (1972): 15–16.

Barbal, Maria. *En la pell de l'altre*. Barcelona: Columna, 2014.

Barrera Beitia, Enrique. *Galegos en Mauthausen*. A Coruña, Spain: Deputacion da Coruña, D.L., 2012.

Bársony, János, and Ágnes Daróczi. *Pharrajimos: The Fate of the Roma during the Holocaust*. Trans. Gabor Komaromy. New York: International Debate Education Association, 2008.

Bartra, Agustí. *Xabola*. Mexico: n.p., 1943.

Bathrick, David. "Teaching Visual Culture and the Holocaust." *Teaching the Representation of the Holocaust*. Eds. Marianne Hirsch and Irene Kacandes. New York: The Modern Language Association of America, 2004. 286–300.

Batiste Baila, Francisco. *Mariner del "Maria Rosa."* Vinaròs, Spain: Antinea, 2007.

– *El sol se extinguió en Mauthausen: vinarocenses en el infierno nazi*. Vinaròs, Spain: Antinea, 1999.

Ben-Dror, Graciela. *La Iglesia Católica ante el Holocausto: España y América Latina, 1933–1945*. Madrid: Alianza Editorial, 2003.

Beneito Lloris, Àngel, Francesc-X. Blay Meseguer, and Natxo Lara Jornet. *Francisco Aura Boronat: resistència i dignitat enfront de la desmemòria*. Alcoi, Spain: Associació Cultural l'Alcoià-Comtat i Cubicat Edicions, 2012.

Benet i Jornet, Josep M. *Material d'enderroc*. Barcelona: Edicions 62, 2010.

Berenbaum, Michael, ed. *A Mosaic of Victims: Non-Jews Persecuted and Murdered by the Nazis*. New York: New York UP, 1990.

Bergen, Doris L. *War & Genocide: A Concise History of the Holocaust*. Lanham, MD: Rowman & Littlefield, 2016.

Bermejo, Benito. *El fotògraf de l'horror: La història de Francesc Boix i les fotos robades als SS de Mauthausen*. Barcelona: RBA, 2015.

– *Francesc Boix, el fotògraf de Mauthausen*. Barcelona: La Magrana, 2002.

– "Re: Información viaje.doc." Message to the author. 17 Mar. 2011. Email.

Bermejo, Benito, and Sandra Checa. "La construcción de una impostura. Un falso testigo de la deportación de republicanos españoles a los campos nazis." *Migraciones y Exilios* 5 (2004): 63–80.

– *Libro memorial: Españoles deportados a los campos nazis (1940–1945)*. Madrid: Ministerio de Cultura, Subdirección General de Publicaciones, Información y Documentación, 2006.

Bermejo, Benito, et al. "Conversació en Commemoració del 70è aniversari de l'Alliberament de Mauthausen." Barcelona: Auditori RBA Diagonal, 2015. Roundtable lecture.

Blanco, Rosa (runawesty). "Tres días Antonio! Tres días!!!" 2 May 2015, 5:34 am. Tweet.

Blatter, Janet, and Sybil Milton. *Art of the Holocaust*. New York: Rutledge Press, 1981.

Boder, David P. *Voices of the Holocaust*. Chicago: Illinois Institute of Technology; Galvin Library, 1946.

Boix Testimony, U.S.A. v. Hans Altfuldisch et al. College Park, MD: National Archives & Records Administration, 1946.

Brenneis, Sara J. *Genre Fusion: A New Approach to History, Fiction, and Memory in Contemporary Spain*. West Lafayette, IN: Purdue UP, 2014.

Buggeln, Marc. *Slave Labor in Nazi Concentration Camps*. Trans. Paul Cohen. Oxford: Oxford UP, 2014.

Burleigh, Michael. *Death and Deliverance: "Euthanasia" in Germany c. 1900–1945*. Cambridge: Cambridge UP, 1994.

Butler, Judith. *Precarious Life: The Powers of Mourning and Violence*. New York: Verso, 2004.

Calcerrada Guijarro, Enrique, and Florencio Pavón Mariblanca. *Republicanos españoles en Mauthausen-Gusen*. Benalmádena, Spain: Caligrama, 2003.

Calvo Gascón, Juan Manuel. *Itinerarios e identidades: republicanos aragoneses deportados a los campos nazis*. Zaragoza: Gobierno de Aragón, 2011.

Camacho, Enmanuel, and Ana Torregrosa. *Mauthausen 90.009: la historia de un español en los campos nazis*. Sevilla: Centro Andaluz del Libro, 2003.

Campillo, Maria. "Memoria literaria y ficción del universo concentracionario." *Una inmensa prisión: Los campos de concentración y los prisiones durante la guerra civil y el franquismo*. Eds. Carme Molinero, Margarida Sala and Jaume Sobrequés. Barcelona: Crítica, 2003. 231–49.

– "Un viatge a l'infern: *Nit i boira*, de Mercè Rodoreda." *Caplletra* 36 (2004): 77–92.

Canciones para después de una guerra. Dir. Martín Patino, Basilio. Prod. La Linterna Mágica, 1976. Film.

Carbos, Toni, and Javier Cosnava. *Prisionero en Mauthausen*. Alicante, Spain: Ediciones de Ponent, 2011.

Carcedo, Diego. *Un español frente al holocausto. Así salvó Ángel Sanz Briz a 5.000 judíos*. Madrid: Temas de Hoy, 2000.

Carrió i Vilaseca, Jacint. *Manresa-Mauthausen-Gusen: deportació i retorn d'un home compromès amb la llibertat*. Manresa, Spain: Centre d'Estudis del Bages, 2001.

Caruth, Cathy. *Unclaimed Experience: Trauma, Narrative, and History*. Baltimore: Johns Hopkins UP, 1996.

Català, Neus. *De la resistencia y la deportación: 50 Testimonios de mujeres españolas*. 1984. Barcelona: Península, 2000.

Cerca del Danubio. Dir. Vega, Felipe. Prod. Canal + España, 2000. Film.

Cercas, Javier. *El impostor*. Barcelona: Literature Random House, 2014.

– *Soldados de Salamina*. Barcelona: Editorial Tusquets, 2001.

Cerezo, Herme. "'En una novela han de suceder cosas que interesan al lector.'" *Siglo XXI*. Sept. 2010.

Checa, Sandra, Ángel del Río, and Ricardo Martín. *Andaluces en los campos de Mauthausen*. Sevilla: Centro de Estudios Andaluces. Consejería de la Presidencia, 2006.

Climent Sarrión, Casimir "Ya es hora ..." *Hispania* 54 (II época). April/May (1976): 11.

Cohen, Eugene S. *Cohen Report (Report of Investigation of Alleged War Crimes Mauthausen – Gusen – Ebensee to Commanding General, Twelfth Army Group, U. S. Army)*. KZ Gusen Memorial Committee Digital Archive, 1945.

El comboi dels 927. Dir. Armengou, Montse, and Richard Belis. Prod. Televisió de Catalunya, 2004. Film.

Constante, Mariano. *Les années rouges: de Guernica à Mauthausen*. Paris: Mercure de France, 1971.

– *Los años rojos: españoles en los campos nazis*. Barcelona: Círculo de Lectores, 2005.

– *Los años rojos: españoles en los campos nazis*. Barcelona: Ediciones Martínez Roca, 1974.

– *Republicanos aragoneses en los campos nazis*. Huesca, Spain: Editorial Pirineo, 2000.

– *Tras Mauthausen*. Barcelona: Círculo de Lectores, 2007.

– *Yo fui ordenanza de los SS*. Barcelona: Martínez Roca, 1976.

De Diego, Joan. Interview by Mercedes Vilanova. No. OH/ZP1/178. Vienna: Archiv der KZ-Gedenkstätte Mauthausen (AMM), 2002.

– "Letter to Mariano Constante." No. 0001. N.d. Barcelona: Museu d'Història de Catalunya/Joan de Diego Archive.

– "Postcard from Joan de Diego to his family." No. 0313. Dec. 1943. Barcelona: Museu d'Història de Catalunya/Joan de Diego Archive.

De las Heras Pedrosa, Carlos. *La prensa del movimiento y su gestión publicitaria (1936–1984)*. Málaga: Universidad de Málaga, 2000.

Díaz Sande, José R. "El triángulo azul. Ripoll – Llorente Entrevista." 28 Apr. 2014. Madridteatro.eu. Web.

Didi-Huberman, Georges. *Images in Spite of All: Four Photographs from Auschwitz*. Chicago: U of Chicago P, 2008.

Diner, Dan. "Icons of European Memory Juxtaposed: The Spanish Civil War and the Holocaust." *The Holocaust in Spanish Memory. Historical Perceptions and Cultural Discourse*. Eds. Antonio Gómez López-Quiñones and Susanne Zepp. Leipzig, Germany: Leipziger UP, 2010. 31–5.

– "Restitution and Memory – The Holocaust in European Political Cultures." *New German Critique* 90 (2003): 36–44.

Dios Amill, José de. *La verdad sobre Mauthausen*. Barcelona: Sírius, 1995.

Doerr, Anthony. *All the Light We Cannot See*. New York: Scribner, 2014.

Dreyfus, Jean-Marc. "Censorship and Approval: The Reception of *Nuit et Brouillard* in France." *Uncovering the Holocaust: The International Reception of Night and Fog*. Ed. Ewout van der Knaap. London: Wallflower Press, 2006. 35–45.

Dreyfus-Armand, Geneviève. *El exilio de los republicanos españoles en Francia: de la guerra civil a la muerte de Franco*. Trans. Dolors Poch. Barcelona: Editorial Crítica, 2000.

Eaglestone, Robert. *The Holocaust and the Postmodern*. Oxford: Oxford UP, 2004.

Egea Pujante, José. *K.L. Mauthausen 5894*. Barberà del Vallès, Spain: Tabelaria, 2003.

Englander, Nathan. *What We Talk about When We Talk about Anne Frank*. New York: Knopf, 2012.

"Entre el sufrimiento y la esperanza: Juan de Diego." Dir. Roig, Montserrat. Prod. RTVE/Sant Cugat, 1984. Television.

Estrada, Isabel. *El documental cinematográfico y televisivo contemporáneo: memoria, sujeto y formación de la identidad democrática española*. Woodbridge, England: Boydell & Brewer Ltd., 2013.

– "To Mauthausen and Back: The Holocaust as a Reference in Spanish Civil War Memory Studies." *The Holocaust in Spanish Memory. Historical Perceptions and Cultural Discourse*. Eds. Antonio Gómez López-Quiñones and Susanne Zepp. Leipzig, Germany: Leipziger UP, 2010. 37–50.

Exilio. Dir. Carvajal, Pedro. Prod. Televisión Española, 2002. Film.

Faber, Sebastiaan. "Javier Cercas y 'El impostor', o el triunfo del kitsch." *Fronterad*. 12 Feb. 2015.

Felman, Shoshana, and Dori Laub. *Testimony: Crises of Witnessing in Literature, Psychoanalysis and History*. New York: Routledge, 1992.

Fernández Areal, Manuel. *El control de la prensa en España*. Madrid: Guadiana de Publicaciones, 1973.

Fernández, James D. *Apology to Apostrophe: Autobiography and the Rhetoric of Self-Representation in Spain*. Durham, NC: Duke UP, 1992.

Ferrán, Ofelia, and Gina Herrmann. *A Critical Companion to Jorge Semprún: Buchenwald, Before and After*. New York: Palgrave Macmillan, 2014.

Ferrándiz, Francisco. *El pasado bajo tierra: Exhumaciones contemporáneas de la Guerra Civil*. Barcelona: Anthropos, 2014.

Ferreras, Juan Ignacio. *La novela por entregas, 1840–1900. Concentración obrera y economía editorial*. Madrid: Taurus, 1972.

A Film Unfinished. Dir. Hersonski, Yael. Prod. Oscilloscope, 2010. Film.

Francés Díez, M. Àngels. *Montserrat Roig: feminisme, memòria i testimoni*. Barcelona: Publicacions de l'Abadia de Montserrat, 2012.

Francisco Boix, un fotógrafo en el infierno. Dir. Soler, Llorenç. Prod. Oriol Porta. S.A.V., 2000. Film.

Fraser, Ronald. *Blood of Spain: An Oral History of the Spanish Civil War*. New York: Pantheon Books, 1986.

Friedlander, Henry. *The Origins of Nazi Genocide: From Euthanasia to the Final Solution*. Chapel Hill, NC: U of North Carolina P, 1995.

Friedländer, Saul. *Reflections of Nazism: An Essay on Kitsch and Death*. Trans. Thomas Weyr. New York: Harper & Row, 1984.

Friedman, Jonathan C., ed. *The Routledge History of the Holocaust*. New York: Routledge, 2011.

Foer, Jonathan Safran. *Everything is Illuminated*. Boston: Houghton Mifflin, 2002.

Gallart Vivé, Ernest. *Los republicanos españoles en el sistema concentracionario del KL Mauthausen: "el Kommando César."* Móstoles, Spain: "Memoria Viva" Asociación para el estudio de la deportación y el exilio español, 2011.

García Gaitero, Prisciliano. *Mi vida en los campos de la muerte nazis*. León, Spain: Edilesa, 2005.

García-Merás, Lydia. "El cine de la disidencia. La producción militante antifranquista (1967-1981)." *Desacuerdos 4. Sobre arte, políticas y esfera pública en el Estado español. Cine y vídeo*. Barcelona: MACBA / Arteleku, UNIA arte y pensamiento, Centro José Guerrero, 2007. 16–41.

Garijo, Eulogio. Interview. No. 38613. Los Angeles: Shoah Foundation Visual History Archive, 1997.

Goldhagen, Daniel Jonah. *Hitler's Willing Executioners: Ordinary Germans and the Holocaust*. New York: Alfred A. Knopf, 1996.

Gómez, Luis. "El detective de Mauthausen." *El País* 5 May 2015, sec. Culture.

Hackl, Erich. "El caso 'Sefarad': industrias y errores del santo de su señora." *Lateral* 78. June (2001): 21, 28.

Halbwachs, Maurice. *The Collective Memory*. 1950. Trans. Francis J. Ditter Jr. and Vida Yazdi Ditter. New York: Harper & Row, 1980.

Halbwachs, Maurice, and Lewis A. Coser. *On Collective Memory*. Chicago: U of Chicago P, 1992.

Halow, Joseph. *Innocent at Dachau*. Newport Beach, CA: Institute for Historical Review, 1992.

Hayes, Peter, and John K. Roth. *The Oxford Handbook of Holocaust Studies*. New York: Oxford UP, 2010.

Heger, Heinz. *The Men with the Pink Triangle: The True, Life-and-Death Story of Homosexuals in the Nazi Death Camps*. 1980. Trans. David Fernbach. Boston: Alyson Publications, 1994.

Hernández de Miguel, Carlos (deportado4443). "Deberíamos estar durmiendo, pero no podemos. Que los SS hayan soltado a Pindado significa que Franco sabe que estamos aquí encerrados." 11 Mar. 2015, 4:19 p.m. Tweet.

– "@deportado4443". Twitter, Inc., 2015. Twitter account.

– (deportado4443). "Durante casi 5 años los alemanes nos han llamado #RotSpanier Hoy será el último día en que tengamos que llevar ese 'nombre' y este uniforme." 5 May 2015, 1:00 a.m. Tweet.

– "Ferroviario, carabinero, deportado…" 2015. Deportados.es. Web.

– (deportado4443). "Me encuentro en el campo de prisioneros de guerra de Trier, Alemania. Somos unos 700 españoles. Los nazis nos mantienen separados del resto." 21 Jan. 2015, 5:00 p.m. Tweet.

– (deportado4443). "¡No traen la comida! Llevamos días recibiendo la mitad de la pírrica ración habitual. Hoy ¡nada! Tengo una sensación extraña. Algo planean." 2 May 2015, 5:05 a.m. Tweet.

– *Los últimos españoles de Mauthausen*. Barcelona: Ediciones B, 2015.

Hernández de Miguel, Carlos, and Ioannes Ensis. *Deportado 4443: Sus tuits ilustrados*. Barcelona: Ediciones B, 2017.

Herrmann, Gina. "Camera Caedens, Camera Vindez: Francesc Boix and Photography at Mauthausen." *The Holocaust in Spanish Memory. Historical Perceptions and Cultural Discourse*. Eds. Antonio Gómez López-Quiñones, and Susanne Zepp. Leipzig, Germany: Leipziger UP, 2010. 115–37.

– "Documentary's Labour of Law: The Television Journalism of Montse Armengou and Ricard Belis." *Journal of Spanish Cultural Studies* 9.2 (2008): 193–212.

– "Entrevista con Montse Armengou." *Journal of Spanish Cultural Studies* 9.2 (2008): 213–23.

– *Written in Red: The Communist Memoir in Spain*. Urbana, IL: U of Illinois P, 2010.

Herzog, Dagmar. *Sex after Fascism: Memory and Morality in Twentieth-Century Germany*. Princeton: Princeton UP, 2005.

Hilberg, Raul. *Perpetrators, Victims, Bystanders: the Jewish Catastrophe, 1933–1945*. New York: Aaron Asher Books, 1992.

Hirsch, Joshua Francis. *Afterimage: Film, Trauma, and the Holocaust*. Philadelphia: Temple UP, 2004.

Hirsch, Marianne. *Generation of Postmemory: Writing and Visual Culture after the Holocaust*. New York: Columbia UP, 2012.

Holzinger, Gregor, and Andreas Kranebitter, eds. *The Concentration Camp Mauthausen 1938–1945: Catalogue to the Exhibition at the Mauthausen Memorial*. Vienna: New Academic Press, 2013.

Horwitz, Gordon J. *In the Shadow of Death: Living Outside the Gates of Mauthausen*. New York: The Free Press, 1990.

Howe, Irving. "Writing and the Holocaust." *Writing and the Holocaust*. Ed. Berel Lang. New York: Holmes & Meier, 1988. 175–99.

Hristova, Marije. "Memoria, olvido y la apertura de las fosas comunes de la Guerra Civil en 1978–1981 y 2000–2006." Groningen, Netherlands: University of Groningen, 2007. Thesis.

Huyssen, Andreas. *Present Pasts: Urban Palimpsests and the Politics of Memory*. Stanford: Stanford UP, 2003.

– *Twilight Memories: Marking Time in a Culture of Amnesia*. New York: Routledge, 1995.

Ich bin Enric Marco. Dir. Fillol, Santiago, and Lucas Vernal. Prod. Prodimag. 2009. Film.

Ioanid, Radu. *The Holocaust in Romania: The Destruction of Jews and Gypsies under the Antonescu Regime, 1940–1944*. Chicago: Ivan R. Dee, 2000.

Jardim, Tomaz. *The Mauthausen Trial: American Military Justice in Germany.* Cambridge, MA: Harvard UP, 2012.

Jaskot, Paul B. *The Architecture of Oppression: The SS, Forced Labor and the Nazi Monumental Building Economy.* London: Routledge, 2000.

Jauss, Hans. *Toward an Aesthetic of Reception.* Trans. Timothy Bahti. Minneapolis: U of Minnesota P, 1982.

Jensen, Erik N. "The Pink Triangle and Political Consciousness: Gays, Lesbians and the Memory of Nazi Persecution." *Sexuality and German Fascism.* Ed. Dagmar Herzog. New York: Berghahn Books, 2005. 319–49.

Junquera, Natalia. "Víctimas del franquismo, vetadas en el acto de memoria del Holocausto." *El País* 27 Jan. 2014, sec. Política.

Klüger, Ruth. *Still Alive: A Holocaust Girlhood Remembered.* New York: The Feminist Press at CUNY, 2001.

Kremer, S. Lillian, ed. *Holocaust Literature: An Encyclopedia of Writers and their Work.* 2 vols. New York: Routledge, 2002.

Kulish, Nicholas, and Souad Mekhennet. *The Eternal Nazi: From Mauthausen to Cairo, the Relentless Pursuit of SS Doctor Aribert Heim.* New York: Vintage Books, 2014.

Labanyi, Jo. "The Languages of Silence: Historical Memory, Generational Transmission and Witnessing in Contemporary Spain." *Journal of Romance Studies* 9.3 (2009): 23–35.

LaCapra, Dominick. *Writing History, Writing Trauma.* Baltimore: Johns Hopkins UP, 2001.

Lágrimas rojas. Dir. Meler, Lucía, and Victor Riverola. Prod. Cameo Media, 2006. Film.

Lang, Berel. *Act and Idea in the Nazi Genocide.* Chicago: U of Chicago P, 1990.

Langer, Lawrence. "Interpreting Survivor Testimony." *Writing and the Holocaust.* Ed. Berel Lang. New York: Holmes & Meier Publishers, 1988. 26–40.

Lazo Díaz, Alfonso. *La Iglesia, la Falange y el fascismo (Un estudio sobre la prensa española de posguerra).* Sevilla: Universidad de Sevilla, Secretariado de Publicaciones, 1998.

Le Chêne, Evelyn. *Mauthausen: The History of a Death Camp.* London: Methuen, 1971.

Lechner, Ralf. *Mauthausen Memorial.* Trans. Nick Somers. Ed. KZ-Gedenkstätte Mauthausen. Vienna: Federal Ministry of the Interior, Section IV/7, 2009. Pamphlet.

Leggewie, Claus. "Equally Criminal? Totalitarian Experience and European Memory." *Eurozine.* 1 June 2005.

Leguineche, Manuel. *El precio del paraíso. De un campo de exterminio al Amazonas.* Madrid: Espasa Calpe, 1997.

Lejeune, Philippe. *On Autobiography*. Minneapolis: U of Minnesota P, 1989.

Lengyel, Olga. *Souvenirs de l'au-delà*. Ed. László Gara. Paris: Editions du Bateau Ivre, 1946.

Lennon, John, and Malcom Foley. *Dark Tourism: The Attraction of Death and Disaster*. London: Continuum, 2000.

Levi, Primo. *The Drowned and the Saved*. Trans. Raymond Rosenthal. New York: Summit Books, 1988.

– *Se questo è un uomo*. Torino: F. DeSilva, 1947.

– *If This Is a Man/The Truce*. Trans. Stuart Woolf. New York: Penguin Books, 1979.

Levy, Daniel, and Natan Sznaider. *The Holocaust and Memory in the Global Age*. Trans. Assenka Oksiloff. Philadelphia: Temple UP, 2006.

Ley 52/2007 (Law of Historical Memory). Madrid: Boletín Oficial del Estado 310, 2007. 53410–16.

Libres. Noticiarios y Documentales NOT N 125A ("Año III"). Madrid: Ministerio de Cultura, 1945. Film.

Life is Beautiful. Dir. Benigni, Roberto. Prod. Miramax, 1999. Film.

Lipstadt, Deborah E. *Denying the Holocaust: The Growing Assault on Truth and Memory*. New York: Free Press, 1993.

Lisbona, José Antonio. *Más allá del deber: La respuesta humanitaria del Servicio Exterior frente al Holocausto*. Madrid: Ministerio de Asuntos Exteriores y de Cooperación, 2015.

Llor, Montserrat. *Vivos en el averno nazi*. Barcelona: Crítica, 2014.

Llorente, Mariano, and Laila Ripoll. *El triángulo azul*. Madrid: Centro Dramático Nacional, 2014.

Loew, Camila. "Portraits of Presence: Excavating Traumatic Identity in Contemporary Catalan Testimonies." *The Image and the Witness: Trauma, Memory and Visual Culture*. Eds. Frances Guerin and Roger Hallas. London: Wallflower Press, 2007. 23–36.

Luengo, Oscar. *La colina de la muerte: basado en la narración de Fermín Arce, prisionero en Mauthausen, N° 4.051*. Bilbao: n.p., 2002.

lumipife. "El martes es el día de la liberación, ánimo queda poco pero con estos salvajes es una eternidad." 2 May 2015, 6:22 a.m. Tweet.

Manent, Albert. *La literatura catalana a l'exili*. Barcelona: Curial, 1989.

Mangini González, Shirley. *Memories of Resistance: Women's Voices from the Spanish Civil War*. New Haven: Yale UP, 1995.

Marsálek, Hans. *Die Geschichte des Konzentrationlagers Mauthausen: Dokumentation*. Vienna: Mauthausen Komitee Österreich, 2006.

Martín Alegre, Sara. "Cercas, Hernández de Miguel and Mauthausen: The Limited Use of the Novel (Fiction or Non-Fiction ...)." *The Joys of Teaching Literature*. Barcelona: Blogs de la UAB, 2015.

Martín Romaní, Agapito. *Sobrevivir a Mauthaussen*. Valencia: n.p., 1997.

Más allá de la alambrada, la memoria del horror. Mauthausen 1939–1945. Dir. Vergara, Pau. Prod. Sorolla Films, 2005. Film.

Massaguer, Lope, and María Ángeles García-Maroto. *Mauthausen, fin de trayecto: un anarquista en los campos de la muerte*. Madrid: Fundación Anselmo Lorenzo, 1997.

Mata Maeso, Ignacio. *Mauthausen: memorias de un republicano español en el holocausto*. Barcelona: Ediciones B, 2007.

Mata, Nacianceno, Ricardo A. Guerra Palmero, and Oliver Quintero Sánchez. *Nacianceno Mata, un canario en Mauthausen: memorias de un superviviente del holocausto nazi*. La Laguna, Spain: Centro de la Cultura Popular Canaria, 2006.

Mauthausen. Prague: KSC Kraj Praha, 1946.

Mauthausen, el deber de recordar. Dir. Sella, Joan, and Cesc Tomás. Prod. Radiotelevisión Española, 2000. Film.

Mauthausen: un regard espagnol. Dir. Fernández Pacheco, Aitor. Prod. Chaya Films. 2007. Film.

Mayans, Marcial. *Testimoniatges i memòries (1936–1945): una nit tan llarga*. Valls, Spain: Cossetània Edicions, 2009.

Melenchón i Xamena, Joanna María. *Mauthausen, des de l'oblit*. Barcelona: Amicron, 2008.

Més enllà de Mauthausen: Francesc Boix fotògraf. Ed. Museu d'Història de Catalunya. Barcelona: Museu d'Història de Catalunya, 2015.

Messenger, David A. *Hunting Nazis in Franco's Spain*. Baton Rouge, LA: Louisiana State UP, 2014.

Milton, Sybil. "The Camera as Weapon: Documentary Photography and the Holocaust." *Simon Wiesenthal Center Annual* 1, Chapter 3 (1984).

Monegal, Ferran. "Mariano Constante, cuatro años en el campo de exterminio de Mauthausen." *La Vanguardia Española* 21 Jan. 1976.

– "Noche y niebla en Mauthausen." *La Vanguardia Española* 30 Nov. 1976.

Morales, Clara. "Un 'vodevil' para contar los horrores de los españoles en Mauthausen." *El País* 24 Apr. 2014, sec. Cultura.

"Muertos en cámara de gas." No. 0469. Museu d'Història de Catalunya/Joan de Diego Archive, Barcelona, c. 1945. Archival document.

Muñoz Molina, Antonio. "El caso Hackl: El autor de Sefarad responde." *Lateral* 79/80. (July/Aug. 2001): 6–7.

– *Sefarad: una novela de novelas*. Madrid: Punto de lectores, 2001.

Munté, Rosa-Àuria. "Una entrevista a Jorge Semprún. La narración de la viviendia de los campos de concentración en la literatura y el documental." *Trípodos* 16 (2004): 127–38.

Murià, Anna. *Crònica de la vida d'Agustí Bartra*. Barcelona: Publicacions de l'Abadia de Montserrat, 2004.

Nazi Concentration Camps – Prosecution Exhibit #230. Dir. Donovan, Navy Cmdr. James B., Navy Cmdr. E. Ray Kellogg, and George C. Stevens. Prod. U.S. Army Signal Corps. 1945. Film.

"Neus Català." Dir. Roig, Montserrat. Prod. Arxiu TVE Catalunya, 1978. Television.

Nichols, Geraldine Cleary. "Exile, Gender, and Mercè Rodoreda." *Modern Language Notes* 101.2 (1986): 405–17.

Nora, Pierre. "Between Memory and History: *Les Lieux de Mémoire*." *Representations* 26 (1989): 7–24.

Nuit et brouillard. Dir. Resnais, Alain. Prod. Argos Films, 1955. Film.

Núñez Seixas, Xosé M. *Camarada invierno: experiencia y memoria de la División Azul (1941–1945)*. Barcelona: Crítica, 2016.

– "Sharing or Witnessing Destruction? The 'Blue Division' and the Nazi Holocaust." *The Holocaust in Spanish Memory. Historical Perceptions and Cultural Discourse*. Eds. Antonio Gómez López-Quiñones and Susanne Zepp. Leipzig, Germany: Leipziger UP, 2010. 65–84.

Pakier, Małgorzata, and Bo Stråth. *A European Memory?: Contested Histories and Politics of Remembrance*. New York: Berghahn Books, 2010.

Payne, Stanley G. *Franco and Hitler: Spain, Germany, and World War II*. New Haven: Yale UP, 2008.

Pérez Domínguez, Andrés. *El violinista de Mauthausen*. Seville: Algaida, 2009.

Permanyer, Luís. "Un libro-monumento." *La Vanguardia Española* 28 May 1977: 78.

Perz, Bertrand, and Jörg Skriebeleit. "Introduction." Trans. Joanna White. *The Concentration Camp Mauthausen 1938–1945: Catalogue to the Exhibition at the Mauthausen Memorial*. Eds. Gregor Holzinger, Andreas Kranebitter, and Association for Remembrance and Historical Research in Austrian Concentration Camp Memorials. Vienna: New Academic Press, 2013 (12–15).

Pike, David Wingeate. *Españoles en el holocausto: vida y muerte de los republicanos en Mauthausen*. Trans. Enrique Benito. Barcelona: Random House Mondadori, 2003.

– *Franco and the Axis stigma*. New York: Palgrave Macmillan, 2008.

– *Franco y el eje Roma-Berlín-Tokyo: una alianza no firmada*. Trans. Patricia Arroyo. Madrid: Alianza, 2010.

– *Spaniards in the Holocaust: Mauthausen, the Horror on the Danube*. London: Routledge, 2000.

Pons Prades, Eduardo. *Los que SÍ hicimos la guerra*. Barcelona: Ediciones Martínez Roca, 1973.

Pons Prades, Eduardo, and Mariano Constante. *Los cerdos del comandante: españoles de los campos de exterminio nazis*. Barcelona: Editorial Argos Vergara, 1978.

"Presentación del libro 'Los S.S. tienen la palabra.' Anoche, en el Instituto de Cultura Italiano." *La Vanguardia Española* 7 Oct. 1972, 30.

Preston, Paul. "Franco and Hitler: The Myth of Hendaye 1940." *Contemporary European History* 1.1 (Mar. 1992), 1–16.

– *Franco: A Biography*. London: HarperCollins, 1993.

– *The Spanish Holocaust: Inquisition and Extermination in Twentieth-Century Spain*. New York: W.W. Norton & Co., 2012.

"El proceso de Nüremberg. Desfile de testigos. Los prisioneros en los campos de concentración acusan." *ABC* 30 Jan. 1946, 9.

"Projecte Stolpersteine a Navàs." Ed. Generalitat de Catalunya Memorial Democràtic. Navàs, Spain: Ajuntament de Navàs, 2015. Web.

Ramón Resina, Joan. "In the Butcher's Den: The Holocaust Through Catalan Eyes." *The Holocaust in Spanish Memory. Historical Perceptions and Cultural Discourse*. Eds. Antonio Gómez López-Quiñones and Susanne Zepp. Leipzig, Germany: Leipziger UP, 2010, 155–66.

Ramos, Galo. *Sobrevivir al infierno: memorias de una víctima del nazismo*. Avilés, Spain: Foto Angelín, 2002.

Razola, Manuel, and Mariano C. [Constante] Campo. *Triángulo azul: los republicanos españoles en Mauthausen, 1940–1945*. Trans. Janine Muls de Liarás. Barcelona: Edicions 62, 1979.

– *Triangle bleu: les républicans espagnols à Mauthausen, 1940–1945*. Paris: Gallimard, 1969.

Ribelles de la Vega, Silvia. *Luis Montero Álvarez Sabugo: en los abismos de la historia: vida y muerte de un comunista*. Oviedo, Spain: Pentalfa Ediciones, 2011.

Rich, Motoko, and Joseph Berger. "False Memoir of Holocaust is Cancelled by Publisher." *The New York Times* 28 Dec. 2008.

Ricoeur, Paul. *Memory, History, Forgetting*. Chicago: U of Chicago P, 2004.

Riggs, Thomas, ed. *Reference Guide to Holocaust Literature*. Farmington Hills, MI: St. James, 2002.

Ríos Carratalá, Juan A. *La mirada del documental*. Alicante: Publicacions de la Universitat d'Alacant, 2014.

Robert, Marthe. "Origins of the Novel." *Theory of the Novel: A Historical Approach*. Ed. Michael McKeon. Baltimore: Johns Hopkins UP, 2000. 57–69.

Rodoreda, Mercè. "Nit i boira." *La Nostra Revista* June 1947: 231–33.

– "Nit i boira." Trans. Clara Janés. *Parecía de seda*. Barcelona: Edicions del Mall, 1985. 56–69.

– *The Selected Stories of Mercè Rodoreda*. Trans. Martha Tennent. Rochester, NY: Open Letter, 2011.

– *Semblava de seda i altres contes*. Barcelona: Edicions 62, 1978.

Rodoreda, Mercè, and Anna Murià. *Cartes a l'Anna Murià, 1939–1956*. Barcelona: LaSal, Edicions de les Dones, 1985.

Rodríguez del Risco, Carlos. "Yo he estado en Mauthausen: Carlos R. del Risco relata en exclusiva para 'Arriba' sus siete años de aventura en el exilio." *Arriba* 26 Apr.–1 June 1946.

Rohr, Isabelle. *The Spanish Right and the Jews, 1898–1945: Antisemitism and Opportunism*. Brighton: Sussex Academic Press, 2007.

Roig, Montserrat. "Carta abierta a Serrano Suñer." *El País* 1 July 1979, sec. Sociedad.

– *Els catalans als camps nazis*. 1977. Barcelona: Edicions 62, 2001.

– "Una generación romántica: Españoles en los campos nazis." *Triunfo* 9 Dec. 1972: 34–7.

– "Una historia provisional." *Tele/eXpres* 10 May 1972: 13.

– "Letter to Josep Ester." No. 0047. Barcelona: Museu d'Història de Catalunya/Joan de Diego Archive, n.d.

– *La lluita contra l'oblit: escrits sobre la deportació*. Barcelona: Amical de Mauthausen i altres camps de concentració nazis, 2001.

– *Noche y niebla: los catalanes en los campos nazis*. Barcelona: Ediciones Península, 1978.

– "El somriure de la Mercè Rodoreda." *Oriflama* April 1972: 26–8.

Romaguera i Ramió, Joaquim, and Llorenç Soler de los Mártires. *Historia crítica y documentada del cine independiente en España: 1955–1975*. Barcelona: Laertes, 2006.

Rosenfeld, Alvin H. *The End of the Holocaust*. Bloomington, IN: Indiana UP, 2011.

Roskies, David G., and Naomi Diamant. *Holocaust Literature: A History and Guide*. Waltham, MA: Brandeis UP, 2012.

Rothberg, Michael. *Multidirectional Memory: Remembering the Holocaust in the Age of Decolonialization*. Stanford: Stanford UP, 2009.

– "Trauma, Memory, Holocaust." *Memory: A History*. Ed. Dmitri Nikulin. Oxford: Oxford UP, 2015. 280–90.

– *Traumatic Realism: The Demands of Holocaust Representation*. Minneapolis: U of Minnesota P, 2000.

Rother, Bernd. *Franco y el Holocausto*. Trans. Leticia Artiles Gracia and Gonzalo Álvarez Chillida. Madrid: Marcial Pons Historia, 2005.

– "Myth and Fact – Spain and the Holocaust." *The Holocaust in Spanish Memory. Historical Perceptions and Cultural Discourse*. Eds. Antonio Gómez López-Quiñones and Susanne Zepp. Leipzig, Germany: Leipziger UP, 2010. 51–63.

Rousset, David. *L'univers concentrationnaire*. Paris: Éditions du Pavois, 1946.

Salabert, Juana. *Velódromo del invierno*. Barcelona: Seix Barral, 2001.

Salou Olivares, Véronique, and Pierre Salou Olivares. *Los republicanos españoles en el campo de concentración nazi de Mauthausen. El deber colectivo de sobrevivir*. Paris: Éditions Tiresias, 2005.

Salvadó i Valentines, Ramon. *Un clam de llibertat: vivències de Josep Simon i Mill, exdeportat de Mauthausen (4.929)*. Saldes, Spain: Abadia Editors, 2003.

San Martín Boncompte, Josep. *Memòria d'exilis i retorns*. Lleida: Pagès Editors, 2008.

Sánchez, Clara. *Lo que esconde tu nombre*. Barcelona: Ediciones Destino, 2010.

– *The Scent of Lemon Leaves*. Trans. Julie Wark. Richmond, VA: Alma, 2012.

"Un idioma sin fronteras." *Andrés Pérez Domínguez y "El violinista de Mauthausen."* Ed. Susana Santaolalla. Radio Exterior de España, 24 Feb. 2010. Radio.

Sanz, Paloma. *Amanece en París*. Madrid: Ediciones Planeta, 2010.

Saunders, Max. "Life-Writing, Cultural Memory, and Literary Studies." *A Companion to Cultural Memory Studies*. Eds. Astrid Erll and Ansgar Nünning. Berlin: De Gruyter, 2010. 321–31.

Schindler's List. Dir. Spielberg, Steven. Prod. Universal Pictures, 1993. Film.

Schmidt, Amy, and Gudrun Loehrer. *The Mauthausen Concentration Camp Complex: World War II and Postwar Records*. Reference Information Paper 115. Washington, DC: National Archives and Records Administration, 2008.

Semprún, Jorge. *The Long Voyage*. 1963. Trans. Richard Seaver. Woodstock, NY: Overlook Press, 2005.

Sentis, Carlos. "Visita al campo de concentración de prisioneros de Dachau." *ABC* 15 May 1945, morning ed.

Serrano i Blanquer, David. *Un cadáver en el espejo: la odisea de Juan Camacho: Gádor, Mauthausen, Montevideo*. Sabadell, Spain: Fundació Ars, 2010.

– *Un català a Mauthausen: el testimoni de Francesc Comellas*. Barcelona: Pòrtic, 2001.

– *Les dones als camps nazis*. Barcelona: Pòrtic, 2003.

– "Edició i recepció de K.L. Reich." *Marges* 61. September (1998): 89–99.

Silva, Emilio. *Las fosas de Franco. Crónica de un desagravio*. Madrid: Temas de Hoy, 2005.

Sinca Vendrell, Amadeo. "Letters from Sinca Vendrell to José Francisco Sedano Moreno." Almería, Spain: n.p., 1981–83. Personal archive.

– *Lo que Dante no pudo imaginar: Mauthausen-Gusen 1940–1945*. Barcelona: Producciones Editoriales, 1980.

– "Mis 20 artículos." Toulouse, France: n.p., 1981.

Sinova, Justino. *La censura de prensa durante el franquismo*. Barcelona: Debolsillo, 2006.

Smith, Sidonie, and Julia Watson. *Reading Autobiography: A Guide for Interpreting Life Narratives*. Minneapolis: U of Minnesota P, 2010.

Sobrevivir en Mauthausen. Dir. Soler, Llorenç. 1975. Film.

Soler, Llorenç. *Los hilos secretos de mis documentales*. Barcelona: CIMS, 2002.

Soo, Scott. *The Routes to Exile: France and the Spanish Civil War Refugees, 1939–2009*. Manchester, England: Manchester UP, 2013.

Spiegelman, Art. *MetaMaus*. New York: Pantheon Books, 2011.

Stanley, Maureen Tobin. "'Parlo...': A Catalan Voice from the Holocaust: Writer and Survivor of Mauthausen Joaquim Amat-Piniella Shatters Francoist Mandated Silence." *Catalan Review* 21 (2007): 69–86.

– "Stills of Mauthausen: The Photographic Memoirs of Nazi Camp Survivor Francesc Boix." *Hispanic Issues On Line Debates* 3. Spring (2011): 39–55.

Staub, Ervin. *The Roots of Evil: The Origins of Genocide and Other Group Violence*. Cambridge, England: Cambridge UP, 1989.

Stokes, Bruce. "Euroskepticism Beyond Brexit: Significant Opposition in Key European Countries to an Ever Closer EU." *Pew Research Center*. 7 June 2016.

Strozier, Charles B. "Supervivencia, testimonio y arte. Españoles en los campos nazis." Ed. Centro Documental de la Memoria Histórica. Salamanca: Ministerio de Cultura, 2010.

Sturken, Marita. *Tourists of History: Memory, Kitsch, and Consumerism from Oklahoma City to Ground Zero*. Durham, NC: Duke UP, 2007.

Suñer Aguas, Raimundo. *De Calaceite a Mauthausen: memorias de Raimundo Suñer*. Alcañiz, Spain: Centro de Estudios Bajoaragoneses, 2006.

Szpilman, Wladyslaw. *Smierc miasta*. Warsaw: Spółdzielnia Wydawnicza Wiedza, 1946.

Taft, Margaret. *From Victim to Survivor: The Emergence and Development of the Holocaust Witness, 1941–1949*. London: Vallentine Mitchell, 2013.

Tillard, Paul. *Mauthausen*. Paris: Éditions sociales, 1945.

Todorov, Tzvetan. *Facing the Extreme: Moral Life in the Concentration Camps*. New York: Metropolitan Books, 1996.

Toran, Rosa. *Amical de Mauthausen: lucha y recuerdo, 1962–1978–2008*. Barcelona: Amical de Mauthausen y otros campos y de todas las víctimas del nazismo de España, 2008.

– *Joan de Diego: tercer secretari a Mauthausen*. Barcelona: Edicions 62, 2007.

– *Vida i mort dels republicans als camps nazis*. Barcelona: Proa, 2002.

Toran, Rosa, and Margarida Sala. *Mauthausen: crònica gràfica d'un camp de concentració = crónica gráfica de un campo de concentración*. Ed. Museu d'Història de Catalunya; Amical de Mauthausen. Barcelona: Viena Edicions, 2002.

Torrús, Alejandro. "PP y PSOE rechazan que el rey pida perdón a los republicanos deportados a los campos nazis." *Público*. 12 May 2015.

"Trasladadas de Ravensbrück a Mauthausen." No. 0460. Museu d'Història de Catalunya/Joan de Diego Archive, Barcelona, c. 1945. Archival document.

Trial of the Major War Criminals before the International Military Tribunal, Nuremberg, 14 November 1945–1 October 1946. Vol. 6. 42 vols. Nuremberg, Germany: n.p., 1947.

United States Holocaust Memorial Museum (USHMM). "Liberation of Nazi Camps." Holocaust Encyclopedia. 2015. Web.

– "Mauthausen." Holocaust Encyclopedia. 2015. Web.

– "Night and Fog Decree." Holocaust Encyclopedia. 2015. Web.

Vilalta i Prat, Joan. *Records d'un moianès a Mauthausen.* Moià, Spain: Associació Cultural Modilianum, 2006.

Vilanova, Antonio. *Los olvidados.* Paris: Ruedo Ibérico, 1969.

Vilanova, Mercedes. *Mauthausen, después: voces de españoles deportados.* Madrid: Cátedra, 2014.

Vives i Clavé, Pere. *Cartes des dels camps de concentració.* Barcelona: Edicions 62, 1972.

White, Hayden V. *Figural Realism: Studies in the Mimesis Effect.* Baltimore: Johns Hopkins UP, 1999.

Winter, Ulrich. "'Acción solidaria:' The Mauthausen Experience in Early Narration." *The Holocaust in Spanish Memory. Historical Perceptions and Cultural Discourse.* Eds. Antonio Gómez López-Quiñones and Susanne Zepp. Leipzig, Germany: Leipziger UP, 2010, 103–13.

Young, James Edward. *The Texture of Memory: Holocaust Memorials and Meaning.* New Haven: Yale UP, 1993.

– *Writing and Rewriting the Holocaust: Narrative and the Consequences of Interpretation.* Bloomington, IN: Indiana UP, 1988.

Zelizer, Barbie. *Remembering to Forget: Holocaust Memory through the Camera's Eye.* Chicago: U of Chicago P, 1998.

Index

Page numbers in italics are references to illustrations.